KNOWING THE TRIUNE GOD

KNOWING THE TRIUNE GOD

The Work of the Spirit in the Practices of the Church

Edited by

James J. Buckley *and* David S. Yeago

William B. Eerdmans Publishing Company
Grand Rapids, Michigan / Cambridge, U.K.

Wm. B. Eerdmans Publishing Co.
255 Jefferson Ave. S.E., Grand Rapids, Michigan 49503 /
P.O. Box 163, Cambridge CB3 9PU U.K.

Printed in the United States of America

06 05 04 03 02 01 7 6 5 4 3 2 1

Library of Congress Cataloging-in-Publication Data

Knowing the Triune God: the work of the Spirit in the practices
of the church / edited by James J. Buckley and David S. Yeago.

p. cm.

Includes bibliographical references.

ISBN 0-8028-4804-4 (pbk. : alk. paper)

1. Trinity. 2. Church. I. Buckley, James Joseph, 1947- II. Yeago, David S.

BT113.K57 2001
231′.044 — dc21

2001040374

www.eerdmans.com

To the Braatens and Jensons,

for their *generosity, hospitality,* and *patience*

Contents

Contributors

James J. Buckley is Professor of Theology and Dean of the College of Arts and Sciences at Loyola College in Maryland. He has published *Seeking the Humanity of God. Practices, Doctrines, and Catholic Theology* (Liturgical Press, 1992). He is co-editor (with L. Gregory Jones) of the journal *Modern Theology* and is currently working on a *Handbook of Ecclesiastical Opposition.*

David S. Cunningham is Professor of Theology and Ethics at Seabury-Western Theological Seminary in Evanston, Illinois. His books include *Faithful Persuasion: In Aid of a Rhetoric of Christian Theology* (Notre Dame, 1992) and *These Three Are One: The Practice of Trinitarian Theology* (Blackwell, 1998). He is currently working on a book tentatively titled *Reading Is Believing,* which uses novels and films to explicate the Apostles' Creed.

Reinhard Hütter is Associate Professor of Christian Theology at Duke University Divinity School. He has published *Evangelische Ethic as Kirchliches Zeugnis* (Neukirchener Verlag, 1993) and *Suffering Divine Things: Theology as Church Practice,* trans. Doug Stott (Eerdmans, 2000). He has also edited (with Theodor Dieter) *Ecumenical Ventures in Ethics: Protestants Engage Pope John Paul II's Ecumenical Encyclicals* (Eerdmans, 1998). He is currently working on a book exploring the interrelationship between "freedom" and "law."

L. Gregory Jones is Dean of the Divinity School and Professor of Theology at Duke University. He is author of *Embodying Forgiveness* (Eerdmans, 1995), the co-author (with Stephen Fowl) of *Reading in Communion* (Eerdmans and SPCK, 1991), and author of *Transformed Judgment* (Notre Dame, 1990). He is also the co-editor of four books and the author of numerous essays and reviews. He is working on a book on the dynamics of remembering and forgetting in Christian life.

Bruce D. Marshall is Professor of Historical Theology at the Perkins School of Theology of Southern Methodist University in Dallas, Texas. He has authored *Christology in Conflict: On the Idea of a Savior in Barth and Rahner* (Blackwell, 1987) and *Trinity and Truth* (Cambridge, 1999). He is currently working on a Christian theology of the Jewish people as well as a book on pneumatology.

Eugene F. Rogers, Jr., is Associate Professor of Philosophical Theology and Chair of the Program in Theology, Ethics, and Culture in the Department of Religious Studies at the University of Virginia. He has authored *Thomas Aquinas and Karl Barth: Sacred Doctrine and the Natural Knowledge of God* (Notre Dame, 1995) and *Sexuality and the Christian Body: Their Way into the Triune God* (Blackwell, 1999). He is currently working on *After the Spirit: The Story of the Holy Spirit Eclipsed by Nature, Grace, and Law* (Westview Press, forthcoming).

A. N. Williams is University Lecturer in Patristics at the University of Cambridge. She has published *The Ground of Union: Deification in Aquinas and Palamas* (Oxford University Press, 1999) and is currently working on a book on conceptions of the intellect in patristic theology.

Susan K. Wood is Professor of Theology and Associate Dean of the School of Theology at Saint John's University in Collegeville, Minnesota. She has authored *Spiritual Exegesis and the Church in the Theology of Henri de Lubac* (Grand Rapids: Eerdmans, 1998) and *Sacramental Orders* (Liturgical Press, 2000).

David S. Yeago is Michael C. Peeler Professor of Systematic Theology at Lutheran Theological Southern Seminary in Columbia, South Carolina. He has written many articles in historical and doctrinal theology and is currently completing *Taking Hold of Christ: The Catholic Shape of Martin Luther's Evangelical Theology.*

1. Introduction

A Catholic and Evangelical Theology?

JAMES J. BUCKLEY AND DAVID S. YEAGO

The central claim of this book is that knowing the triune God is inseparable from participating in a particular community and its practices — a participation which is the work of God's Holy Spirit. Why say this, now?

A first step in answering this question is the specific circumstances of the book's origin. Several years ago Carl Braaten and Robert Jenson founded the Center for Catholic and Evangelical Theology, headquartered in Northfield, Minnesota. The Center sponsors regular conferences on theological matters, and publishes *Pro Ecclesia: A Journal of Catholic and Evangelical Theology.* In addition, the Center has also sponsored meetings among theologians interested in "Catholic and Evangelical theology." The authors here were members of one such group, originally called "The Dogmatics Project." This group was "Catholic and Evangelical" — Anglican (Cunningham and Williams), Lutheran (Hütter, Marshall, and Yeago), Methodist (Jones), Roman Catholic (Buckley and Wood), and one raised Presbyterian, with a Lutheran conscience, who reads Catholics and Orthodox, and attends Episcopal services (Rogers); at times the group included Greek Orthodox and Baptist participants as well.

Thanks to the generosity of Carl and LaVonne Braaten and Robert and Blanche Jenson, this group met in Northfield, Minnesota, once or twice a year for several years, beginning in 1991. At our meetings, we discussed papers on a wide range of topics central to the future of a Catholic and Evangelical theology — from the doctrine of the Trinity to emerging theologies of the Jewish people. Eventually it was time to ask whether our conversations were leading in any distinctive direction. Did we have something to say as a group about the best direction for what the Center calls a "Catholic and Evangelical theology"?

This volume is our answer to that question to date. But we did not proceed deductively by arguing for an abstraction called "Catholic and Evangelical theology" to add to the pantheon of modern and postmodern theologies. The label has a past and present that is suggestive but hardly forms a monolithic school of thought. For example, in the nineteenth century, William Augustus Muhlenberg, the Anglican grandson of a famous Lutheran leader, proposed the formation of "an Evangelic and Catholic Union" of "the two distinctive elements" of the "Protestant Episcopal Church" — the primitive Catholicism of the early church and the restored Catholicism of the Reformation.[1] But an aspiration to "evangelical catholicity" is also deeply embedded in the Lutheran tradition; "evangelical catholic" has recently served as a party label in intra-Lutheran controversy.[2]

The label also has a connection with what moderns call "The Radical Reformation." That is, George Hunston Williams identified "Evangelical Catholics" as one subspecies of the "Evangelical Rationalists" of the Reformation era, exemplified by Erasmus, Lefevres, and Juan de Valdes.[3] Still further, in the Reformed tradition, Karl Barth once expressed "a horror of mystical, High-Church, Evangelical-Catholic dilettantism"; but he could say, decades later, that he preferred "evangelical-catholic" to "evangelical"[4] — and Thomas Torrance's essays on evangelical and catholic unity in east and west carry on this tradition.[5] A more liberal theological tradition

1. Rev. William Augustus Muhlenberg, D.D., "Suggestions for the Formation of an Evangelic and Catholic Union [1870]," in Rev. William Augustus Muhlenberg, D.D., *Evangelical Catholic Papers,* First Series, compiled by Anne Ayres (Suffolk Co., N.Y.: St. Johnland Press and Stereotype Foundry, 1985), no. 9, pp. 31-460.

2. Jaroslav Pelikan, *Obedient Rebels: Catholic Substance and Protestant Principle in Luther's Reformation* (New York: Harper & Row, 1964), chapters 11 and 14; Carl E. Braaten and Robert W. Jenson, eds., *The Catholicity of the Reformation* (Grand Rapids: Eerdmans, 1996).

3. George Hunston Williams, ed., *Spiritual and Anabaptist Writers: Documents Illustrative of the Radical Reformation* (Philadelphia: Westminster, 1957), pp. 22-24.

4. Karl Barth, *Epistle to the Romans,* trans. Edwyn C. Hoskyns (London: Oxford, 1933; 1972 reprint), p. 21 (1924 Preface). For what Barth may have meant, see Dieter Voll, *Hochkirchlichen Pietismus* (München: Chr. Kaiser Verlag, 1960), translated by Veronica Ruffer as *Catholic Evangelicalism. The acceptance of evangelical traditions by the Oxford Movement during the second half of the nineteenth century* (London: Faith Press, 1963), where "evangelical catholics" are Methodists. For a later, positive reference to "evangelical catholic," see *Ad Limina Apostolorum: An Appraisal of Vatican II,* trans. Keith R. Crim (Richmond, Va.: John Knox, 1968), p. 18.

5. *Theology in Reconciliation: Essays Towards Evangelical and Catholic Unity in East and West* (London: G. Chapman, 1975).

speaks of "the public Church" as a coalition of "mainline, evangelical, and catholic."[6]

Among Roman Catholics, "evangelical" has usually meant "non-Roman Catholic."[7] But Catholics also have a tradition of evangelical Catholicity, and Avery Dulles has recently spoken of "the birth of a new Catholicism which, without loss of its institutional, sacramental, and social dimensions, is authentically evangelical."[8] Charles Colson and Richard John Neuhaus have brought together American Evangelicals (quite different, on many scores, from the largely Continental Evangelical theologians mentioned so far) and Catholics to speak to their "common mission" as well as "the gift of salvation."[9]

We could go on. Our point is that, *if* all these groups and individuals share something theologically, it certainly does not add up to a party line. We certainly wish to embrace *a* Catholic and Evangelical cause. In calling the spirit in which we do theology "Catholic and Evangelical" we mean that we intend to engage the whole of the Christian tradition, in its diversity and richness. At one level, this means that we believe modern and constructive theology is authentically Christian and ecclesial when it is contiguous with the prior theological tradition — this much is implied when we affirm our belief in the communion of saints. At another level, it implies an ecumenical conviction: that theology which is to be heeded is not simply the theology of the church to which a particular writer belongs, but the theology of all Christians. The Roman Catholic is to listen to Luther and Barth; the Presbyterian is to listen to Aquinas, and everyone is to listen to the theology of the church in the patristic age. But we have no interest in announcing a new theological

6. Martin Marty, *The Public Church: Mainline, Evangelical, Catholic* (New York: Crossroad, 1981).

7. E.g., John A. Bain, *The New Reformation: Recent Evangelical Movements in the Roman Catholic Church* (Edinburgh: T. & T. Clark, 1906), which is about Roman Catholics leaving the Catholic Church.

8. Avery Dulles, "John Paul II and the New Evangelization," *America* 166, no. 3 (February 1992): 52-72 (quote here from p. 70). But, for an earlier "liberal" Catholic movement, see Friedrich Heiler, *Evangelische Katholitizität.* Gesammelte Aufsätze und Vorträge Ban I (München: Ernst Reinhardt, 1926), a collection of essays on the unity of the Church by a Roman Catholic, dedicated to "the martyrs of evangelical Catholicism of the last fifty years": Ignaz Döllinger, Herman Schell, George Tyrrell, Eduard Herzon, and Friedrich von Hügel.

9. See the original document and responses in Charles Colson and Richard John Neuhaus, *Evangelicals and Catholics Together: Toward a Common Mission* (Dallas: Word, 1995); "The Gift of Salvation," *First Things* 79 (January 1998): 20-26. For responses, see subsequent issues of *First Things* as well as Norman L. Geisler and Ralph E. MacKenzie, eds., *Roman Catholics and Evangelicals: Agreements and Differences* (Grand Rapids: Baker Books, 1995), esp. pp. 494-502.

school, or restoring an old one. We simply aim to do theology in a way that reflects and generates "Catholic and Evangelical" dialogue and debate.

It should not be surprising, given this history, that the unity of the volume is not provided by a single philosophical perspective or global ethical agenda. We found ourselves disagreeing about issues raised by traditional and modern and postmodern philosophies as well as about the joys and griefs of contemporary economic and political life. Those who think that theological coherence depends on first elaborating a common philosophical framework, methodological program, or social-ethical commitment may find it difficult to see any unity in this volume at all. Each essay has its own distinctive shape. There will thus be no substitute for reading each of the chapters on its own terms. However, we believe that the diversity of the essays only underlines our central thesis: that what unifies theology as a coherent enterprise of inquiry and dialogue is the work of the Spirit in the practices of the Church. That is, it is the concrete context of ecclesial practice that constitutes the framework of reflection *within which* agreements and disagreements over various methodological strategies and philosophical gambits and ethical projects are contained.

Thus, one reason for this volume at this time is the specific circumstances that brought us together. But what holds the essays together without dissolving their distinctiveness? Our first step in holding together the unity-in-diversity of the volume was to divide the nine essays into three parts. Part One centers on the way in which a particular communal practice gives rise to our knowledge of the triune God. For Reinhard Hütter, knowledge of God arises as we undergo the work of the Spirit sacramentally operative in, with, and under the core practices that mark out the unique public space of the Christian Church. David Yeago argues that the context of ecclesial practice both forms and demands a distinctive enterprise of "understanding" the scriptures as the formative discourse of the Spirit. And Susan Wood proposes that Christian worship contains within itself a distinctive mode of "participatory" knowledge of the triune God.

Part Two focuses more on particular ways in which the interrelation of knowledge and practice in Christianity gives distinctive shape to both. A. N. Williams presents the inseparability of love and knowledge, especially in Augustine; theology is thus inseparable from prayer, but prayer is likewise inseparable from the engagement of the mind with God. Gregory Jones re-reads the catechumenate as a set of practices that shape Christian practical wisdom on the way into God's dazzling light. David Cunningham argues that the tradition of finding "vestiges of the Trinity" throughout our personal and political lives, far from a reduction of the Spirit's work to ours, is in the service of articulating God's triune mystery.

The essays in Part Three respond implicitly to the concern that binding knowledge of God to church practice will insulate Christian practitioners from repentance and challenge, making of the Church a self-enclosed and self-satisfied enclave. These three essays therefore focus on the significance of "others" — "strangers," "Israel," and "separated brothers and sisters" — for the knowledge of God, calling the Church to be drawn by the Spirit's work to unexpected places. Buckley argues that the Spirit is in ecumenical movement as the Church recognizes and repents of its divisions, resisting the temptation either to forget them or to grant them the final word over the Spirit's work on the Church as a wounded body. Marshall takes up the even deeper division between Church and synagogue, asking about the relationship of the Christian worship of the triune God to the knowledge of God in Israel. Gene Rogers offers a re-reading of the natural knowledge of God in the broader Gentile world, arguing that a trinitarian construal of "natural knowledge of God" mandates hospitality to the stranger.

Readers will quickly see that there is no sharp division of topics or *loci* among these essays. Thus there is no neat division between Parts One and Two, nor are any of the essays in Parts One and Two untouched by the disputed questions that arise regarding the Church's identity in its mission to the world. Hütter's account of the relation between *pathos, poiesis,* and *praxis,* Yeago's incorporation of hermeneutics into a missionary ecclesiology, Wood's appeal to philosophies of participatory knowledge, Williams's Augustinian anthropology, Jones's neo-Aristotelian notion of practices, Cunningham's trust in the work of the Trinity throughout the world — all these suggest (in partly conflicting ways) how the Spirit's working of knowledge of God in the practices of the Church is inseparable from the mission of the Church to a world created, fallen, and redeemed.

What is it, then, that unifies the three parts? It is, we think, the book's central theme: knowing the triune God is inseparable from participating in a particular community and its practices — a participation which Christians link with the work of God's Holy Spirit. Consider each of the major elements of the book's title.

1. What Does It Mean to *Know* the Triune God?

Scriptures, especially Paul and John, speak of faith and knowledge as inseparable (e.g., Romans 6:8; John 10:38). From this point of view, our title raises no more (or no fewer) problems than does Scripture for the theologians, pastors, and educated Christians to whom we address this book. Or we could put the point this way. We confess faith's knowledge of the triune God when we profess the ancient creeds. But we also confess the triune God in the very gathering to hear the scriptures and eat the body and blood of Christ, with or without the ancient creed. This practice includes as an essential ingredient our hope of knowing the God who, as Father and Son and Spirit, creates the world and elects Israel as a blessing unto the nations and pours himself out even unto death, sending the Spirit to gather and abide with the communion of saints. On one level, "knowing the triune God" creates no problem: it is the knowledge embedded in our faith as lived and confessed.

Nonetheless, perhaps especially in our time, saying that we hope to *know* the triune God by the gift of the Spirit in the practices of the Church is a dangerous claim. It is dangerous mostly because it confesses a difficult hope — our trust in a God who bears the sins of the world to bring us to share God's own triune life and love. But it is also dangerous because modernity as well as postmodernity include a luxurious garden, or desert wilderness, of theories and practices of "knowing" that all too often eclipse the singular habits of mind and heart required to know *this* God. In such a context, knowing and believing become competitors. Ordinary Christ-believing Christians, educated as well as uneducated, are then tempted to sequester their believing from their knowing, ignoring the various ways each is ingredient of the other in Scripture and tradition and our lives together today.

But, in the face of the temptation to isolate believing and knowing, there is another temptation to seek some comprehensive, systematic, or programmatic account of the relationship between knowledge and practice, in order to defend ourselves in advance from those who would play the two off each other, or isolate them from each other, or complain that we have ignored the insights of one or other "epistemology" or personal or political practice. Theologians have succumbed to this temptation every time they have discovered or created a new methodology to pull the theological train. But we are not only thinking here of theologians like ourselves. We are thinking of the ways that comprehensive claims to know from one systematic theology or one psychology or social theory can infect local congregations as well as the universal Christian communion of saints and then eclipse the triune communion that is the center of our faith.[10]

The authors here have tried to resist the temptations to isolate faith and knowing, or to provide a comprehensive account of their relationship as a

10. See, for an example, Philip Kenneson, "Selling [Out] the Church in the Marketplace of Desire," *Modern Theology* 9 (1993): 319-48. The entire issue is on "Ecclesiology and the Culture of Management."

preliminary to "knowing the triune God." We have resisted partly because of limitations of the nine of us and partly to resist the familiar Christian temptation to think that Christian communal identity depends upon all manner of minute agreements in theory and practice before we can worship and witness and work together.

Our actual procedure in this volume, which makes no attempt to provide such an all-encompassing account, may suggest a more complex approach. Christians, we might say, have two *prima facie* options. On the one hand, we may construct quite comprehensive accounts of knowledge and practice, carefully showing how all kinds of knowledge and practice relate to all other kinds; the "all other kinds" would include Christian knowing and practice (always recognizing the singularity of Christian knowledge and practice as response to the triune God). For this strategy we might think of the Cappadocians and Augustine, at least in one dimension of their thought, or of Rahner and Pannenberg in our own day. Or else we may remain skeptical of all such accounts precisely because of the risk that they will envelop and eclipse the singularity of Christian knowledge of the triune God in the practices of the Church. For this second strategy we may think of Kierkegaard's rightful insistence on the singularity of Christian practice and knowledge over against modern systems out to sublate us — or less idiosyncratically, Barth's insistence that for theology, relating to such comprehensive teachings is itself a matter of skilled practice, to be accomplished only *ad hoc* and without finality. In the older Christian tradition, we may think of Irenaeus's celebration of the concrete *depositum fidei,* what the Church has received from the apostles, over against the speculative systematics of *gnosis,* or the insistence of the medieval Cistercians that true knowledge of God and creatures depends on — and may finally be identical with — a certain kind of ascetic-liturgical schooling of the affections.

We have not ruled out either of these broad options in advance of their application to specific theological issues, in the context of the work of the Spirit in and on the Church. The burden on those who take the first tack is to do justice to what is essential for Christian communal identity, and avoid the reduction of Christian knowledge to a mere "case in point" of some more general kind of knowing. The burden on those who take the second tack is to relate the singular Christian knowledge of God to other human knowing, and avoid the isolation of the knowledge of God in a special "religious" sphere.

What unites this book therefore is not a particular epistemological strategy (e.g., a strategy that relies on an account of what it means to know anything and everything), but an agreement about the context from which such strategies must move and the form of life to which they must be made congenial. That context and life-form is the communion of the Church, understood in terms of the specific practices that make it distinctive among human communities. We might not agree about which of the broad epistemological strategies mentioned above does best justice to the distinctive communal life and practice of the Church, and the knowledge contained therein, but it is clear that either strategy could be pursued in ways that would be *inappropriate* to that setting. A "universalist" epistemology that reduced the Christian knowledge of God to a mere symbolic mediation of abstract universal truths would fail the test, but so would a "particularist" epistemology that reduced "knowledge" to a finally non-cognitive "authenticity" produced by a lonely convulsion of the individual will.

Rather than any *a priori* epistemological program, it is this agreement about the communal setting of the Christian knowledge of God, and the involvement of that knowledge with ecclesial practice, that produces certain further broad agreements about the *character* of the Christian knowledge of God that seem to be discernible in these essays. Over against a certain kind of "liberalism," both Catholic and Evangelical, there seems to be broad consensus in this volume, implicit or explicit, that the Christian knowledge of God is properly cognitive, that is, that it involves assent to truth-claims which can be articulated in sentences. Over against Neo-Kantian and existentialist theologies, whether of Evangelical or Catholic provenance, which reduce the knowledge of faith to the "passive" determination of the will by divine action or a transcendental apprehension of "mystery," there seems to be broad agreement here with Barth's claim that the "Church which utters the Creed, which comes forward with the tremendous claim to preach and to proclaim the glad tidings, derives from the fact that it has *perceived* [*vernehmen*] something . . . and it wishes to let what it has perceived be perceived again."[11] Or we might cite Anselm, commenting on Romans 10:17:

> We should understand the statement "faith comes by hearing" to mean that faith comes from what the mind apprehends or conceives through hearing, not in the sense that the mind's conception alone produces faith in a person, but in the sense that there can be no faith without some conception.[12]

11. Karl Barth, *Dogmatics in Outline,* trans. G. T. Thompson (New York: Harper, 1959), p. 23 (translation altered).

12. Anselm, "On the Harmony of the Foreknowledge, the Predestination, and the Grace of God with Free Choice," ch. 6, in *Anselm of Canterbury: Trinity, Incarnation, and Redemption — Theological Treatises,* ed. Jasper Hopkins and Herbert Richardson (New York: Harper, 1970), p. 181 (translation altered).

Both Barth and Anselm (as well as Paul!) have in view the bond between Christian knowledge and liturgical practice: what Christians know about God can and must be proclaimed in sermons and doxologies, summed up and confessed in creeds, sung forth in hymns. It is a knowledge embedded in communal practice and just so must be the kind of "saleable" knowledge that can be *shared,* not only a "deep," wordless (and just so inalienably private) affection of the inner life.

But at the same time, over against a certain kind of "conservatism," both Evangelical and Catholic, there seems to be equal agreement in these essays, implicitly or explicitly, that the Christian knowledge of God, though it is a communicable and therefore "saleable" knowledge, cannot be grasped or shared in abstraction from the web of concrete practice from which it arises and in which it lives. Knowing is articulated in teaching, and in teachings about teachings. But, to revise Austin Farrer's proverb, we cannot know that which we can *only* know.[13] Knowing is an ingredient of our dealings with things — and, in this sense, an ingredient of our practices. The Church can state its faith, but what Christians *say* about the triune God cannot be adequately explicated without reference to what Christians most characteristically *do* in worship and obedience to that God.

Over against any sort of abstract "propositionalism," therefore, whether of Catholic or Evangelical provenance, be it a "manualist" presentation of the knowledge of faith as a free-standing system of axioms and deductions, or the reduction (for the purposes of evangelistic "church-marketing") of Christian knowledge to an easily grasped "content" separable from any given "form" of life or practice, there seems to be broad agreement here with the view of Irenaeus as articulated by Thomas Torrance:

> . . . knowledge of the truth of God or the truth of the Gospel is not given in an abstract or detached form but in a concrete embodied form in the Church, where it is to be grasped within the normative pattern of the faith imparted to it through the teaching of the apostles, and is therefore to be grasped only in unity and continuity with the faith, worship, and godly life of all who are incorporated into Christ as members of his Body.[14]

13. *Faith and Speculation: An Essay in Philosophical Theology* (New York: New York University Press, 1967), pp. 1-51, esp. p. 22: There is "no thought about any reality about which we can do nothing but think."

14. Thomas F. Torrance, *The Trinitarian Faith: The Evangelical Theology of the Ancient Catholic Church* (Edinburgh: T. & T. Clark, 1988), p. 33.

This does not mean that Christian claims cannot be understood by "outsiders," but it does mean that "outsiders" will have to pay close attention to the interrelations of Christian belief with Christian practice in order to understand Christian claims. And it means that coming to *share* those claims, to join in *making* them, involves more than a change occurring inside one's head. It means entering into the "concrete embodied" articulation of those claims that occurs in the life of the Church, in the interplay of word and sign, articulate confession and significant practice, by which alone the truth about God can be truthfully uttered (so Christians have classically believed) under the conditions of this life.

This is a kind of agreement that leaves many issues open, and the authors of this volume would undoubtedly parse the remaining questions in very different, sometimes opposing, ways. Readers will want to keep their eyes and ears out for such disagreements. We have nonetheless found it to be *sufficient* agreement to sustain several years of lively and fruitful conversation. We suggest that this experience at least raises the question: What *kind* of unity does theology need? More specifically: Does theology need *more* unity, or *another kind* of unity, than the Church does? Or is it sufficient unity for the theological enterprise that it share in those things that unify the Church, that it be shaped by participation in the Church's *communio?* Is modern academic theology's never-ending quest for a unifying method or program *only* a sign of authentic intellectual seriousness, or is it (also) a kind of compensatory obsession, a reaction to the fragmentation and occlusion of theology's ecclesial setting by Christian divisions?

2. Who or What Is the Church, and Why Do We Focus on Its "Practices"?

All this talk about the Church and its communion raises another set of questions for this book which could easily be articulated as critique. What does it mean to speak of "the Church" when all that is available to us are *churches* — the confessionally divided denominations left behind by the schisms of the last millennium? How can we speak of theology "sharing in those things that unify the Church" when the Church is not in fact unified?

Here again we believe that this book displays a certain kind of coherence without offering a systematic program. This is not a book of ecumenical theology, though it is an example of ecumenical theologizing. While we have different relationships to formal ecumenical dialogue, none of us believes that the separated post-Reformation confessional traditions provide an adequate setting for the theological enterprise. Truly "Catholic and Evangelical" theology cannot simply be Roman Catholic or Anglican or Methodist or Lutheran or Reformed theology, nor indeed can it be simply "Western" theology isolated from the traditions of the Christian East. Each of us, in this volume and elsewhere, finds it natural and necessary to transgress denominational borders and bring into dialogue themes and figures of the Christian past and present often assumed to be irrevocably at odds with one another.[15]

At the same time, none of us is willing to take the insufficiency of the divided confessions as reason for theology to stand apart from actual Christian communities and their life. None of us seems disposed to compensate for the fragmentation of the Church's communion by looking for a unifying center in the private depths of religious subjectivity or a moral-political imperative of the enlightened conscience or a definition of the "essence of Christianity" achieved by the application of a superior academic methodology.

Focus on ecclesial practice is once again central to the alternative modeled here. Not all contributors would find sufficient Hütter's Luther-inspired description of the Church as a public space constituted by a distinctive mesh of practices, but none would want to describe the Church *less* concretely. As a convergent line of thought from the Catholic side of the post-Reformation divide, one might think of Vatican II's discussion of the Church in terms of its constituent "elements of sanctification and truth" (which are, in effect, what most of us call "practices") "many" of which can exist even in separated "ecclesial communities" outside the visible structure of the Catholic Church.[16]

If the Church is understood in this way primarily in terms of the singular practices through which it is formed and bound to God, then theology which is oriented to those practices can share in that which unifies the Church even when the Church is divided. The way in which several of these essays take shared patterns of liturgical worship as a locus for theological reflection is one example of this. Such theology may even hope to be an unpretentiously prophetic theology of and for the one Church in the midst of the divided churches. This modestly prophetic character of a Catholic and Evangelical theology has been succinctly described by one of the founders of our feast in terms most of us could accept:

15. It is perhaps worth noting that, among the authors of these essays, some of the non-Catholics have written extensively on Aquinas, while others have written on the Orthodox Palamas; the non-Reformed have written on the Reformed Barth, and some of the non-Lutherans on the Lutheran Bonhoeffer.

16. Cf. Vatican II, *Dogmatic Constitution on the Church,* ch. 8 in *Decrees of the Ecumenical Councils,* ed. Norman Tanner (London/Georgetown: Sheed & Ward and Georgetown University Press, 1990), pp. 854-55.

> To live as the church in the situation of a divided church — if this can happen at all — must at least mean that we confess we live in radical self-contradiction and that by every churchly act we contradict that contradiction. Also theology must make this double contradiction at and by every step of the way.[17]

The orientation to constitutive Christian practices, to the "elements of sanctification and truth" shared by Christian communities across their divisions, is, at least in this book, the "churchly act" by which theology goes about "contradicting the contradiction" of Christian disunity in a concrete way even when the ecumenical theme is not explicitly or intentionally to the fore. Buckley's intentional engagement of the theme presupposes this orientation, first of all simply in its assumption that such matters as the way stories are told and memory cultivated in Christian communities are proper objects of disciplined theological concern.

The best way to understand further what we mean by "practices" is by attending to the specific examples of them in particular chapters. Thus, by "practices" we include theology itself in the service of the variety of "constitutive practices" of the Church (Hütter); sundry uses of the Bible in the life of the Church (Yeago); the practices of baptism (Jones) and Eucharist and other sacraments (Wood); a full variety of personal and communal prayer (Williams); the quest to interpret "marks of the Trinity" throughout our world (Cunningham); the efforts of the wounded body to find the Spirit's healing work as we learn to pray and think together, again (Buckley); the many practices involved in re-figuring our relationships to the Jewish people and the God of Israel (Marshall); the diverse practices of hospitality it takes to welcome the blessing of strangers among us (Rogers).

What more must be said about ecclesial practices? There is no need to repeat about "practices" what we said earlier about "knowing." That is, we have not aimed to agree on a comprehensive list of practices, or a theory thereof — even as we recognize that some of the essays above move toward such comprehensive theories. But there are two features of "practices" that we think all the authors share. First, one ingredient of the practices of the Church is that the goods of these practices are (in Alasdair MacIntyre's phrase) *internal* to them. MacIntyre means that such goods can be specified in terms of examples — and "they can only be identified and recognized by the experience of participating in the practice in question."[18] Negatively put, such practices are

17. Robert W. Jenson, *Systematic Theology* (New York: Oxford, 1997), vol. 1, p. vi.

18. Alasdair MacIntyre, *After Virtue* (Notre Dame: University of Notre Dame Press, 1981), pp. 174-90.

not mere instruments to attain some external end. There is a temptation in North American culture to make the practices of the Church instrumental to other practices — perhaps the "private" spiritual exercises of Catholic and Evangelical pietisms or liberal/conservative practices of a more "public" religion. But the practices summarized in the previous paragraph are practices whose goods are internal to them, practices recognized by participating in them — or, if we do not know how to so participate, learning to participate in them from their best practitioners.

Second, standard descriptions of "practices" usually take them to be a kind of "doing" or "making" clearly distinct from "suffering." The authors in this volume make no such distinction. Our "practices" include "suffering" as well as "making" or "doing." MacIntyre's definition of a practice describes it as "any coherent and complex form of socially established cooperative human activity" enacted in such a way that "human powers to achieve excellence, and human conceptions of the ends and goods involved, are systematically extended."[19] As fruitful as this definition is for many purposes, it does not readily include what Reinhard Hütter has called the *pathos* of the church — the practice it takes to endure, the compassion it takes to be a passionate people, the way that *passio* is genuine *actio*. More generally, for all these essays, "the practices of the Church" are the practices of the body of Christ whose ultimate trust is in the Head who has patiently endured death for us, and called us to communion with God in this *pathos*.

It would be possible, we suppose, to read these essays as variously inclined toward practice as passion and action, perhaps a modern version of the sixteenth-century dispute over the *sola fide* (faith alone) and *fides caritate formata* (faith formed by love). None of the essays here directly addresses that dispute, although all the authors would share the "convergence" between Catholics and Evangelicals reached in the twentieth century on issues of justification.[20] Not all Catholics and Evangelicals (especially but not only Ameri-

19. *After Virtue*, p. 175. This is not the place to try to articulate whether this is a substantial or marginal critique of MacIntyre's philosophy on this score. Compare MacIntyre's response to philosophical criticisms of his practices in *After MacIntyre: Critical Perspectives on the Work of Alasdair MacIntyre*, ed. John Horton and Susan Mendus (Notre Dame: University of Notre Dame Press, 1994), pp. 283-304, and the theological criticisms in Stanley Hauerwas and Charles Pinches, *Christian Among the Virtues: Theological Conversations with Ancient and Modern Ethics* (Notre Dame: University of Notre Dame Press, 1997). And now see MacIntyre's own self-correcting arguments on behalf of vulnerability in *Dependent Rational Animals: Why Human Beings Need the Virtues* (Chicago and La Salle, Ill.: Open Court, 1999).

20. The literature is enormous. A good place to start is the discussion generated by Karl Lehman and Wolfhart Pannenberg, eds., *The Condemnations of the Reformation Era: Do They Still Divide?* trans. Margaret Kohl (Minneapolis: Fortress, 1990 [German original 1986]); Karl

can Evangelicals) share in this convergence.[21] But what is most crucial is that we would agree that any contradicting of our self-contradictory disunity can only endure if it is our authentic response to the genuine work of the triune God among us. For example, we are confident that the goods of these practices are internal rather than external to them because they are the work of the Spirit shaping us into a community of Jew and Greek, the people of a new heaven and new earth. We are confident that these are not the practices of a self-evidently "practical" church because these are practices as the patient response to the Spirit of Jesus, who trains us to be a people of faith and hope and love in truly unexpected ways. In short, it is only if the practices of the Church (in which the triune God is truly known) are the creation of that God that they are the authentic practices of the Church. But who is the triune God, and why do we focus on the Spirit?

3. Who Is "the Triune God"?

The triune God of whom we write is the God attested and discerned in the Church's liturgy of Word and Eucharist, whose marks we find throughout the cosmos but who is self-identified as the God of Israel, incarnate in the singular Jesus, drawing near to give life in the Spirit's Pentecostal mission to the world through the Church.

In the link it posits between trinitarian faith and ecclesial practice, this volume is not proposing something fundamentally novel. Whether modern trinitarian theology is a renewal or eclipse of traditional trinitarian theology is a good subject to dispute.[22] But some crucial strands of modern trinitarian theology have been at the heart of many of the central theological achievements of the twentieth century. From Barth (for many Reformed and some Lutheran Christians) and de Lubac or Rahner (for many Roman Catholics), as well as important Eastern Orthodox influences such as Bulgakov and Lossky, the sort of trinitarian theology whence we borrow has proceeded

---

Lehman, Michael Root, and William G. Rusch, eds., *Justification by Faith: Do the Sixteenth-Century Condemnations Still Apply?* (New York: Crossroad, 1997).

21. For one discussion, see the entire issue of *Pro Ecclesia* 7, no. 4 (Fall 1998), although the Vatican's May 1999 acceptance of the Joint Declaration by Catholics and Lutherans (after its seeming rejection earlier in 1998) was not anticipated by most of these essays.

22. See Bruce Marshall's argument that much recent trinitarian theology (including strong contrasts between Eastern and Western approaches to the Trinity) "embodies not so much the renewal as the eclipse of trinitarian theology as an ongoing tradition of inquiry" in "The Trinity" in *The Blackwell Companion to Theology* (forthcoming).

from the realization that trinitarian doctrine codifies *the knowledge of God given in Christian particularity:* in the movement of the stories of Israel and Jesus, in the patterns of the Church's prayer and liturgy, in the logic of mission and ministry.[23]

It is worth noting, in light of what was said above about Christian practice and the unity of the theological enterprise, that the trinitarian "renewal" in twentieth-century theology has been a striking example of a theological conversation that has crossed not only the borders between denominations but also the sometimes more closely guarded barriers of academic methodology. There has in effect been an ongoing colloquy, by now spanning three or four theological generations, in which it is possible to hear voices as different as those of Barth and Rahner, Moltmann and Stăniloae,[24] Jenson and LaCugna, as participants in a shared enterprise, or at least a common conversation, despite their very different confessional traditions, epistemologies, and socio-political commitments. This surely has something to do with the recognition, present in the Protestant, Catholic, and Orthodox initiators of the trinitarian renewal, that in accounting for Christian trinitarianism one is up against the deep structures of Christian identity, with that which is constitutive of what is "Christian" in a profound and epistemically basic way.

This account of the relation between trinitarian faith and doctrine, on the one hand, and distinctive ecclesial language and practice, on the other, is what separates the trinitarianism of the authors of these essays from older and more recent attempts at a speculative retrieval of trinitarian teaching like Tillich's view of the Trinity as "the unity in a manifoldness of divine self-manifestation" at the end of a systematic theology.[25] Such attempts typically tend to unhook trinitarian belief from Christian particularity and transform it into an abstract cosmological or ontological explanatory scheme. It also distinguishes the con-

23. For an eloquent recent example, cf. Boris Bobrinskoy, *The Mystery of the Trinity* (Crestwood, N.Y.: St. Vladimir's Seminary Press, 1999). The Orthodox have been especially insistent on the role of liturgy and prayer in sustaining the trinitarian character of Christian faith and life even when trinitarian theology as an intellectual enterprise has not been at its best.

24. Cf. Moltmann's "Geleitwort" to volume 1 of the German edition of Stăniloae's dogmatics: Dimitru Stăniloae, *Orthodoxe Dogmatik* ("Ökumenische Theologie," Band 12), trans. Hermann Pitters (Zurich: Benziger, 1985), pp. 9-13. For an English translation of part of this work (but not of Moltmann's introduction), cf. Dimitru Stăniloae, *The Experience of God,* trans. and ed. Ioan Ionită (Brookline, Mass.: Holy Cross Orthodox Press, 1994).

25. Paul Tillich, *Systematic Theology* (Chicago: University of Chicago Press, 1963), vol. 3, pp. 283-94. Such revisionary proposals (whose father is Friedrich Schleiermacher) are not to be confused with those who go further, embracing a kind of intentionally heterodox Gnosticism; for a reading of Hegel along these lines, see Cyril O'Regan, *The Heterodox Hegel* (Albany, N.Y.: State University of New York Press, 1994).

cerns and commitments of these authors from much that is done and said today in the name of "Spirit" and "spirituality." Insofar as the Spirit is the Spirit of the Father and the Son, identified in gospel-narrative and the rhythms of liturgical invocation, the conclusion is hard to avoid that some, at least, of what now goes by the name of "spirituality" has little to do with the Spirit at work in the practices of the Church and attested in the gospel narrative; it is more like a renewal of pagan animisms, now made relevant to the depths of the enchanted subjectivities of late- and post-modernity.[26]

All of the essays in this book, by contrast, work within the framework of a trinitarian apprehension of God grounded in the particularities of Christian practice and continuous, at least by intention, with the consensus of the ancient councils. Issues of trinitarian theology come most directly to the fore in Cunningham's reconsideration of the "vestiges of the Trinity" in the created world, in Williams's exposition of Augustine's account of the relation of intellect and prayer in the knowing of the triune God, and in Marshall's inquiry into the implications of trinitarian belief for Jewish-Christian dialogue. Indirectly, trinitarian theology is very much at issue in those essays that emphasize the doctrine of the Spirit, especially Hütter's presentation of theology as a practice arising within the sphere and under the pressure of the Spirit's church-constituting action, Yeago's attempt to relate inspiration and interpretation within the context of a doctrine of the Spirit's mission to gather the Church as a sign of Christ, and Buckley's account of the Spirit's movement in view of the Church's divisions. But this raises a fourth question about the common theme embodied in the book's title.

4. Why Does Our Title Focus Attention on the *Spirit* of God?

More precisely, our title juxtaposes the Spirit both to *theology* and to *the practices of the Church,* and this double juxtaposition may indeed suggest something about the broad consensus that unites our essays.

On the one hand, by associating the Spirit with Church practices, the title may hint at a certain resistance to modernist assumptions that would separate the two. Theologians as otherwise different as Fergus Kerr and John Milbank have described the importance to cultural and political modernity of a clear dividing line between the inner and the outer, with an inward realm

26. See L. Gregory Jones, "A Thirst for God or Consumer Spirituality? Cultivating Disciplined Practices of Being Engaged by God," in *Spirituality and Social Embodiment,* ed. L. Gregory Jones and James J. Buckley (Oxford: Blackwell, 1997), pp. 3-28.

of private subjectivity marked off clearly from the outward realm of secular public objectivity.[27] The internalization of such dichotomies in modern religious thought has yielded enormous pressure towards associating "Spirit" with the private realm of inward subjectivity, as well as towards a hierarchical ranking of the inner and the outer. The inner world of the private self has been identified as the locus of authentic contact with transcendence, while bodily disciplines, ritual forms, and outward practices seem always to attract the adjective "mere" to mark their lower significance for the life of the spirit.

While such classical-modern dichotomies and hierarchies are under attack from several different directions in "postmodern" high culture, they still retain enormous cultural power, not only in the various subcultures of contemporary spirituality, but also and not least in the academic study of religion and theology. By contrast, it would be fair to say that the essays in this volume proceed on different assumptions. Hütter's essay indeed provides a deliberate alternative, a vision in which bodily communal practice is the primary location for our "suffering divine things" under the impress of the Spirit. But a comparable dissent from modern assumptions is surely implicit in Wood's description of a knowledge of God acquired through participation in liturgical practice, in Yeago's exploration of the patristic claim that the "understanding" of Scripture is dependent on communal context, in Jones's insistence that Christian spirituality requires the kind of catechesis that is the work of the Spirit.

On the other hand, by associating *theology* with this juxtaposition of "Spirit" and "practices," our title hints at an account of the complex point of departure of theological reflection as practiced in these essays. Reinhard Hütter has spoken elsewhere of the core practices of the Church as "enhypostasized" in the Spirit;[28] not all of us are equally happy with this application of christological categories to a pneumatological issue, but his formulation at least suggests the complexity of the starting-point of a mode of theological reflection that is *both* Evangelical *and* Catholic. Such a mode or style of theological reflection must begin *both* from God's always-precedent action and grace (Evangelical emphasis) *and* from the holy catholic Church, the communion of saints, which is likewise also always prior to the thinking and pondering of the individual theologian (Catholic emphasis). And it must begin from these two as, in some proper sense, *one single starting-point:* in the

27. Fergus Kerr, *Theology after Wittgenstein* (Oxford and New York: Blackwell, 1986); John Milbank, *Theology and Social Theory* (Oxford and New York: Blackwell, 1990).

28. Reinhard Hütter, *Suffering Divine Things: Theology as Church Practice,* trans. Doug Stott (Grand Rapids/Cambridge: Eerdmans, 2000).

Spirit, beginning with God's action and beginning with the Church and its practices are *one* beginning, in a unity in which the divine and the human are neither divided nor confused.

Much would need to be said to develop such formulations into a proper theological position, and undoubtedly there would be differences and disagreements in the diverse ways in which the authors of these essays would execute that development. The editors chose to make Hütter's the lead essay in the collection precisely because it brought this underlying theme, which we regard as crucial to the project, so clearly into focus. Some of the rest us have given generous indications of how we would go on to work out this issue; others have been more reticent.

The unity of the essays does not therefore lie in agreement with any *single* account, whether Hütter's or another, of the relation between the Holy Spirit and the practices of the Church. What binds them together is rather their friendliness to the notion that it is with *some* acknowledgment of God's action as bound up with Church practice, and with *some* acknowledgment of Church practice as the locus of God's action, that theology best begins. And this brings us back to the beginning of this introduction for it is precisely here that we have found sufficient unity for an extended and coherent theological conversation.

As in the cases of knowing and other practices, or the arguments over when practices of active resistance and when practices of patient endurance are called for, we have left many questions with regard to the Spirit unanswered. But what may be important about the essays in this book, and the theological alternative they represent, is that none of their authors shows any signs of attraction to the notion that the theological task is to find or construct a place in the world for "s/Spirit." On the contrary, the assumption in these essays is that the action of the Spirit has already united divine and human, inner and outer, public and private, soul and body, in the communion of the Church and in the distinctive discourse, institutions, and practices that make up its life. This precedent action of the Spirit is discerned and followed, but not constructed or constituted, by theology.

Some of the authors of these essays are drawn to theological projects in which it might be attempted to describe in some systematic way the work of the Spirit constituting the ecclesial locus of theological reflection. Others are content simply to live in that space and ponder what goes on there and consider how human lives are formed, how human joys and sorrows are engaged, and how the world and its powers are challenged thereby. Again, we would encourage readers to look for such differences and find a way beyond them that we have not. But the starting-point, a starting-point in the midst of the public, ecclesial work of the Spirit, rather than in the privacy and alienation of the modern or postmodern self, is on the whole shared by all, and constitutes, we as editors hope, one of the contributions of this book to the contemporary theological scene.

In all of this, what kind of an audience are we addressing? We presume an audience of educated Christians, from both Catholic and Evangelical traditions. We assume that what has bound us together as a group will also bind us to our audience: participation in the life and practice of the Church, and a common commitment to thoughtful inquiry into the implications and significance of that life and that practice. We do not assume therefore that what we have to say will be of much interest to theologians willingly isolated from the Church, nor to Church members willingly isolated from the disciplines of theological reflection and inquiry.

Some essays will be easier reading than others; all will require patient attention and even study. We ourselves have debated these essays and criticized one another. We hope that readers will find their way through each chapter, asking not only how they move on their own but also how they contribute to the larger theme encapsulated in our title and subtitle. What, readers might ask, does this essay have to say about knowing the triune God? About the role of the Spirit in the practices of the Church? About specific practices that constitute the Church, and their relationship to still other practices? About the Catholic and Evangelical identity of the Church of the third millennium? Where might one essay benefit from the insights of another? And where might we all have to repent? If the reader disagrees with the proposal of one of the essays, then what is the alternative and how does it bear on the work of the Spirit in the practices of the Church? Such are the sorts of questions we recommend readers keep in mind.

There are many other perspectives and themes that would have been desirable to include. We wished that participants in the group who represented other ecclesial traditions had not been prevented by prior commitments from contributing. An ecclesial epistemology with any claim to completeness would, moreover, have included more about the many gods who try to challenge the triune God; about the challenges to Christian mission and Christian practice from the diversity and interdependence of cultures on a global stage; about the challenge of the competing catholicities of Islam and Buddhism, or about the political witness of the Church in a world at once totalitarian and democratic, tribal and imperialist. We do not aspire to completeness, but to a preliminary sketch, on the basis of which readers might wish to continue thinking with the Church Catholic and Evangelical.

In and with its faults, we dedicate this volume to the Braatens and

Jensons — for their generosity in calling together a group of theological strangers, for their warm and exquisite hospitality when we assembled, and most of all for their astounding patience in letting this volume take its own shape in its own time. We wish we had more to give back. But this is it, for now.

I. SOURCES OF KNOWING THE TRINITY

2. The Church

The Knowledge of the Triune God: Practices, Doctrine, Theology

REINHARD HÜTTER

Introduction

The goal of the following chapter[1] is to retrieve an understanding common to almost all Christians until roughly about two hundred years ago: *that the church is the location where we come to know God, surely not in every possible way,*[2] *but in the one decisive way, namely as the One who saves us and draws us into the fullness of the divine life — all of this through faith in the crucified and risen Jesus Christ.* The church itself is nothing else than the thankful creature of God's saving work, not a proud executor but a glad recipient. Yet this receiving embodied in practices is precisely the way in and through which the Holy Spirit works the saving knowledge of God. For this very reason not only the Catholics but also the Reformers could call the church the "mother of faith."[3]

Yet the great schism of the Western church, its ensuing religious wars,

1. This is a strongly abbreviated and condensed version of my book *Suffering Divine Things: Theology as Church Practice,* trans. Doug Stott (Grand Rapids, Eerdmans, 2000).

2. For a discussion of the way the very structure of creation can support in suggestive ways our knowledge of the triune God cf. Chapter 7, "Interpretation," by David Cunningham. For a fuller account cf. David Cunningham, *These Three Are One: The Practice of Trinitarian Theology* (Oxford: Blackwell, 1998).

3. Cf. Martin Luther, *Weimarer Ausgabe,* 40/1, 664, 15-21.

and the mutual doctrinal condemnations opened the door to a basic skepticism regarding the very possibility of coming to know the triune God in and through the church's practices and teachings. Instead, the intellectual avant-garde of the seventeenth and eighteenth centuries felt forced to fall back onto a rational knowledge of God that could be metaphysically warranted and assured. Both the late medieval developments in rational theology and the increased retrieval of antique thinking during the Renaissance facilitated this move considerably.[4] Yet this metaphysically assured knowledge of God itself proved to be unstable. It was the very project of Kant's critical philosophy to show that the existence and knowledge of God can in no circumstances fall under the competence of a rational metaphysics.[5] Rather, the idea of God is a necessary consequence of the human being as moral agent. Another "Copernican revolution" of sorts had taken place: the human subject becomes the fixed point for whom the idea of God is a necessary working hypothesis of practical reason.[6]

What is the point of the church under these radically changed circumstances? The church, now just an aggregation of individuals, is the location for moral motivation and improvement, with Jesus being the paradigm of perfect morality.[7] It was Schleiermacher's great achievement to overcome this radical reduction of the saving knowledge of God to a model of the moral life by establishing the category of "religion" as an entity fundamentally different from metaphysics and morals and therefore immune to Kant's critical philosophy. Religion roots in a pre-reflective and ultimately ineffable feeling of radical dependence over against the universe in its totality as experienced by the subject.[8]

4. For some different yet mutually supportive accounts of this complex intellectual development cf. Michael Buckley, *At the Origins of Modern Atheism* (New Haven/London: Yale University Press, 1987), Michael Allen Gillespie, *Nihilism Before Nietzsche* (Chicago/London: University of Chicago Press, 1995), J. B. Schneewind, *The Invention of Modernity: A History of Modern Moral Philosophy* (Cambridge: Cambridge University Press, 1998), and Jeffrey Stout, *The Flight from Authority: Religion, Morality, and the Quest for Autonomy* (New Haven/London: Yale University Press, 1981).

5. Immanuel Kant, *Critique of Pure Reason,* B 611-71. For a good general introduction cf. Arsenij Gulyga, *Immanuel Kant: His Life and Thought* (Boston: Birkhäuser, 1987), and Otfried Höffe, *Immanuel Kant* (Albany, N.Y.: State University of New York Press, 1994).

6. Immanuel Kant, *Critique of Practical Reason,* A 223-38. For a good overview and introduction cf. Bernard M. G. Reardon, *Kant as Philosophical Theologian* (Totowa, N.J.: Barnes & Noble, 1988).

7. Immanuel Kant, *Religion Within the Limits of Reason Alone,* B 137-44. Cf. Reardon, *Kant as Philosophical Theologian,* pp. 125-28.

8. Cf. Friedrich Schleiermacher, "Second Speech: On the Essence of Religion," in *On Religion: Speeches to Its Cultured Despisers,* trans. R. Crouter (Cambridge/New York: Cambridge

The church now is the community of those religiously moved to express and communicate and thereby interpret and understand their ineffable religious experience. Consequently, Jesus becomes the paradigm of this very religiosity.[9]

What is significant is that in both the "Kantian church" of moral motivation and the "Schleiermacherian church" of religious communication, the moral and/or religious subject antecedes the church. The fixed point is the subject to whom the "church" stands in a functional relationship of service — be it of a moral or a religious kind. In other words, *the subject is the end of the church.* And the result of this is nothing else than the modern "denomination" and the service-jargon pervasive in contemporary church growth talk. And this is not surprising. Where the subject is the end of the church, the market becomes the means.[10]

The point of the following proposal is not to overcome this problematic by heralding some "postmodern turn" that might simply relieve us from our predicament. The postmodernity presently celebrated seems to be nothing less than an intensification of the very turn to the subject — yet at the same time having lost the utopian assurances once connected to it by the Enlightenment. The following, rather, is to be understood as an exercise in theological remembrance in the face of the modern turn to the subject and its postmodern mass application. Yet my proposal does not suggest a return to "pre-modern" securities either. Rather, in a conflictual and thus critical relationship to modernity it is the attempt to remember *theologically* what is at stake in the church being the church for knowing the triune God. The church is gifted with a promise that it carries in its very way of being the church. This promise is nothing less than a knowledge of God that both saves and transforms. Yet this is a knowledge that depends on the church's practices and in this significant sense antecedes us as individuals. Only by being drawn into these very practices, which in their very core are the church's make-up, does that knowledge of God come about that we do not own, but that ultimately will own us. In this very specific way *the church will turn out to be the end of the subject* — precisely in its modern sense where knowledge presupposes the subject's self-positing and ultimately will to power.

And what would it mean if theology were to be itself reconceived in light of this theological remembrance? What if theology were neither a hermeneutics of

---

University Press, 1988); *The Christian Faith,* trans. H. R. Macintosh and J. S. Stewart (Edinburgh: T. & T. Clark, 1948), p. 4.

9. Cf. Schleiermacher, *The Christian Faith,* pp. 3, 93-94.

10. For an excellent analysis and critique of this dynamic cf. Philip D. Kenneson and James L. Street, *Selling Out the Church: The Dangers of Church Marketing* (Nashville: Abingdon Press, 1997).

"values" to be distilled from the moral paradigm "Jesus" nor a description or re-imagination of the religious subjectivity paradigmatically encountered in Jesus?

Theology, I will claim, has to be understood as a distinct practice that comes necessarily with the church (— yet without being constitutive of the church!). As an ecclesial practice, theology precisely realizes the fact that the knowledge of God cannot be achieved "nakedly," be it in form of the "thereness" of an "objective" knowledge (early modern metaphysics) or be it in form of that "knowledge" which is the construct of the poietic subject (modern religiosity after Kant). Rather, Christian knowledge of God can only be gained by suffering God's saving activity as it engages us in word and sacrament as well as in the rest of the church's core practices and by committing us to the preaching and teaching of the gospel *(doctrina evangelii)* through those specifications that needed to be formulated as ways of holding on to the gospel in the face of its distortion (*doctrina definita;* doctrine). In other words, if the church is the end of the subject because the Holy Spirit becomes the agent of the triune God's knowledge through the church's core practices and teaching, "to do theology" appropriately means to do it in relationship to both the church's core practices and to doctrine. This claim is clearly an affront if one assumes that the subject is the end of the church. Yet under the presupposition here entertained that the church is the end of the subject, this understanding of theology is its necessary implication.[11]

Naked "Knowledge of God" and the Modern Dilemma: God "Reified" or God "Construed"

Yet before we move into more explicitly theological considerations we have to realize what the specific dilemma is under which we encounter the question of the knowledge of God in modernity: "Knowledge of God" is an oxymoron as long as we understand it strictly along the lines of knowledge-of-something-as-acquired-according-to-the-universal-standards-of-knowledge. Under the epistemological conditions of modernity, essentially two dominant ways out of this oxymoronic situation were developed.

First, since God is not part — or even the totality — of that which can be "known," i.e., of the created world, God cannot be known in the strict sense at

11. The latter approach by no means excludes the fact that philosophy (metaphysics), science, and humanities are significant conversation partners conveying relevant knowledge. Yet what they do not convey is the knowledge of God through which we are being drawn into God's own life.

all. All we can do is consciously construe "similes" that most accurately reflect our pre-reflective and essentially ineffable experiences of the transcendent and communicate them to others. This communication is essential for a full development of human selfhood in relationship to others and to the transcendent. The estrangement inherent in this kind of "knowledge of God" is transparent in the poietic nature of the "similes" that theological construction puts in place for the ineffable "mystery" of the divine. Thus, the oxymoronic situation is solved by giving up the expectation of a genuine knowledge in relationship to God. There might be intimations of the divine as poietically construed by the pious consciousness, but there is no genuine knowledge of God.[12]

Second, since God is to be understood as the omnipotent Creator of the world, it is quite conceivable that God conceived of ways that allow for a genuine knowledge of God under the conditions of a created world, be it via human reason's immediate participation in divine reason or via a particular corpus of divinely inspired texts, or via a particular deposit of faith that potentially contains all the knowledge of God to be unfolded and mediated by an infallible magisterium. Here there is a form of "worldly knowledge" to be acquired "under the conditions of the world" as any other knowledge can be acquired. Some particular aspect of the created world has to be claimed so that God can be known "univocally," i.e., under the general conditions of knowledge as constitutive of this world.[13] "God" becomes a "thing" to be "known." Here the oxymoronic situation is solved by getting rid of "God" in relationship to knowledge. There is a knowledge of a "God," who has essentially ceased to be God.[14]

12. This is fundamentally Schleiermacher's route, taken in response to the epistemological problematic defined by Kant's critical philosophy. Cf. Schleiermacher, *The Christian Faith,* p. 50.

13. Here I have in mind the modern understanding of metaphysics as onto-theology (based on a univocal concept of being and represented in various modern systems such as Descartes, Leibniz, Wolff, and Hegel). Martin Heidegger was the most consequential critic of this modern mode of metaphysics, to the degree that all recent deconstruction of metaphysics as onto-theology is fundamentally indebted to his thought. Cf. esp. his *Identity and Difference,* trans. Joan Stambaugh (New York: Harper & Row, 1969) and in Heidegger's footsteps cf. esp. Walter Schulz, *Der Gott der neuzeitlichen Metaphysik* (Pfullingen: Verlag Gnther Neske, 1957), pp. 31-56. For a critical re-lecture of Heidegger's reading of Descartes, cf. Jean-Luc Marion, *On Descartes' Metaphysical Prism: The Constitution and the Limits of Onto-theo-logy in Cartesian Thought,* trans. Jeffrey L. Kosky (Chicago: University of Chicago Press, 1999).

14. Cf. the penetrating criticism of this way of knowing "God" under the conditions of the world, Jean-Luc Marion, *God Without Being: Hors-texte* (Chicago/London: University of Chicago Press, 1991), pp. 53-107. (But cf. the way Marion nuanced and qualified his critique of

An earlier attempt at overcoming this modern dilemma was Hegel's speculative sublation of the two alternatives in the human spirit's participation via philosophical reflection in the absolute Spirit: Knowledge of God is possible insofar as we participate via speculative reason in God's own self-knowledge. The decisive problem in this still deeply influential way of thinking is the fact that the radical difference between Creator and creature is erased in the (self-) movement of spirit. The "knowledge of God" is saved by Hegel in and through the human spirit's reflective activity completed in the standpoint of absolute Thought.[15]

Karl Barth's Solution and Its Pneumatological Instability

One of the lasting achievements of Karl Barth and the theological movement he initiated was to keenly see this modern dilemma and at the same time not to succumb to the Hegelian temptation, namely to ultimately identify the human mind's self-reflexivity with God's self-knowledge, or at least a genuine moment of it. The crucial reason that allowed Barth to stay free from the Hegelian temptation was his insight into the noetic effects of human sin. *Post lapsum* humanity not only has lost any genuine community with God that might allow for a participatory knowledge of God. Rather, humanity finds itself in a position of radical estrangement from and even enmity toward God — a situation in which knowledge of God can only be experienced as a radical judgment of the human knower and, at the very same time, as the radical justification "in Christo" of this very knower.[16] Therefore, the knowledge of

---

Aquinas's alleged "onto-theology" in his "Saint Thomas d'Aquin et l'onto-théo-logie" in *Revue Thomiste* 95 [1995]:31-66.) It should be noted that I am narrating, obviously in strokes all too broad, a primarily Protestant problem. To do justice to the Roman Catholic engagement of and partial complicity in modern onto-theology is another, and, for that matter, highly complex, story. In such an account one would have to attend to the intellectual struggle between traditional, neo-scholastic Thomism and the *Nouvelle Théologie* (with Transcendental Thomism playing its own unique role). For an accessible introduction to this struggle from a nuanced Thomist perspective, cf. William J. Hill, O.P., *Knowing the Unknown God* (New York: Philosophical Library, 1971).

15. G. W. F. Hegel, *Phenomenology of Mind,* trans. J. B. Baillie (New York: Humanities Press, 6th ed. 1966), ch. 8, "Absolute Knowledge." Cf. Søren Kierkegaard's penetrating critique of Hegelianism, especially in his *Philosophical Fragments,* trans. D. F. Swenson, rev. Howard V. Hong (Princeton: Princeton University Press, 1962).

16. This is preeminently the case in Barth's *The Epistle to the Romans,* trans. E. C. Hoskyns (Oxford/New York: Oxford University Press, 1933). Cf. on the "knowledge of God" without Christ: "But what does 'apart from and without Christ' mean? *The wrath of God is revealed*

God is possible only as God's self-giving knowledge.[17] Barth had to develop the knowledge of God as God's self-communication *in actu,* in order to preserve God's freedom from the modern claim to the self's epistemic primacy (Kant)[18] or supremacy (Fichte).[19] At the same time, Barth integrated genuine concerns of modernity into his account by construing human selfhood and freedom relationally so that in the encounter with God's self-communication the human is not only judged and justified in Christ but also genuinely set free in relationship to God, the enactment of which are faith and witness. "In" this knowledge of God *in actu* this "freedom as relationship," to which humanity was destined from the beginning, is both fully revealed and restored.[20]

---

against all ungodliness and unrighteousness of men. These are the characteristic features of our relation to God, as it takes shape on this side of the resurrection. Our relation to God is *ungodly.* We suppose that we know what we are saying when we say 'God'. We assign Him the highest place in our world: and in so doing we place Him fundamentally on one line with ourselves and with things. We assume that He *needs something:* and so we assume that we are able to arrange our relation to Him as we arrange our other relationships. We press ourselves into proximity with Him: and so, all unthinking, we make Him nigh unto ourselves. . . . Secretly we are ourselves the masters of this relationship. We are not concerned with God, but with our own requirements, to which God must adjust Himself. . . . And so, when we set God upon the throne of the world, we mean by God ourselves. In 'believing' on Him, we justify, enjoy, and adore ourselves. Our devotion consists in a solemn affirmation of ourselves and of the world and in a pious setting aside of the contradiction. . . . Such is our relation to God apart from and without Christ, on this side [of the] resurrection, and before we are called to order. God Himself is not acknowledged as God and what is called 'God' is in fact Man. By living to ourselves, we serve the 'No-God'" (p. 44). Cf. on the dialectic of judgment and grace in God's self-communication in Christ: "We have to see Adam and Christ, the old and the new world, the dominion of sin and the dominion of righteousness, linked together in a strict dialectical relationship. We have seen them apparently pointing to one another, determining one another, and authorizing one another. We have been careful, however, to emphasize (vv. 15-17) the dialectical character of this relation. The first is dissolved by the second; the reverse process is impossible" (p. 188). And: "The continuity of the relation between sin and grace, Saul and Paul, forms the actus purus of an invisible occurrence in God. The unity of the divine will is divided only that it may be revealed in overcoming the division" (p. 189). But cf. also *CD* I/1 ¶5.4. On the inner logic of this dynamic cf. Bruce McCormack, *Karl Barth's Critically Realistic Dialectical Theology: Its Genesis and Development 1909-1936* (Oxford: Clarendon Press, 1995), pp. 245-62.

17. "The Truth itself has proclaimed to us that Truth is Truth and that we originally participate in it: — *The Spirit himself beareth witness with our spirit, that we are children of God*" (Karl Barth, *The Epistle to the Romans,* p. 298).

18. Cf. Gulyga, *Immanuel Kant,* for the best recent intellectual biography. For the best and, at the same time, most accessible introduction to Kant's transcendental idealism cf. Sebastian Gardner, *Kant and the Critique of Pure Reason* (London/New York: Routledge, 1999).

19. Cf. Michael Allen Gillespie, *Nihilism Before Nietzsche,* pp. 64-100, for the crucial impact the early Fichte had on nineteenth-century thought and literature.

20. Cf. *CD* IV/3.2 ¶71.2 and idem, "The Gift of Freedom: Foundation of Evangelical Eth-

But how, we might ask, is *theology* being construed from this perspective in relationship to the knowledge of God? For Barth, theology is the dialectical practice of reflecting on the witness of God's past self-communication in constant expectation of God's future self-communication. Being stretched out between memory and hope, between the witness of Scripture and the mandate of proclamation, theology critically examines the church's performance of witnessing to God's self-communication by preaching the gospel.[21] Barth deployed the philosophical concept of a "realist actualism"[22] as a way of overcoming the modern dilemma in regard to the knowledge of God. This concept allows Barth to differentiate categorically between God and God's act of self-communication on the one hand and all "traces" of this self-communication in humanity's witness to it on the other hand, be it Scripture, the witnessing acts of baptism and the Lord's Supper, church doctrines, and the teachings of the church fathers as well as of later theologians. Insofar as they are faithful witnesses they are to be taken seriously. But since they are just that, witnesses, the danger of reification, of mixing up God with one of the reflections of God's self-communications can thereby be avoided.[23] On the other hand, Barth's concept allows him to keep in check any modern claims to the poietic primacy (or supremacy) of the knowing subject.

Yet Barth has to pay a high price for his highly intricate way of coping with the modern dilemma of the knowledge of God. His "actualistic" solution imprisons as much as it liberates. Why? Because it leads to the eclipse of the Holy Spirit's distinct economy and mission. Barth understands the Holy Spirit as God's self-enactment, or better put, as the enacted relationship, first as the inner-trinitarian relationship between Father and Son, and second, as the actualization of God's self-revelation in the human being, thus setting one free to be a believing and responding agent.[24] What is lost in this pneumatological ac-

---

ics," in idem, *The Humanity of God*, trans. Thomas Wieser (Atlanta: John Knox Press, 1978), pp. 69-96.

21. Cf. *CD* I/1 ¶1 and 7.

22. Cf. George Hunsinger, *How to Read Karl Barth: The Shape of His Theology* (New York/Oxford: Oxford University Press, 1991), pp. 30ff., 43-49, and Bruce McCormack, *Karl Barth's Critically Realistic Dialectical Theology*, pp. 129ff.

23. Cf. *in nuce* already his essay "Church and Theology," in Karl Barth, *Theology and Church: Shorter Writings 1920-1928*, trans. L. P. Smith (New York: Harper & Row, 1962), pp. 286-306, and extensively *CD* I/2 ¶21-24.

24. Cf. most clearly *CD* I/1, ¶450: "The creature needs the Creator to be able to live. It thus needs the relation to Him. But it cannot create this relation. God creates it by His own presence in the creature and therefore as a relation of Himself to Himself. The Spirit of God is God in His freedom to be present to the creature, and therefore to create this relation, and therefore to be the life of the creature." Cf. also *CD* I/1, ¶470: "[The Holy Spirit] is the common element, or, better, the fellowship, the act of communion, of the Father and the Son."

count is (a) the Holy Spirit as distinct trinitarian "identity" *(hypostasis)*[25] and (b) the Spirit's distinct economy as enacted through the Spirit's works.[26]

The severe limitation of Barth's pneumatology is mirrored in the very way his concept of the knowledge of God and of theology finally is unable to fully overcome the modern dilemma. Barth's central concept of "actualism" makes the dialectical discourse of theology a *conditio sine qua non* for avoiding to be pierced by either one of the modern dilemma's horns. Only the ongoing dialectic of the theological discourse itself on the one hand keeps the witness (Scripture, church doctrine, theological teaching) "fluid" (i.e., preserves it from becoming a reified knowledge of God) and on the other hand prevents any poietic activity from the theologians' side by committing and submitting them to the ongoing discourse with all the significant interlocutors (Scripture, church doctrine, theological teaching etc.).[27] This is the reason why the *Church Dogmatics* is essentially a discourse without beginning or end.[28] In the very enactment of a discourse, the dialectical theologian practices a subtle sublation of both ends of the modern dilemma. Yet Barth achieves this only by means of a sleight-of-hand. The one who practices the dialectic of sublation, of the ongoing suspense for the sake of the ever-new inbreaking of God's self-communication, is the individual theologian in the enactment of an ongoing theological discourse. While thus the noetic primacy (or supremacy) of the human might be held in check, the primacy of the human as the condition for the possibility of practicing the ongoing suspense of theological discourse is implicitly but *de facto* reaffirmed in Barth's concept.[29]

25. Cf. Robert W. Jenson, "You Wonder Where the Spirit Went," in *Pro Ecclesia* 2 (1993): 296-304.

26. The emphasis on the Holy Spirit's own economy is especially strong in Eastern Orthodox theology. Yet one can also find it in the Western tradition — arguably on the basis of Eastern-Orthodox influences — i.e., among Lutheran theologians like Peter Brunner, Wolfhart Pannenberg, and Robert W. Jenson. (It is not an accident that the latter two were students of Peter Brunner at the University of Heidelberg.)

27. Cf. the exchange between Erik Peterson and Karl Barth regarding the nature and task of theology in relationship to doctrine, in Reinhard Hütter, "The Church as Public: Dogma, Practice, and the Holy Spirit," in *Pro Ecclesia* 3 (1994): 334-61, esp. pp. 340ff. and more extensively in Hütter, *Suffering Divine Things*, pp. 95-115.

28. Cf. Ernstpeter Maurer, *Sprachphilosophische Aspekte in Karl Barths "Prolegomena zur Kirchlichen Dogmatik"* (Frankfurt/New York: Peter Lang, 1989).

29. While I disagree with his constructive turn, I largely agree with the issues Erik Peterson raised critically over against Barth in his essay "Was ist Theologie?" in *Theologische Traktate* (Munich: Kösel, 1951), pp. 9-43. Cf. also Oswald Bayer's critique along similar lines in the long and very astute analysis of Barth in his *Theologie* (Gütersloh: Gütersloher Verlagshaus, 1994), pp. 310-88, esp. pp. 310-18, and my *Suffering Divine Things*, pp. 95-115.

One way out would be to succumb again to the Hegelian temptation and claim that the discourse itself reflects the Spirit's self-enactment in history, which would only deepen the question of how to achieve a knowledge of God that is not primarily self-knowledge. Yet both Kierkegaard and Barth make a serious return to this path impossible. Another way out would be to rethink the question of how the knowledge of God and theology relate by rethinking the inner connection between the church, doctrine, and theology. The guiding concept will be "pathos" in its original meaning: being formed and thus qualified by the knowledge of God as embodied in the church's constitutive practices and in doctrine — both of which will have to be understood as the Spirit's works. In the following, we will take this course.[30]

The Holy Spirit's Economy and the Knowledge of God

It is necessary to approach the question of the knowledge of God — following Barth's initial direction — by starting from a much more substantive pneumatology, one that takes the Holy Spirit's distinct economy into account. Following the lead of Eastern Orthodox theologians,[31] this move will allow us to understand the church's existence and mission in the closest connection with the Holy Spirit's person and mission. In addition, it will permit us to develop a pneumatological notion of doctrine that allows for understanding the knowledge of God as a distinct "pathos," a "suffering" through which the Spirit recreates us and draws us into his sanctifying mission. My thesis is the following: *The knowledge of God is achieved in and through the reception of the gospel proclaimed and taught (doctrina evangelii), which takes place via the church's constitutive practices and via doctrine (dogma; doctrina definita).* There might be potential and partial knowledge of God separate from these practices and from doctrine, yet sav-

30. For an extended version of the following cf. my *Suffering Divine Things,* pp. 116-45.

31. Cf. among many John D. Zizioulas, *Being as Communion: Studies in Personhood and the Church* (Crestwood, N.Y.: St. Vladimir's Seminary Press, 1985); John D. Zizioulas, "Die pneumatologische Dimension der Kirche," in *Internationale katholische Zeitschrift Communio* 2 (1973): 133-47; Nikos A. Nissiotis, *Die Theologie der Ostkirche im ökumenischen Dialog: Kirche und Welt in orthodoxer Sicht* (Stuttgart: Evangelisches Verlagswerk, 1968); Nikos A. Nissiotis, "Der pneumatologische Ansatz und die liturgische Verwirklichung des neutestamentlichen," in Felix Christ, ed., *Oikonomia: Heilsgeschichte als Thema der Theologie* (Hamburg/Bergstedt: Berg, 1967), pp. 302-9; Dimitru Stăniloae, *Theology and the Church* (Crestwood, N.Y.: St. Vladimir's Seminary Press, 1976).

ing knowledge of God — that knowledge we suffer by being drawn into God's triune life — is the reception of the gospel through which the Holy Spirit recreates us. Most crucial in this regard is (1) to develop an understanding of how the church is to be understood as the Spirit's work through which he fulfills his own sanctifying mission in the triune economy of salvation, (2) how the *doctrina* as corresponding to the church's core practices is to be understood similarly as the Spirit's work, and (3) how theology as distinct ecclesial discourse-practice is completely in-formed by the Spirit's works, namely both by the church's core practices and by doctrine. The knowledge of God has to be understood as constituting theology's *pathos* in that its discourse is completely informed, or better, qualified, by doctrine and the constitutive practices through which it receives the saving and sanctifying knowledge of the triune God. Thus, theology's discourse depends upon the prior existence of the knowledge of God as it is embodied in both the church's constitutive practices and the gospel as specified through doctrine. Its very *pathic* character reflects theology's complete dependence on the Spirit's works. These works constitute the Spirit's own distinct public, whose telos is the fulfillment of the Spirit's sanctifying mission in the triune God's economy of salvation.

The Church's Constitutive Practices: The Spirit's Sanctifying Work

While it might be possible to draw upon a number of theologians at this point in order to underwrite the following claim, it makes most eminent sense to draw upon Martin Luther's theology. Not only is he the preeminent Reformer, acknowledged both by Melanchthon and Calvin as their senior and teacher. More importantly, he offers an ecumenically as well as theologically helpful way of perceiving the church as the Holy Spirit's work in the third part of his treatise "On the Councils and the Church."[32] In this text, probably the best summary of Luther's mature ecclesiology, he develops a much richer and denser account of the relationship between the Holy Spirit and the church than we tend to find in the standard Protestantism of "word and sac-

32. Martin Luther, "On the Councils and the Church," in *Luther's Works,* vol. 41 (Philadelphia: Fortress Press, 1966), esp. pp. 143-78. For a list of core practices that is fully reflective of the Mennonite theological tradition cf. John Howard Yoder, *Body Politics: Five Practices of the Christian Community Before the Watching World* (Nashville: Discipleship Resources, 1992). Yoder focuses on Binding and Loosing, Baptism, Eucharist, Multiplicity of Gifts, and Open Meeting.

rament." Luther claims that we have to understand a set of particular practices as the church's constitutive marks. In them we not only unquestionably encounter "church," but also the Spirit's concrete works through which he fulfills his own sanctifying mission in the triune economy of salvation. Luther lists the following practices as the constitutive marks of the church:

- Proclamation of God's word and its reception in faith, confession, and deed[33]
- Baptism[34]
- Lord's Supper[35]
- Office of the keys[36]
- Ordination/offices[37]

33. "Now, wherever you hear or see this word preached, believed, professed, and lived, do not doubt that the true *ecclesia sancta catholica,* 'a Christian holy people,' must be there, even though their number is very small. . . . And even if there were no other sign than this alone, it would still suffice to prove that a Christian holy people must exist there, for God's word cannot be without God's people, and conversely, God's people cannot be without God's word" (Martin Luther, "On the Councils and the Church," p. 150). Cf. Chapter 4 in this volume, "The Liturgy," by Susan Wood for an account of how worship informs our knowledge of the triune God.

34. "That too is a public sign and a precious, holy possession by which God's people are sanctified" (Martin Luther, "On the Councils and the Church," p. 151).

35. "Third, God's people, or Christian holy people, are recognized by the holy sacrament of the altar, wherever it is rightly administered, believed, and received, according to Christ's institution. This too is a public sign and a precious, holy possession left behind by Christ by which his people are sanctified so that they also exercise themselves in faith and openly confess that they are Christian, just as they do with the word and with baptism" (Martin Luther, "On the Councils and the Church," p. 152).

36. "Fourth, God's people or holy Christians are recognized by the office of the keys exercised publicly. . . . Now where you see sins forgiven or reproved in some persons, be it publicly or privately, you may know that God's people are there. If God's people are not there, the keys are not there either; and if the keys are not present for Christ, God's people are not present. Christ bequeathed them as a public sign and a holy possession, whereby the Holy Spirit again sanctifies the fallen sinners redeemed by Christ's death, and whereby the Christians confess that they are a holy people in this world under Christ. And those who refuse to be converted or sanctified again shall be cast out from this holy people, that is, bound and excluded by means of the keys, as happened to the unrepentant Antinomians" (Martin Luther, "On the Councils and the Church," p. 153).

37. "Fifth, the church is recognized externally by the fact that it consecrates or calls ministers, or has offices that it is to administer. There must be bishops, pastors, or preachers, who publicly and privately give, administer, and use the aforementioned four things or holy possessions in behalf of and in the name of the church . . ." (Martin Luther, *Luther's Works* vol. 41, p. 154). "Now wherever you find these offices and officers, you may be assured that the holy Christian people are there; for the church cannot be without these bishops, pastors, preachers, priests; and conversely, they cannot be without the church. Both must be together" (Martin Luther, "On the Councils and the Church," p. 164).

– Prayer/doxology/catechesis[38]
– Way of the cross/discipleship[39]

What we find in Luther's account is a way to conceive the Holy Spirit's sanctifying work as concretely embodied and thus mediated in distinct communal practices.[40] For Luther, they clearly not only identify the church but make it "church" in the strict sense. This is why I tend to call them "core practices." Obviously each of these practices can be warranted christologically. This becomes clear in the way each of them is shaped in a unique way by the preaching and teaching of the gospel in its doctrinal specification. And each of these practices is open to misunderstanding, distortion, and abuse, as Luther is himself quite aware of. Therefore, each of the core practices needs to be normed by the proclamation and teaching of the gospel as it is specified in doctrine *(doctrina definita)*. Thus, Luther opens the avenue toward a *pneumatological ecclesiology:* the church is to be understood as a web of core practices which at the same time mark and constitute the church. These practices are the Spirit's works through which the Holy Spirit enacts his sanctifying mission in the triune economy of salvation.[41]

38. "Sixth, the holy Christian people are externally recognized by prayer, public praise, and thanksgiving to God. Where you see and hear the Lord's Prayer prayed and taught; or psalms or other spiritual songs sung, in accordance with the word of God and the true faith; also the creed, the Ten Commandments, and the catechism used in public, you may rest assured that a holy Christian people of God are present" (Martin Luther, "On the Councils and the Church," p. 164). Cf. Chapter 5 in this volume, "Contemplation," by Anna Williams and Chapter 6, "Baptism," by L. Gregory Jones for detailed accounts for how prayer and catechesis have traditionally functioned as practices in which the formation in knowing the triune God took place.

39. "Seventh, the holy Christian people are externally recognized by the holy possessions of the sacred cross. They must endure every misfortune and persecution, all kinds of trials and evil from the devil, the world, and the flesh (as the Lord's Prayer indicates) by inward sadness, timidity, fear, outward poverty, contempt, illness, and weakness, in order to become like their head, Christ. And the only reason they must suffer is that they steadfastly adhere to Christ and God's word . . ." (Martin Luther, "On the Councils and the Church," p. 164f.).

40. For a denser reading and spelling out of a number of those practices and their implications for the knowledge of the triune God cf. Chapter 4, "The Liturgy," by Susan K. Wood, Chapter 5, "Contemplation," by Anna Williams, and Chapter 6, "Baptism," by L. Gregory Jones.

41. Next to the ecclesial core practices, a whole range of other practices need to be mentioned, practices inherent to the church and integral to faith. One of them is theology as ecclesial discourse, a practice to which I will come further down. Cf. my "The Church as Public: Dogma, Practice, and the Holy Spirit," pp. 334-61, esp. pp. 355f., for a list of other practices. For the recovery of the significance of one important Christian practice, which actually is an implication of Luther's first core practice (proclamation of God's word and its reception in faith, confession, and deed), cf. L. Gregory Jones, *Embodying Forgiveness: A Theological Analysis* (Grand Rapids: Eerdmans, 1995).

Doctrine: The Knowledge of God Received — or: The "Form" of Theology's Pathos

So far we have identified the church's constitutive practices and their relationship to the Holy Spirit. Yet how do they relate to the knowledge of God? In an immediate sense, as I will show. In order to do that it is first necessary to clarify that which is received in the context of and through the church's core practices: It is the gospel proclaimed and taught in one, or as Luther puts it, the *"doctrina evangelii."* In the proclamation of God's word, in baptism, and in the Lord's Supper, the gospel addresses and claims us in both tangible and specific ways; in the form of the ordained office, prayer, doxology, catechesis, and the suffering walk of discipleship, the gospel engages us in a personal, intellectual, and deeply existential way. The gospel proclaimed and taught *(doctrina evangelii)* is the very point of the core practices, their telos. It is both the core practices' criterion and justification for a faithful enactment and embodiment of God's redeeming and reconciling work, the economy of salvation.

Yet the gospel proclaimed and taught does not exist without its normative specification. Or stronger: without its normative specification, the gospel could neither be proclaimed nor taught. The gospel has a specific intention that is open to misunderstanding and/or distortion. And precisely in order to remain faithful and hold on to the gospel's intention, its normative specification becomes necessary. The canon of Scripture,[42] the *regula fidei,*[43] and the creeds are from early on reflections of this necessity. The gospel proclaimed and taught requires its own normative specification. This is the very task of doctrine, or in its specific ecumenically pronounced form, of "dogma." Far from being an estrangement of the gospel, doctrine enables the gospel's proclamation and teaching![44]

Thus, it is crucial to differentiate between the gospel *(doctrina evangelii)* and doctrine *(doctrina definita)*. The gospel is, in its core, nothing else than Christ's own presence in the promise. Received in faith, Christ thus becomes faith's "form."[45] Traditionally put, in Christ as the "form of faith" both faith's

42. Cf. Chapter 3, "The Bible," by David S. Yeago for an account that forcefully shows how Scripture has functioned in this way in the tradition.

43. Cf. the very instructive essay on the "rule of faith" for theological statements by Bengt Hägglund, "Die Bedeutung der 'regula fidei' als Grundlage theologischer Aussagen," in *Studia theologica* 12 (1958): 1-44.

44. For a more extensive discussion of the relationship between doctrine and core practices cf. my *Suffering Divine Things*, pp. 134-45, and esp. Eeva Martikainen, *Doctrina: Studien zu Luthers Begriff der Lehre* (Helsinki: Luther-Agricola-Gesellschaft, 1992).

45. Here I draw upon the Finnish Luther research of Tuomo Mannerma's school. For a fine introduction to this significant movement towards rereading Luther's theology in light of the

content *(fides quae creditur)* and the act of faith *(fides qua creditur)* are inseparably one. Faith's form, Christ's presence, realizes both together. This is the fundamental "pathos" of Christian existence — fully identical with the saving knowledge of God. What is most crucial is that "faith's form" cannot be isolated either from the church's core practices or from doctrine, since such an attempt would mean to abstract Christ's presence in the believer from the Spirit's works, from the Spirit's means of conveying and enacting this qualification which *is* the gospel proclaimed and taught. Christ's saving presence cannot be separated from the Spirit's sanctifying mission as enacted through his particular works, the church's core practices. This is why doctrine needs to be carefully distinguished from the gospel yet cannot be separated from it, because the latter is secured through the specifications of the former. In other words, doctrine is another form of enactment of the gospel in analogy to the church's core practices — yet under a different aspect: Doctrine's "pathos," its own qualification through the gospel, is constituted by the binding formulation of the gospel's proclamation and teaching in the context of its internal challenge, distortion, or rejection. Doctrine is thus completely qualified by the gospel in committing itself in a binding way to a distinct teaching and by distinctively rejecting a particular theological teaching or set of teachings. Thus the saving knowledge of God, the gospel proclaimed and taught, is mediated and specified both by the church's core practices and by doctrine.[46]

Yet another important distinction needs to be made in order to fully unpack the relationship between the church and the knowledge of God. Not only is doctrine *(doctrina definita)* to be distinguished from the gospel *(doctrina evangelii)*, it also needs to be distinguished from any given particular consensus of theological teaching *(dogmatics)*, which is a phenomenon belonging to the ongoing ecclesial practice of theology. While this distinction is crucial in that the latter *(dogmatics)* is not binding, the former *(doctrina definita)* cannot exist independently from the latter. Doctrine is in constant need of re-appropriation, of re-interpretation, and of re-communication[47]

dialogue with Eastern-Orthodox theology cf. Carl E. Braaten and Robert W. Jenson, eds., *Union with Christ: The New Finnish Interpretation of Luther* (Grand Rapids: Eerdmans, 1998).

46. This move preserves the critical moment in Karl Barth precisely by offering a pneumatological account that is more concrete — according to Luther's rule implicit in the pneumatological ecclesiology of his "On the Councils and the Church": The more pneumatological the more concrete!

47. For a very fine recent exercise in re-interpreting and re-communicating Christian doctrine via the works of theologians who were most formative in its development and in retrieving the comprehensive soteriological telos of doctrine cf. Ellen Charry, *By the Renewing of Your*

lest it become a reified quasi-knowledge of God substituting for the gospel itself. This task of preventing doctrine from turning the saving knowledge of God into an ossified formulaic knowledge shapes theology as a distinct ecclesial practice. Yet it is important to understand that there is no transference of "accumulative effect" from theological teaching or dogmatics to doctrine/dogma. In other words, no theology as such, even if it finds widest acceptance and is deeply formative, becomes thereby "doctrine" or "dogma" — not even the theology of an Augustine, Aquinas, or Luther! The latter requires a distinct and always new "the Holy Spirit and we have decided . . ." (Acts 15:28), in other words, a binding confession of faith of the whole church through its appropriate channels. This always and only occurs as a reaffirmation of the one gospel *(doctrina evangelii)* under the conditions of its serious challenge, distortion, or rejection *inside* the church.[48]

While particular theologians had either directly or indirectly a decisive influence on the shaping of doctrine, the authority of their respective theologies is categorically different from the doctrines/dogmas they were formative in shaping. In other words, the authority of the theology of the Cappadocians Basil the Great, Gregory Nazianzen, and Gregory of Nyssa is categorically different from the Creed formulated at the *Second Ecumenical Council* (Constantinople 381), the authority of Augustine's theology from the 25 canons of the *Synod of Orange* (529), the authority of Luther's and Melanchthon's theology from the *Augsburg Confession* (1530) and the *Book of Concord* (1580), the authority of Calvin's theology from the *Synod of Dort* (1618/19), and the authority of Barth's theology from the *Barmen Declaration* (1934). To illustrate the most recent: While Barth's theology is not doctrine (*pace* some Barthians!), the *Barmen Declaration* (the drafter of which Barth was) *is*, because it was accepted as such by the subscribing *Confessing Churches* as a way to hold on to the gospel, thereby being completely qualified by the gospel, while at the same time rejecting a distinct set of heretical teachings promoted by the so-called "German Christians."

Let us summarize: The gospel is the saving knowledge of God received in word and sacrament. Each of the church's core practices (as the Holy Spirit's

---

Minds: The Pastoral Function of Christian Doctrine (Oxford: Oxford University Press, 1997). Chapter 3, "The Bible," Chapter 5, "Contemplation," Chapter 6, "Baptism," and Chapter 7, "Interpretation," can also be read in this way.

48. One of the most intricate problems facing and challenging this very account is, of course, the disunity and deep doctrinal disagreement between the churches. This fundamental problem is addressed by James J. Buckley in Chapter 8, "The Wounded Body." Cf. also Ephraim Radner, *The End of the Church: A Pneumatology of Christian Division in the West* (Grand Rapids: Eerdmans, 1998).

works) enacts the gospel in a particular way "pathically": participating in these practices provides the ongoing occasion for "suffering" the Spirit's sanctifying work, for growing in faith. *Doctrine reflects its own distinct pathos by holding fast to the gospel in the liminality and the binding character of its concrete affirmations and rejections.*

Thus, saving knowledge of God means to be engaged and transformed by the Spirit's sanctifying works and thereby to be increasingly drawn into God's triune life. There is no immediate knowledge of the God of the gospel in abstraction from being engaged by and drawn into the church's core practices and from being kept accountable by doctrine. Yet both, core practices and doctrine, are in need of another particular practice which is not constitutive of the church, but integral to its being the public through which the Spirit's sanctifying mission is fulfilled.

The Church and the Knowledge of God

In order to fully appreciate the nature and function of theology as an ecclesial practice in relationship to the saving knowledge of God, an intermediate step in ecclesiology is necessary. The reason for this seeming detour has to do with the fact that in a history in which church and culture were for a very long time virtually identical, the specific nature and location of Christian theology had been forgotten or eclipsed. While the relationship between church and society, Christianity and culture, has changed dramatically in recent decades, the implications for theology have only rarely been drawn.[49]

As the work of the Spirit, the church participates in the Spirit's sanctifying mission. In this precise sense the church is the Spirit's public. Only if we understand rightly the church as a public of its own kind, as the Spirit's public, will we be able to fully appreciate theology's particular location and function in relationship to the gospel and doctrine. In which way now is the church to be understood as a public of its own kind?

49. Most notable exceptions are George Lindbeck, Robert W. Jenson, Stanley Hauerwas, and John H. Yoder, all of them, of course, with Karl Barth in the background.

The Church as Public: A Political Analogy[50]

Here it will be helpful to draw on the insights of political theory. By way of interpreting Plato and Aristotle, Hannah Arendt[51] develops a structural notion of "public," of which the Greek polis is only one unique instantiation. Any public is defined by a particular set of normative convictions, embodied in constitutive practices and directed toward a distinctive telos.

One can easily see how the Greek polis would be one particular instantiation of this notion of "public." First of all, the polis was a specific space circumscribed by the city walls. A totally open and unstructured space (a seemingly endless plain, for example) would contradict one of the central purposes of the polis, namely to be a space for the free citizens to come together to speak, act, and cooperate. In addition, and much more importantly, the laws of the polis prescribed its constitutive practices and underwrote its normative convictions. Thus, just as much as a polis had a wall surrounding and defining it spatially, its laws were what made it possible as a unique public. The laws preceded the public; they were the result of a *poiesis,* an intentional production in order to provide the distinct practices through which praxis, the political activity of free citizens, was made possible. And third, it was a very particular telos that characterized the whole enterprise of the polis in its distinction for the *oikos:* the escape from the endless cycle of production and reproduction, from the fragility and finality of mortal life into a space where heroic *praxis* (both in speech and act) would be praised by equals and where a specific kind of immortality in the memory of the polis could be achieved.[52] This telos, in addition, was precisely what informed the kind of freedom (ἐλευθερία) for which the polis stood.[53]

This structural notion of a public as suggested by Hannah Arendt helps us to understand also a "democratic society" or a "university" as distinctive publics, each defined by a particular telos, circumscribed by constitutive

50. Here I draw heavily on my essay "The Church as Public." Cf. my *Suffering Divine Things,* pp. 158-71, and Bernd Wannenwetsch, *Gottesdienst als Lebensform: Ethik für Christenbürger* (Stuttgart: Kohlhammer, 1997), pp. 135-70.

51. Hannah Arendt, *The Human Condition* (Chicago: University of Chicago Press, 1958), esp. pp. 194-99.

52. Cf. Arendt, *The Human Condition,* and John Milbank, *Theology and Social Theory: Beyond Secular Reason* (Oxford: Blackwell, 1990), pp. 332-36.

53. Cf. Heinrich Schlier, article "ἐλεύθεορος, ἐλευθερόω, ἐλευθερία, ἀπελεύθερος," in *Theological Dictionary of the New Testament,* vol. II, ed. Gerhard Kittel, trans. G. W. Bromiley (Grand Rapids: Eerdmans, 1964), pp. 487-502, esp. pp. 487-92.

practices and underwritten by normative convictions. Similarly, we have to understand the *Torah* and especially the Decalogue as defining the public in which God's covenant people Israel's praxis of "following the way" could take place.[54] The *Torah* is, thus, not an idiosyncratic limitation of an otherwise "free" existence, but rather the very condition of the possibility of Israel's praxis of following the way of God — the latter being the defining telos of Israel as a distinct public. The Torah's binding nature creates precisely the "space," the public that makes this *praxis* possible in the first place.[55]

In a similar way we have to understand the church's doctrine and core practices as constituting and defining the church as a distinct public the telos of which is nothing less than the triune God's economy of salvation. Pentecost initiated an eschatological, albeit very concrete, "*novus ordo seclorum*."[56] A new public was created; the *ekklesia* of the eschatological polis (Hebrews 13:14) was gathered. After initial struggles, it became increasingly clear that it was not the life according to the *mizvot* anymore that constituted and informed this public most fundamentally.[57]

Rather, the *ekklesia* was constituted and informed, christologically and pneumatologically, by the *kerygma*[58] and by peculiar practices (especially the breaking of the bread and baptism).[59] The earliest creeds, the scriptural

54. Cf. Frank Crüsemann, *Bewahrung der Freiheit: Das Thema des Dekalogs in sozialgeschichtlicher Perspektiv* (Munich: Kaiser, 1983), and my way of relating his insights to an analogy between church and polis in *Evangelische Ethik als kirchliches Zeugnis* (Neukirchen-Vluyn: Neukirchener Verlag, 1993), pp. 259-65.

55. It was not essential for Israel as public to function as a state. Under certain circumstances it might have been necessary, under others it would have been counterproductive. But it was a central crisis for Israel whenever it was squeezed out as a public in its own right, whether through oppression and persecution (as in medieval and early modern Christendom), through the pressure of assimilation (as in the Enlightenment and post-Enlightenment periods), or — *horribile dictu* — through annihilation (as in the Holocaust). (By mentioning these three eclipses of Israel as public in one single sequence I imply by no means that the Holocaust might be an instance in any way comparable to the other two.)

56. Cf. the backside of any United States one dollar bill.

57. Cf. Jürgen Roloff, *Die Kirche im Neuen Testament* (Göttingen: Vandenhoeck & Ruprecht, 1993).

58. Still very instructive in this regard is Heinrich Schlier's essay "Kerygma und Sophia. Zur neutestamentlichen Grundlegung des Dogmas," in *Die Zeit der Kirche: Exegetische Aufsätze und Vorträge* (Freiburg: Herder, 2nd ed. 1958), pp. 206-32.

59. For a very strong reminder that the triune God is no other than the God of Israel and that the identification of precisely this God is at stake in the liturgy, cf. Chapter 9, "Israel," by Bruce Marshall. For another strong reminder that the *ekklesia* represents the strangers, the Gentiles that were added on "against the very nature" of Israel and the importance of this insight for ecclesial identity cf. Chapter 10, "The Stranger," by Eugene F. Rogers, Jr.

canon, the *regula fidei,* and the office of ministry that provided the continuation of the kerygma and the kerygma's practices were the elements that distinguished the church as an identifiable public both in distinction from the theologico-political public of the *Pax Romana*[60] and from Judaism.[61]

The Church as the Public of the Triune Economy of Salvation

It is important to remember that what we have elaborated in relationship to Greek politics is an *analogical* argument. The church is *not* just another instantiation of the overarching genus "polis." It is, rather, a public in a distinctive way such that the character of its "public nature" is defined neither by the genus "polis" nor by the "public" of modern civil society but by its own very particular and concrete designations.

From early on the church signaled in a very self-conscious way that it saw itself as a public in its own right in distinction from the *polis.*[62] The church did that by drawing in its self-description also upon the "other" of the polis, namely the *oikos* or household. Ephesians 2:19 clearly shows in its terminology how the church could be understood as something similar to a polis *and* to an oikos, though not identical with either one: "So then you are no longer *(xenoi)* and aliens *(paroikoi),* but you are citizens *(sympolitai)* with the saints and also members of the household *(oikeioi)* of God" (NRSV).[63] If we take this sentence in all its radicality, we have to conclude that the *ekklesia* explodes the framework of antique politics, which is precisely built on the strict dichotomy between *polis* and *oikos,* or, in John Milbank's wonderful formulation: "[T]he polis itself . . . was partly constituted as a machine for minimizing the oikos, or as a kind of cultural bypass operation to disassociate continuity and succession from wombs and domestic nurture. Hence a virtue (like Christian virtue) that can also be possessed by women, and be exercised as

60. For an interesting analysis of the theologico-political reality of the *Pax Romana* in contrast to Jesus and the early Christians cf. Klaus Wengst, *Pax Romana and the Peace of Christ* (Philadelphia: Fortress, 1987).

61. For an excellent account of the complex interrelationship of early Judaism and the *ekklesia* cf. N. T. Wright, *The New Testament and the People of God* (Minneapolis: Fortress Press, 1992).

62. For a differentiated historical account cf. Wayne A. Meeks, *The Origins of Christian Morality: The First Two Centuries* (New Haven: Yale University Press, 1993), pp. 37-51.

63. Cf. Joachim Gnilka, *Der Epheserbrief.* Herders theologischer Kommentar zum Neuen Testament, vol. 10 (Freiburg/Basel/Wien: Herder, 1971), pp. 152-54, and Heinrich Schlier, *Der Brief an die Epheser: Ein Kommentar* (Düsseldorf: Patmos, 1957), pp. 118-45, esp. pp. 140ff.

much in the home as in the forum (and perhaps also as much by the immature as the mature) cannot be 'virtue' in the same 'political' sense at all: it must be an entirely transvalued virtue."[64] Thus, the *ekklesia* was nothing less than a revolution of the antique political superstructure of *polis* and *oikos.* God's own *oikonomia,* God's own saving activity — encompassing all of creation and culminating in the *eschaton* of a new heaven and a new earth — becomes the characterizing telos of a public in its own right. Here, those who are by definition excluded from the antique *polis* and relegated to the *oikos*[65] (women, children, and slaves) become through baptism "*sympolitai*" of that unique public that is governed by God's *oikonomia,* God's household-rule. This is what the apostle Paul refers to in Galatians 3:27-29: "As many of you as were baptized into Christ have clothed yourselves with Christ. There is no longer Jew or Greek, there is no longer slave or free, there is no longer male and female; for all of you are one in Christ Jesus. And if you belong to Christ, then you are Abraham's offspring, heirs according to the promise" (NRSV). It is exactly this *oikonomia* of God, the church's characterizing telos, which the key practices embody and doctrines safeguard.

The Church as Public and Its Distinct Practice of Discourse: Theology

Yet next to its core practices each distinct public is characterized by a unique *discourse practice* which in an ongoing way thematizes the public's defining telos in relationship to the public's underlying convictions and constitutive practices. Each public needs its own discourse practice in order to remain faithfully oriented to its telos. While this discourse practice is in a unique way "critical" in that it consciously thematizes the public's telos, its practices, and convictions in relationship to the public's performance, the discourse practice is in no way a neutral arbiter independent from the binding convictions and constitutive practices of the respective public. Rather, being completely informed by the public's distinct telos constitutes its very freedom in relationship to both the binding convictions and the constitutive practices. In other words, the "critical" attitude of theology as ecclesial discourse practice rests in the concreteness of its freedom in relationship to doctrine and the

64. John Milbank, *Theology and Social Theory,* p. 364.

65. Aristotle, *Politics,* 1253bff. For an excellent discussion of these matters from a modern socio-political and feminist perspective cf. Jean Bethke Elshtain, *Public Man, Private Woman: Women in Social and Political Thought* (Princeton: Princeton University Press, 1981), esp. pp. 40-54.

core practices. The freedom of theology is precisely constituted and shaped by the same telos that informs the core practices and doctrine. Thus, the critical nature of theology as ecclesial practice remains concrete and limited by its own accountability to the gospel and to doctrine. In this regard, theology as ecclesial discourse practice is distinct from the abstract and negative freedom that modern theology characteristically has claimed for itself over against doctrine and the core practices of the church.

Therefore, as long and insofar as the church exists as a public in its own right, the teaching and the theological exploration of those convictions and practices that constitute it, continue. The discourse practice of theology is a practice of the church as public only insofar as it is bound to those convictions and rules that constitute it as a public. This is precisely why theology makes sense only as an ecclesial practice bound to those norms (doctrines) that constitute the public that is the church. A theological discourse that attempts to justify or critique the church's constitutive convictions and practices on alien grounds is unavoidably part of another public constituted by other normative convictions and practices.

We said earlier that doctrine is in constant need of re-appropriation, of re-interpretation, and of re-communication lest it become a reified quasi-knowledge of God substituting for the gospel *(doctrina evangelii)* itself. Now it has become clear how the core practices together with doctrine constitute the church as a distinct public that requires its own discourse practice, theology. Yet core practices can become distorted and doctrines reified. It is the specific task of theology as ecclesial practice to help avoid or overcome both dangers.

This task of preventing doctrine from turning the saving knowledge of God into an ossified formulaic knowledge and of preventing practices from becoming unfaithful to and distortive of the gospel shapes theology as a distinct ecclesial practice. It is easy to identify theology's three central aspects in relationship to doctrine. There is, *first,* the task of re-appropriation *(fides quaerens doctrinam),* in which specific appropriations and interpretations of doctrine are developed and continuously tested in particular traditions of discourse.[66] There is, *secondly,* the task of perceiving and judging how specific doctrines inform particular contexts in which the church finds itself and what kind of challenge particular contexts raise for the communication and presentation of particular doctrines. And this, the presentation and communication (catechesis) of the gospel in light of its doctrinal specification constitutes the *third* task of theology as ecclesial practice in relationship to doctrine.

66. One can reasonably make the claim that the major efforts of doctrinally committed ecumenism belong to this aspect, or better put, fulfill it most precisely.

These tasks of theology in relationship to doctrine are crucial because it is doctrine that relates normatively to the core practices — not theology itself (*pace* many contemporary theologians!). Theology as ecclesial discourse practice, rather, is the occasion of bringing doctrine and core practices into that kind of interface that they constructively and critically inform each other, since *both* are ways through which the saving knowledge of God is mediated. And they need each other, or to put it technically: the relationship of "lex orandi, lex credendi" is a two-way street.[67] Yet doctrine, insofar as it is itself normed by and accountable to the witness of Scripture, has the right of way in this mutual traffic managed by theology as ecclesial practice.

Yet despite this important role theology is in no way the final arbiter between doctrine and practice. Rather, theology is itself nurtured and formed through the church's core practices. Without being rooted in the very life of these practices theology becomes a stale enterprise cut off from its living subject. Without being kept accountable to doctrine, theology becomes in all of its interpretive, imaginative, and speculative moves a free-floating enterprise, or in other words, a bad form of philosophy. In both cases, theology loses its vital contact with its subject matter, the saving knowledge of God, the gospel proclaimed and taught *(doctrina evangelii).*

Theology as Ecclesial Practice and the Knowledge of God

So far we have been sketching an alternative route for the Christian knowledge of God under the conditions of modernity, an alternative that will both avoid the temptation of reification and construction and, in addition, avoid the pneumatological instability of Barth's still eminently significant proposal about how to overcome the modern dilemma regarding the knowledge of God. This other "way out" was to approach the question of the knowledge of God by rethinking the relationship between church, doctrine, and theology under the aspects of "pathos," of being formed and thus qualified by the knowledge of God as embodied in the church's constitutive practices and in doctrine — both of which will have to be developed as the Spirit's works.

It has become clear that the *pathos* of theology as ecclesial practice consists

67. Cf. in detail Chapter 4, "The Liturgy," by Susan K. Wood. Cf. for a very instructive example of how to travel this two-way street as a Methodist systematic theologian, Geoffrey Wainwright, *Doxology: The Praise of God in Worship, Doctrine, and Life. A Systematic Theology* (New York: Oxford University Press, 1980). An older, yet still important Lutheran example is Peter Brunner, *Worship in the Name of Jesus,* trans. M. H. Bertram (St. Louis: Concordia Publishing House, 1968).

precisely in the circumstance that the knowledge of God cannot be achieved "nakedly," be it in the form of the "thereness" of an "objective" knowledge or be it in the form of that knowledge which is the construct of the poietic subject. Christian knowledge of God can only be gained by suffering God's saving activity as it engages us in word and sacrament as well as through the rest of the core practices, and by committing us to the gospel's proclamation and teaching *(doctrina evangelii)* through doctrine *(doctrina definita).* In other words, our knowledge of God is subject to the same *eschatological condition* to which our whole being is subject. We find ourselves engaged by and in the Spirit's beginning and increasing work *(opus inchoatum)* of sanctification.[68] The knowledge of God we are thereby drawn into is saving, yet not total; concrete, yet not complete; distinct, yet not comprehensive; "clothed" by embodied practices and normative doctrine, thus perceived "like in a mirror dimly," yet still not "face to face." It is not insignificant that the last practice Luther enumerates as a mark of the church is the way of the cross. The knowledge of God that we suffer in faith — embodied in and lived through the core practices — as the Holy Spirit's sanctification can ultimately be reflected only in a theology of the cross. Because only here, in the cross of Christ, we find the immovable difference secured between the love that is God's full knowledge of us achieved in Christ's cross — when we were still sinners, radically estranged from God — and our love, the full knowledge of God that is the completion of the Spirit's sanctifying work.

To use a biblical analogy: The core practices and doctrine surround us like a tent. By being engaged in them practically and intellectually we find ourselves "clothed" with the knowledge of *God for us* in Christ. But being precisely "clothed" this way we long for the full knowledge of God that completely transforms us into the likeness of the One who is the knowledge of God and who knows us better than we know ourselves since he took our human lot upon himself. Through his crucifixion and resurrection we have the promise of "suffering" a last knowledge of God, namely of being "clothed with our heavenly dwelling."[69]

68. This is the way Luther describes the Spirit's work in his exposition of the third article of the Apostles' Creed in the *Large Catechism.* Cf. *The Book of Concord,* ed. Theodore G. Tappert (Philadelphia: Fortress, 1959), p. 418.

69. "For we know that if the earthly tent we live in is destroyed, we have a building from God, a house not made with hands, eternal in the heavens. For in this tent we groan, longing to be clothed with our heavenly dwelling — if indeed, when we have taken it off we will not be found naked. For while we are still in this tent, we groan under our burden, because we wish not to be unclothed but to be further clothed, so that what is mortal may be swallowed up by life. He who has prepared us for this very thing is God, who has given us the Spirit as a guarantee" (2 Cor. 5:1-5).

The Spirit and the Spirit's works are precisely the guarantee that the knowledge of God, which we suffer by being engaged by them, is a knowledge neither at our disposal nor of our making, but the beginning of a final "clothing," a last "suffering" that will include that knowledge of God of which the apostle Paul says: "Then I will know fully, even as I have been fully known" (1 Cor. 13:12).[70]

70. Cordial thanks to the co-authors of this volume for their constructive and critical input, to the two editors Jim Buckley and David Yeago for their patience and editorial help, to Carl E. Braaten and Robert W. Jenson, who made the whole project possible, and to Stanley Hauerwas and Joseph L. Mangina for their helpful suggestions at critical moments.

3. The Bible

The Spirit, the Church, and the Scriptures: Biblical Inspiration and Interpretation Revisited

DAVID S. YEAGO

Those who are situated outside the church are not able to acquire any understanding of the divine discourse.

St. Hilary of Poitiers[1]

I. Scriptural Interpretation and Ecclesial Location

In its claim that the church is somehow a privileged locus for scriptural interpretation, this saying of St. Hilary represents the mind of the whole premodern Christian tradition, up to and even beyond the sixteenth-century Reformers. As such, it also represents precisely the sort of presumption against which, from its origins, modern hermeneutic theory protested. Against accounts of scriptural interpretation as a mysterious transaction between a supernatural object — *sermo divina* — and specially "situated" interpreters, modern hermeneutics declared authentic interpretation to be an essentially open, secular, and methodical business. Among Protestants especially, polemic against interpretive privileges claimed for popes and bishops was gradually

1. "*Qui extra Ecclesiam positi sunt, nullam divini sermonis capere possunt intelligentiam.*" *In Matthæum,* 13, 1, in Hilaire de Poitiers, *Sur Matthieu,* vol. 1, Sources Chrétiennes 254 (Paris: Cerf, 1978), p. 296.

generalized into a rejection of the very idea of privileged interpretation. All interpretive "situations" were declared equal; the only relevant distinctions among interpreters would be unavoidable differences in technical preparation and natural talent. Moreover, every text would as such be defined as a secular phenomenon, *sermo humana,* presenting no *unique* challenges to the interpreter, and therefore in principle to be treated like any other text.

The history of this hermeneutic shift is replete with the ironies characteristic of Christianity's passage through modernity. Protestant attacks on *clerical* interpretive privilege were originally founded on convictions about the status of the *whole* Christian people as a royal priesthood (1 Pet. 2:4-10), recipient of the baptismal anointing by virtue of which *all* share in "privileged" insight (1 John 2:27). But by its increasing reliance on formal notions of Scripture's "perspicuity," Protestant polemic doubtless helped undermine, not only the interpretive privilege of the clergy, but that of the church itself: if the sense of the text was abstractly perspicuous, then it was no longer clear why the assembly of believers was better situated to interpret it than anyone else. At the same time, this rejection of privileged interpretation has been subject to the usual ironies of egalitarianism. The status elite was replaced by a meritocratic elite, with its own mythos and mystique; the priest and prophet, qualified to interpret the text by divine charisma, yielded to the professor, qualified by guild certification.

The outcome is that the church has not only been denied the unique interpretive significance claimed for it by St. Hilary, it has been firmly relegated to interpretive irrelevance, or worse. For much modern biblical scholarship, even when it has wanted ultimately to serve the church, the church has figured essentially as a community of hermeneutical amateurs, whose spiritual pretensions make it all the more dangerous as a purveyor of mystification and misinformation. Even with all that has changed, hermeneutically, in recent decades, biblical instruction in mainline seminaries still all too often regards the experience students have had of the Bible in the church to be its great problem, the obstacle that must be bulldozed if students are to be initiated into responsible interpretive practice.

Valid interpretation may therefore take place within the church, on this modern view, but the church's own distinctive life and belief must be transcended in order to secure that validity. Indeed, valid interpretation takes place within the church only to the extent that representatives of *another* community, the community of critical scholars, are awarded a monopoly on interpretation. Such scholars may also, of course, be devoted members of the church, but that is not understood to have any essential bearing on their interpretive competence. Though it might be widely agreed that pastoral wisdom and a deep knowledge of the church's tradition are a collateral advantage for a biblical scholar in the church, few in mainline churches would regard these qualities as themselves already constituting an essential dimension of interpretive competence. This is precisely what divides us from Hilary and the earlier Christian tradition.

This essay will attempt to retrieve some of the assumptions underlying Hilary's declaration, and thus contribute to a doctrine of the *inspiration of Scripture* with consequences for scriptural interpretation as a distinctive practice *intra ecclesiam.* It will argue that classical Christian scriptural interpretation took place within a comprehensible theological horizon that has by no means become obsolete or irrecoverable; though we cannot repristinate the exegesis of the Fathers, the great medievals, and the Reformers, we *can* rejoin the tradition in which they stood. Over against *both* the hermeneutics of critical modernity *and* its inveterate foe, the Protestant doctrine of plenary verbal inspiration, this essay will suggest that classical scriptural interpretation proceeded from a rich and complex sense of Scripture's place and role within the economy of salvation; Scripture functions as a quasi-sacramental instrument of the Holy Spirit, through which the Spirit makes known the mystery of Christ in order to form the church as a sign of his messianic dominion. The church's knowledge of Scripture as inspired has therefore interpretive consequences; it calls for a specific art, or perhaps a concatenation of arts, of faithful reading, exposition, and application by which Christ is glorified and the church built up in its distinctive life and mission.

It has, of course, become somewhat easier to argue for a distinctively ecclesial practice of interpretation in the present-day hermeneutical climate; indeed, dissatisfaction with modernity's abstract methodological universalism has erupted on so many fronts and for so many reasons that it is probably not possible to say even in the most general terms that a unified counter-position is emerging. One broad strand of dissatisfaction, however, may be specially pertinent to Hilary's dictum, for it shares with the patristic tradition an interest in the "situatedness" of interpretation, often marked with the notion of "context": both texts and their readers, it is said, are located in "contexts" and the business of interpretation is therefore inevitably "contextual."

It will be best to consider this line of thought in an elementary form. As we seek to "understand" a text, it is more and more agreed, we must in the process make decisions for which modernist hermeneutics cannot fully account. Even if we recognize in "the text itself" — however construed — a givenness of sense that properly exercises a decisive control over understanding, there are nonetheless interpretive judgments to be made that "the text itself" cannot determine. Examining the text — by whatever methods — and ascertaining what the text says does not bring to an end the task of *understanding* what is said. "Understanding" in any full sense involves — or so we would ordinarily suppose — appreciating the *force and implications* of what the text says, its relation to our beliefs and its bearing on our thought and action, the ways in which it might confirm or call into question or make more complicated a wide range of ideas and attitudes and behaviors.[2]

This generates interpretive questions that can neither be settled *a priori* by appeal to method, nor answered in any immediate way by further observation of the text itself. The answers seem inevitably contingent, in ways that need closer examination, on particular interpreters and what they bring with them to the interpretive enterprise, generating unavoidable diversity: two different interpreters, with equal philological and historical competence, exercising exemplary attentiveness to the text, may nonetheless "understand" the same text in very different ways, depending on the answers given to such questions. To what issues and inquiries and perplexities does what is said in this text pertain? On what realms of practice and perception and belief and concern does it press? What might we see differently, what might we do differently, because we have grasped what is said here?

It is here that a broad stream of contemporary hermeneutics moves in directions that make Hilary seem, if not readily accessible, then at least less remote. If the enterprise of understanding a text raises questions whose answers must be supplied, not by the *a priori* exigencies of method, nor by appeal to the very words of the text, but by the active reflection and judgment of interpreters, then modernity's insistence that there are only two kinds of interpreters, competent and incompetent, falls to the ground. The different ways in which interpreters are "situated" will bear unavoidably on the conduct of the enterprise of understanding.

This point is often made with a critical edge turned towards the interpre-

2. This is essentially Barth's distinction between *explicatio* and *meditatio:* understanding involves not only determining "the sense of the text itself, what it does actually say" but also "the act of reflection on what Scripture declares to us." Cf. Karl Barth, *Church Dogmatics* I/2 (Edinburgh: T. & T. Clark, 1956), pp. 726-27. At this point, however, I am not yet distinguishing Barth's *meditatio* from his *applicatio.* I am also trying, with these formulations, to avoid taking a position prematurely in contemporary debates about objectivity and interpretation. Later I shall suggest that there are *theological* reasons for Christians to suppose that they are *discovering* rather than *producing* meaning in the scriptures, but I want this to appear as clearly as possible as a *theological* necessity, not a principle of general hermeneutic theory. It is another question whether, as Barth suggests, the specifically theological exigencies of Christian interpretation of Scripture might not, precisely as such, have general hermeneutical consequences. Cf. Karl Barth, *CD,* pp. 465-66.

tive meritocracy: if the Bible is read differently among the poor than among middle-class academics, this cannot be explained simply in terms of the ignorance of the former and the expertise of the latter. At their best, the poor read the Bible with a lively concern for the implications of what it says amid the distinctive miseries and challenges of their "context." Middle-class academics not only have a different education, they live in a different "context" and so have different interests, often unacknowledged behind the façade of meritocratic objectivity.

But this appeal to the interpretive dispositions of the poor needs closer examination. Talk of "interests" brings us up against the "postmodern" temptation to reduce the enterprise of understanding to a mere series of moves in a struggle for dominance, so that "understanding" the text comes to mean no more than "using" it to advance our ends. Yet surely the Christian poor do not read the Bible as they do simply because they consciously or unconsciously calculate it to be in their interests. Rather, their interpretive practices reflect and embody deeply held beliefs about what is the case in the universe at large. If they read the scriptures as bearing immediately on their situation, it is because they believe that the whole world is presided over by one "who executes justice for the oppressed; who gives food to the hungry" (Psalm 146:7) — one to whom tyranny and hunger are matters of pressing concern. Believing also that the scriptures embody the will and word of this engaged and partisan God, they cannot reasonably understand them otherwise than as pressing urgently and concretely upon the miseries and challenges of their "context."

This suggests two points of some importance. First, there is an ambiguity in the notion of "context" so insistently flourished in contemporary discussion. In reality, the "contextuality" of understanding involves *two* crucial contexts, not just one. There is the context of social, political, and economic conditions, which is most often intended by the term. But by itself this "context" has *no* immediate implications for interpretation and understanding; it acquires such implications only within another "context," that of the interpreter's *beliefs* about the world at large, the historical situation, and the text to be interpreted. It is this *context of belief* that sets the interpreter, the text, and the social-historical situation into concrete relations with one another, and so brings them to bear on one another. The Bible is not read as it is by the Christian poor simply because they are poor, but also because of what they believe to be true about God and the world, about poverty, and for that matter about the biblical texts themselves. It is in large measure because understanding and interpretation are always situated in belief-contexts as well as social-historical contexts that equally poor Christians can disagree quite vigorously with one another, as well as with the detached and comfortable, about the proper bearing of Scripture on their situation.[3]

This point is connected with another. For those who believe that the scriptures are the word of a God for whom much is at stake in feeding the hungry and executing justice for the oppressed, understanding what the scriptures say as bearing directly on the life of the poor requires no complex hermeneutical technique. Indeed, within the context of those beliefs, such an understanding of the texts is not only natural and unforced, but in a certain sense *obligatory.* For those who hold such beliefs, reading, say, the narrative of the Exodus with the detached curiosity of a university professor of Semitic philology is what would require *effort,* indeed the deliberate suppression of knowledge pertinent to understanding. Such effort is, of course, what modernist hermeneutics requires of its initiates, insisting that beliefs of *that* sort be checked at the door of the temple of science. Modern academic culture has regarded this as the heroic asceticism of the objective truth-seeker; to a disillusioned contemporary eye it may seem more like a mechanism for controlling what truth-claims are allowed to reach the public square, excluding from the public discourse any rabble of poor people, old-believers, mystics, and apocalyptic crazies who might disrupt the peace of the secular city.

Christian biblical interpretation, as it took form in the patristic era, was in any case founded on the conviction that the church, as a corporate body, *knows something* of the most immediate relevance to the interpretation of both the scriptures of Israel and the apostolic testimony. Thus Athanasius, commenting on Acts 2:25-36, sums up Peter's interpretation of Psalm 16:8-11 as follows:

> Now David and all the prophets have died, and the tombs of all of them are here in our midst; but the resurrection that has now taken place *(hē de gegomenē nun anastasis)* has shown that the things that were written *(ta gegrammena)* pertain to Jesus.[4]

3. It is of course true that not all Christians see the world in this way, so that one could argue that these beliefs are really the by-products of socio-economic status. But it is equally true that not all *poor* people see the world in this way — only those formed within the biblical tradition. What I am claiming does not require that belief-contexts and socio-economic contexts be neatly distinguishable, nor is it a denial of the important truism that self-interest tints all that we do, including our interpretive practice. I am claiming only that the traffic runs both ways, that our beliefs shape the kind of significance we ascribe to the social context and even the concrete directions taken by our self-interest — including the ways in which we estimate what our interest is.

4. *Against the Arians* II, 16. Cf. Robert L. Wilken, "*In novissimis diebus:* Biblical Promises, Jewish Hopes and Early Christian Exegesis," in Wilken, *Remembering the Christian Past* (Grand

Knowing the resurrection that has now taken place, the apostolic company can hardly help reading the scriptures of Israel in a new way. The "things that were written" are the same — what they say has not changed — but they are understood quite differently, in the light of new insight into what they pertain to, what they are *about.* Paul van Buren has written:

> That little group of Jews who had seen Jesus as their rebbe and had seen him executed by the Romans were at a loss to know what to say or even how to talk about him. So, they did what any good Jew of the time would have done. They went to their one source of wisdom and understanding; they turned to their tradition, their scriptures, and there they found the words they needed. For them and for their successors, their Bible, their Jewish scriptures, became their ABC's and their grammar book for talking about Jesus.[5]

What is somewhat masked in this way of putting things is the context of *belief* in which this move was made. Peter does indeed turn to Scripture to find a language in which to talk about resurrection and the risen one; but it is only because he believes that a particular resurrection has taken place that it seems natural, and in a sense rationally obligatory, to take the scriptures as bearing on Jesus. Further, Peter does not simply turn to the scriptures in a spasm of ethnic loyalty, as "his tradition"; he turns to them because he believes that they embody the word and will of the one who by raising the Lord Jesus from the dead has disclosed the ultimate *skopos* of all his words and purposes.

The church knows about the resurrection that has now taken place, and seeks to understand Scripture in the light of this knowledge. This is brought into focus in historic liturgies when the gospel lesson is read: the congregation rises and cries out before and after the reading: "Glory to you, O Lord!" — "Praise to you, O Christ!" The acclamations establish a "context" in which to understand the words read aloud: these are the deeds and utterances of one who is living and at large, not dead and confined to the tomb, one who is present and able to act, who has indeed been enthroned as Lord and Christ. The liturgical practice thus embodies a claim to relevant *knowledge* that gives a distinctive shape to the enterprise of understanding the scriptures.[6]

This suggests a further point of great importance: what the church knows

---

Rapids: Eerdmans, 1995), pp. 95-119. Cf. also Wilken's study, "St. Cyril of Alexandria: The Mystery of Christ in the Bible," *Pro Ecclesia* (1995): 454-78.

5. Paul van Buren, "Authenticity without Demonization," *Journal of Ecumenical Studies* 34 (1997): 342.

6. Cf. many of the other essays in this volume, especially Susan K. Wood, "The Liturgy."

that is relevant to interpretation is never more than partially available in articulated, discursive form. While articulate truth-claiming — "Jesus is risen!" — is essential to the church's life, its articulate claims are never fully intelligible apart from a context of embodied social practice that bespeaks the risen Christ in a whole range of both verbal and more-than-verbal ways. The fullness of what the church knows is embedded in the form of ecclesial life, in the normative rituals and institutions and patterns of interaction that constitute the church as a singular people. One can see an awareness of this in the famous riposte of Irenaeus to the gnostic denigration of the flesh:

> How can they say that the flesh, which is nourished with the Lord's body and with his blood, goes to corruption and does not share in life? Let them therefore either change their views or else let them quit [celebrating the sacrament]. But our view is in harmony with the Eucharist and the Eucharist in turn supports our view. For we offer to God that which is his own, proclaiming consistently the communion and union of flesh and Spirit. For as the bread, when it receives the invocation of God, is no longer ordinary bread, but the Eucharist, made up of two realities, earthly and heavenly, so also our bodies, when they receive the Eucharist, are no longer subject to corruption, but have the hope of resurrection to eternity.[7]

The Gnostics separate flesh and Spirit, but the eucharistic rite joins them in a complex network of juxtapositions: the eucharistic bread is identified with God as his own gift, now returned to him, and at the same time the earthly element is joined to the heavenly reality of the risen Christ. By participation in this joining of heaven and earth, our corruptible bodies are themselves joined to eternity by way of a promised resurrection. The rite itself *performs* the judgment that flesh and Spirit belong together; those who believe otherwise should in all consistency forswear eucharistic worship. Thus Irenaeus brings to bear *knowledge* embedded in the church's practice, a knowledge of the destiny of the ordinary and corruptible that is ultimately knowledge of what may be hoped for in light of "the resurrection that has now taken place."

A brief look at Martin Luther may show how the main lines of this ecclesial hermeneutic were received by the Reformers, as well as summarizing the argument so far. In his famous response to Erasmus's claims about the obscurity of Scripture, Luther insists that Scripture has a twofold clarity, inward and outward. The inward clarity of Scripture, "located in the heart's understanding," is altogether the work of the Holy Spirit, for "all those who do not have the Spirit of God have an obscured heart" that can have no true un-

7. Irenaeus, *Against Heresies* IV, 18, 5. Adapted from the translation in *ANF* 1:486.

derstanding of the scriptures no matter how well acquainted with them it may be.[8] By contrast, Luther is often supposed to have initiated the turn to historical criticism by defining the *outward* interpretation of Scripture as a purely technical problem, capable in principle of resolution by anyone with proper philological tools.[9]

But in reality Luther does *not* present the outward clarity of Scripture as a simple property of the text; he describes it rather as "located in the ministry of the word" *(in verbi ministerio posita),* that is, in the network of ecclesial communicative practice within which both text and interpreter are situated. With respect to outward clarity, "nothing whatever remains obscure or ambiguous, but all things whatsoever that are in Holy Scripture have been brought out into a most certain light through the word, and declared to the whole world."[10] This is explicated by way of a distinction between the *verba* of Holy Scripture and its *res* or subject-matter:

> I do indeed grant that many passages in the scriptures are obscure and abstruse, not because of the majesty of their *res,* but because of our ignorance of terms and grammar, yet these do not at all hinder a knowledge of all the *res* in the scriptures. For what more august thing could lie hidden in the scriptures, now that the seal has been broken and the stone rolled away from the tomb, and that supreme mystery has gone forth, that Christ the Son of God became a human being, that God is one and triune, that Christ suffered for us and will reign eternally? Are not these things known and sung about even on the street-corners? Take Christ from the scriptures and what more will you find in them? Therefore the *res* contained in the scriptures have all been brought forth, although some passages are still obscure because the words are unknown.[11]

8. Martin Luther, *De servo arbitrio, WA* 18:609. Since for Luther, we receive the Spirit of God only through participation in what he calls the "external word" in the church, this point already requires his agreement with Hilary.

9. Thus Peter Stuhlmacher paraphrases *claritas externa* as "the clarity and perspicuity of the outward, philologically analyzable meaning of the text." See Stuhlmacher, *Historical Criticism and Theological Interpretation of Scripture,* translated and with an introduction by Roy A. Harrisville (Philadelphia: Fortress, 1977), p. 34.

10. Luther, *De servo arbitrio,* p. 609. The "word" here, it must be noted, is not Scripture itself; typically for Luther, it serves as a kind of shorthand for the Christian community's whole testimony to Christ in speech and sign.

11. Luther, *De servo arbitrio,* p. 606. It was pointed out by one respondent to this essay that Jews would have an obvious riposte to Luther's "Take Christ from the scriptures and what more will you find in them?" But that is precisely the point: Luther's question presupposes a particular community that has a specific reason for being interested in these texts and a particular set

Scripture is "outwardly" clear, therefore, not because there is no obscurity in its words, but because we know what Scripture is *about,* to what *res* it pertains.

> Thus the same *res,* most openly declared to the whole world, is at one point spoken of in the scriptures in clear words, and at another still hides in obscure words. It makes no difference, so long as the *res* is in the light, if some sign of it is in darkness, while in the meantime there are many other signs of the same *res* in the light. Who would say that a public fountain was not in the light because those who are in an alley do not see it, even though everyone in the marketplace does see it?[12]

This is a knowledge that we bring with us to the scriptures; we acquire it from the apostolic preaching that has made Christ known throughout the world.

> The things of supreme majesty are no longer in hiding but have been brought forth and expounded in the very marketplaces and public squares, for "Christ has opened our minds so that we might understand the scriptures" (Luke 25:45), and "the gospel has been preached to every creature" (Mark 16:15), "into all the earth their sound has gone forth" (Romans 10:18), and "all things which have been written were written for our instruction" (Romans 15:4). Likewise: "All divinely inspired Scripture is useful for teaching" (2 Timothy 3:16).[13]

The knowledge thus communicated is essentially christological and trinitarian, focused in proclamation of "the resurrection that has now taken place." Or as Luther puts it, the seal has been broken, the stone has been rolled away from the tomb, and the mystery has come forth: "that Christ the Son of God became a human being, that God is one and triune, that Christ suffered for us and will reign eternally."

To be sure, this knowledge is itself not textually unmediated; as Luther indicates, it is imparted through manifold forms of witness and proclamation in the Christian community, in which the texts of Scripture also play a role. Scripture is outwardly clear insofar as we approach it within the context of teaching, preaching, catechesis, and liturgical celebration in which there has

---

of convictions about their pertinence. Of course, therefore, Luther's question will seem odd or even silly to those who do not bring Christian beliefs about Jesus Christ to their reading of the scriptures — that is just the point being made here about the significance of belief-contexts for interpretation.

12. Luther, *De servo arbitrio,* p. 606.

13. Luther, *De servo arbitrio,* p. 607.

been set before us the *res* to which Scripture's *verba* pertain. The church's knowledge is thus not prior to engagement with Scripture in the sense that it proceeds from some pure immediacy of intuition or feeling. Everything the church knows, it knows by attending to testimony, listening to words and performing rites that have been *given* to it.[14] Nor is the church's knowledge prior to Scripture in any static or absolute way; indeed, every formulation of what the church knows must always be tested and authenticated and corrected through continuous engagement with Scripture. But the clarity of Scripture depends upon its interpreters' location within the apostolic tradition, the web of testimony that identifies the *res* to which the words of the texts pertain. That testimony is prior to every *particular* interpretive engagement with Scripture, and the knowledge it communicates is what makes it possible for the church to recognize Scripture as *sermo divina* in the first place.

This knowledge of the *res* of Scripture, received from the apostolic preaching and the ecclesial practices that extend it from age to age, gives a distinctive shape to the interpretive encounter with Scripture's *verba.* Luther certainly recognized the philological and historical dimensions of interpretation, but scriptural understanding is not therefore reduced to methodologically ruled philological-historical analysis, the local application of a general hermeneutic. On the contrary, to understand the *verba* is to understand them as signs of the christological *res,* and so as "instruction" and "teaching" for a people that venerates and proclaims this *res.* The sign has not yet been brought out "in the light" until it has been read in the "context" of shared faith in the one who was crucified for us and will reign eternally. Philological and historical tools and procedures are thus taken into the service of an essentially theological and ecclesial enterprise of understanding.

14. Here it is possible only to point to the neglected work of Heinrich Schlier, who argued, through studies of the "kerygmatic formulae" in the New Testament, that the apostolic gospel took "textual" form from the very beginning, in the sense of fixed verbal formulation. Cf. his remarkable essay, "Kerygma und Sophia — Zur neutestamentlichen Grundlegung des Dogmas," in Heinrich Schlier, *Die Zeit der Kirche: Exegetische Aufsätze und Vorträge* (Freiburg: Herder, 1966), pp. 206-32. Debate over Schlier's proposal bogged down in the details of his reading of 1 Corinthians (cf. his own concessions on this point, p. 313), and even more damagingly, was distorted by polemical reactions to his entry into the Roman Catholic Church in 1953. Consequently, the full significance of his thesis has seldom been explored: that Christianity came into the world not as an "experience" only subsequently "expressed" in textual monuments but precisely as a *new textuality,* which in its concrete givenness provides human thought and experience with a genuinely new starting-point.

II. Inspiration: What the Church Knows about the Scriptures

From its origins, the Christian community has held that its knowledge of "the resurrection that has now taken place" contains *a knowledge about the scriptures themselves.* One might put the point thus: that there is *testimony* to the resurrection is not something secondary, added on to the event only after the fact; it is provided for from within the event itself. The testimony of the prophets and apostles is in a real sense an aspect of the resurrection-event itself, so that if the church knows "the resurrection that has now taken place," it is just thereby in a position to identify the prophetic and apostolic scriptures as *sermo divina,* "divine discourse."

In the subsequent Christian tradition, the notion of Scripture's "inspiration" proved the most durable way of articulating this unity of the resurrection-event with its double attestation by the prophets and apostles. Paul provides the theological underpinnings in one of his knottiest probes of the logic of the faith (1 Cor. 2:6-16). To understand what God has given us in the crucified and risen Messiah, he writes, is to know the incomprehensible mystery of God's eschatological presence with his people: "what no eye has seen, nor ear heard, nor the human heart conceived, what God has prepared for those who love him" (2:9). To acquire such knowledge would be to probe the "depths of God" (2:10), to share in God's privileged knowledge of his own inner reality (2:11). Just such participation, Paul startlingly insists, is what has been given to the church: "Now we have received not the spirit of the world, but the Spirit that is from God, so that we may understand the gifts bestowed on us by God. . . . We have the mind of Christ" (2:12, 16). Thus the church's witness is not simply surrendered to the insubstantial relativity of the "human, all-too-human" but is informed by the divine witness of the Spirit: "And we speak of these things not in words taught by human wisdom but in words taught by the Spirit, interpreting spiritual things by spiritual things" (2:13).[15]

It was into this theological framework that the later church, emboldened by 2 Timothy 3:15-17,[16] placed the prophetic and apostolic scriptures. The scriptures are "God-breathed," divine discourse, the abiding gift precisely of "words taught by the Spirit" in which to speak of "spiritual things"; just so, they are able to "communicate the wisdom" *(sophizein)* that leads to salvation

15. My translation; NRSV obscures Paul's contrast between two kinds of *logos* in the first part of the verse. In the last clause NRSV has "interpreting spiritual things to those who are spiritual," thus anticipating v. 14, but it seems more natural to take this as elaborating the "words — words" contrast.

16. As well as 1 Peter 1:10-12, which cannot be more than mentioned here.

(v. 15). The Spirit in whose power the Lord Jesus came into the world (Matt. 1:20; Luke 1:35), the Spirit of him who raised Jesus from the dead (Rom. 8:11), is the very one who "spoke by the prophets" (Nicene Creed) and taught the apostolic witnesses, bringing to their remembrance all that the Lord had said to them (John 14:26). This same Spirit is poured out on all the baptized, and only those who "walk in the Spirit" by taking part in the church's distinctive life come to an authentic understanding of the divine discourse. "Those who are unspiritual do not receive the gifts of God's Spirit, for they are foolishness to them, and they are unable to understand them because they are spiritually discerned" (1 Cor. 2:14).[17] Thus Hilary's prayer at the beginning of his great work *On the Trinity:* "We look to you . . . to call us to participation in the prophetic and apostolic Spirit, so that we may grasp their words in no other *sensus* than they uttered them. . . ."[18]

The doctrine of inspiration has not been a favorite theme in recent theology, even when it professes "post-critical" ambitions, for understandable reasons: no one who proposes a doctrine of scriptural inspiration with direct interpretive relevance can hope to avoid the dreaded charge of "fundamentalism," one of the most potent weapons of modernist hegemony. Recent essays in hermeneutics have therefore tended to lean on more formal notions of "scripture" or "canon" that mark out in a general way typical functions of sacred texts in religious communities. This is illuminating as far as it goes, but it is difficult in this way to say much about the *specific* role of Scripture in the *Christian* community. That is the function of the notion of inspiration: to

17. "Spiritual" here is best glossed as "inwardly and outwardly participant in the life of the church on which the Spirit is poured out." It indicates not a special detached inner experience but something like the "full, conscious, and active participation" in ecclesial practice of which Vatican II spoke. Cf. Vatican II, *Constitution on the Sacred Liturgy,* par. 14. On this whole theme, cf. the thoughtful discussion in William M. Thompson, *The Struggle for Theology's Soul: Contesting Scripture in Christology* (New York: Crossroad, 1996), pp. 1-32, as well as the essays by Reinhard Hütter and Susan Wood in this volume; compare also the extended discussion of "The Epistemic Role of the Spirit" in Bruce Marshall, *Trinity and Truth* (Cambridge: Cambridge University Press, 2000).

18. Hilary, *De Trinitate,* I, 38, in S. Hilari, *De Trinitate, Praefatio, Libri I-VIII,* CCSL 62, ed. P. Smulders (Turnhout, Belgium: Brepols, 1979), p. 36. "Sensus" can be translated "meaning" but also "outlook" or "frame of mind"; it seems best not to smooth out the ambiguity. Cf. the injunction of Vatican II that "since Holy Scripture is to be read and interpreted in that same Spirit in which it was written, for a right construal of the sense of the sacred text one must consider no less carefully the content and unity of Scripture as a whole, taking account of the living tradition of the whole church and the analogy of faith." Vatican II, *Constitution on Divine Revelation,* 12. Cf. Ignace de la Potterie, "Interpretation of Holy Scripture in the Spirit in Which It Was Written (*Dei Verbum* 12c)," in *Vatican II: Assessment and Perspectives: Twenty-Five Years After (1962-1987),* ed. Rene Latourelle, vol. 1 (New York: Paulist, 1988), pp. 220-66.

specify the Christian community's distinctive knowledge of the biblical texts and their role in the economy of salvation.

It can at least be said that a revival of the older Protestant doctrine of inspiration, against which historical criticism fought its famous battles, is by no means what is advocated here. In that version, the doctrine of inspiration really functioned to ground the doctrine of perspicuous propositional revelation, according to which God speaks by propounding universally accessible true propositions for our belief.[19] Plenary verbal inspiration explains how there can be a book made up of inerrantly true propositions that everyone can understand: such a book can be, it was taught, because God produced it in a miraculous way. The aim of the whole construction was to undermine as massively as possible Roman Catholic arguments for an authoritative teaching office in the church; that such a theory was concocted precisely during the heyday of philosophical foundationalism in European culture was likewise no accident.

In this version, the doctrine of inspiration was developed with surprisingly little reference to the larger economy of the Spirit; indeed, by grounding perspicuity in the divine oversight of the production of the texts, rather than, with Luther, the ongoing apostolic witness, it tended to isolate Scripture and its individualistically conceived interpreter from any wider context. Thus Protestant theology sowed the seeds of its own dethronement by historical criticism and general hermeneutical theory. A renewed account of scriptural inspiration must focus on what the seventeenth century neglected: it must locate the scriptures within the redemptive economy of the Spirit, and thereby recover the church's distinctive knowledge of these texts.

The proper mission of the Spirit in the trinitarian work of salvation is to glorify the God of Israel to the nations by making known and glorifying Jesus the Messiah, crucified and risen, as the Lord and Savior sent to fulfill all God's promises. The Spirit thus bears witness to Jesus as the *Son* of the God of Israel and to the God of Israel as the *Father* of Jesus and in so doing is obliquely revealed as *the Spirit of the Father and the Son.* The acknowledgment of Jesus evoked by the Spirit's witness is properly cognitive, involving the mind's assent, but this "knowledge" is inseparable from *adherence* to Jesus, from communion with him and through him with the Father; in this way the witness of the Spirit confers participation in eternal life even now.

19. My understanding of the modern Protestant doctrine of plenary verbal inspiration has been shaped by Robert Preus, *The Inspiration of Scripture: A Study of the Theology of the Seventeenth Century Lutheran Dogmaticians* (Edinburgh: Oliver and Boyd, 1955), and Carl F. H. Henry, *God, Revelation, and Authority* (Dallas: Word, 1979).

This knowledge and communion, moreover, are concretely inseparable from the social reality of the one, holy, catholic, and apostolic church. The church, as an actual earthly-historical community, the renewed Israel gathered to the crucified and risen Messiah, is the *sign* that the Spirit plants on the earth as witness to the Father and the Son. The Spirit bears witness, and *the church is the witness the Spirit bears.* The knowledge of God provided by the Spirit is thus inscribed in the concrete institutions and practices of the ecclesial life that the Spirit displays before the nations; knowing "the only true God and Jesus the Messiah whom he has sent" (John 17:3), and so experiencing a foretaste of eternal life, is not separable from participation in the "sanctification" (v. 17) of the disciples, for it is through the unity of his people that the unity of Jesus with the Father is made known to the world (vv. 22-23).

It is within this context that we must locate the biblical texts if we are to understand them as "inspired." The scriptures are, most basically, a crucial element within the concrete ecclesial witness of the Spirit by which the witness of faith, hope, and love is formed. Scripture is the standing testimony of the Spirit to the church, for the purpose of forming the church itself as the Spirit's testimony to the nations. The goal of the Spirit's gift can thus be summed up as *aedificatio ecclesiae,* the building-up of the church; the *telos* of Scripture's presence in the life of the church is the formation of the church's earthly-historical common life in such a way that the corporate existence of the Christian people in the world bears witness to the Messiah Jesus and to the God of Israel who sent him for the world's salvation.

We can say more about the *specific* role of Scripture in the work of the Spirit by considering two of Scripture's most elementary features. First, the scriptures are a body of *discourse,* language that is syntactically ordered, semantically significant, and pragmatically pointed. Thus something, or rather a variety of things, is *said* in the scriptures; they present us with intelligible utterance. Second, the scriptures are at the same time *texts,* that is, discourse *written down* to become an enduring "thing-in-the-world." As such the scriptures display properties characteristic of written texts, in particular a combination of persisting self-identity across time and circumstance combined with inability fully to predetermine the contexts in which they will be read and pondered.

To describe the biblical texts as "inspired scriptures" is thus to affirm that the Holy Spirit has made the *discourse* of these texts his own. Through the scriptures, the Spirit bears witness to the Father and the Son *in* the church, in order to make *of* the church a sign that glorifies the Father and the Son before the nations. What these texts say, therefore, is "what the Spirit says to the churches" (Rev. 3:22) to this end.[20] Scripture is in this sense *divine* discourse: it is human speech, articulated in human language, which the Spirit has formed and gathered together and made his own, in order to render utterable and intelligible "the gifts bestowed on us by God" (1 Cor. 2:12) in Jesus Christ. Such utterability and intelligibility are necessary for the Spirit's public glorification of the Father and the Son through the church, for the "mystery" or the "witness" of God cannot be proclaimed in plausible words of human wisdom but only by the "demonstration" or the "display" of the Spirit and of power.[21] Nor is this entirely different from saying that the scriptures are "God-breathed" or "inspired" in that they are "useful for teaching, for reproof, for correction, and for training in righteousness" (2 Tim. 3:16), for the witness of the Spirit requires not only words as its medium but also the life of a people formed by the wisdom and power of God present in the crucified Messiah.

The *textual* character of the scriptures is thereby taken up and put to work *sacramentally;* the scriptures function as a quasi-sacramental means through which the Spirit's rule as "lord and life-giver" (Nicene Creed) becomes concretely effectual in the church. In its written *fixity* as an object, its self-identity across changes of time and circumstance, Scripture intrudes on the church the one witness of the one Spirit; the persistent diachronic *sameness* of the scriptures is a concrete point of reference for the discernment of spirits. As an object in the world, Scripture retains its own specific density and particularity as it passes through time. The texts are what they are, and they say what they say; no interpretation, however valid, is ever *exactly* "the same" as the text. In this way Scripture brings to bear the Spirit's transcendence of the church's life and understanding; it is always possible to turn from what we already know and experience to the scriptural texts in their abiding particularity, and in so doing we turn sacramentally away from ourselves to hear the word of the Lord.[22]

20. In trinitarian perspective, of course, what the Spirit says is also what the Father and the Son say; the Spirit bears witness on behalf of the Father and the Son in the unity of the divine nature. To say that Scripture is the discourse of the Spirit is also to say that it is the word of the Father and the word of the Son. But for our purposes clarity may be served by a consistent focus on the Spirit.

21. 1 Corinthians 2:1, 4. The manuscripts of 2:1 waver between *musterion* and *marturion;* either makes the point.

22. In an earlier essay, I argued that Philippians 2:5-11 and the Nicene Creed make *substantially* the same claim about Jesus' relationship to the God of Israel. I would not retract anything in that argument, but the *next* point to be made is that "*substantially* the same" is not "*exactly* the same." Paul and Nicea do say "the same thing" *in crucial respects,* but there are also

Finally, as an enduring object in the world, Scripture is capable of being read and pondered again and again in changing contexts and circumstances. What the scriptures say can thus be continually read and reread, related to new challenges and new knowledge, brought to bear on shifting realms of concern, conviction, and conduct. In this way, the scriptural texts serve as a sacramental locus of the Spirit's presence as perpetual *giver of life* in the church; through these selfsame texts, the Spirit speaks *continually* to the Christian people, provoking new prophecy for new situations and bringing forth from the "depths of God" (1 Cor. 2:10) new insight into God's mystery.

The *possibility* of this continual *relecture* arises from the simple durability of the scriptures as written texts. Textually fixed discourse endures into new situations and contexts and can always be given new readings, display new implications, and so yield new understanding, in new circumstances. But the logic of inspiration implies not only the general point that it is always possible to read texts anew in new contexts, but also that in doing so with *these* texts the church is built up by the Spirit to be a communal sign before the nations glorifying the Father and the Son. The faithful reading of the scriptures yields not only imaginative possibility but divine guidance and divine formation.

"Faithfulness" in this context must in part mean something like "consistency with all relevant knowledge," consistency with what the church, *as* church, *knows* about the scope and function of the scriptures within the economy of the Spirit. Faithful interpreters must therefore resist those hermeneutical regimes, despite their continuing authority in contemporary high culture, that tell them that "real science" begins with the suppression of such distinctively ecclesial knowledge. On the contrary, we must recover a sense of ecclesial interpretation as an ordered practice of reading and understanding in its own right, with its own standards of cogency and competence — a practice of interpretation that is capable, indeed, of absorbing and making its own use of much that is produced by other interpretive enterprises, but cannot be reduced or subjected to any of them.

In the remainder of this essay, we shall consider several aspects of what it means to practice faithfulness in the ecclesial interpretation of Scripture, and so to read Scripture *intra ecclesiam*, from within the church as a decisive *cog-*

---

respects in which they are not *exactly* the same. To that extent, Nicea cannot *replace* Paul, however faithfully it may follow him; and when the church turns from its achieved understandings to wrestle again with the canonical texts, expecting to be instructed thereby, it sacramentally acknowledges the Spirit's transcendence of its own mind and experience. Cf. David S. Yeago, "The New Testament and the Nicene Dogma: Contribution to the Recovery of Theological Exegesis," *Pro Ecclesia* 3 (1993): 152-64. Reprinted in Stephen Fowl, ed., *The Theological Interpretation of Scripture: Classical and Contemporary Essays* (Oxford: Blackwell, 1997), pp. 87-100.

nitive context for interpretation. In the process, it should become clear that the faith of the church, in which belief in Scripture's inspiration is enfolded, does indeed have hermeneutical consequences; it founds a distinctive enterprise of interpretation with aims and arts and excellences peculiarly its own. Our considerations will follow the general outline of Barth's three moments of interpretation: the descriptive moment or *explicatio* (III), the reflective moment or *meditatio* (IV-V), and the appropriative moment or *applicatio* (VI).[23] At no point will it be possible to do more than allow the distant prospect of a renewed ecclesial practice of interpretation to come into view.

III. "How Sweet Are Your Words": Faithfulness as Deference

What the church knows about Scripture gives the church compelling reasons for deferential and indeed reverent *attentiveness* to the particularity of the texts in all their detail. It is *this* discourse, what is said in *these* writings, textually fixed in just *this* fashion, which the church knows as the "divine discourse" of the Holy Spirit. So the notion of a "faithful" reading of the inspired scriptures always includes *fitness with regard to what the texts say* in their concrete fixity and density. The first mandate of faithful ecclesial reading is therefore: "Pay attention, meticulous attention, to what the scriptures say; strive to do justice to the way the words go in the text."

This is a point, it should be noted, at which ecclesial interpretation may connect, for its own reasons and in its own way, with certain modern concerns; the freedom from modernist *hegemony* advocated here is not a blanket antimodernism. In the first place, ecclesial interpretation connects here with currents in modern literary hermeneutics, beginning in Renaissance humanism, that have emphasized descriptive fidelity to the literary structure and movement of the text ("close reading") as a mark of interpretive validity. This has points of contact with the church's own tradition of *meditatio* or *lectio divina,* involving a kind of constant close grappling, orally and aurally as well as mentally, with the very words of the sacred texts. Indeed we should not be surprised to discover that modern humanistic "close reading" has one root precisely in medieval monastic *lectio:* the humanists in some measure transferred the church's reverence for the divine discourse of Holy Scripture to the

23. Cf. note 2, above. *Meditatio,* which attempts to grasp the unity of Scripture's diversity, will be discussed in two sections looking at two crucial dimensions of scriptural unity: the diachronic unity of the Old and the New Testaments and the synchronic unity of the canonical whole in relation to the plurality of its parts.

human "excellence" of a cultural canon. Reformation-era exegetes already strove to recover humanist interpretive practice for the ecclesial context, enriched by the technical tools of analysis humanist critics had developed through engagement with the ancient rhetoricians.[24]

In the second place, such deferential attentiveness to the words of Scripture has a proper and necessary *historical* dimension, another point of contact with modernist concerns. What is at stake is not so much the reconstructive historical enterprise associated with form and redaction criticism — finding the "original meaning" of the text in its context of origin — but rather a concern with the historical particularity of the *language* of the text. Every text is written in some conceptual-linguistic tradition from which it receives codes and usages, conceptual tools and metaphorical formations, images and figures. This received conceptual and linguistic substance may of course be used in innovative and even subversive ways, but that is just what we will fail to see if we are ignorant of the conventions with which the text operates. Precisely in order to take *what the text says* seriously, therefore, we must grasp as clearly as we can the background of shared conceptual-linguistic usages and understandings that it takes for granted and employs for its own ends.

The scriptures come to the church from Israel: not only the Old but also the New Testament is written from within an overwhelmingly *Jewish* linguistic and conceptual matrix, to which we must attend carefully if we are to follow the divine discourse set forth in the texts. Otherwise we will often miss the point of what is said, because we will miss the resonances of the discourse, the expectations it evokes (and perhaps turns upside-down) within the linguistic and conceptual world it assumes. This was put charmingly and precisely by the seventeenth-century English scholar John Lightfoot:

> For . . . when all the books of the New Testament were written by Jews, and among Jews, and to Jews; — and when all the discoveries made there, were made in like manner by Jews, and to Jews, and among them; — I was always fully persuaded, as of a thing past doubting, that the New Testament could not but everywhere taste of, and retain, the Jews' style, idiom, form,

24. Thus Luther drew on both traditional monastic culture and the "rhetorical criticism" of his day when he directed: ". . . you should meditate, not only in the heart, but also externally constantly handle and rub together, read and reread, the oral speech and written words in the book, persistently paying attention to and thinking over what the Holy Spirit intends thereby" (Martin Luther, "Preface to the German Writings," *WA* 50:657). "Handle and rub together" are quasi-technical terms from medieval meditation practice, while "what the Holy Spirit intends" reflects humanist understandings of texts as purposeful rhetorical unities aiming at particular *skopoi.*

> and rule of speaking. . . . For it is no matter, what we can beat out concerning those manners of speech on the anvil of our own conceit, but what they signified among them in their own ordinary sense and speech.[25]

In the writings of the Old Testament the church always has at hand the most important port of entry into the conceptual world of the apostolic witness; at least one of the functions of the Old Testament in the church is to serve as a kind of conceptual school for Gentile believers, a means of sharing concretely in the "mind of Christ" (1 Cor. 2:16), which is certainly always the mind of a Jew.

Historically, this necessary initiation into the conceptual and linguistic world of the prophets and apostles has most often been informal, the by-product of formative practice; consider the extent to which daily recitation of the Psalter in the Divine Office shaped the environment in which much traditional biblical interpretation took place. Such practice has doubtless often had to work against the grain of Christian anti-Judaism, yet the sheer presence of the Psalms and other Old Testament texts in the church's prayer has in some measure undermined the immemorial Gentile Christian tendency to regard the New Testament as the liberation of God's word from Israelite particularity. There is no substitute for such practices of intensive engagement with the words of the sacred texts, yet the contemporary explosion of our knowledge of the early Jewish context of primitive Christianity provides a resource for an ecclesial exegesis in which attention to the words of Scripture in their Israelite-Jewish particularity might become a matter of *intentional* concern.

This first mandate is, it should be noted, a point at which theological commitments seem to impinge unavoidably on contemporary debates that this essay has attempted on the whole to avoid; a question at least arises here about the capacity of a "constructivist" hermeneutics, which regards the text as the simple *product* of the hermeneutical conventions of the "interpretive community," to do justice to what Christianity has meant by the inspiration of Scripture. The church has a deep commitment to the belief that it has *received* Scripture from the prophets and apostles, and ultimately from the Spirit, and does not in any simple sense *construct* it; the Christian tradition is

25. John Lightfoot, *Horae Hebraicae,* cited in Stephen Neill and N. T. Wright, *The Interpretation of the New Testament, 1861-1986* (Oxford: Oxford University Press, 1988), p. 314. Or as Barth wrote in the 1930s: "The Bible as the witness of divine revelation is in its humanity a product of the Israelitish, or to put it more clearly, the Jewish spirit. . . . The cry of dismay which is heard so strongly today is quite justified: we and the men of all nations are expected by Jews not only to interest ourselves in things Jewish, but in a certain and ultimately decisive sense actually to become Jews" (*Church Dogmatics* I/2, p. 510).

likewise committed to an interpretive stance of *deference*, indeed *loving* deference, towards the words of Holy Scripture, enacted in practices of attentive and persistent *lectio*.

The important insight in constructivism is that what particular interpreters make of particular texts is always at least partly dependent on what they bring with them, on what they know, or think they know, and believe relevant, about the world, the texts themselves, and their relation to one another. Such knowledge or putative knowledge is learned and shared in communities, and to this extent it is right to say that different interpretive communities will inevitably engage in very different sorts of interpretive practice with the same texts and understand them in correspondingly different ways. For example, social historians of ancient Israel do not, as such, write sermons on the book of Deuteronomy; the assumptions that social historians bring to the reading of Deuteronomy offer no *entrée* to this form of interpretive practice. Nor will a social historian make of Deuteronomy 8 (for example) what a Christian preacher might: a word spoken to a living community "for teaching, for reproof, for correction, and for training in righteousness" (2 Tim. 3:16), perhaps calling into question very specific features of its present life. In this way it is proper to say that an interpreter "situated outside" the believing community cannot hear the text as divine discourse, the Spirit's witness confronting the community.

But this wholesome repudiation of the Enlightenment myth of the abstractly rational, socially and historically locationless *interpreter* does not seem to authorize collapsing the distinction between *what the text says* and what the interpreter or interpretive community is in a position to *make* of it. That Christian readers hear Deuteronomy 8 as a word addressed to themselves corporately, or that they find themselves obligated to make reference to Jesus Christ in construing its implications, is a function of the beliefs they bring with them to the interpretive enterprise. But that Deuteronomy 8 warns the elect people against faithlessness and idolatry, and threatens them with destruction like any other nation, and that these warnings have specific resonances within the Pentateuchal narrative, is not the outcome of decisions made by the interpretive community.[26] It is rather the outcome of de-

26. It may be objected that these remarks caricature the "constructivist" case; after all, Stanley Fish himself has granted that texts exert pressure on interpreters: "The fact that the objects we have are all objects that appear to us in the context of some practice, of work done by some interpretive community, doesn't mean that they are not objects or that we don't have them or that they exert no pressure on us" (Stanley Fish, *Doing What Comes Naturally: Change, Rhetoric, and the Practice of Theory in Literary and Legal Studies* [Chapel Hill, N.C.: Duke University Press, 1989], p. 153). But if this is taken seriously, then much of the sound and fury Fish

cisions made by *others,* by those who brought the text into its present form; as interpreters we must see what we can and should make of what those others have wrought, just as, in analogous ways, we are constantly coming to terms throughout our lives with choices made by others and their outcomes. It is in just this "otherness" of the scriptures, in the contingency in which they come to us from outside the reach of our individual or corporate control, that the church encounters sacramentally the freedom and authority of the Spirit of God.

IV. The Unity of Scripture: The Old and the New

When the church recognizes the biblical canon as inspired Scripture, it approaches the texts as the discourse of the Holy Spirit, the discourse therefore of *one single speaker,* despite the plurality of their human authors. Thus a distinctive kind of *unity* is ascribed to the scriptures: the church receives the canon, in all its diversity, as nonetheless a *single* body of discourse, which serves the consistent purpose of a single authoritative agent.[27]

There are, of course, important non-theological ways in which one can speak of the biblical canon as a unity. The biblical texts represent a relatively coherent literary, conceptual, and theological tradition, and so can be read as a unity in tradition-historical perspective. One can also study the phenome-

---

has directed against textual autonomy can be little more than rhetorical overstatement, including his sophisticated mockery of the young woman whose question provided the title for his earlier book *Is There a Text in This Class? The Authority of Interpretive Communities* (Cambridge, Mass.: Harvard University Press, 1980). For a thoughtful argument that attention to interpretive practice undermines sweeping constructivist claims, cf. Francis Watson, *Text and Truth: Redefining Biblical Theology* (Grand Rapids: Eerdmans, 1997), pp. 95-126.

27. This is in effect to confess the Holy Spirit's "authorship" of the canon. However, the Latin *auctor* does not exactly mean "writer"; the *auctor* is one from whom we receive a text, one who stands behind it and invests it with his or her own *auctoritas.* To say that the Spirit is the *auctor* of Scripture is not necessarily to say that the Spirit *wrote* the texts, but that the Spirit has appropriated them and invested them with the specific *auctoritas* proper to his saving mission. The texts *written* by Isaiah or Matthew or Paul have been appropriated by the Spirit, so that we now rightly read them as the Spirit's own discourse, backed by the Spirit's authority, and directed towards the Spirit's ends. Charles Wood's analogy is helpful here: in his *Notes on the New Testament,* John Wesley lifted large tracts of text actually *written* by Johann Albrecht Bengel, yet in doing so Wesley made them his own, backed them with his own name, and deployed them for his own purposes, so that we have no qualms either about taking the whole of the *Notes* as a work "authored" by John Wesley or in reading them as aimed at the formation of "the people called Methodists" (Charles Wood, *The Formation of Christian Understanding: An Essay in Theological Hermeneutics* [Philadelphia: Westminster, 1981], pp. 67-68).

non of intertextual echo among the biblical texts, as later texts appeal to earlier ones and reinterpret them. Moreover, there is no reason why a purely literary analysis could not take seriously a biblical canon, Jewish or Christian, as a unified whole, received as such by an important community of readers. There seems to be no rational imperative that forces us to regard the formation of the canon as less significant than, say, the redaction of the Pentateuch; if the latter can be taken seriously as the composition of a single literary work out of diverse pre-existing parts, so too can the former.

However, even though the church can recognize such literary and historical unities and exploit them in its own interpretive practice, the unity of the canon as Holy Scripture is a distinctively *theological* unity implicit in the notion of "inspiration." The church reads the scriptures as the discourse of a single divine agent, the Holy Spirit, who has a unified purpose: to bear witness to Jesus in his unity with the Father. The discourse that Isaiah addressed to the inhabitants of Zion, or the first evangelist addressed to the so-called "Matthaean community," or Paul addressed to the Thessalonians, is thus received by the Christian community as the discourse addressed by the *Spirit* to the church of *every* time and *every* place. Literary and historical unities may be assumed into this theological unity, but the latter cannot be derived from them; moreover, the specific unity of the texts as inspired Scripture may well authorize reading them as mutually interpretive in ways that go beyond anything for which literary and historical considerations can account.

Furthermore, the distinctive unity ascribed to the texts by the doctrine of inspiration is also compatible with acknowledgment of their literary and historical *diversity* and even *disparity,* considered simply as historical artifacts. Much of the vitality of the church's scriptural interpretation arises precisely from the commitment to framing a very diverse body of texts in a larger unity of divine purpose and action. *What these diverse texts say,* in their concrete detail, is *what the one Spirit says* to the churches to make Christ known; the church must therefore *both* attend minutely to what the texts say *and* seek to construe that diverse discourse coherently as the unified utterance of the Spirit.

Thus a second mandate of faithfulness may be formulated: "Seek within Scripture's diversity the *unity* of the Spirit's witness to Jesus Christ for the church." The Spirit's witness has a specific aim: to make Christ known in his unity with the one who sent him, to make the crucified known as Lord and Messiah. Thus to read the scriptures as the discourse of the Spirit is to read them as a single complex testimony to Christ; in Luther's terms, the *res* of which all these words are signs is Jesus Christ, the Son of God born in the last days of the Virgin, crucified for us, and risen from the dead to reign eternally.

Thus our second mandate may also be formulated thus: "Do not suppose that you have understood these signs, in their employment by the Spirit, until you have grasped how they pertain to Jesus Christ and his messianic dominion."

While this rule has considerable implications for a wide range of church practice,[28] it is most obviously challenging with regard to the Old Testament. Not only has the interpretive faithfulness enjoined here been especially obnoxious to modernity, the difficulty of reading the Old and New Testament scriptures as a single witness has been felt from the beginning. Indeed, interpreting the scriptures of Israel as the Spirit's testimony to Jesus Christ, discerning and arguing and displaying the unity of the two-part Christian canon, may be called the central task of ecclesial exegesis; it is arguably the root from which *all* Christian theology, as a distinctly ecclesial practice of reflection, has grown.[29]

The most important point to be made here is that there is no "method" of a *formal* kind — historical or literary, critical or allegorical or typological — by which the unity of the Christian canon can be set forth in abstraction from theological argument and judgment. To put it another way, the hermeneutics that displays this unity just *is* classical Christian theology, insofar as it presents and argues and ponders certain central *judgments of identity* that span the divide between the two testaments. The most important of these judgments are (i) that the one who sent Jesus, and raised him from the dead, is self-identically the God of Israel, the God attested in the Old Testament scriptures; (ii) that the church of Jesus Christ is continuous, to be sure across massive and radical transformation, with the covenant people of the Old Testament; and (iii) binding these together, that Jesus Christ is the *one* word that God speaks to his people, so that whatever is "word of God" in the Old Testament must be read as a moment within the protracted utterance of what is conclusively articulated only in the paschal mystery of Good Friday and Easter — in "the resurrection which has now taken place."[30]

28. For example, it would seem to imply a rule, "Do not interpret any part of Scripture as good advice about managing stress," which could have drastic implications for much contemporary preaching.

29. Cf. Hans Urs von Balthasar, *The Glory of the Lord,* vol. 7: *Theology: The New Covenant* (San Francisco: Ignatius, 1989), pp. 103-14.

30. Cf. Robert W. Jenson, "Hermeneutics and the Life of the Church," in *Reclaiming the Bible for the Church,* ed. Carl E. Braaten and Robert W. Jenson (Grand Rapids: Eerdmans, 1995), pp. 89-105. For the role played by these judgments in classical Christian Old Testament interpretation, cf. Wilfried Hagemann, *Wort als Begegnung mit Christus: Die christozentrische Schriftauslegung des Kirchenvaters Hieronymus* (Trier: Paulinus, 1970), pp. 117-36. Compare also the classic account of Henri de Lubac, *Medieval Exegesis,* vol. 1: *The Four Senses of Scripture,* trans. Mark Sebanc (Grand Rapids: Eerdmans, 1998), pp. 225-67, and the commentary by

To comprehend the Christian canon as a unity is essentially to present and unpack and argue these judgments in one's reading of the texts; in early Christianity, the development of a unified reading of the two-part canon, and the development of trinitarian theology, christology, and ecclesial self-definition, were not two developments but one. Within the framework of these judgments, traditional Christian exegesis employed a diverse organon of procedures to draw out and display the bearing of the two testaments on one another; the persuasiveness of these moves finally derived, however, not simply from "methodological" convictions about typology, allegoresis, and the like, but from the theological judgments just described.

We can see this framework in operation in Gregory the Great's rationale, in the "Preface" to his *Moralia in Job,* for taking the great Old Testament faithful, including Job, as christological figures. In the night of human sin, Gregory writes, God has provided a series of witnesses, who appeared in turn to illumine different aspects of the good that humankind has suppressed or forgotten. Thus the "night" is not simply lost time; it moves towards a promised future as night moves towards morning, as the sequence of rising and setting stars moves towards the rising of the Morning Star. The Old Testament scriptures are thus construed as a narrative moving towards Christ as *telos.* But the relation between Christ and the Old Testament saints is more than merely sequential, as Gregory goes on to say:

> All the elect led the way for the Morning Star by living well, and promised him by prophesying in both actions and words *(et rebus et vocibus).* There was no righteous person who was not figurally his herald. For it was surely appropriate that in themselves they should all show forth that Good by virtue of which all of them were good and which they knew would benefit all.[31]

In this scriptural astronomy, the Morning Star is the source of the light that shines from all the earlier stars; the crucified and risen Christ is the *bonum* by which all his predecessors were good and holy. Therefore the saints prophesy him not only by verbal prediction but also by bearing his form: insofar as

---

Susan K. Wood, *Spiritual Exegesis and the Church in the Theology of Henri de Lubac* (Grand Rapids: Eerdmans, 1998), pp. 25-51. These issues also seem central to the call for a new biblical theology in both Christopher R. Seitz, *Word Without End: The Old Testament as Abiding Theological Witness* (Grand Rapids: Eerdmans, 1998), and Francis Watson, *Text and Truth: Redefining Biblical Theology* (Grand Rapids: Eerdmans, 1997).

31. Gregory the Great, *Moralia in Iob, Praefatio,* VI, 14, in *Moralia in Iob, Libri I-X,* ed. M. Adriaen, CCSL 143 (Turnhout, Belgium: Brepols, 1979), p. 19.

their lives display some aspect of the *bonum,* the good that God intends for his people and his world, they anticipate and elucidate the reality of Jesus Christ, who *is* that good in person.

Yet there is no sense, for Gregory or other classical exegetes, that the Old Testament stories thereby cease to be coherently particular stories of vocation and discipleship and suffering; the christological *skopos* does not rob them of what might be called an *ecclesial* sense, as paradigmatic narratives of the deeds and sufferings of the covenant people, with which the church claims to be continuous, albeit across vast transformations and changes.[32] Indeed, Gregory sees this simultaneity as itself christologically grounded:

> But because our Redeemer has shown himself to be one person in union with the church which he has taken to himself — for of him it is said, "He is the head of us all," and of his church it is said, "The body of Christ, which is the church" — anyone who signifies Christ in himself sometimes portrays him from the perspective of the head and sometimes from the perspective of the body, so that he speaks with the voice not only of the head but also of the body.[33]

According to this rule of the unity of the Lord with his body,[34] Christ and the church together form *one single complex whole* to which "the things that were written" must be read as pertaining. The christological pertinence of the stories of Job or David or Abraham does not prevent them from being read as exemplary stories of discipleship, vocation, and membership in God's people, nor can we set Scripture's "realistic" narrative depiction of "believable individuals and their credible destinies" against christological relevance.[35] On the contrary, discipleship, vocation, and membership in God's people are essentially *forms of participation in Christ,* so that the more the Old Testament nar-

32. Even the Gentile Job is interpreted in light of the church's continuity with the ancient covenant people: he is a *prophetic sign* of that continuity, a Gentile who testifies by his own life that Jews and Gentiles are summoned to the same good.

33. Gregory the Great, *Moralia in Iob,* VI, 14, pp. 19-20.

34. Cf. Augustine, *De doctrina christiana,* book III, par. 44.

35. Cf. Hans Frei's remarks on typology in the introduction to *The Eclipse of Biblical Narrative: A Study in Eighteenth and Nineteenth Century Hermeneutics* (New Haven: Yale University Press, 1974), pp. 10-16, here p. 15. It is part of the problem of the relations between literary theory and theological argument in this great book that Frei can leave the impression that what modern hermeneutics most crucially lost was the *technique of figuration,* whereas I want to suggest that the critical loss was the distinctively churchly knowledge of Christ in its relevance to interpretation. It was when christological conviction ceased to function as public knowledge that figural readings began to look arbitrary and "primitive."

rative renders credible stories of life in the covenant, the more it prophesies and prefigures Christ. "There was no righteous person who was not figurally his herald."

Two remarks may be in order about challenges that a reappropriation of this exegetical tradition must face. First, the detailed connections that can plausibly be made between the two testaments undoubtedly change from era to era, not simply due to arbitrary changes in the culturally dominant *Zeitgeist,* against which ecclesial disciplines of thought and imagination, if actually practiced, might be some defense, but also because of changes in what we believe to be true and pertinent to the understanding of the texts. The specifically ecclesial knowledge explored in this essay is never the *only* knowledge that properly bears on our reading of Scripture, and this constitutes one source of interpretive change with which even the most resolutely non-relativistic hermeneutics must reckon.

It may be then that both the modern accumulation of knowledge about the historical circumstances in which the texts originated, as well as our heightened awareness of historical distance, have rendered it permanently impossible for us to repeat in our own voice many specific exegetical moves with which older Christian interpreters sought to display the unity of the canon; this essay should not be read, therefore, as calling for a simple *repristination* of pre-modern exegesis.[36] Having made this necessary stipulation, however, it seems equally important to warn that we cannot know *a priori* to what extent or in what cases the impossibility holds; we cannot know what might seem plausible and persuasive within an interpretive community that took the church's knowledge as seriously, and meditated on it as deeply,

36. James Kugel has recently asserted that all ancient biblical interpreters, Jewish and Christian, shared the assumption that "the Bible is a fundamentally cryptic document. That is, all interpreters are fond of maintaining that although Scripture may appear to be saying X, what it really means is Y, or that while Y is not openly said by Scripture, it is somehow implied or hinted at in X" (James Kugel, *The Bible As It Was* [Cambridge, Mass.: Harvard University Press, 1997], p. 18). I wonder how much of what is genuinely unassimilable in pre-modern exegesis derives from *this* assumption rather than the theological framework described in this essay. Thus it seems to be one sort of procedure to relate the *pattern and movement* of the drama in the Song of Songs to the relationship of Christ and the church. It seems a different *kind* of move when Bernard, for example, interprets the two breasts of the bride as *compassio* and *congratulatio,* readiness to share the sorrows and joys of others (cf. *In Cantica Canticorum,* X, 1). Historians have labored to distinguish these *methodologically,* as typology vs. allegory (Daniélou) or *allegoria facti* vs. *allegoria verbi* (De Lubac). But it may be more useful to distinguish them in terms of the beliefs that authorize them: Bernard and others may find the *first* sort of move plausible partly because they share the beliefs described in this essay, but make the *second* sort of move because they *also* believe Scripture to be "a fundamentally cryptic document."

as modern scholarship has done with historical research and historical consciousness. We have reason to approach the Christian exegetical tradition without too many provisos, preconditions, and fixed securities: much that seems strange and even perverse to us may turn out to be thoroughly defensible within a context of belief that we may want to share.

The second remark concerns something more difficult, yet is not unrelated to the first. It is clear that from an early time, the attempt to display the unity of the canon as testimony to Jesus Christ assumed a deeply *anti-Jewish* character: to set forth Christ as the *skopos* of the whole Scripture was to "triumph" over the Jews and demonstrate the worthlessness of *their* exegesis. In light of widespread agreement today that Christian attitudes towards Judaism require drastic correction, the very idea of a reading of the scriptures of Israel in light of a distinctively ecclesial knowledge may seem unpromising and even impermissible.

Yet this may simply be an important case in which, because we do not share *all* relevant beliefs with earlier exegetes, we will rightly read Scripture differently than they did, even though we may share with them crucial governing assumptions and thus stand recognizably in their tradition. Nearly all pre-modern Christian exegetes were supersessionists; they believed that the Jewish people had been irrevocably expelled from covenant standing before God. Therefore they treated Jewish exegesis as illegitimate from the outset: Jews were interlopers who had no *right* to read the law and the prophets as divine discourse. That belief is rightly now widely recognized to be contrary to Scripture; for Paul, who speaks most extensively to this point, it is not the "rejection" but the "gifts and a calling" of the Jewish people that are irrevocable (Rom. 11:28-29).[37]

There seems no reason why a renewed ecclesial exegesis, rejecting supersessionism, could not regard Jews and Judaism in a new way: not as cheats to be exposed but as appointed interlocutors — indeed, given their prior and irrevocable covenant standing, *privileged* interlocutors, whose rejection of the church's reading of Israel's scriptures is rightfully a constant provocation, calling at all times for a careful word in response.[38] To regard

37. On supersessionism, cf. Bruce Marshall, "Christ and the Cultures: The Jewish People in Christian Theology," in *The Cambridge Companion to Christian Doctrine,* ed. C. Gunton (Cambridge: Cambridge University Press, 1997), pp. 81-100, as well as his essay in this volume.

38. The Jewish contestation of the Christian reception of the ancient scriptures, which I am suggesting Christian exegetes should take quite seriously, is something different from the currently widespread charge that a Christian reading of those scriptures is a violent expropriation of the "property" of the Jewish people, the prototype of all the damage done by Christians to Jews over the centuries. In reality, Christian and Jewish ways of reading the scriptures both

Jews and Judaism in this way might indeed be the hermeneutical force of Paul's warning precisely to Gentile believers: "Therefore do not be haughty, but be afraid."[39]

At the same time, it is important to be clear about the goal of such a reoriented interpretive enterprise. Christians cannot aim at producing a Christian exegesis of the Old Testament that Jews would not contest: so long as there is schism between the church and the Jewish people, Christians will be unable to be faithful to what they have received from the apostles of the Lord without coming into disagreement with Jews. The goal suggested here would be neither to conciliate Jews nor yet to triumph over them, but simply to give them an answer, "in gentleness and reverence" (1 Pet. 3:15-16) in which they were genuinely *heard.* Such hearing, we may be confident, will tend to produce Christian readings of the scriptures that are more faithful, more profound, and more edifying to the church, however little they may persuade the Jewish interlocutors whose questions and arguments have provoked them. In this way the church's exegesis might acknowledge at least one dimension of the irrevocable gifts and calling of the Jewish people: they continue to teach the Gentiles the ways of the Lord their God, even across the chasm of separation that we cannot, in this age, finally bridge or eliminate.

---

rest on decisions made by *Jews:* Jewish readings rest on a majority decision to interpret Scripture in light of codified oral tradition in the context of the synagogue after the destruction of the temple and the dispersion from the land; Christian readings rest on a minority decision to interpret Scripture in light of the apostolic proclamation of Jesus' enthronement as Lord and Messiah, in the context of a common life ordered around baptism and Eucharist, after Jesus' crucifixion and its startling aftermath. Gentile Christians receive both the ancient scriptures and this way of reading them from the Jewish apostles of the Lord; it would be an act of presumption, of astonishing Gentile "high-mindedness" (Rom. 11:20), to suppose that we were now able to know the Lord Jesus without the testimony of the "oracles of God" (Rom. 3:2). That could only imply naïve confidence in our innate religious perceptions as adequate "testimony" to God's redemptive purpose; such confidence has been common in modern theology but hardly does honor to Israel as a light to the Gentiles. Nor is Israel honored by reduction of the whole question to ethnic identity-politics. The point is surely not that the Torah and the Prophets "belong" to Jews as a beloved ethnic heirloom, as "Danny Boy" might be said to "belong" to the Irish. The issue is *the truth about God,* which Jews as a chosen, priestly people believe is distorted in the Christian reception of the scriptures. It does not follow from the undeniable fact that many Jews and Christians today would be uncomfortable joining the issue at this level that either community is taken seriously by anything less. Cf. Jon Levenson, *The Hebrew Bible, the Old Testament, and Historical Criticism: Jews and Christians in Biblical Studies* (Philadelphia: Westminster/John Knox, 1993), for a study that resists accounting for Jewish-Christian differences in scriptural study at any level beneath the theological.

39. Romans 11:20; my translation.

V. The Unity of Scripture: The Whole and the Parts

For the Christian tradition, to regard the canon as a unity is not to regard it as a flat surface, on which every point is level with every other point. Rather, the canon is treated as an intricately structured whole, with a definite center, the figure of Jesus the Messiah, crucified and risen, and a definite point and purpose, the upbuilding of the church as sign and witness to his unity with the Father who sent him. This has implications for our understanding of "faithfulness to Scripture" as a *norm of ecclesial teaching and practice.*

The tendency of contemporary scholarship is to identify mature understanding of the texts with clear perception of their irreconcilable *differences,* in the confidence that it is always a good thing to become more "aware of diversity." The idea of a coherent scriptural norm that could measure church practice is thus generally viewed as a remnant of fundamentalist simple-mindedness.

Despite a certain amount of radical posturing, such scholarship is quite *conservative* within the mainline denominations in which it is most devoutly practiced. In those denominations, "diversity" is the existing *status quo;* indeed, mainline denominations are perhaps best described as institutional vessels designed to enclose extreme religious plurality. In such settings, criticism that privileges difference and diversity *protects* denominational institutions from disruptive normative claims that might upset their fragile containment of highly centrifugal factions. If no coherent appeal can be made to a shared norm of scriptural faithfulness, we are all allowed to continue on our parallel tracks, doing and saying the different and incompatible things — conservative, liberal, or centrist — with which we feel comfortable. Every party within the church is thus reduced to a *club,* boosters of a favorite style or commodity, and therefore to a phenomenon that mainline denominationalism is equipped to manage.

In all this, modernist hermeneutics covertly trades on the very understanding of scriptural authority it deplores in fundamentalism. Scripture's authority seems automatically called in question by internal diversity only because the canon is conceived from the start as a mere accumulation of pieces, each equally authoritative because it is "in the Bible." The only coherence such an unstructured heap could have would be simple uniformity among its parts; the demonstration of tension and difference among the parts would already refute its integrity as canon, reducing it to a mere anthology of ancient Israelite and early Christian literature, a resource but not a norm for contemporary religiosity. If Elisha's floating axehead (2 Kings 6:5-7) is legendary, then the testimony to Jesus' resurrection is called into question; if the canon is shown to have a periphery, it follows that it cannot have a center.

A rather different perception of the canon can be discerned in the older Christian interpretive tradition. To begin with, complex judgments about the shape and structure of the canon seem to be at work in traditional patterns of *liturgical* engagement with the texts. To return to an earlier example: that *both* an epistle text *and* a gospel text have been read at the Eucharist, but with the gospel reading in the place of emphasis, with the assembly called at that point to rise and greet the present Lord, bespeaks a subtle sense of intertextual relationship within the canonical whole. The exposition of the faith in the epistles is essential, one might paraphrase, but only insofar as it orients us to the concrete figure of the Messiah, Jesus of Nazareth himself in his narrated particularity. Likewise there are doubtless judgments about the center implicit in the extreme prominence of the Psalms in traditional liturgical usage.

Other such perceptions are implicit in traditional *exegetical practice,* especially the procedures post-Reformation Protestants liked to call "interpreting Scripture from within Scripture" or "rightly dividing the word of truth" (cf. 2 Tim. 2:15, KJV). These procedures were not, by and large, *invented* by Protestants, but were drawn chiefly from the anti-Gnostic and anti-Arian exegesis of the Fathers, taking up the patristic norm of interpretation according to "the rule of the faith."[40] Early Protestants had an interest in codifying these exegetical rules of play, but the fruit of their labors was typically not so much the systematic elaboration of a method as the partial description of a traditional practice.[41]

In the relatively concise list of Johann Gerhard, the first rule lays down the general principle of scriptural intertextuality: "The sense of Scripture is to be construed from within Scripture itself."[42] The second rule is concerned with unity: "All interpretation of Scripture should be governed by the analogy of the faith," summarized in the Apostles' Creed.[43] Likewise the third: "More obscure and uncommon *(pauciora)* texts are to be explicated on the basis of

40. Cf. Paul M. Blowers, "The *Regula Fidei* and the Narrative Character of Early Christian Faith," *Pro Ecclesia* (1997): 199-228.

41. Perhaps the greatest such work was the *Clavis Sacrae Scripturae* of the Lutheran theologian Matthias Flacius Illyricus (1520-1575). For a modern reprint of key portions of this work, cf. Matthias Flacius Illyricus, *De Ratione Cognoscendi Sacras Literas/Über den Erkenntnisgrund der heiligen Schrift,* Latin-German Parallel-Edition, ed. Lutz Geldsetzer (Düsseldorf: Stern-Verlag Janssen & Co., 1968).

42. Johann Gerhard, "De Scriptura Sacra," ch. 24, sec. 529, in *Loci Theologici,* vol. 1, ed. E. Preuss (Berlin: Schlawitz, 1863), p. 237.

43. Gerhard, "De Scriptura Sacra," p. 238.

the more clear and common *(pluribus)* ones."[44] The three rules that follow call for deference to the particularity of the texts: the "native sense of words and the idiomatic meaning of phrases" is to be construed from the original languages; articles of faith can only be established by appeal to the *sensus literalis,* to the "proper and native significance" of the words; and careful attention must be given to "what is aimed at (the *skopos*) in each passage, as well as the context and order of the parts."[45] The final rule defines exegesis as a communal and convivial enterprise rooted in tradition: "In scriptural interpretation we both can and should make grateful use of the labors of both ancient and more recent teachers of the church."[46]

Crucial to Gerhard's understanding of Scripture's unity here is the notion of the *analogia fidei,* received from the Fathers. It brings to bear the conviction that the scriptural witness has a *center* — identifiable in Scripture itself but summed up in the Apostles' Creed — and that the whole canon in all its parts should be read and understood in relation to that center. Gerhard's rationale for this rule appeals directly to Scripture's inspiration: as the discourse of a single agent, the scriptural canon should be interpreted congruently with the known intentions of that agent. Therefore even if we cannot always get at "the sense intended by the Holy Spirit" in every passage, we can at least "take care to avoid proposing anything contrary to the analogy of the faith."[47]

At the same time, Gerhard equates this point with another, which is less persuasive and sets the stage for later difficulties. He assumes not only that Scripture should be read in light of the intentions of the Spirit, but also that no scriptural text can be at odds with those intentions: "Since all Scripture originates in the immediate breathing of the Spirit, and is *theopneustos,* therefore also all things in it are equally true *(synalēthē)* and supremely harmonious among themselves, so that nothing in it steps out of place as contrary or inconsistent or self-contradictory."[48] We stand here at the beginning of the dogmatic slurring of the ragged particularity of the texts that will eventually provoke historical-critical attack, and also at the beginning of that conception of the canon as a flat, undifferentiated surface that fundamentalists and critics still tend to share.

Yet in Gerhard there are interesting complexities: if this were the *whole*

44. Gerhard, "De Scriptura Sacra," p. 239.

45. Gerhard, "De Scriptura Sacra," p. 239. The insistence on original languages is more humanist than patristic, but is not without patristic precedent (Origen, Jerome).

46. Gerhard, "De Scriptura Sacra," p. 240.

47. Gerhard, "De Scriptura Sacra," p. 238.

48. Gerhard, "De Scriptura Sacra," p. 238.

truth, it is hard to see why we would need a rule mandating interpretation "according to the analogy of the faith" at all, or why the Apostles' Creed would be required as a practical norm for exegesis, or why it is needful to distinguish between "obscure" and "clear" passages of Scripture. None of this seems to reflect a homogenous, tensionless Scripture, and yet these are just the points at which Gerhard is most faithful to traditional exegetical *practice.* That practice, one could claim, contained a recognition that the relation between textual particularity and canonical unity is more complicated than many theories of inspiration have been able to acknowledge, while it continued to treat "faithfulness to Scripture" as a meaningful and operationally practicable goal.

Faithfulness to Scripture is achieved, for that tradition, by a distinctive art of reading whose crucial moves are mandated or at least authorized by Christian beliefs about God, Christ, the world, and the scriptural canon itself. A faithful reading is one that is clearly governed from the *center* of the canonical witness, yet allows that center to be illumined and explicated by the linguistic and literary particularity of specific texts, with even contrary or tensive texts being permitted to speak so far as this is possible without displacing the center. Within this framework, *ad hoc* but reasoned argument is possible about, for example, the way particular texts should be ranked and weighted with regard to particular issues, or what constitutes the "clearer and more common" line of witness on a specific topic within the canon.[49] What makes such arguments possible, however, is a shared ecclesial knowledge that enables identification of the Spirit's intentions and thus of the *skopos* of the canonical witness.

In this way, the art of "interpreting Scripture from within Scripture" contains an implicit *critical* dimension, which could be made explicit in response to modernity's manifold moral critique of Scripture. Over and over, though most recently and powerfully by feminists, the argument has been made, not without plausibility, that scriptural authority is destructive, perpetuating cruelties and oppressions from which cultural enlightenment might otherwise

49. I recall, in this connection, the observation made in conversation by my colleague, Professor Agneta Enermalm, that the prominence of Galatians 3:28 in some arguments about the role of women in the church is justified by the *baptismal* context of that verse, a context therefore in which the foundations of ecclesial identity are on the table. While not a knockdown blow, this is surely a reasonable consideration to adduce in reflecting on how to order and weigh the various conflicting statements and attitudes concerning women within the canon. One might also point to the difficulty — noted already by John Chrysostom — of squaring the hierarchical scheme invoked in 1 Corinthians 11:3 with Nicene Christology as further reason for taking not that text but Galatians 3:28 as the canonical center in this matter.

free us. The most natural response for many modern Christians has been to retreat from the textual mediation of Christian faith altogether; authority has been lodged instead in some variant of a "simple gospel" or original *kerygma,* the expanding contemporary experience of the Spirit, or another experientially immediate norm.[50]

However, if Paul is right, such Christianity, cut free from textual positivity, *cannot* have as its theme the eschatological wisdom of God in the crucifixion of the Messiah: for that "no eye has seen, nor ear heard, nor the human heart conceived" (1 Cor. 2:9). To make *that* wisdom our theme, we need the "words taught by the Spirit" (1 Cor. 2:13) of which the apostle speaks. The wisdom that leads to salvation cannot therefore be acquired without the labor of engagement with the *grammata,* the holy writings (2 Tim. 3:15); if the *gramma* kills without the *pneuma* (2 Cor. 3:6), this does not mean that "spirit" is available in sheer immediacy, floating free of the dense flesh of the texts. Even Paul, so often claimed by those who would celebrate pneumatic immediacy, cannot state the good news without the twofold "according to the scriptures" of 1 Corinthians 15:3-4. The eschatological community that has drunk of the Spirit (1 Cor. 12:13), on which "the ends of the ages have come," nevertheless needs "admonition" on the basis of "what has been written" (1 Cor. 10:11). "For whatever was written in former days was written for our instruction, so that by steadfastness and by the encouragement of the scriptures we might have hope" (Rom. 15:4).[51]

50. This is in effect what Luther and Calvin knew and opposed as "enthusiasm." Cf. Luther in the 1537 *Smalcald Articles:* "In these matters which concern the oral, external word, we must insist that God gives no one his Spirit or grace except through or with the foregoing external word, so that we are on guard against the Enthusiasts, that is, spirits which boast that they have the Spirit without and prior to the word, and judge, interpret, and stretch the Scripture or the spoken word as they please accordingly. . . . All this is the old devil and the old snake who made Adam and Eve into Enthusiasts, led them away from God's external word to spirit-mongering and their own darkness. . . . In sum: enthusiasm clings to Adam and his children from the beginning to the end of the world, implanted and introduced as a poison in them by the old serpent; it is the origin, power, and force of all heresy, including that of the Pope and Mahomet. Therefore we should and must persist in holding that God will not deal with us human beings except through his external word and sacrament. Everything else which is boasted of concerning the Spirit without this word and sacrament is the devil . . ." (*BSELK,* 455-56). Just as this issue divided Luther and Calvin from contemporaries with whom they shared important goals, such as reform of the exercise of power in the church, so today this same issue unfortunately shows every sign of having the potential to bring into conflict those who share goals such as reforming Christian attitudes to women and Judaism.

51. Notice the continuity of 2 Timothy 3:15-16 with 1 Corinthians 10:11 and Romans 15:4: the *didaskalia* in 2 Timothy echoes the *didaskalia* in Romans 15:4, while "reproof" and "correction" take up the "admonition" of 1 Corinthians 10:11. Modern scholarship predictably empha-

For those who refuse the turn to a textually unmediated gospel, yet share concerns about abusive employments of Scripture, what is left is the possibility of a critique of Scripture from *inside* rather than *outside* the canon, building on the ancient rule of exegesis "according to the analogy of the faith." However much we may need to distinguish what Paul or Matthew says from what God says, this cannot be accomplished by some direct access to divine purpose unmediated by the textual witness of which Paul and Matthew are parts. It must be achieved through the art of reading just outlined, in which particular texts, even when cross-grained and difficult, are allowed so far as possible to speak in their own voice, yet interpretation is governed from the center of the canon, and the particularity of the passage must find its place within the *skopos* of the whole.

An example that far predates contemporary ideological conflicts in the church is the treatment of Hebrews 6:4-6 and 12:16-17 in the exegetical tradition. From the time of the Novatian controversy in the mid-third century, "catholic" exegetes were unanimous that these texts *could not* be taken to say what modern criticism would insist they *do* say: that those who have been initiated into the Christian faith and then renounce it cannot be restored to salvation. The texts *may* not be taken to say this, for so read they contradict the sense of the canon as a whole. The young Luther put the case bluntly: ". . . if there were no repentance, the entire Epistle to the Galatians would amount to nothing, since it is not the so-called actual sins that are censured in this epistle, but the greatest sin, namely, the sin of unbelief, because of which they had fallen away from Christ to the Law."[52] Thus if the texts from Hebrews are taken in their apparent sense, Paul was wrong to strive to restore the Galatians to true faith, for the Galatians were precisely such as had "shared in the Holy Spirit and tasted the goodness of the word of God" (6:4-5; cf. Gal. 1:6, 3:1-5), yet had fallen away.

Therefore the exegetes, from Chrysostom through Aquinas to Calvin, interpret these texts in the prior knowledge that "in this world there is no sin of which a person cannot repent."[53] But two things are important about this tradition. First, the principle to which the reading of the texts must conform *is itself textually mediated.* The exegetes appeal not to a "simple gospel" of divine mercy, nor to the church's developing experience of the Spirit, but to the

---

sizes the differences between the Pastorals and the "genuine" Pauline epistles, but 2 Timothy 3:15-16 can just as well be read as commentary integrating a whole nexus of "genuine" Pauline concern.

52. Martin Luther, "Lectures on Hebrews," *LW* 29:182.

53. Thomas Aquinas, "Super Epistolam ad Hebraeos Lectura," par. 291, in *Super Epistolas S. Pauli Lectura*, vol. 2, ed. Fr. Raphael Cai, O.P. (Turin: Marietti, 1953), p. 400.

consensus of the canon: the governing principle is evident from many places.[54] Paul struggling with the Corinthians and Galatians is the primary witness, but grouped around him stands a whole chorus of canonical figures and voices calling for the restoration of the lapsed. Chrysostom in particular provides a miniature biblical theology of repentance, drawing together material from the Psalms, prophets, and wisdom-writings, as well as the gospels and epistles, to display a persistent pattern of scriptural invitation to the fallen.[55]

Second, the tradition does not take their tension with the canonical consensus as grounds to denigrate and suppress these problematic texts. Instead, there is a real effort to let them speak, to give them a voice. Hebrews 6:6 does not say that the *restoration* of the fallen is impossible, but rather their repeated *renewal (palin anakainizein);* it therefore teaches the impossibility of a second baptism (Chrysostom and many others). Or else it warns simply of the peril of those who willfully renounce Christ and "rush on in their obstinacy unto destruction" (Calvin).[56] As for Esau (in 12:16-17), he is not an example of the impossible, a true penitent denied forgiveness, but the very type of *false* penitence, weeping not from godly sorrow but from "pride and wrath" (Chrysostom). As Aquinas says laconically: "Esau was sorry, not because he sold his birthright, but because he lost it."[57] Thus even though interpretation must be governed from the center, it does not follow that there is nothing serious to be said from the periphery.

Here as elsewhere in this essay, all that can be done is gesture towards an opening that might be explored and widened by those prepared to take the church's knowledge seriously as "context" for biblical interpretation. Could the tradition's *implicit* recognition of difficulty and tension within the canon be made *explicit,* to acknowledge that not only certain texts, but also certain widespread *features* of the texts (e.g., ways of representing women), are in specific respects at odds with the Spirit's purpose, and therefore permanently liable to lead us astray? Could this be done without recourse to a textually unmediated norm lodged in our heads and hearts, but established by painstaking argument from *within* the canon, "interpreting" — and sifting — "Scripture from within Scripture"?[58] Could this be done without the depressing

54. John Chrysostom, "Homilies on Hebrews," Homily 9, par. 8, in *NPNF,* First Series, vol. 14, p. 411.

55. Chrysostom, "Homilies on Hebrews," pp. 411-12.

56. John Calvin, *Commentaries on the Epistle of Paul the Apostle to the Hebrews,* trans. J. Owen (Grand Rapids: Baker, reprint 1996), p. 139.

57. Aquinas, par. 694, *Super Epistolas,* p. 489.

58. Recently Francis Watson has offered an interesting proposal for such an internal cri-

mimicry of totalitarian politics so common in modernist *Sachkritik,* where problematic texts are denounced as "enemies of the people" and thereafter appear in public discourse only as objects of repeated ritual vilification?[59] Could we sustain the burden of complexity involved in holding that certain aspects of the texts are inherently problematic, precisely in view of Scripture's own *skopos,* while affirming that even these aspects of the texts have a function within the canonical whole? Might there be connections between such a position and classical notions of the Spirit's kenotic "accommodation" and "condescension" in Scripture, such that Scripture itself is affirmed to be both inherently problematic and the indispensable *sermo divina* through which alone we have access to the deep things of God?

VI. *Applicatio:* What the Spirit Says to the Churches

The church to which Scripture is given is an actual historical community whose life is *extended in space and time.* By the logic of inspiration, the textually fixed discourse of the scriptures is addressed by the Holy Spirit to the church of *every* time and *every* place; at every moment of its temporal career and in every place where it assembles, the church rightly reads the biblical canon as relevant and formative for its own life, as a *sacramental* discourse through which the Holy Spirit is present as lord and life-giver. Some thoughts on this claim of the constant *applicability* of the scriptural texts to the life of the Christian people must conclude this essay.

In one contemporary rite of ordination to the pastoral ministry, the ordaining bishop reads 1 Corinthians 4:1-2, along with other New Testament texts, as an address to the newly ordained: "This is how one should regard us, as servants of Christ and stewards of the mysteries of God. Moreover, it is required of stewards that they be found trustworthy."[60] It may be helpful to focus our thoughts about the applicative dimension of ecclesial interpretation on the questions raised by this use of this text in this setting.

What is likely to strike anyone formed by historical criticism is the way in

---

tique of Scripture by Scripture; cf. esp. Watson, *Text, Church and World: Biblical Interpretation in Theological Perspective* (Grand Rapids: Eerdmans, 1994), pp. 155-219.

59. It is not only recent politically engaged exegesis that I have in mind here; many contemporary exegetes learned this sort of denunciatory *Sachkritik* from Bultmannian arraignments of New Testament writings regarded as deviating from pure Pauline *kerygma.*

60. *Occasional Services: A Companion to the "Lutheran Book of Worship"* (Minneapolis: Augsburg, 1982), p. 197. The other passages read are 1 Timothy 6:11-12, Acts 20:28, and 1 Peter 5:2-4.

which the referent of the first-person plural pronoun shifts when this text is read in a present-day service of ordination. In Paul's context, the "us" in 1 Corinthians 4:1 refers to the "anthrōpoi" of 3:21, to Paul and Apollos and Peter ("Cephas"), the "human leaders" (NRSV) to whom the Corinthians had formed divisive loyalties. As 4:6 makes clear, the whole of chapters 3 and 4 constitutes an extended discussion of this problem; 4:1-2 provides an alternative description of "human leaders" within the context of eschatological wisdom (cf. 3:18ff.) that Paul is trying to bring to bear on the divisions in the Corinthian church.

When these verses are put into the mouth of a bishop at an ordination, the "us" seems to acquire a different or at least significantly expanded referent: it seems to indicate "us clergy," "we ordained ministers," thus for the first time including the newly ordained in that vocational plural. Or else, if the words spoken by the bishop are nonetheless heard as words of Paul, the "us" is expanded to include present-day Christian clergy in a single group with Paul, Apollos, and Peter. In either case, there is a hermeneutical problem. The Christian ordained ministry as we know it did not exist when Paul wrote these words to the Corinthians; whatever he took himself, Apollos, and Peter to have in common, it was not "ordination" as practiced in Christian churches today or even in the second or third century. Therefore it cannot have been within the scope of his intention, as historical research can reconstruct it, to make any statement whatsoever about contemporary clergy and their duties. What then is the rationale, if any, for the employment of this text in a rite of ordination?

It is, of course, possible within the historical-critical framework to attempt to *mitigate* the discontinuity between the "original meaning" of the text and its contemporary use. There are certainly points of *analogy* between the group to which Paul was referring and the Christian clergy today: both are authority-figures, for example, and both are identified in special (though different) ways with the preaching of the gospel. Therefore we might conclude that what Paul said about himself, Apollos, and Peter could legitimately provide "talking-points" for discussion of contemporary pastoral ministry; though the proper "meaning" of 1 Corinthians 4:1-2 is locked in the first century, what Paul says might nonetheless be found "meaningful" by those in a comparable situation today.[61]

But notice how this approach construes the relationship between text, in-

61. This is more or less the way of relating "what it meant" and "what it means" embodied in the division of the influential *Interpreter's Bible* into parallel "exegetical" and "homiletical" tracks.

terpreter, and contemporary audience. What we have in the text is the documentary record of Paul's address to other people, about a different matter, under conditions that have long since passed away and can only be reconstructed with extreme difficulty and uncertainty. The contemporary interpreter — say, the preacher at an ordination — is placed before this record of the past and left to find in it some occasion for present speech capable of *mattering* in some way to a contemporary audience.

Inevitably, under these conditions, the interpretive task presents itself as that of finding something "meaningful" to say to the hearers, some way in which this ancient and alien text could play a role in their acknowledged world and speak to problems of which they are conscious. The perceptions and felt needs of the audience thus constitute the framework within which the text must be made to function, even when its relevance is claimed to be startling or transforming. Used in this way, the root significance of the "meaningful" is very close indeed to that of the "satisfying." The text is in effect *commodified,* defined as a commodity that the interpreter is commending on the market, under the norm of subjective value. The preacher's claim that "this text speaks to *you*" becomes difficult to distinguish in principle — though it may certainly be very different in sophistication and moral seriousness — from similar claims about canned beer or fast food.

This model is so pervasive in contemporary preaching that it is easy to miss how differently the text is brought to bear in the liturgical setting.[62] The address in which 1 Corinthians 4:1-2 appears is preceded by the invocation of the Spirit with laying on of hands and the conferral of the stole, symbolic of the yoke of obedience to Christ; it concludes with an exhortation to faithful and disciplined ministry.[63] In this context, the words of Paul do not appear as a resource in which the ordained may find relevant themes and challenging possibilities, despite their distant historical provenance. They appear as immediately formative words, which articulate the intentions of the Spirit just invoked upon the ordained, and delineate the shape of the obedience just symbolically laid upon their shoulders. They do not offer to speak meaningfully within the horizon of the perceptions and desires of the ordained; they

62. Cf. the critical survey of contemporary preaching theory in Charles Campbell, *Preaching Jesus: New Directions for Homiletics in Hans Frei's Postliberal Theology* (Grand Rapids: Eerdmans, 1997), pp. 117-86.

63. "Care for God's people, bear their burdens and do not betray their confidence. So discipline yourself in life and teaching that you preserve the truth, giving no occasion for false security or illusory hope. Witness faithfully in word and deed to all people. Give and receive comfort as you serve within the Church. And be of good courage, for God has called you, and your labor in the Lord is not in vain" (*Occasional Services,* p. 197).

prescribe for them the horizon within which they will from now on live. They say, in effect: "*This* faithfulness is what you will desire from now on; whatever needs and problems may have seemed pressing up till now, henceforth *these* are the really urgent issues."

Moreover, the liturgical order also suggests a rationale for speaking and hearing words written long ago with such immediacy. The prayer in which the laying on of hands is embedded says, in part:

> We thank you that by his death your Son has overcome death and, having been raised by your mighty power, has ascended above all the heavens, that he might fill all things. We praise you that Christ has poured out his gifts abundantly on the Church, making some apostles, some prophets, some pastors and teachers, to equip your people for their work of ministry for building up the body of Christ.[64]

In the invocation that follows, this outpouring of *gifts* is identified with the outpouring of the *Spirit.*[65] What is evoked thereby is the new "context" of Easter and Pentecost, in which the church lives as the people gathered and formed by the Spirit to bear witness to Christ as his body in the world. It is within *this* context that the liturgical use of 1 Corinthians 4:1-2 makes sense; Paul's words from long ago are joined to the present occasion within a *continuum of divine purpose and divine action.*

Referring to himself, Apollos, and Peter, Paul speaks of human leadership in the community gathered and shaped by the Spirit. In the prayer just cited, *the worshiping assembly identifies itself as that same community,* and confesses that the outpouring of the Spirit continues to occur concretely in its midst, in the immediate present. Within this continuum, the discernment of analogies between Paul's words and the present occasion is not the attempt to construct a narrow and unsteady bridge correlating events in the distant past with our concerns. It is rather the discernment of the intentions of the one Spirit whose action and purpose *already* bind together the Corinthian assembly and the present-day church in one redemptive economy. "Relevance" is not established by coordinating the text with the expectations, perceptions, and felt needs of the hearers, but by bringing the hearers themselves into the realm, inhabited alike by Paul, the Corinthian believers, and the contemporary church, where the intentions articulated in the text hold sway. The ordained

64. *Occasional Services,* p. 196. Cf. Ephesians 4:7-13.

65. "Eternal God, through your Son, Jesus Christ, pour out your Holy Spirit upon *name* and fill *him/her* with the gifts of grace [for the ministry of Word and Sacrament]" (*Occasional Services,* p. 196).

are brought by the act of ordination itself into a place of responsibility whose God-intended shape is articulated in the Scripture passages with which the bishop addresses them.

Three additional remarks may bring out the implications of this example. In the first place, the continuum of divine purpose into which the ordination rite places Paul's words about human leadership is precisely that into which 2 Timothy 3:15-17 places the whole phenomenon of "Scripture." As Christ is said in the ordination prayer to pour out the Spirit "to equip your people for their work of ministry for building up the body of Christ," so in 2 Timothy, Scripture's "inspiration" is related to its usefulness "for teaching, for reproof, for correction, and for training in righteousness, so that everyone who belongs to God may be proficient, equipped for every good work" (vv. 16-17).[66] The divine project of forming a people to make Christ known among the nations is the context in which canon and church come together; the texts are carried into the assembly and brought to bear on its life by the energy of that divine intention, which has made them its instruments.

In the second place, what was described as "bringing the hearers into the realm where the intentions articulated in the text hold sway" is a complex and multidimensional business. In one sense, that realm is the whole creation, for the Messiah attested in Scripture is lord over all things in heaven and on earth, judge of the living and the dead. In this sense, one "enters" the realm where the intentions in the text hold sway through *conversion of mind and heart,* casting away illusion to live in the light of truth. In another sense, though, that "realm" is *the church itself,* precisely as the community that knows and confesses "the resurrection that has now taken place" and seeks to be formed by that truth in thought, word, and deed. Within this double framework, there are other, analogous modes of such "entry": vocational change, as in ordination, altering one's "placement" within the community; repentance, confession, and absolution; transforming experiences of renewal and rededication; regular congregational worship; and the daily practice of recollection, meditation, and prayer.

Yet complex as it is, this notion has a clear focus: in all these diverse modes of "entry" we have essentially to do with *baptism* and its ongoing implications for Christian life. It is essential to the structure of baptism that it is at once the sacrament of *faith,* in which Christ is confessed and his lordship acknowledged, and the sacrament of *initiation,* by which the baptized are received into the community that attests and represents Christ's lordship

66. The Greek words translated "equip" are different in 2 Timothy 3:17 and in Ephesians 4:12, on which the ordination prayer is based, but the thought is unmistakably similar.

amidst the nations. Baptism is thus the *illumination* by which we enter the domain of truth, and the *incorporation* by which we enter the church and take part in its mission.[67] In the discernment of personal vocation, the restoration of the penitent, the experience of spiritual renewal, and the regular offices of corporate worship and private devotion, we have to do with different but not unrelated ways in which baptismal identity is enacted and reclaimed.

The "applicative" dimension of scriptural interpretation is therefore essentially an exercise in the *anamnēsis* of baptism. The texts become formative when readers and hearers approach them in mindfulness of baptismal identity:

> In Holy Baptism our gracious heavenly Father liberates us from sin and death by joining us to the death and resurrection of our Lord Jesus Christ. We are born children of a fallen humanity; in the waters of Baptism we are reborn children of God and inheritors of eternal life. By water and the Holy Spirit we are made members of the Church which is the body of Christ. As we live with him and with his people, we grow in faith, love, and obedience to the will of God.[68]

In such remembrance of baptism, the whole community encounters Scripture much as the newly ordained encounter the texts read by the bishop: in the knowledge that something has been done to us, that our lives have been placed within a new horizon and set on a new track. We have been made witnesses to a particular truth, citizens of a new city, subjects of a specific lordship, and in all this we have fallen under the sway of the Spirit of God. Those who remember this, and approach the scriptures in this knowledge, are in a position to read and hear them as *sermo divina,* "words taught by the Spirit" so that we may understand the gifts of God (cf. 1 Cor. 2:12-13). Without ceasing to be historically particular words, reflecting contingencies of language and circumstance, they nonetheless come into our midst as bluntly formative, delineating the geography of the new world in which we have been brought to live, and articulating the shape of the divine intention by which we are now to be formed.[69]

Third, reading and applying Scripture within the baptismal domain of

67. Cf. the study of the baptismal catechumenate by L. Gregory Jones, in this volume.

68. *Lutheran Book of Worship* (Minneapolis: Augsburg, 1978), p. 121. I have drawn on the liturgies of my own denomination here simply because I know them best; equivalents could be found in other traditions.

69. On baptism as the context for Christian preaching, cf. William Willimon, *Peculiar Speech: Preaching to the Baptized* (Grand Rapids: Eerdmans, 1992), esp. pp. 1-23.

the Spirit means reading them within a regular ecology of divine gift, within which Scripture is a distinctive but not exclusive articulation of the Spirit's intentions. The scriptures are the Spirit's formative gift to the church, but they are not the *only* gift the Spirit bestows. The whole earthly-historical life of the church is lived as the constant reception and exercise of the gifts of the Spirit. In addition to Scripture, the Spirit bestows on the church forms and practices of worship; orderings of ministry; wise teachers; exemplary lives; holy icons; fruitful traditions of theological reflection, spiritual practice, preaching, and pastoral care; movements of renewal; historic determinations of the norms of doctrine; and so on. All these are comprehended in the promise that the Spirit of truth will lead the church into "all the truth" by glorifying Jesus and making him known (John 16:13-14).[70]

Some of these gifts, like the canon of Scripture itself, are permanently and irreversibly bestowed on the church, and so their relevance to the church's life is indefinitely renewable; others are more local and transitory in their significance.[71] As none of these gifts can be properly interpreted and appreciated except in the light of Holy Scripture, so in turn the scriptures must be interpreted and appreciated in light of the whole fabric of gift that makes up the earthly-historical life of the Christian people. Everything in the church's life that the church acknowledges as the gift of the Spirit is therefore potentially a relevant point of reference for the interpretation of Scripture.

Thus persons ordained according to the rite discussed above will find in the liturgical calendar of their denomination fifteen figures commemorated as exemplary "pastors and bishops."[72] These diverse lives may properly be re-

70. This has implications for our understanding of the divine *origination* of the scriptures. The older Protestant doctrine of inspiration focused on this; inspiration was the miracle that produced a perspicuous book of inerrantly true propositions. The account developed here can get along with a far more modest account of the Spirit's role in the *production* of the texts. We need not insist that the Spirit's guidance of the biblical writers was of an entirely different *order* than his guidance of the bishops at Nicea, or St. Francis of Assisi, or the iconographer Andrei Rublev; in each case, persons were formed by the Spirit's witness embodied in the life and practice of the covenant community so that their speech and action might play a role in the Spirit's formation of the community. To be sure, Scripture, the Nicene dogma, the example of Francis, and Rublev's *Old Testament Trinity* do not play the *same* role; Scripture is the Spirit's own discourse to the church in all times and places, while the Nicene dogma, the life of Francis, and Rublev's icon are in different ways *interpretations* of that discourse. But this is the point: Scripture's uniqueness is located in the *end* for which the Spirit guided its genesis, not in the *mode* of that guidance.

71. On this distinction, cf. Bruce Marshall, "The Church in the Gospel," *Pro Ecclesia* (1992): 27-41.

72. Those commemorated are Ambrose of Milan, the Norwegian bishop Eivind Berggrav, Clement of Rome, Gregory the Great, George Herbert, Irenaeus of Lyon, James of Jerusalem,

garded as *commentary* on 1 Corinthians 4:1-2, for here, or so one Christian community has judged, are lives and ministries genuinely formed by the very intentions of the Spirit articulated in that text. Paul's description of church leaders as servants of Christ and stewards of God's "mysteries," of whom trustworthiness is required, is thus taken as a theme on which the Spirit plays many variations, from the world-historical impact of Pope John XXIII to the obscure death by scurvy of the obscure Rasmus Jensen, the first Lutheran minister in North America, on a Danish exploration vessel in 1620. Such lives display something of the range of the text's *applicatio* in the realm of the Spirit's working, and so contribute to our understanding of the text.[73] To return to the dictum of St. Hilary with which this essay began, those who stand *extra ecclesiam,* in an interpretive posture from which such lives, with others of the Spirit's gifts, are not visible, lack an essential prerequisite for understanding the scriptures as *sermo divina,* "useful for teaching, for reproof, for correction, and for training in righteousness" (2 Tim. 3:16).

VII. Conclusion

"Let anyone who has an ear," writes the Christian prophet, "listen to what the Spirit is saying to the churches" (Rev. 2:29). This essay has been an attempt to imagine possessing such ears, to describe the conditions under which it would be possible to interpret Scripture as divine discourse, what the Spirit is saying to the churches. Such considerations call us to an arduous and countercultural discipline, running against the grain of much that is still potent in the contemporary culture as well as in modern churches of the "mainline" variety. To recover not only the fortuitous hearing of Scripture as the

---

Rasmus Jensen, Pope John XXIII, the Bavarian pastor-theologian Wilhelm Loehe, Martin of Tours, Henry Melchior Muhlenberg, Nicholas of Myra, and the Swedish archbishops Nathan Söderblom and Johan Olof Wallin. Cf. *Lutheran Book of Worship,* "Lesser Festivals and Commemorations," pp. 10-12. The list is lopsidedly Lutheran, but the picture could be balanced by many others listed simply as "saints" as well as martyrs, missionaries, theologians, and "renewers of the church." Cf. Philip H. Pfatteicher, *Festivals and Commemorations: Handbook to the Calendar in "Lutheran Book of Worship"* (Minneapolis: Augsburg, 1980).

73. We will of course *also* come to see the limitations and sins of the saints; Galatians 5:17 holds good throughout the church's historical existence, and so even the most exemplary life is shaped *not only* by the Spirit but *also* by the flesh. The same is true of everything else we acknowledge as gifts of the Spirit, including Scripture itself: in none of them do we encounter *only* the Spirit and not *also* the flesh. But we cannot learn to make such distinctions except from *within* the concrete interplay of witness with witness; we do not have within ourselves a pure apprehension of the Spirit as an Archimedean point from which to sit in judgment.

word of God, which certainly continues to occur in the churches, but an ordered enterprise of interpretation that approaches Scripture *as* the discourse of the Spirit, would require an uncommon simultaneous measure of freedom of mind and attentiveness to tradition, as well perhaps as the humility to learn from those who have never been permitted full access to either the benefits or the temptations of modern academic high culture.

In the end, however, what is in view is simply one dimension of that distinctively ecclesial identity and mission which the churches of the northern hemisphere need so urgently, in their diverse ways, to recover and disentangle from the confusions and corruptions engendered by Christian disunity and the persistence of Constantinian habits of mind in a post-Constantinian situation. For if these reflections on inspiration have made anything clear, it is that practices of reading and interpreting Scripture enact the church's sense of its own identity and vocation. A church community that can get along without a distinctive ecclesial enterprise of scriptural interpretation is therefore a community with little awareness of distinctive being and calling, one whose life is so to speak on loan from its host society. Renewal of the church requires not only new ideas about the church, but renewed practices of being the church, and chief among these are practices of understanding and applying the scriptures.[74]

74. I am conscious of the challenge implicit here: renewal requires not essays on hermeneutics but models and examples of ecclesially situated exegetical-theological practice. An essay like this has value only as the necessary throat-clearing prior to such engagement.

4. The Liturgy

Participatory Knowledge of God in the Liturgy

SUSAN K. WOOD

How do we know God? Can we acquire a dispassionate, objective knowledge of God? Do we know God in order to have faith, or do we have faith in order to know God? Do we know God only with our mind or with our whole body? This essay responds to these questions by claiming that our participation in the liturgy gives us access to a certain kind of knowledge of God, which I am identifying as participatory knowledge.[1] This knowledge is mediated through the symbol system of the liturgy, including the scriptures, liturgical actions, sacraments, and prayers. It requires the commitment of faith in order to work. It takes place not individually, but in the context of community. It is primarily a knowledge of who God is for us within a trinitarian economy wherein God sends the Son to give the Spirit that we may be constituted into the body of the Son and return to the Father in his gift of himself and our gift of ourselves. In learning who God is for us, we know indirectly who God is in Godself, for they are one and the same.[2] Although not irrational or without reason, reason is not the primary avenue through which this knowledge is ac-

1. This essay has greatly benefited from discussions of the Dogmatics Colloquium of the Center for Catholic and Evangelical Theology, my colleagues at Saint John's University, Collegeville, Minnesota, and the Liturgical Theology seminar of the North American Academy of Liturgy.

2. The Arian controversy illustrates this. Athanasius championed the divinity of Christ because if Christ were not God he could not save. We also have Karl Rahner's famous dictum: "The economic Trinity is the immanent Trinity" (*The Trinity* [New York: Crossroad, 1974], p. 22).

quired since God is not a consequent idea. Rather, we acquire this knowledge by entering into the symbolic time and space of liturgical action. Within the liturgy we enter a formative environment that shapes our vision, our relationships, and our knowing.

Participatory knowledge of God within the liturgy is more analogous to kinesthetic knowledge than rational knowledge. It is a knowledge gained through action.[3] It is an incarnate, embodied knowledge. Theodore Jennings characterizes ritual knowledge as "primarily corporeal rather than cerebral, primarily active rather than contemplative, primarily transformative rather than speculative."[4] We learn what balance feels like by riding a bicycle rather than listening to explanations. By being fed, by hearing the words of forgiveness, by being caught up in the paschal events of death and resurrection liturgically made present, we learn God's sustaining, self-diffusive love. By entering into praise and thanksgiving we know who we are in relationship to God and God's sovereignty. Within the liturgy we come to know ourselves and God because the liturgy orders our relationships: my relationship to others within the body of Christ sacramentally constituted within the Eucharist, my relationship to God as recipient of God's graciousness, my relationship to the world by being not only sent, but missioned and commissioned to live ethically within history what has been experienced in the meta-historical time and space of the liturgy. In short, in the liturgy we do not acquire knowledge *about* God; we acquire knowledge *of* God.

Participatory knowledge within the liturgy is a personal knowledge in the biblical sense of knowing. It is experiential knowledge acquired by entering into a relationship. We cannot know without being known. We cannot know or be known without being transformed. Thus it is not an acquisition of an object, something we call knowledge, but an expansion of relationship, a broadening of horizon, a creation of something new within us. When we know God within the liturgy, we know God in relation, in creative and transformative activity. We also know ourselves in God. Personal knowledge is characterized by this reciprocity.

Two clarifications are required to clarify the claims made here: to note what is not implied in this thesis and to define what is meant by liturgical prayer. This claim does not mean that we do not have a knowledge of God

3. This is also a characteristic of ritual knowledge identified by Theodore W. Jennings in "On Ritual Knowledge," *Journal of Religion* 62 (1982): 116. What Jennings describes as ritual knowledge would include knowledge within the liturgy, although he situates ritual more broadly and generally.

4. Jennings, "On Ritual Knowledge," p. 115.

outside the liturgy. It does not imply that the content of this knowledge of God is different in the liturgy than it is outside the liturgy. It does make a claim, however, that the manner in which we know God within the liturgy is different. In other words, it does not make a claim that what we know about God is different, unique, or only accessible through the liturgy, but it does make a claim that *how* we know God is different.

Liturgical Prayer

Within the Roman Catholic tradition liturgical prayer is the official public worship of the church.[5] Although the summit and center of the liturgy is the Eucharist or Lord's Supper, liturgical prayer also includes official rites and the other sacraments of the church as well as the Liturgy of the Hours, the prayer consisting of the psalms, canticles, hymns, and readings, which sanctifies life by turning to God at "ritual moments symbolic of the whole of time."[6] Although there is a variety of prayer and ritual that is liturgical, in this essay I will tend to refer to the Eucharist most often as paradigmatic of liturgical prayer.

Because it is official, liturgical prayer is under the official regulation or recognition of the church. This means that the church recognizes it as its official prayer and oversees it. It also means that it takes place in communion with the local bishop.

Because it is public, it normally requires an assembly of believers visibly gathered together. This, however, has not been without interesting exceptions in the history of the church. Peter Damian is reported to have asked whether a hermit celebrating Mass alone should say, "The Lord be with you." He replied to his own question with a resounding "yes," with the implication that there is a public dimension to this prayer even when celebrated alone. The *Constitution on the Liturgy,* the first document promulgated by the Second Vatican Council in 1964, emphasizes that liturgical services are not private functions. It stipulates that "rites which are meant to be celebrated in common, with the faithful present and actively participating, should as far as possible be celebrated in that way rather than by an individual and quasi-privately."[7] In another vein, Roman Catholic priests are required to pray the Divine Office, the

5. For a good overview of what constitutes the liturgy see Mary Collins, "Liturgy," in *The New Dictionary of Theology,* ed. Joseph Komonchak, Mary Collins, and Dermot Lane (Collegeville, Minn.: The Liturgical Press/Michael Glazier, 1987), pp. 591-601.

6. Robert Taft, *The Liturgy of the Hours in East and West: The Origins of the Divine Office and Its Meaning for Today* (Collegeville, Minn.: The Liturgical Press, 1986), p. 361.

7. *Constitution on the Liturgy,* 26-27.

Liturgy of the Hours, one of the liturgical prayers of the church, privately if they do not pray it in common. It is not considered to be any less liturgical even though it does not occur in the context of an assembly. However, even when recited individually, it remains "the voice of the Church" rather than the voice of an individual.[8] Even clerics who are not obliged to attend office in choir are encouraged to pray at least some part of the Divine Office in common. Thus it seems fair to observe that the church's daily prayer, the Liturgy of the Hours, presumes a gathering of the Christian people at various times of the day in households, monasteries, and local churches. As Robert Taft notes, "traditionally the Liturgy of the Hours is something that a group celebrates, not something an individual reads."[9]

What distinguishes liturgical prayer from other prayer of the church is that it is a corporate gesture of praise of God neither originating from nor directed toward any one individual or group in the church. It is the church as church glorifying God. Individuals who participate in the liturgy participate on behalf of and in the name of the church. It is an exercise of the priestly office of Jesus Christ by the whole church, his mystical body, including the head, that is, Christ, and the members — baptized Christians. Thus it is the prayer of Christ carried on in his body, the church.

Individual piety is subsumed into the corporate prayer of the church. Henri de Lubac, in his book on the Apostles' Creed, notes that the subject of "Credo," the subject who professes faith in the creed, the "I" in "I believe," is not the individual believer in isolation, but the church. It is first the church as a community that believes in its Lord; then with it and in it, I as an individual am led to personally proclaim "I believe."[10] Here we recall that the context of the creed is liturgical: either baptism or the Eucharist. Additionally, in the liturgical revision the congregation now recites "We believe." Clearly, the individual professes faith, but the liturgical context of this profession emphasizes the ecclesial role in an individual Christian's faith formation as well as an individual's interconnectedness with other Christians.

The liturgy is more than a certain kind of prayer service in which we worship God according to certain rubrics. The liturgy is really the Christian economy enacted and realized symbolically. It is the Father coming to us in Christ who gives us the Spirit so that we may be united in Christ and return to the Father. The exitus-reditus of the Christian economy is not only recounted within

8. *Constitution on the Liturgy,* 99.

9. Taft, *The Liturgy of the Hours in East and West,* p. 362.

10. Henri de Lubac, *La Foi chrétienne: essai sur la structure du Symbole des Apôtres* (Paris: Aubier-Montaigne, 1970), p. 227.

the readings of the liturgy and commemorated according to the liturgical year, but our own participation in those events is made possible sacramentally.[11] Liturgical prayer is related to the paschal mystery, an expression that refers to the mystery of our salvation through the power of Christ's life, death, and resurrection. The Eucharist or Lord's Supper proclaims and celebrates the life, death, and resurrection of Jesus Christ and thus is the summit of liturgical worship. However, this same paschal mystery of Christ's dying and rising is also evident in a principal way in baptism, Sunday, and Easter, and also commemorated in matins and vespers, funerals and feasts. The annual cycle of the liturgical year celebrates successive aspects of the mystery of salvation in Christ.

Liturgical prayer encompasses more than ritual prayers addressed to God. It is more than a collection of prayers printed on paper. In addition to the text of the rite, liturgical prayer includes an assembly of believers, the public reading of scripture, music, gesture and movements, vesture, various ritual objects, and the ordering of ritual space and its furnishings. It is the liturgical event encompassing a ritual whole inclusive of ritual and symbolic gestures as well as the liturgical text, that discloses theological and spiritual meanings. Finally, although prayers of lament and supplication are common in liturgical prayer, the dominant sentiments expressed within this prayer are praise and thanksgiving for God's deeds on behalf of God's people and eschatological hope for the final realization of the kingdom of God.[12]

Although some ecclesial communions are more liturgical than others — here one thinks of the Orthodox, Roman Catholics, and Anglicans — many communions issuing from the Reformation are reviving their practice and theology of liturgical prayer. One sign of this is a more frequent celebration of the Lord's Supper. However, even if a particular Sunday service consists of readings, sermon, and hymns, this is arguably "liturgy" in that it is the activity of an assembly of baptized Christians, involves an order of worship, and an observation of the paschal mystery around the great feasts of Christmas and Easter as well as other biblical feasts. Thus there may be "high" or "low" liturgical sensibilities among Christian denominations, but what is meant in this essay as "participatory knowledge of God in the liturgy" is accessible to all Christians within their communal worship. What is necessary is an assembly of Christians who intend to pray, a connection between this prayer and the

11. In other words, "What was visible in our Redeemer has passed into the sacraments (Quod itaque Redemptoris nostri conspicuum fuit, in sacramenta transivit)" (Leo I, *Sermo, De Ascensione II*).

12. See Thomas J. Madden, "Liturgy," in *The New Dictionary of Sacramental Worship* (Collegeville, Minn.: The Liturgical Press/Michael Glazier, 1990), p. 741.

life, death, and resurrection of Jesus Christ, and the recognition on behalf of a church that this prayer is its official prayer.

Thus Bible study in and of itself would not meet these criteria, because the intention is study rather than prayer, even though there might be a prayer to the Spirit for guidance. A Bible study group is also most likely not a church's official assembly of Sunday worship. There is a continuum between liturgical prayer and many other church activities since an interpretation of a biblical text is influenced by a church's liturgical use of it, and even the self-identity of a church is derived from its self-expression in its public, official prayer. It is not the intent of this essay to precisely determine for churches, who do not routinely use the word "liturgy" to describe their prayer, which activities might be termed "liturgical." It is the intent, however, to be inclusive in the sense that the way of knowing God within the liturgy, which is to say within a complexus of symbols that include biblical text, preaching, song, gesture, etc., applies to the public worship of these groups as well.

In the final analysis, the liturgy is the place where an ecclesial group preserves its traditions, symbols, and texts and expresses its self-identity. These traditions, symbols, and texts are also operative extra-liturgically, but they derive their primary meaning from their liturgical context. The liturgy is also the place where the community enacts the truth it knows about God. In the words of Gordon Lathrop:

> Whatever else the Sunday assembly of Christians is intended to do, there can be wide ecumenical agreement on this: the Sunday assembly means to say the truth about God. Indeed, we hold the gathering intending to proclaim the truth about God to whoever will listen — the assembly, visitors, the larger world, ourselves — and thereby to re-immerse those listeners in a view of the world as it stands before God.[13]

Tacit Knowledge

The participatory knowledge acquired within the liturgy is similar to what Michael Polanyi calls "tacit knowledge." It is not really a question of tacit knowledge versus another kind of knowledge, though, since for Polanyi all knowledge is either tacit knowledge or rooted in tacit knowledge.[14] In tacit

13. Gordon Lathrop, "At Least Two Words: The Liturgy as Proclamation," in *Liturgy: We Proclaim* 11, no. 1 (1993): 1.

14. Michael Polanyi, *Knowing and Being* (Chicago: University of Chicago Press, 1969), p. 193.

knowing there is an attending from and an attending toward. We interiorize particulars to which we are not attending and which therefore remain unspecified for us. We attend from these particulars towards a comprehensive entity that connects them in a way we cannot identify.[15] Yet, paradoxically, the whole does not exist apart from the particulars that comprise it. In other words, we only notice the whole when we are not fixated on the details within it. Polanyi cites our perception of a physiognomy or the production of vocal sound as examples. It is the interplay of features which comprise a physiognomy, but we cannot perceive the whole if we focus too closely on any individual feature. We do not see a face if we focus on the nose. Sound loses meaning if we attend to the motion of tongue and lips. Polanyi notes that "the belief that, since particulars are more tangible, their knowledge offers a true conception of things is fundamentally mistaken."[16] To Polanyi's example we can add the example cited earlier of riding a bicycle. It is not by attending to the tensions within muscles that we learn balance. It is the Gestalt, the perception of the whole in the interplay of the particulars, that is the true conception of things.

It is not by looking at things, but by *dwelling* in them that we understand them.[17] Indwelling constitutes a type of empathetic knowledge. I have identified this empathetic knowledge with a kind of kinesthetic knowledge. We sense the movements within ourselves, without attending to the particulars. This allows us to experience the world from another perspective. Another way of saying this is to say we "indwell" a complexus of particulars and in this indwelling we can perceive the whole. Polanyi describes religious ritual as "the highest degree of indwelling that is conceivable."[18] This is so, he suggests, because the experience of worship is comparable to a mystic's surrender, closer to sensual abandon than to exact observation. He describes ritual as a sequence of "things to be said and gestures to be made which involve the whole body and alert our whole existence" in such a way that the true participant is completely absorbed in them. The surrender within worship "corresponds to the degree to which the worshiper dwells within the fabric of the

15. Michael Polanyi, *The Tacit Dimension* (Garden City, N.Y.: Anchor Books, 1967), p. 24.

16. Polanyi, *The Tacit Dimension*, p. 19.

17. Polanyi, *The Tacit Dimension*, p. 18; *Knowing and Being*, p. 148.

18. Michael Polanyi, *Personal Knowledge* (Chicago: University of Chicago Press, 1958), p. 198. Polanyi contrasts this indwelling, however, with that of other kinds of knowledge in that it is never enjoyed, never consummated; we never achieve complete understanding. He notes that the ritual of worship is expressly designed to induce and sustain a state of "anguish, surrender and hope." Christianity fosters mental dissatisfaction by offering us the comfort of a crucified God.

religious ritual."[19] The religious ritual, as a Gestalt, becomes a world within the interplay of symbols, a world in which the interplay of elements mutually inhere and cohere in such a way that each part derives its meaning from the whole at the same time that it contributes to the meaning of the whole.

With respect to the liturgy, we must ask what is the "face" known in the liturgy. What is the "whole"? The answer is the paschal mystery of salvation in Christ Jesus. This is the "whole" that gives meaning to all of the liturgy. This paschal mystery of salvation is not only christological, it is trinitarian, for the Father sends the Son who lives, dies, rises, and sends the Spirit that we, too, may ascend to the Father through Christ in the power of the Holy Spirit. The "face" of the liturgy is about this trinitarian economy of everything being recapitulated in Christ in the return to the Father. This is the "whole," not only of eucharistic liturgy, but also the Liturgy of the Hours.[20] Because the "whole" of liturgy is this paschal mystery and economy of salvation in its entirety, to focus on any one part in exclusivity is to miss the whole. Thus, to reduce a theology of Eucharist to the confection of the "real presence" misses placing that presence in the movement of return to the Father in the power of the Holy Spirit. To emphasize the role of the Liturgy of the Hours in the sanctification of the hours of our day in a narrow sense misses its eschatological meaning. These "parts" are necessary for the "whole," but the meaning of the whole is greater than any part.

Biblical Texts within a Liturgical Context

One of the most striking illustrations of this interplay of various liturgical elements — the proclamation of the scriptures, the presence of companion believers, the great prayer of Thanksgiving including the Last Supper narrative — lies in the interpretation of biblical texts within a liturgical context. With Louis-Marie Chauvet we can assert that "in a completely literal sense the liturgical assembly (the ecclesia in its primary sense) is the place where the Bible becomes the Bible."[21] The text assumes its meaning within the Gestalt of

19. Polanyi, *Personal Knowledge.*

20. Robert Taft shows that "the hours take their meaning not from the Eucharist, nor from Christian daily life as opposed to an otherworldly eschatological expectation, nor from the natural cycle of morning and evening, nor from personal devotion and edification as distinct from the work of the community," but from the paschal mystery (*The Liturgy of the Hours in East and West,* p. 334).

21. Louis-Marie Chauvet, *Symbol and Sacrament: A Sacramental Reinterpretation of Christian Existence,* trans. Patrick Madigan and Madeleine Beaumont (Collegeville, Minn.: The Liturgical Press, 1995), p. 212.

its liturgical context. The interpretation that emerges from the liturgical juxtaposition of selections from the Old and New Testaments within a liturgy commemorating the paschal mystery functions according to typology rather than the historical-critical method. There is a reciprocal relationship between the text and the community. First, the texts belong to a canon accepted by the community, thereby indicating an authority accorded the texts by the community. Second, the reading of this text gives the community its identity since the texts proclaim a past experience of the People of God as the living Word of God for today. The function of ordained ministry within the assembly is to guarantee both the apostolicity of what is read and to assure that these texts function as an exemplar of the community's identity.[22]

Chauvet points out that these four constitutive elements of the Liturgy of the Word — texts of past events accepted as authoritative, texts proclaimed as living today, their reception by a community recognizing its own identity in them, and ministry that guarantees their apostolicity and exemplarity — parallel the four constitutive elements of the biblical text as the Word of God. First there are the instituted traditions of the community gathered in the oral and later written forms and finally into the biblical corpus as such. Then the hermeneutical process interprets this in relation to the present, thus rewriting the text in relation to the present. As an example of this one can cite Israel's interpretation of the Exodus in the light of the Babylonian captivity. The community becomes the agent in this process as it writes itself into the book it is reading. Finally there is the canonical sanction of this reading by legitimate authority.[23]

In both instances we have event and interpretation. The Christian scriptures join both Testaments in the light of the death and resurrection of Jesus Christ. The event that is interpreted is historical in two senses: first, it recounts a past event. Second, that event is transposed into the present life of the ecclesial community in its remembrance. It is precisely the proclamatory nature of the Word, affirmed in faith within the liturgy, that moves the text from its identity as a literary narrative to an interpretation of a past event as now present in the life of the community. The historicity of the liturgical moment grounds the aesthetic interplay of symbols within a historical and sacramental realism whereby the narrative is no longer a literary story, but the very life of the community. In short, the very word becomes sacramental, making present under symbol the event it recounts. As a proclamatory speech-act, liturgical proclamation is performative; it accomplishes what it proclaims. This means

22. Chauvet, *Symbol and Sacrament,* p. 210.

23. Chauvet, *Symbol and Sacrament,* p. 212.

that the salvation event proclaimed in the scriptures is accomplished in the present time in the life of the assembly. In its proclamation the church gives its interpretation in faith of its present experience in terms of the proclaimed event.

The question arises as to whether approaching the text in the context of liturgy dispenses with the historical-critical method, whether it represents a retreat from history to allegory. According to Jean Daniélou a typological reading of the biblical text notes the correspondences between different moments of sacred history. This occurs when we identify Adam as the "figure" of Christ (Rom. 5:14) or the Flood as a type of baptism (1 Pet. 3:21).[24] Daniélou, citing Thomas Aquinas before him, emphasizes that a typological reading of Scripture is not a sense of the Scripture, that is, a sense of the text, but is a sense of the events themselves. Most specifically, it is an interpretation of the events from an eschatological perspective. Daniélou identifies the source of typology as the plan of salvation. In other words, the events in the history of Israel prefigure the events at the end of time that appear to us in Christ. A typological reading is thus necessarily eschatological.

Here the liturgical context of the scriptural interpretation is crucial. There is a profound congruence between (1) the eucharistic symbol of meal that commemorates a past meal, and sacrifice, which becomes present now and anticipates a future eschatological banquet; and (2) a liturgical reading of the scriptures that proclaims a past event which becomes the autobiography of the present community, and yet also has an eschatological meaning of future completion. In liturgical time, the past, present, and future are present simultaneously as the community commemorates past saving events, celebrates them as present in the life of the community, and anticipates final fullness in the future.[25] This same compression of past, present, and future exists in both the symbolism of meal and the symbolic interpretation of bibli-

24. Jean Daniélou, "Symbolisme et théologie," *Interpretation der Welt: Festschrift für Romano Guardini zum Achzigsten Geburtstag* (Würzburg: Echter-Verlag, 1965), p. 670.

25. Thomas J. Talley explains the relationship between the past, present, and future thus: "By virtue of the resurrection, Christ is now transhistorical and is available to every moment. We may never speak of the Risen Christ in the historical past. The event of his passion is historical, but the Christ who is risen does not exist back there, but here, and as we live on this moving division line between memory and hope, between the memory of his passion and the hope of his coming again, we stand always in the presence of Christ, who is always present to everyone. This is where the real substance of our anamnesis lies." Cited by Robert Taft in "What Does Liturgy Do? Toward a Soteriology of Liturgical Celebration: Some Theses," *Worship* 66, no. 3 (May 1992): 200. In other words, the past is present in the resurrected Christ who is transhistorical. See also Robert Taft, "Toward a Theology of the Christian Feast," in *Beyond East and West: Problems in Liturgical Understanding* (Washington, D.C.: The Pastoral Press, 1984), pp. 1-13.

cal text. The entire liturgical action represents a future eschatological fullness symbolically represented in the present time. The assembly, however, experiences the tension between the "already" and the "not yet" as it experiences itself as a pilgrim people and finds itself in a posture of waiting until all is gathered into one.

The text itself becomes a sacramental symbol. Just as the Christian assembly represents Christ and the sacramental species represent Christ, a liturgical reading of the text is primarily christological. This means that the texts are used liturgically to interpret the Christ event by way of the historical events to which the texts bear witness. The events of the Testaments are interpreted through this lens. The historical event represented in Jesus is the eschatological completion of the events that prefigure him. Perhaps one of the mistakes we have made in the past is to attempt to read Christ into the Exodus or some of the messianic prophecies instead of reading the Exodus and the prophecies into Christ. The first would be a form of Christian eisegesis. The latter respects the historical-critical location of the text at the same time it treats the two Testaments as a unity and explicates the Christ event in continuity with the Jewish tradition. Arguably this is also how Paul read the Scriptures in relationship to Christ, and the Jews in exile read the Exodus before him. The Old Testament becomes an interpretation of the New, which in turn becomes paradigmatic of the community's life in Christ. Within this reading, the Exodus becomes a paradigm of Christ's passage from death to life and the Christian's passage from sin to grace. It is precisely the context of the liturgical action that changes the interpretation of the scriptural text.

Reception of the Word

Our interpretation of the scriptural text is not only shaped by the interplay of symbols within the liturgy, but within the liturgy we also hear the Word of God differently than when we read it privately. George Worgul reminds us that ritual allows us to interpret our life experiences within the complexus of meaning that ritual celebrates and enables us to live that meaning more fully.[26] Within the Eucharist the paschal mystery becomes the interpretative key for our life experiences. We interpret our lives in terms of our identity in Christ, our passage from death to life within the paradox of the Cross, our vocation to live a life poured out for others. Worgul comments that "ritual de-

26. George S. Worgul, "Ritual," *The New Dictionary of Sacramental Worship*, p. 1101.

mands that role become autobiography."[27] This means that ritual is never play-acting, but that we ourselves assume the identity that we enact. Within the eucharistic liturgy this means that we put on Christ, become the body of Christ, individually, yes, but especially corporately. As Paul says, "I have been crucified with Christ; yet I live, no longer I, but Christ lives in me" (Gal. 2:20). In knowing Christ, we put on Christ. In putting on Christ we know him almost kinesthetically, as it were, in our sinews and bones, by acting like him, by seeing the world through his eyes.

In liturgy the assembly conforms itself to the patterns of relationships expressed liturgically. We repeat in our own lives and become the mystery we celebrate. We become conformed to Christ in his self-offering and his passage from death to life and thus are remade into a new humanity. This is how ritual becomes autobiographical so that the texts proclaimed are not just about a past event in salvation history, but recount the transformation that is taking place in us now. The story of the paschal event in Christ becomes our story.

That in the liturgy we have a proclaimed word and not merely a collection of venerable and sacred texts is crucial. In the act of proclamation, of standing before the community and speaking the word aloud, we become the word we utter. At this moment the narrative is no longer a literary story, but the very life of the community. The past events of that story are transposed into the present life of the ecclesial community in the very process of repeating and remembering it. The liturgy constitutes a living transmission of the word, a word transmitted within the very life of the community. In short, the very word received in faith becomes sacramental, making present under symbol the event it recounts.

As proclamation is different from silent reading in our armchair at home, so preaching in a liturgical context is something quite different from an academic lecture. The purpose is not primarily to communicate information, but to elicit faith. This difference is between a knowledge *about* God, the kind of knowledge theologians communicate, and knowledge *of* God, the knowledge acquired through participation in the liturgy. In effective preaching, those who preach must first resonate with the Word of God and let that word elicit faith within themselves. Then they speak the word, not as disembodied or separate from themselves, but as owned and appropriated by the self so that it resonates with the faith in the hearer. In effective preaching there is a resonance or movement of recognition between the speaker and the hearer. A word in the heart of one person resonates with a similar word in the heart of another. Something familiar is recognized, but there is

27. Worgul, "Ritual," p. 1104.

also something of a recognition experience, for the word also brings something new to awareness.

Liturgy becomes an interpretive key for our experiences whenever this encounter with the word in human proclamation occurs. We recognize our own experience and faith in the word we hear proclaimed. In this encounter our own experience is validated, but even more importantly, a community of faith is formed in the encounter out of the mutual recognition of shared faith and common experience. It is by dwelling within the Christian story that we are formed into a Christian community as we assume that story as our own.

As Richard Gula tells us, our conscience as a Christian people is concerned as much with "seeing" as with "choosing."[28] Christian beliefs have a great deal to do with shaping what we see. The real world of our moral choices includes imagination, vision, habits, affections, and other non-rational factors. To understand moral behavior, we need to pay attention first not to moral rules, but to the images shaping the imagination and the stories giving rise to these images. We live more by stories than we do by rules. We make our decisions more out of the beliefs we live by and the habits we have formed than out of the principles we have learned. The vision that forms all this is a community achievement, the result of internalizing the beliefs and values. Moral conversion is a matter of repatterning the imagination so as to see dimensions of reality that were not available to us before. Gula tells us that vision informed by story gives rise to character, and our choices and action arise out of the character that has been formed. This is another way of saying that action follows being. As we are, so do we act. As God is, so God acts. What we are, our character, is shaped by how we pattern our world and imagine ourselves within it. The liturgy repatterns our imagination according to the values and relationships enacted within it.

Parables, for example, reshape our imagination as they invite us to see the world and relationships in a new light. They do not articulate rules and principles, but give us something to "see." They address our imagination at the same time they invert our usual way of seeing things. Take as an example the parable of the Good Samaritan. We are used to being told in homilies that we should be good Samaritans. This means that we are supposed to help the

28. The material in this section is a summary of Richard Gula, *Reason Informed by Faith* (New York: Paulist Press, 1989), pp. 141-50. See also Iris Murdoch, "Vision and Choice in Morality," in *Christian Ethics and Contemporary Philosophy,* ed. Ian Ramsey (New York: Macmillan, 1966); Stanley Hauerwas, "The Significance of Vision: Toward an Aesthetic Ethic," in *Vision and Virtue* (Notre Dame: University of Notre Dame Press, 1981), pp. 30-47; and Craig Dykstra, *Vision and Character: A Christian Educator's Alternative to Kohlberg* (New York: Paulist Press, 1981).

poor traveler in the ditch. Bernard Brandon Scott suggests that this parable actually reverses this scenario. Rather than identifying with the hero, the Good Samaritan, in this parable the hearer is forced to identify with the half-dead and be saved by a mortal enemy. The only other alternative for an Israelite hearing the story is to dismiss the narrative as not like real life since there is no Israelite other than the man in the ditch with whom the hearer can identify. It is not an Israelite who helps his mortal enemy, a Samaritan, but the reverse: an Israelite who accepts help from a Samaritan. Thus the parable subverts the type of story where one is encouraged to come to the aid of those not normally deserving of aid. What happens is that the story subverts the effort to order reality into the known hierarchy of priest, Levite, and Israelite. Insiders and outsiders are no longer separated in terms of universal categories. In this parable, according to Scott, "the Samaritan is not the enemy but the savior, and the hearer does not play hero but victim."[29] That makes us not the do-good Samaritan, but the person in the ditch. In this scenario the transformation asked of us is not to help someone who differs from us racially or culturally, but to accept help where we don't look for it and would rather not find it. What happens if we are the person in the ditch? Are we willing to accept the help of a Samaritan, someone of a social class or ethnic group from whom we would rather not receive help? This parable not only dissolves the usual boundaries between insiders and outsiders, it reverses our expectations of who has to negotiate those boundaries. In this case, it is not the person with resources, but the person in need. The parable enables us to "see" and imagine an aspect of the Christian story in a new way.

Gordon Lathrop suggests that parables are not just one example of this kind of reversal that invites a new vision, but that all liturgy is essentially parabolic.[30] This is certainly true of the paschal mystery, which orders all liturgy and proclaims that life proceeds through death. The boundaries between insiders and outsiders are overcome in Jesus' inclusive meal fellowship. Any social hierarchy is reversed in Jesus' instruction to wash one another's feet or in the image of a crucified Christ. When we dwell within the liturgy we dwell within this parabolic world with all its reversals.

29. Bernard Brandon Scott, *Hear Then the Parable: A Commentary on the Parables of Jesus* (Minneapolis: Fortress Press, 1989), pp. 189-202.

30. Gordon Lathrop offered this suggestion during a discussion of an earlier version of this paper in the Liturgical Theology Seminar of the North American Academy of Liturgy January 5, 1998.

Liturgy as Interpretative Lens and Knowledge of God

To indwell the liturgy is to interiorize it. According to Polanyi, when we have tacit knowledge of such things as language, a probe, or a tool, we interiorize these things and make ourselves dwell in them. In his words, "Such extensions of ourselves develop new faculties in us; our whole education operates in this way; as each of us interiorizes our cultural heritage, he grows into a person seeing the world and experiencing life in terms of this outlook."[31] The liturgy becomes an interpretative lens that bestows meaning on the world. To be a Christian is not simply to assent to a series of propositional statements that articulate the faith. To be a Christian means to be in the world in a certain way and not in another way because one's relationships are constituted by the primary relationship of what it means to be united to the Father through Christ in the Spirit. To be a Christian is to be transformed according to the patterns of the liturgy. This relationship, described in the scriptures and enacted in the liturgy, is dynamic rather than static.

Just as the early monks memorized the scriptures in order to interiorize them for the purpose of praying unceasingly, the Christian repeatedly participates in the liturgy so as to imprint that economy in his or her very being. When we try to live the gospel and the relationships forged within the liturgy, we fall short. We need to return to the pattern again and again to "get it right," to be reminded (the anamnesis) of God's activity for us so that we don't forget, and to renew our strength — which to no small extent is drawn from our common efforts and identity as a community. Examples of this new way of seeing in the liturgy include a table fellowship inclusive of sinners and tax collectors, the redefinition of power as service, of the quest for life as a passage through death, and a redefinition of social and religious boundaries.

Finally, we experience the knowledge of faith in our lives before we reflect upon it. Knowledge is an activity, a process,[32] and we literally act our way into knowing by entering into the relationships constituted by the liturgy. Liturgy becomes the ritual action by which we live and enact the faith. Faith here is understood in the most dynamic sense of the term, which far exceeds intellectual assent. It is trust, commitment, and participation in God. The dynamism of the liturgy ritually expresses the dynamic relations of faith.

The consequences for theological study are found in the fact that worship provides the parameters for thinking about Scripture and theology by keeping these reflections oriented toward their proper object, God, and within their

31. Polanyi, *Knowing and Being,* p. 148.
32. Polanyi, *Knowing and Being,* p. 132.

proper context, the Christian community. It is in liturgy that we encounter the reality and mystery of God, the object of our study. This encounter grounds our knowledge of God in the primary narratives, in the symbols and concepts of the faith we seek to understand. There is a connection, however, between the practice of the church and worship and the formulation of the church's belief in dogma. As David Power expresses it, "dogma expresses meaning, that is to say, the lived and at least incipiently theoretical approach to the truths of faith that guide a church in its quest for community with God in Jesus Christ."[33] The truths are lived and practiced in worship before they are expressed dogmatically. For example, the church baptized in the name of the Father, Son, and Spirit and prayed to the Father through Christ in the power of the Spirit long before it developed a doctrine of the trinitarian relationships in the fourth-century Councils of Nicea (325) and Constantinople (381).[34]

The relationship between dogma and worship, however, is really reciprocal. In addition to worship giving rise to doctrine, doctrine, on the other hand, ensures right worship. The liturgy as experienced is itself already formed by a great deal of "secondary theology." This is evident not only in the texts, but in such gestures as genuflections and elevations at the narrative of institution. The worship extended to Christ and represented in the very performance of the eucharistic prayer would be idolatrous unless Christ is held to be divine.

At the risk of an oxymoron, participatory knowledge of God within the liturgy is a mediated immediate knowledge of God.[35] It is mediated because the complexus of liturgical elements mediates the meaning of the liturgy which is God, the object of our doxology. However, we attend from these elements toward their meaning. Although in a second, more reflective moment, we may attend to the theology of each of the individual elements that comprise the liturgy, within well-executed liturgy the particular elements do not impinge on our consciousness in their particularity. Rather we are unaware of them as we are caught up into the primary symbols and larger movement of

33. David M. Power, *The Sacrifice We Offer* (New York: Crossroad, 1987), p. 139.

34. Sarah Coakley argues for a rational defense of the doctrine of the Trinity from the practice of prayer in "Why Three? Some Further Reflections on the Origins of the Doctrine of the Trinity," in *The Making and Remaking of Christian Doctrine: Essays in Honour of Maurice Wiles*, ed. Sarah Coakley and David A. Pailin (Oxford: Clarendon Press, 1993), pp. 29-56.

35. As Avery Dulles notes, authors such as Rahner speak paradoxically of "mediated immediacy" in their theology of revelation. Dulles states: "The inner presence of God cannot be known and cannot achieve itself except insofar as it becomes mediated, or mediates itself, in created symbols. The symbols, however, do arouse a genuine awareness of the divine itself — an awareness that always surpasses all that we can say about it" (*Models of Revelation* [Maryknoll, N.Y.: Orbis Books, 1983, 1992], pp. 148-49).

worship. Ideally, many liturgical elements have a transparency. They do not call attention to themselves, but by means of them we are drawn into the worship and knowledge of God. This is similar to the experience described by Polanyi: when I point my finger at an object I mean that object, and so this object is the meaning of my pointing finger.[36] I attend not to my finger, but at the object to which I am pointing. The object of our knowing, God, is mediated by the elements of worship, but there is a surplus of meaning that exceeds the sum of the parts much as a physiognomy exceeds each of the individual features.

This type of experience is a kind of contemplation. According to Polanyi, in contemplation "we cease to handle things and become immersed in them"; there is a "complete participation of the person in that which he contemplates."[37] However, the contemplation proper to the liturgy is not the detached contemplation of thought. All the senses are brought to bear in the liturgical act of indwelling. We are impressed with the objects, sights, smells, sounds. We indwell the liturgy not only by being present, but by being impressed with its various elements, as a coin is impressed by a stamp. We even physically ingest the object of our faith. The point of this impression is to be formed and shaped so as literally to assume the form of Christ. In this regard we have only to recall the words of St. Augustine: "Become what you eat, the body of Christ." As in the gospels, where physical healing is a sign of spiritual healing, the forgiveness of sin, so the physical indwelling that occurs at the liturgy is the material dimension of the contemplative indwelling and union that occur there. Thus there is a mediated immediacy in our knowing. The result is a union at every level of our being. Knowing becomes a function of communion.

To speak of indwelling and communion sounds like mysticism — and so it is. However, this is not a flight of the alone to the alone, but a communion with and knowledge of God through the materiality of bread and wine shared together. This is what Kenneth Leech calls a "flesh-based spirituality."[38] The materiality of sign and symbol inherent to the liturgy belongs to the incarnational order. Eucharistic liturgy points to the fulfillment of the incarnation in the redemption of the material world. Eucharistic bread is "the symbol of all bread shared." The common life centered on the breaking of bread has social consequences. The bread has often been seen as the symbol of human labor and human struggle, placed upon the altar so it can be sanctified. In the words of the prayer at the Preparation of the Gifts, it is bread

36. Polanyi, *Knowing and Being,* p. 189.

37. Polanyi, *Personal Knowledge,* p. 197.

38. Kenneth Leech, *True Prayer* (San Francisco: Harper & Row, 1980), p. 75.

"which earth has given and human hands have made." Similarly, the wine has been seen as symbolizing human fellowship and mirth. Liturgy becomes the microcosm of the work that God is doing in the world, that is, transforming it into his body. This is the theme of Romans 8, which speaks of all creation being set free from its bondage to decay, obtaining the freedom of the glory of the children of God, groaning in labor pains as we wait for adoption and redemption, the reconciliation of all things in Christ. Thus worship, knowledge of God, and respect for the material order are inseparable. The condemnations of the Monophysites, Arians, and Iconoclasts illustrate how attempts to drive a wedge between the material order and the divine have been judged heretical.[39] Liturgical worship, because it belongs to the incarnational order, cannot be privatized or spiritualized, but has an ethical dimension that is social and historical. Knowledge of God leads us into *diakonia,* service, which is public and political as it seeks to translate Christian love into the structure of our societal life.

The God we come to know in the liturgy is God-for-us. We know who Christ is in the Eucharist within the context of the eucharistic action. In his critique of scholastic metaphysics, Louis-Marie Chauvet shows the inadequacy of conceiving the reality of eucharistic presence in terms of a metaphysical substance understood in itself.[40] Relying on the philosophy of Heidegger and the idea that we do not know a thing in itself until we know what a thing is for, he maintains that one cannot conceive of the *esse,* that is, the ultimate reality of Christ in the Eucharist without reference to Christ's *ad-esse,* the ultimate reality of being for the church. Furthermore, the *ad-esse* is constitutive of the sacramental esse.

This means that God's "being-for" is part of what it means for God to be God. To be God is to be in relationship, to be not in self-sufficient isolation, but ecstatically toward and for another.[41] Doctrines, particularly those of the Trinity, incarnation, and redemption, tell us these truths about God in the

39. The Monophysites taught that Christ had only one nature, a divine one, and that worship moved us away from the human to the divine. The Arians taught that Jesus was a creature subordinate to the Father since the divine essence of God could not be communicated. The Iconoclasts forbade religious images.

40. This material summarizes Chauvet, *Symbol and Sacrament,* pp. 389-98. He acknowledges that Thomas Aquinas strongly emphasizes the connection between the Eucharist and the Church, but notes that Thomas does not allude to this connection in his analysis of transubstantiation.

41. For a discussion of the ecstatic nature of God within a trinitarian and eucharistic framework see John Zizioulas, *Being as Communion* (Crestwood, N.Y.: St. Vladimir's Seminary Press, 1985).

code language peculiar to theology and church councils. However, in the anaphora, the eucharistic prayer, we experience again the economy of the Father sending the Son who gives his life for us and is present among us sacramentally by the power of the Spirit in order that we may become one body in Christ, a "living sacrifice of praise." The sending of the Son and the Spirit results in a communion whose purpose is doxology, the return to the Father in praise and thanksgiving. Within the eucharistic liturgy we have the Trinitarian relationships, a commemoration of Christ's becoming human and dying for us, and a sacramental representation of that final messianic banquet, the image of eschatological redemption. Knowledge that is codified in doctrine is lived in the liturgy.

Chauvet illustrates this "being-for" of God within the liturgy with Heidegger's analysis of a pitcher. A pitcher cannot be adequately known by science, which can only pronounce on its materials, its shape, and its use. A pitcher's essence or "thingness" does not consist in the matter of which it is constructed, but "in the emptiness that holds which in turn rests on an 'outpouring.'" The pitcher's essence is to be shaped for this possibility of pouring out. Heidegger plays on the double meaning of the verb *schenken,* which means both to "pour" and "to offer" a drink at the same time, and concludes that "the pouring pitcher unfolds its being as the pouring which offers."

Chauvet extends this analysis to the bread of the Eucharist. Noting the social instituting of bread as a symbol for what one shares during a meal, Chauvet concludes that the essence of bread unfolds itself in the "symbolic act of religious oblation" where "bread is never so much bread as in the gesture of thankful oblation where it gathers within itself heaven and earth, believers who 'hold fellowship' in sharing it, and the giver whom they acknowledge to be God." In this experience of bread a "new communion of life is established with God and between themselves."

The *ad-esse* of the Eucharist is also the body of Christ given for us and broken for us. This is certainly the meaning of Luke's text: "Then he took a loaf of bread, and when he had given thanks, he broke it and gave it to them saying, 'This is my body, which is given for you. Do this in remembrance of me'" (22:19). To adequately know the real presence of Christ in the Eucharist it is not enough to assert his real substance; we know this presence when we know what Jesus did with the body and for whom. This means that the real meaning and knowledge of the eucharistic presence is only acquired through the entire eucharistic action, which represents sacramentally Christ's self-giving for us. Again, this is not a commemoration of a past event, but that past event brought into the present through sacramental symbol. The *ad-esse* of the Eucharist is always new for us in this time.

One of the problems associated with religious knowledge is identifying the criteria for authenticity. When is it a true knowledge of God and not a deception or false knowledge? The dialectic between creedal professions of faith and the ritual enactment of faith offers constraints on both. For example, the God known and worshiped within the liturgy is trinitarian. The Trinity is professed in creed, and the liturgical economy of worship offered to the Father in the Son by the power of the Holy Spirit is trinitarian. A unitarian profession of faith or a unitarian liturgical economy would be false. Thus one looks for a correspondence between what a community professes and how that community prays. If this correspondence is missing, either we have false worship or false belief.

A second criterion for true knowledge of God, however, is the ethical dimension of the liturgy. Our knowledge of God within the liturgy is true when it patterns our imagination and behavior according to the parabolic structure of the gospel. The test of true liturgy and true knowledge of God is how they form and transform us to live outside of the liturgy. Any number of individuals, for example, have claimed to have received messages from God asking them to perform atrocious acts against other human beings. The action belies the message. Similarly, the conduct of Christians verifies or falsifies what they claim to know of God.

Conclusion

We must now ask whether the liturgy is a necessary avenue for knowing God within the Christian tradition. Polanyi notes that "a true understanding of science and mathematics includes the capacity for a contemplative experience of them, and the teaching of these sciences must aim at imparting this capacity to the pupil."[42] If this is true of science and mathematics, how much more true this must be for a knowledge of God. If so, this means that "a true understanding of God includes the capacity for a contemplative experience of God, and a teaching about God, the study of theology, must aim at imparting this capacity to the pupil." The question is how we live in what we know so as to acquire this capacity for contemplation. Contemplation requires that we submerge ourselves in that which we contemplate. Attachment rather than detachment is the condition of this type of knowledge. What this requires first is a faith commitment.

Beyond this some Christians might respond that we can indwell the real-

42. Polanyi, *Personal Knowledge,* pp. 195-96.

ity of God by internalizing the scriptures. However, one of the significant differences among the Christian churches is how those scriptures are interpreted. As Wainwright notes:

> The liturgy was, and *mutatis mutandis* remains for us, the locus in which the story of the constitutive events is retold in order to elicit an appropriate response in worship and ethics to the God who remains faithful to the purposes which his earlier acts declared. As the book in which the original stories have been deposited, developed, and classically defined, the scriptures subserve that continuing function of the liturgy.[43]

Here Wainwright seems to point to a reciprocal relationship between the biblical text and the liturgy. The liturgy is the interpretative lens for the Bible, while the scriptures are necessary for the community's response to God in worship and ethics. Thus some liturgical context, interpreted as the presence of the paschal mystery, appears necessary for a Christian reading of the canon.

Third, we need a community that hands on from generation to generation what is tacitly known in its tradition.[44] Tradition shapes our power of perception so that we perceive in the Christian symbols what the church perceives. Avery Dulles, following Polanyi, tells us that tradition "is grasped not by objective knowledge — that is to say, by looking at it — but by participatory knowledge — that is, by dwelling in it."[45] He notes that tradition functions most effectively when we are not expressly conscious of it. What is finally achieved is a "tacit, lived awareness of the God to whom the Christian scriptures and symbols point." The Second Vatican Council in the *Dogmatic Constitution on Divine Revelation* states that this tradition is passed on in the church's doctrine, life, and worship.[46] Thus the liturgy embodies the community's identity at the same time that the community provides the norm for interpreting liturgical symbols.

Finally, conversion is both the product of indwelling and what is needed to participate more intensively in a symbol system. Ultimately, it is connaturality with the symbol that enables us to resonate with it. Lest this seem

43. Geoffrey Wainwright, *Doxology: The Praise of God in Worship, Doctrine, and Life* (New York: Oxford University Press, 1980), p. 153. See also Louis Bouyer, "Liturgie et Exégèse Spirituelle," *La Maison-Dieu* 7 (1946): 29-50; Jean Daniélou, *The Bible and the Liturgy* (Notre Dame: University of Notre Dame Press, 1956).

44. Avery Dulles, *The Reshaping of Catholicism* (San Francisco: Harper & Row, 1988), p. 86.

45. Dulles, *The Reshaping of Catholicism,* p. 86.

46. *Dogmatic Constitution on Divine Revelation,* 8.

impossibly circular, we have only to recall that Aristotle and Plato, from the ancient tradition, and Thomas Aquinas, in the medieval, held that to discover concretely what is just or prudent or brave or chaste, it is useless to argue deductively. I can only arrive at this knowledge by asking a person who has the virtue who then knows what this virtue is by consulting his or her own inclinations.[47] When we know something connaturally, we have the virtue in question embodied in ourselves and are thus co-natured with it.[48] When we are asked about a moral virtue, we give the right answer by looking at and consulting what we are and the inner bents or propensities of our own being or, in Jacques Maritain's words, listen to "the inner melody that the vibrating strings of abiding tendencies made present in the subject."[49]

Strictly speaking, virtue cannot be taught. Conversion is necessary in order to have an intuitive insight into the Good or God, for only then do we possess the value, virtue, or divine life within us with which we can resonate. Conversion results in charity, which is to say love, which unites us to God.[50] Maritain notes that John of St. Thomas's great achievement was to show that in mystical experience love grows into an objective means of knowing that unites the intellect with the thing known.[51] This wisdom or knowledge of the divine occurs through taste and affective union rather than discursive reason. This requires contemplation not only of the scriptural text, but of the liturgical symbol within the lived worship of the church. It is not a direct and immediate contemplation of God in Godself, but contemplation by indwelling through the mediation of the complexus of symbols.

Polanyi does not speak of connaturality in connection with tacit knowl-

47. For Thomas Aquinas on knowledge of chastity through connaturality see his discussion on wisdom in the *Summa Theologiae,* II-II, 34, 2.

48. Jacques Maritain is one of the few to attempt a quasi-definition of connatural knowledge: "A kind of knowledge which is produced in the intellect but not by virtue of conceptual connections and by way of demonstration. . . . We shall give the right answer, no longer through science, but through inclination, by looking at and consulting what we are and the inner bents or propensities of our being.

"In this knowledge through union or inclination, connaturality or congeniality, the intellect is at play not alone, but together with affective inclinations and the dispositions of the will, and is guided and directed by them. It is not rational knowledge, knowledge through the conceptual, logical and discursive exercise of reason. But it is really and genuinely knowledge, though obscure and perhaps incapable of giving account of itself, or of being translated into words" ("On Knowledge Through Connaturality," *The Review of Metaphysics* 4 [1951]: 473-74).

49. Jacques Maritain, *Man and the State* (Chicago: University of Chicago Press, 1951), pp. 91-92.

50. Aquinas, *Summa,* I-II, 14, 1.

51. Jacques Maritain, *Range of Reason* (New York: Charles Scribner's Sons, 1952), p. 24.

edge through indwelling; nor does Maritain speak of tacit knowledge. However, since the meaning of symbols cannot be explained fully, but can only be experienced — because they cannot be invented at will, but must be discovered — they have the power to communicate with us only through some sort of connaturality. Participation in a symbol can occur only because of some kind of affinity with it. Light and darkness, oil, bread and wine, water — these have their power because they resonate with something primordial within us. The connatural element within tacit knowledge explains why outsiders can wander into the liturgy or some other symbol system and be unaffected until they have been initiated into that community. Initiation into a specific symbolic community is a process of conversion through which an individual acquires the qualities with which to resonate with the symbol.

Inevitably the question arises whether, in such discussions of the liturgy as this one, we romanticize or idealize the liturgy or make claims about it and for it that cannot be substantiated. In this post-liturgical movement era we need to be critical, honest, and hardheaded about the claims we make for the liturgy — especially in ecumenical conversations. Someone invariably says: "What liturgy do you go to? What you describe is not my experience. Is this the experience of professionally religious people who live with this every day through both Office and daily Eucharist, but not of the ordinary Christian, the person in the pew, who only attends a Sunday service? Does such a view of liturgy reflect more the wish of the author than reality?" How can we reconcile such claims with what is often a rather mundane liturgical experience?

Liturgy is rightfully criticized if it becomes empty ritual or if it becomes a manipulation of symbol in order to receive a desired response from the divine. The key to authentic liturgy is whether or not what is celebrated within the liturgy affects how we attempt to live outside of the liturgy. The liturgy represents symbolically the pattern of Christian relationships. The interplay between the attempt to live inclusive, self-giving relationships outside the liturgy and the pattern of inclusivity and self-offering represented within the liturgy gives life to our liturgical experience. The liturgy does not need to evoke intense emotional experiences or be celebrated with high drama in order to achieve its purpose, although aesthetics do make a difference.

The primary liturgical symbols are simple: a gathered assembly, a proclaimed biblical text, bread and wine, oil, water. The symbols are ordinary. The participatory knowledge of God in the liturgy simply requires that we place ourselves in the formative environment of the liturgy so as to acquire the perspective expressed there, to experience ourselves as active members of a worshiping community, and through the liturgical rite to be caught up into the doxological return to the Father through Christ in the power of the Spirit.

We are formed by the dailiness and commonality of liturgical prayer. Perhaps significantly, Polanyi refers to this kind of knowledge here as tacit. As such it is silent, inferred, unexpressed. We are formed into a pattern, identified as Christian, and thus assume a way of being in the world. This is neither esoteric nor necessarily highly emotional.

Polanyi's epistemology challenges the stereotype of scientific and mathematical knowledge as being objective and capable of study by an impersonal, objective, detached observer. In its effort to find acceptance by the Academy and to prove its objective, scientific character, the academic study of theology often detaches itself from its grounding in a faith community.[52] If Polanyi's theory of tacit knowledge as applied to the knowledge of God within the liturgy is correct, this detachment is very misguided. The object of such study becomes the mediatory elements that are attended in participatory knowledge. Although these are legitimate objects of inquiry, what happens is that such study becomes fragmented and cut off from the context that integrates and unites them. What is needed now is the integration of the various ways of knowing God. This involves, first of all, relocating them in their proper context: the public worship of the church.

52. See David Kelsey, *To Understand God Truly: What's Theological About a Theological School?* (Philadelphia: Westminster, 1992), ch. 3, "Excellence as *Wissenschaft* and Professionalism," pp. 78-100.

II. FORMATION IN KNOWING THE TRINITY

5. Contemplation

Knowledge of God in Augustine's De Trinitate

A. N. WILLIAMS

I. The Unity of the *De Trinitate*

In the prefatory letter placed at the beginning of the *De Trinitate* at Augustine's request, he bewails the pirated portions of his manuscript that had been circulating for some time.[1] His main objection to these unauthorized versions is that they are incomplete, and as such violate the treatise's close-knit structure. The prospect of the parts being read in isolation from one another troubled him so much that he released the complete manuscript before he had polished it to his own satisfaction. Contemporary readers would do well to heed Augustine's concern for the unity of the treatise, for a reading based on part of it will yield conclusions quite different from those based on an interpretation that seeks its internal connections. When one presses the nature of the work's coherence, the *De Trinitate* shows itself to be deeply concerned with a distinctively Christian epistemology, and one that has much to teach contemporary Christianity.

From one perspective, there is nothing new about the claim that the treatise is concerned with religious epistemology, for it is often assumed that the second half of the work functions as a venture in natural theology in which Augustine examines numerous *vestigia trinitatis,* triform structures in the

1. I am grateful to my former colleague Peter Hawkins, ever the acute reader of texts, for his comments on this essay.

human mind that parallel the divine Trinity. Viewed in this way, the treatise's epistemological claim is that because we are like God, we can come to knowledge of God by looking at ourselves. There are numerous objections counting against this reading, however.

One immediate reason to reject this interpretation of the *vestigia's* function is that Augustine explicitly denies one can extrapolate from natural world to God. To begin with, he is wary of the possible misuse of reason in theology. The purpose of his treatise, Augustine tells us in its opening pages, is to refute the sophistry of those deceived by a misguided use of reason (I.1). Second, he is aware of the difficulties inherent in extrapolation from creation to God, because of the profound difference between the Uncreated and the created. He concludes the prologue to Book IX by saying:

> What we have to avoid is the sacrilegious mistake of saying anything about the trinity which does not belong to the creator but rather to the creature, or which is fabricated by vain imaginings.[2]

In places he specifies the nature of the fundamental differences between creature and Creator: God is eternal and creation temporal (XIV.4); the creature is material, while God is not (I.27). At other times he dispenses with reasons altogether and simply asserts the vast disparity between God and ourselves (XV.11 and 39).

If he is doubtful about the possibility of reasoning from creation to God, he flatly denies the value of meditating upon ourselves as a theological end:

> This trinity of mind is not really the image of God because the mind remembers and understands and loves itself, but because it is also able to remember and understand and love him by whom it was made. . . . If it does not do [this], then even though it remembers and understands and loves itself, it is foolish. (XIV.15; cf. XV.51)

Indeed, reflection on the self only serves to show the limitations of our understanding:

> From myself indeed I understand how wonderful and incomprehensible is your knowledge with which you have made me, seeing that I am not even

2. Quotations from the *De Trinitate* follow the translation of Edmund Hill, *The Trinity* (*The Works of Saint Augustine,* I.5 [Brooklyn, N.Y.: New City Press, 1991]). The terms he uses to designate humanity differ from those I prefer, but I have of course let his usages stand in quotations from his translation. Latin glosses follow the text of the *Corpus Christianorum* edition (Series Latina, L), ed. W. J. Mountain (Turnhout, Belgium: Brepols, 1968).

able to comprehend myself whom you have made; and yet *a fire burns up in my meditation* (Psalm 39:3), causing me to seek your face always. (XV.13)

Even more than the explicit statements questioning the possibility of natural knowledge of God, the work's structure argues against reading it as a natural theology, since one can only deem it such by privileging its second half. The first half, comprised of Books I-VIII, treats the divine Trinity exclusively, as Augustine reminds us in his own summary, which he begins by demonstrating the unity and equality of the Trinity from the scriptures (XV.5). The nature of the Trinity having been established, and elaborated at some length, he then moves in Books IX-XV to seek analogies that might aid *understanding:*

> Let us believe that Father and Son and Holy Spirit are one God, maker and ruler of all creation . . . that they are a trinity of persons related to each other, and a unity of equal being. But let us seek to understand this, begging the help of him whom we wish to understand; and as far as it is granted us let us seek to explain what we understand. (IX.prol.)

The *vestigia,* then, are a tool for penetrating belief and grasping it yet more fully, not a means for establishing the content of faith independently of, or prior to, Scripture.

If, taking Augustine's insistence of the unity of the treatise seriously, we acknowledge the distinctive features of each half and trace the connections between them, we reach a theological epistemology, but a rather different one from that assumed by a natural theology. If the *vestigia* are read together with the doctrine of God elaborated in Books I-VIII, the *De Trinitate* yields a distinctively Christian understanding of the knowledge of God rather than the generic conclusions of a natural theology. According to this model, the relation of trinitarian persons to one another, and the relation of God and humanity, are relations constituted by knowledge and love. Knowledge, like love, is a unitive force (to borrow a Dionysian phrase); thus knower is bound to known, lover to the beloved, and knowledge and love are united to one another. This Augustinian epistemology thus proposes three kinds of unity: of the divine persons, of human persons and God, and of knowledge and love themselves as constituent principles of these personal relations. While the issue of intra-trinitarian relations could be taken to be purely theological, and indeed esoteric, the relation of God and humanity pertains equally to the realms of ascetical and mystical theology (spirituality in modern parlance). Thus, although the *De Trinitate* can with some justice be read as a theological treatise, and a rather technical one at that, it also represents a systematic pursuit of the implications of doctrinal statements for spiritual life.[3] As the divine persons are united through knowledge and love, so ought human persons be united to God.

In simultaneously pressing the questions of both "school" theology and mystical theology, the *De Trinitate* suggests another kind of unity, a disciplinary one. This unity of theology, systematic and mystical, could in Augustine's time be taken for granted. In our time, in contrast, academic theology has been reduced to a set of propositions about God that are at least by intention free from the supposed subjectivity and irrationality of spirituality, and spirituality has been reduced to a set of sentiments that are likewise intentionally free from the supposed aridity and narrowness of academic theology. This internal division within what was once a single discipline correlates with a polarity in modern conceptions of the knowledge of God. In the context of academic theology, knowledge of God means mastery of information, knowledge-about. In the context of the spiritual life, on the other hand, knowing God means having a personal relationship from which mastery of information is virtually excluded; it is apparently possible to love God without knowing much about him.[4] This kind of knowledge might be characterized as acquaintance-with.[5] The unwritten conventional wisdom of contemporary Christianity suggests that one must choose between these varieties of knowledge, either speaking theologically or in adoration, but not both, lest one contaminate the other.

3. Cf. John C. Cooper, "The Basic Philosophical and Theological Notions of Saint Augustine," *Augustinian Studies* (hereafter *AS*) 15 (1984), where he claims Augustine's "basic notion" (i.e., throughout his works) is the concept of spiritual quest (p. 95). Similarly, Ronald A. Nash suggests that throughout his writings, Augustine insists that knowledge is not to be sought for its own sake, but so that through it we may attain happiness (*The Light of the Mind: St. Augustine's Theory of Knowledge* [Lexington: University Press of Kentucky, 1969], p. 3). Likewise, Robert J. O'Connell suggests that in the *De Trinitate,* Augustine reiterates his conviction that the primary task of inquiry is to discover how we are to become happy ("Action and Contemplation," in *Augustine: A Collection of Critical Essays,* ed. R. A. Markus [Modern Studies in Philosophy] [Garden City, N.Y.: Anchor, 1972], p. 47).

4. Cf. John Macquarrie, "Theology and Spirituality," in *Paths in Spirituality,* 2nd ed. (Harrisburg, Pa.: Morehouse, 1992), and "Prayer and Theological Reflection," in *The Study of Spirituality,* ed. Cheslyn Jones, Geoffrey Wainwright, and Edward Yarnold (New York: Oxford, 1986; hereafter *SS*).

5. The terms *knowledge-about* and *acquaintance-with* are not those of Dewey J. Hoitenga, Jr., but his description of the elements of knowledge in Augustine's thought resembles the analysis given here. See "Faith Seeks Understanding: Augustine's Alternative to Natural Theology," in *Augustine: Presbyter Factus Sum,* ed. Joseph T. Lienhard, Earl C. Muller, and Roland Teske (Collectanea Augustiniana) (New York: Peter Lang, 1998; hereafter *APFS*). Thomas Merton is also thinking in similar terms, although he does not use these words. See *New Seeds of Contemplation* (New York: New Directions, 1962), pp. 13 and 254-55.

Augustine's conception of the knowledge of God, on the other hand, encompasses both theology and spirituality, because he portrays it as the fruit of contemplation. A contemplative knowledge does not seek to establish truth by hard-won deduction, but rather to nourish understanding and "enable it to rise up to the sublimities of divine things" (I.2). This rising up Augustine tends to characterize with optical images (contemplation, gazing, beholding, as well as seeing, vision, and sight[6]). Nevertheless, contemplation is difficult (I.3 and 4), and requires mental purification (I.3). It does not *establish* belief, for that is the function of Scripture (I.4); yet knowledge of God comprises not simply the intellectual act of reflection on Scripture, but also the various movements of the will implied by spiritual purification and the love of God. This notion of knowledge differs markedly from knowledge of God as conceived in the twentieth century, inasmuch as it unites school theology with mystical theology. Because it grounds and permits such a unitive theology, Augustine's conception of religious epistemology is one that modern Christianity would do well to recover.

II. Axioms of Augustine's Theology and Anthropology

Our first task in teasing out these themes in the *De Trinitate* is to examine the way in which Augustine characterizes the knowledge of God, and we shall start by seeking the sense in which his treatise portrays God as personal. The misgivings a twentieth-century thinker might have about the term *personal* — that it is unscriptural, comes with suspicious psychological baggage, and suggests a false analogy between God and humanity — are paralleled by Augustine's own unease about it. He surveys various possibilities for labeling the three Persons, showing the inadequacies of each:

> What are we left with then? Perhaps we just have to admit that these various usages were developed by the sheer necessity of saying something. . . . Human inadequacy was trying by speech to bring to the notice of men what is held about the Lord God its creator, according to its capacity. . . . So human inadequacy searched for a word to express three what [quid tria], and it said substances or persons. (VII.9; cf. V.10)

Despite the arbitrariness that he sees in using the term *person,* Augustine nevertheless deems it properly applied to God: "it is not one thing for God to be

6. For references to contemplation, see the section below; as examples of gazing, see I.2 and I.4; beholding, XV.5 and 39. References to sight and seeing abound, cf. XI.1-5, 9-10, 14-19.

and another for him to be person, but altogether the same [non enim aliud est deo esse, aliud personam esse sed omnino idem]" (VII.11). He then proceeds from this assumption of God as personal to identify the divine persons with knowledge and love, explaining the relations among them as having a specifically trinitarian structure. In so doing, he employs two distinct insights of trinitarian theology.

On the one hand, he freely makes use of a strategy of appropriation to identify knowledge, word, and wisdom with the second person of the Trinity, and charity with the third (XV.29, 30, and 37). Thus, the terms in which the Son and the Spirit are chiefly conceived are as knowledge and love, activities that are associated preeminently with persons.[7] On the other hand, with a nod to the notion of perichoresis, Augustine insists that the divine persons are inseparable: "just as Father and Son and Holy Spirit are inseparable, so do they work inseparably" (I.7; cf. IV.30). This unity comes from not simply a unity of operation, but a coinherence: "these three are together God because of their inexpressible mutuality [ineffabilem coniunctionem]" (VII.8; cf. XV.43). Thus, Augustine does not, as he is sometimes charged, locate the unity of the Trinity solely in the unity of substance, but also in the inseparability of persons (VI.9). If we put the insights from the side of perichoresis together with those from the side of appropriation, we find that as the Word and Spirit are inseparable in the unity of the Trinity so, we may surmise, must knowledge be inseparable from love of God.

Unity of substance, while by no means more important than personal mutuality, provides a second theological basis for the unity of knowledge and love. The converse of the appropriation strategy is that whatever is predicated of one person is rightly predicated of all three (V.9); the inseparability of charity and truth is grounded not only in the relations of the divine persons, but also in simplicity. Thus, while much contemporary spirituality seems to suggest that one must choose between charity and truth, either loving God or speaking theologically, Augustine refuses to do so. Rather, he pursues the implications of divine simplicity for Christian life: "in that supremely simple nature substance is not one thing and charity another, but substance is charity and charity is substance" (XV.29). As the Trinity exists, so ought we, so that "just as Father and Son are one not only by equality of substance but also by identity of will, so these men, for whom the Son is mediator with God, might be one not only by being of the same nature, but also by being bound

7. I do not, therefore, think Bernard Lonergan is quite right in maintaining that for Augustine *person* simply denotes what there are three of in God ("The Depersonalization of Dogma," in *A Second Collection,* ed. William F. J. Ryan and Bernard J. Tyrrell [Philadelphia: Westminster, 1974], p. 25).

in the fellowship of the same love" (IV.12). Thus, whatever one thinks of the doctrine of simplicity (and some these days do not think much of it[8]), what Augustine has done here is by contemporary standards extraordinary: he has taken a recondite doctrine and pursued its significance for both theology and spirituality, showing its inseparability from both.

From either the perspective of divine simplicity or the perspective of trinitarian relations, then, Augustine deems knowledge and love to be inseparable. The grounding of our knowledge of God is further established by the structures of Augustine's anthropology, the vestiges of the Trinity in the human person. Whether or not his searching for *vestigia trinitatis* in the human person constitutes a legitimate form of natural theology, and whether or not any form of natural theology is legitimate, the restless tracery of Books IX through XV of the *De Trinitate* reflects an elementary principle of Christian Neo-Platonism: like knows like:[9] "While any knowledge has a likeness to the thing it knows, that is, to the thing it is the knowledge of, this knowledge by which the knowing mind is known has a perfect and equal likeness" (IX.16). We are able to know God, in however limited a fashion, because we are in some sense similar to God, and as we shall see, the essential points of that similarity lie in our capacities to reason and to love.

The *vestigia* furnish the essential elements of the Augustinian doctrine of the *imago Dei.* Augustine concurs with the tradition before him in locating that image in the intellect: "What we have to find in the soul of man, that is, in the rational or intellectual soul, is an image of the creator which is immortally engrained in the soul's immortality [immortaliter immortalitati eius est insita]" (XIV.5; cf. XV.39). Yet human intellect, even as its divine likeness establishes our ability to know God, also distinguishes humanity from God, because it falls radically short of the divine (IV.1). The point of claiming any sort of similarity, then, is not to place humanity on a dangerously similar level to God, as is sometimes thought, but merely to ground any sort of relation between God and humanity at all.[10]

8. For an example of a recent critique of simplicity, see Nicholas Wolterstorff, "Divine Simplicity," in *Philosophical Perspectives, 5: Philosophy of Religion,* ed. James E. Tomberlin (Atascadero, Calif.: Ridgeview, 1991).

9. Cf. John Burnaby, *Amor Dei: A Study of the Religion of St. Augustine* (London: Hodder and Stoughton, 1938), p. 67.

10. Cf. Eugene TeSelle's claim that Augustine does not say the mind is like God in every respect, but only in being able to remember, understand, and love specifically God (*Augustine the Theologian* [New York: Herder & Herder, 1970], p. 308). Nash maintains that the most crucial problem of Augustinian epistemology was the difficulty of relating the human aspect of knowledge to the divine, and that knowledge is possible because of the *imago Dei* and direct divine aid in the quest for knowledge (*The Light of the Mind,* pp. 67 and 111).

The *vestigia* also extend Augustine's anthropology beyond a conventional statement of the *imago Dei,* inasmuch as many of his triads point simultaneously to the intellectual and the volitional dimensions of the person. Some focus entirely on the activities of the will: the lover, being loved, and love in VII.14 and IX.2; the lover, what is loved, and love in XV.10. Others encompass movements of both the mind and the will: memory, understanding, and will in IV.30, X.17-19, XIV.8 and 10; the mind, love, and knowledge in IX.4, 6, 7, 8, 15, and 18; and memory, understanding, and love in XIV.13 and XV.42 and 43. The implication of these dually based triads is that humanity resembles God not simply in possessing the faculties of intellect and will, but in that these operate conjointly in the human person, just as they do in the divine Trinity.

While the *imago Dei* and the *vestigia* provide the basis of human relating to God, in Augustine's thought the image is never static; rather, it is the point of departure in a transformative process of growth towards God: "the image of God will achieve its full likeness of him when it attains to the full vision of him" (XIV.24). What accomplishes this transformation is the mind's turning toward God: "This trinity of the mind is not really the image of God because the mind remembers and understands and loves itself, but because it is also able to remember and understand and love him by whom it was made. And when it does this it becomes wise" (XIV.15). The image of God in humanity is therefore both given and yet to come.[11] The fact of some sort of likeness in nature is the foundation upon which grace works to bring us to glory.

Our relation to God thus lies both in our nature's innate, if partial, resemblance to God, and in our participating in the activities that characterize the Trinity: knowing and loving. Augustine's doctrine of the *imago Dei* and the *vestigia trinitatis* in human nature constitutes a claim he makes principally, not about natural knowledge of God, but about two kinds of unity in human engagement with God: the bonding of human intellect and will to the divine persons, and the unity of knowledge and love in God and in us. What Augustine's theology consistently suggests — its doctrine of God and its anthropology alike — is a doctrine of sanctification and a blueprint for understanding the knowledge of God as pertaining to both theology and spirituality, an epistemology in which knowledge of God is distinct among forms of

11. Cf. Edmund Hill, "Karl Rahner's Remarks on the Dogmatic Treatise *De Trinitate* and St. Augustine" (*AS* 2 [1971]). "The image is something we have to realise, to construct in ourselves; it is something which sin has defaced and grace is operating to restore," p. 79. Cf. also Étienne Gilson, who maintains the image of God in the soul is for Augustine the ever-present possibility of participation [in God] (*The Christian Philosophy of Saint Augustine,* trans. L. E. M. Lynch [New York: Random House, 1960], p. 219).

knowing, one in which the intellect cannot function without the will. To grasp the Augustinian notion of the knowledge of God, we must therefore look not only to what he says specifically of knowledge, but also of love, and of the relation between knowing and loving.[12]

III. Knowledge in the *De Trinitate*

Anyone who turns to the *De Trinitate* seeking to understand Augustine's notion of the knowledge of God must begin by noting his distinction between knowledge *(scientia)* and wisdom *(sapientia):* "action by which we make good use of temporal things differs from contemplation of eternal things, and this is ascribed to wisdom, the former to knowledge" (XII.22; cf. XII.25). While knowledge, as wisdom's precursor, is necessary and good (XV.10; cf. XIV.3), Augustine evidently worries about the worldly associations of *knowledge* (XII.21), which is why he prefers to use *wisdom* in connection with knowledge of God.[13] To elucidate the Augustinian notion of knowledge of God, then, one must often look to loci where he discusses wisdom, even though wisdom is not a standard category used in theology today.

The reader of the *De Trinitate* notices immediately a personal dimension to the knowledge of God:

> Our knowledge is therefore Christ, and our wisdom is the same Christ. It is he who plants faith in us about temporal things, he who presents us with the truth about eternal things. Through him we go straight toward him

12. The reading presented here resembles in some respects that of F. Bourassa ("Théologie trinitaire chez Saint Augustin," *Gregorianum* [Part I] 58 [1977]: 675-725 and [Part II] 59 [1978]: 375-412). Bourassa also insists on the dual focus in the treatise on love and knowledge, and gives brief attention to transformation, contemplation, and beatitude. Bourassa, however, sees these elements of Augustine's theology communicated primarily through the *vestigia,* rather than through the mutuality of the Trinity and the unity of substance. He also is not concerned to press his reading as implying an epistemology, or a statement about the relation between theology and spirituality.

13. I thus reluctantly differ from Andrew Louth. He reads Augustine to be saying in Book XII that one must relinquish *scientia* in order to embrace *sapientia* ("Augustine," in *SS,* p. 143). It seems to me that Augustine rather maintains that the rational and practical part of the mind, which deals with worldly things and produces *scientia,* is "drawn off" from the part of the mind that contemplates, but is thereby precisely *not* divorced or separated from the mind as a whole, or the mind that contemplates eternal things (XII.3, 4). If the two parts of the mind are not separated, it does not seem that their products would be, either.

> [per ipsum pergimus ad ipsum], through knowledge toward wisdom, without ever turning aside from one and the same Christ, *in whom are hidden all the treasures of wisdom and knowledge* (Col. 2:3). (XIII.24)

Here we see the distinctiveness of Augustine's epistemology: to know God certainly entails mastery of information, but it also entails personal contact. Knowledge of God is personal knowledge in the fullest sense, in that it encompasses both knowledge-about and acquaintance-with. It is in the first instance because Augustine locates knowledge in the realm of the personal, identifying knowledge, wisdom, and truth with a divine person, that he refuses to separate knowledge and love.

The identification of wisdom with God, however, also distinguishes God from humanity: "Our knowledge . . . is vastly dissimilar to [God's] knowledge. What is God's knowledge is also his wisdom, and what is his wisdom is also his being or substance" (XV.22).[14] While the doctrine of simplicity to which Augustine alludes here became a commonplace of Western theology, we need to note it carefully, for this doctrine is what prevents Augustine's strong conception of the *imago Dei* and his search for *vestigia trinitatis* from compromising the distinction between God and creation.

A third consequence of identifying wisdom with God is that wisdom's operation is governed by the same logic that governs trinitarian operations. We can speak of wisdom, yes, but this wisdom as Augustine understands it is never removed into some realm where the intellect functions alone. It is when the mind remembers and understands and *loves* its Maker that it becomes wise (XIV.15). Wisdom is distinct from love, but without love there can be no wisdom: "Who will say that there is any wisdom where there is no love?" (XV.12). As we examine Augustine's conception of the mind's engagement, then, we must constantly bear in mind that his view of the intellect extends beyond the modern notion. The inseparability of knowledge and love in the *De Trinitate* testifies to Augustine's holistic anthropology: there is no possibility of the true engagement of one human faculty with God in the absence of the engagement of the whole person.[15]

14. Cf. Bourassa (1977): "la difficulté qu'éprouve la raison devant une telle proposition [la doctrine de la Trinité] vient de sa propre faiblesse, que seule peut surmonter la Vérité divine reçue dans l'Église" (p. 686).

15. This point is overlooked by commentators with surprising regularity. For example, contra Harnack, Robert E. Cushman asserts that Augustine is clear about the relation of faith and knowledge, but both Cushman and Harnack neglect to consider love ("Faith and Reason," in *A Companion to the Study of St. Augustine,* ed. Roy W. Battenhouse [New York: Oxford University Press, 1955], p. 250). Likewise, William J. Collinge claims the *De Trinitate* represents a

Because Augustine's view of the mind is rather broader than the contemporary one, he does not fall into this century's trap of polarity: either one must choose the naked intellect alone, or eschew the mind entirely lest it corrupt the spirit. Augustine's view, novel in our time, is that humanity's restless longing for God embraces the mind: he assumes that one would *want* to use one's mind: "the more the thing is known without being fully known, the more does the intelligence desire to know what remains" (X.2). Thus we touch on the chicken-and-egg problem of the relation between knowledge and love in the treatise, which we will pursue more fully later. For the moment, we need note only Augustine's focus on the mind's desire.[16]

The desiring mind, the mind that seeks to complete itself by finding God (X.6), belongs to this life; to the next belongs the intellect's rest in consummation: "There we shall see the truth without any difficulty, and enjoy it in all its clarity and certitude. There, there will be nothing for us to seek with the reasonings of the mind [mente ratiocinante], but we will perceive by direct contemplation [contemplante] why the Holy Spirit is not a son, though he proceeds from the Father" (XV.45). Two points are notable here. First, to understand Augustine's notion of the intellect, one must take into account his understanding of contemplation, because while contemplation is portrayed as distinct from "the reasonings of the mind," it is also akin to them as their more perfect form. Second, Augustine's conception of paradise provides a sharp corrective to modern notions of spirituality, inasmuch as eternity will apparently be spent in the reflection on issues today considered purely technical.

Augustine does not merely expand the notion of mind, however, for his estimation of it is not uncritical. As we have noted, he is suspicious of the purely secular dimensions of intellectual activity. He differs from the variety of anti-intellectualism that pervades today's church by excluding only some forms of intellectual activity rather than all. Thus, as noted earlier, the *De Trinitate* opens with a stern warning against "an unseasonable and misguided love of reason" (I.1). His quarrel, then, is with wrongful *use* of reason, rather than with the mind itself. Indeed, he predicates not only knowledge of God but what we would call spiritual progress upon the advances of the mind: "[The Word] is precisely sent to anyone when he is known and perceived by him, as far as he can be perceived and known according to the capacity of the

---

movement from faith to understanding ("*De Trinitate* and the Understanding of Religious Language," *AS* 18 [1987]: 128), but does not mention the essential role of love in this process, an omission of which the usually scrupulous Hill is also guilty ("Unless You Believe, You Shall Not Understand: Augustine's Perception of Faith," *AS* 15 [1984]: 51-63).

16. This point is noted also by Rowan Williams in his article in *APFS*, "The Paradoxes of Self-Knowledge in the *De Trinitate*," p. 122.

rational soul either making progress toward God or already made perfect in God" (IV.28). Acquaintance-with inevitably fosters knowledge-about. Because Augustine conceives of the mind's growth in this way, he can enter into the act of speculative contemplation that is the *De Trinitate* itself:

> The God himself we are looking for will help us, I confidently hope, to get some fruit from our labours and to understand the text in the holy psalm *Let the heart of those who seek the Lord rejoice; seek the Lord and be strengthened; seek his face always* (Psalm 105:3). (XV.2)

Looking for God thus entails intimate contact with what we seek,[17] and not only contact, but love: "Let us set out along Charity Street together," he says, "making for him of whom it is said 'Seek his face always'" (I.5).

IV. Love in the *De Trinitate*

If Augustine's notion of the intellect differs from modern notions, so too does his view of love. If intellect and heart are not in conflict in his thought, it is because of the particular way in which he conceives them. As our examination of knowledge indicated the difficulty of separating knowledge and love in Augustine's thought, so his very definition of love will show the same: "in this question we are occupied with about the trinity and about knowing God, the only thing we really have to see is what true love is, well in fact, simply what love is. . . . True love is that we should live justly by cleaving to the truth [haec est autem uera dilectatio ut inhaerentes ueritati iuste uiuamus]" (VIII.10). To understand what knowledge of God is then, as well as to understand theology, one must love; love, in turn, binds one to the God of truth and justice, and loving justly implies a binding to one's neighbor. Augustine continues on from the definition of love cited above to say: "for the love of men by which we wish them to live justly we should despise [contemnamus] all mortal things. In this way, we will be ready and able even to die for the good of our brethren" (VIII.10). Indeed, he flings an impatient response at those who make of love a difficulty:

> Let no one say, "I don't know what to love." Let him love his brother, and love that love; after all, he knows the love he loves with better than the

17. Cf. Donald E. Daniels, "The Argument of the *De Trinitate* and Augustine's Theory of Signs," *AS* 8 (1977): "Augustine's doctrine of knowledge runs parallel to his doctrine of grace" (p. 50).

> brother he loves. There now, he can already have God better known to him than his brother, certainly better known because more present, better known because more inward to him, better known because more sure. (VIII.12)

Thus, Augustine's view of love is not far from the Dionysian maxim so important to Aquinas, "love is a unitive force": "This is the love which unites all good angels and all the servants of God in a bond of holiness, conjoins us and them together, and subjoins us to itself [coniungit inuicem nobis et subiungit sibi]" (VIII.12).

If love unites the people of God, it also binds us to those outside the community of faith and indicates the principles that govern our intellectual discourse with them:

> People ask us these questions [regarding the Trinity] to the point of weariness. . . . if we confess to our questioners that these matters live permanently in our thoughts because we are carried away by a love of tracking down the truth, then they can demand us by right of charity that we should show them what conclusions we have been able to reach on the subject. (I.8; cf. I.4)

Love here both impels the Christian to pursue the truth assiduously, and requires that she engage those who reject her beliefs. Far from being the refuge of the intellect, then, charity is its goad.[18]

It is not surprising, therefore, that Augustine claims that love, specifically love of virtue, perfects intellectual growth: "If [the Incarnation] is difficult to understand, then you must purify your mind with faith, by abstaining more and more from sin, and by doing good, and by praying with the sighs of holy desire that God will help you to make progress in understanding and loving" (IV.31). Here we see the warp and woof of his epistemology: if desiring acquaintance, you would grow in knowledge, call on the One you love, that you may know more truly. In the specific case of knowledge of God, it is only through acquaintance-with that we progress towards knowledge-about.

While Augustine generally seeks to link love and knowledge, there is nevertheless one respect in which he values charity because it works not with knowledge, but against it. If charity perfects the intellect, it is in part because it checks the pride that Augustine fears will often accompany knowledge

18. Contrast T. J. van Bavel, who gives three reasons that we must speak, in Augustine's view, none of which pertain to charity, "God in between Affirmation and Negation According to Augustine," *APFS*, p. 83.

(XII.21). Thus while there can be faith without charity, this kind of faith is of no use (XV.32). And so we are brought, once more, to the relationship of knowledge and love.

V. The Ordering of Knowledge and Love

As we have seen, it is virtually impossible to specify what knowledge and love are independently for Augustine, and it is to the precise nature of their intertwining that we now turn. Their relationship in the *De Trinitate* is complex, both in the sense that Augustine finds it difficult to specify one logic of relation, but also in the sense that he grounds their ordering in several different ways.

One of these is to compare the logic of divine relations with that of the *vestigia.* In so doing, Augustine hopes to show that as knowledge and love exist inseparably in God, so must they exist inseparably in humanity. Rather than viewing the *vestigia* as a means of reasoning from humanity to God, we can take Augustine to be offering a certain model of knowing God, one in which there can be no naked knowledge but only knowledge garbed in love. This unity is evident in the chief among the human triads he presents in the *De Trinitate,* that of memory, understanding, and will. The relation among these he compares to the relation among the divine persons:

> When I name my memory, understanding and will, each name refers to a single thing, and yet each of these single names is the product of all three; there is not one of these three names which my memory and understanding and will have not produced together. So too the trinity together produced both the Father's voice and the Son's flesh and the Holy Spirit's dove, though each of these single things has reference to a single person [cum ad personas singulas haec singula referantur]. (IV.30)

Augustine's concern here is not to stress that each human being in some way reflects the Trinity (though he clearly thinks it does) but to claim that the distinct activities of remembering, understanding, and loving are as inseparable as the Father, Son, and Spirit.[19] His point is not so much that human beings

19. Mary T. Clark insists that intellect and memory are functions of the one soul, but does not address the necessity of love in Augustine's schema, "Augustine on Person: Divine and Human," *APFS,* p. 108. Thus, to be a perfect image, one needs to integrate *sapientia* and *scientia* (p. 109), but she makes no mention of love. While Rowan Williams acknowledges the dual focus of knowledge and love, he reads Augustine as claiming these are both necessary to the mind to know *itself* ("The Paradoxes of Self-Knowledge in the *De Trinitate,*" p. 122). This emphasis on

resemble God — as we have seen, he is as acutely aware of the ontological divide as any other Christian thinker — but that what is inseparable in God must also be inseparable in us. The *vestigia* provide not a lesson in anthropology or natural theology, but in epistemology. Specifically, they make a strong claim that the knowledge and love of God are as inseparable as the persons of the Trinity.

A second way of asserting the unity of knowledge and love is to point to the unity of human nature itself: "These three then, memory, understanding and will, are not three lives but one life, not three minds, but one mind. So it follows of course they are not three substances but one substance" (X.18). The inseparability of the three faculties consists in their being of one life and one mind, so that memory and understanding pertain to life and not only to mind, and will pertains to mind and not only life. Although these three elements of the human person are conceptually distinct, and perhaps actually distinct, they cannot function in isolation from one another.

However, Augustine does not insist upon the arguments from anthropology or even from theology with the vehemence he accords the argument from the strictly logical relation of knowledge and love. To the question of the ordering of these two he returns again and again in Books VII-X. His primary argument, a qualified one as we shall see, is that we cannot love what we do not know. Despite his small caveats, he stresses this point firmly and often. He asks: "Who can love what he does not know?" (VIII.6) and: "could [we] love the thing we believe and do not yet know from its likeness to what we do know? But of course this is simply not so" (VIII.8), and: "How can [the mind] love what it does not know?" (IX.3). As the text progresses, the rhetorical questions yield to flat statements: "It is quite certain nothing can be loved unless it is known" (X.2). A few chapters later, the claim has become an axiom upon which he bases another argument: "But what is [the mind] loving? If itself, how, since it does not yet know itself and no one can love what he does not know?" (X.15).

Augustine does make one small qualification to this claim of the logical precedence of knowledge over love, a qualification necessary in virtue of the particular object of the knowledge and love that he is considering. He takes pains to deny that we can only love that which we know completely, since such perfect knowledge of God certainly does not belong to this life, and he makes a pastoral allowance for growth in faith. Thus, he states, we can indeed

---

self-knowledge characterizes his essay as a whole. Similarly, J. F. Worthen claims that the ascent in which we are engaged in reading the *De Trinitate* is a focusing ever more inwardly on the functioning of our own mind ("Augustine's *De trinitate* and Anselm's *Proslogion:* 'Exercere Lectorem,'" *APFS,* p. 519).

love the God in whom we believe, even though we have not yet seen him (VIII.8), even though we must believe before we can understand *(ibid.)*.

While the knowledge that precedes love need not be complete, Augustine hastens to qualify even this qualification, lest he be taken as undermining the necessity of knowledge: "'He loves to know the unknown' is not the same as saying 'He loves the unknown'" (X.3). The unknown element of our relationship with God does not mean that relationship can be real when there is no knowledge whatsoever; he continues: "it can happen that a man loves to know the unknown, but that he should love the unknown is impossible" (X.3). To arrive at this conclusion Augustine does not rely only on his axiom stipulating the necessary relation between love and knowledge. Rather, he investigates the nature of knowing to discover in precisely what sense one can be said to love the unknown:

> "To know" is not put groundlessly in that first sentence ["He loves to know the unknown"] because the man who loves to know the unknown loves not the unknown but the actual knowing. And unless he had known what this was, he would not be able to say with confidence either that he knew something or that he did not know something. (X.3)

Even as Augustine concedes that the kind of knowledge of God that precedes love need not be complete, he rejects yet more thoroughly the devaluation of knowledge by claiming that we *love* to know. His claim is no doubt intended to be descriptive — such is the nature of the case, he says. In our time, in an age when knowledge is often treated as the enemy of faith and theology as somehow destructive of the love of God, we may ruefully concede that the love of knowledge and the desire to know seem rather less than universal. In our time the claim could therefore be taken not as descriptive, but prescriptive.

The prescriptive element in Augustine's thought is not merely a lesson contemporary Christians may draw from the *De Trinitate;* it is also something he on occasion explicitly presses:

> Anyone who has a lively intuition of these three [the Trinity] (as divinely established in the nature of his mind) [quae tria in sua mente naturaliter diuinitas instituta quisquis uiualiter perspicit] and of how great a thing it is that his mind has by that which even the eternal and unchanging nature can be recalled, beheld and desired — it is recalled by memory, beheld by intelligence, embraced by love [reminiscitur per memoriam, intuetur per intelligentiam, amplecitur per dilectionem] — has thereby found the image of that supreme trinity. (XV.39)

Here he posits several principles we have already observed: on the one hand, the trinitarian structure of the *imago Dei* and its epistemological significance, on the other, the inseparability of knowledge and love. There is yet another theme, however: the transformative power of the trinitarian dynamic. The *imago* is given both in nature and through grace; it is both present and yet to be found. One finds it by a "lively intuition" of the divine Trinity, and one exercises that intuition, Augustine implies, by the exercise of memory, understanding, and will, by beholding and embracing. Thus he prays: "let me seek your face always and with ardor. . . . Let me remember you, let me understand you, let me love you. Increase those things in me until you refashion me entirely" (XV.51).

VI. Contemplation

The rubric under which Augustine above all understands the mind's transformative engagement with God is contemplation *(contemplatio)*, and to comprehend what he means by knowledge of God, we must grasp the significance of contemplation in his thought. Up until now, the differences we have observed between Augustine's thought and the prevailing winds of contemporary Christianity have pointed to differing estimations of the intellect; now we will see a gap in the attitude towards prayer. The size of that gap is evident in the frequency with which the term *contemplation* is used in Augustine's, as in patristic and medieval thought, and by its virtual absence from later, and especially twentieth-century, theology.[20]

For Augustine, as we have already seen in passing, contemplation does not signify an advanced form of prayer.[21] What it does designate is a form of

20. The contemporary writer who has treated contemplation most thoroughly is Thomas Merton, and he would count as an important exception to this statement if he were considered a theologian. Generally, he is not, although a sign of change in this regard may be his inclusion in *A New Handbook of Christian Theologians,* ed. Donald W. Musser and Joseph L. Price (Nashville: Abingdon, 1996). While he clearly conceives contemplation as a form of prayer that transcends theological reflection (*New Seeds of Contemplation,* pp. 1-2, 4-5), he also includes within its scope the kind of unity of knowledge-about God and acquaintance-with that Augustine advocates (pp. 13 and 253-55). Merton also acknowledges the need to communicate the fruits of contemplation, and while he is probably thinking in terms of ascetical theology, his understanding of this communication of fruits could easily include theology in general (pp. 268-69; see also *Contemplative Prayer* [New York: Herder and Herder, 1969], pp. 98-99, 104, 144).

21. *Pace* Dom Cuthbert Butler, who considers contemplation in Augustine under the rubric of mysticism (*Western Mysticism: The Teaching of SS. Augustine, Gregory and Bernard on the Contemplative Life* [New York: Dutton, 1924], *passim*). On the other hand, Burnaby insists upon

knowledge of God. Making use of the distinction we have already explained between wisdom and knowledge, he allies contemplation with the former: "contemplation of eternal things . . . is ascribed to wisdom. . . . wisdom belongs to contemplation" (XII.22). Since Augustine's wisdom corresponds to what we would more naturally call knowledge of God, he has here effectively equated that knowledge with contemplation. The first point to note, whose significance will become clearer as we go along, is that while in modern terms contemplation is a mental activity, and knowledge the product of such activity, the status of contemplation in Augustine's thought is ambiguous, seeming to belong exclusively neither to activity nor to product.

No more does contemplation belong exclusively either to the intellect or to the will. The engagement of the human person with God requires, as we have seen, the application of both: "What does knowing God mean but beholding him and firmly grasping him with the mind? [et quid est deum scire nisi eum mente conspicere firmeque percipere?]" (VIII.6), Augustine writes, implying by *beholding* both the regard of devotion and understanding, and by *grasping* both comprehension and the reach of desire. His general rubric for this grasping and beholding is contemplation, and as such, it is clearly not construed as a form of wordless prayer practiced by the spiritually adept, as is the tendency in modern usage, but as a binding of the mind to God.[22]

The mind, however, encounters God in this way not only because of intellectual, but also spiritual preparation: "it is difficult to contemplate and have full knowledge of God's substance. . . . That is why it is necessary for our minds to be purified" (I.3); and: "the rational mind is meant, once purified, to contemplate eternal things" (IV.24; cf. XIII.24). Augustine's reason for insisting on purification is both spiritual and theological, pointing on the one hand to humanity's sin and need for grace, and on the other to the ontological divide and the salvific effect of the Incarnation. Yet he integrates these concerns seamlessly, assuming the alliance of spiritual and intellectual faculties inasmuch as both are directed to the same object: "to contemplate God, which by nature we are not, we would have to be cleansed by him who became what by nature we are and by what sin we are not" (IV.4). Because of the modern associations of contemplation with advanced forms of prayer, the significance of this claim is easily missed; but if we bear in mind that Augustine equates contemplation with wisdom and that he uses wisdom to denote

---

Augustine's view of contemplation as the task of all Christians, not only those who have reached extraordinary heights in prayer (*Amor Dei*, pp. 61 and 64).

22. Indeed, Nash defines reason in Augustine's thought as contemplation of the truth (*The Light of the Mind*, p. 64).

what we would call knowledge of God, we begin to see the far-reaching implications of his doctrine of contemplation.

First, there can be no knowledge of God without cleansing. The spiritual dimension of knowledge of God cannot, therefore, be removed to some corner labeled "spirituality" and ignored by theologians. Second, in this specific case of knowledge, knowledge of God, the mind's object is also its means to that object. Precisely because of the strong sense of the divide between God and humanity, in terms of both ontology and sin, we can come to God only through God.[23] A similar precept is familiar to modern readers in the form of attacks on natural theology which insist that knowledge of God is possible only because of divine self-disclosure and that theology must therefore be based on Scripture alone. Augustine's position departs from the same assumption but reaches a slightly different conclusion: because of the ontological divide and sin, humanity can come to knowledge of God only through intimate contact with God, a contact that surely includes reading Scripture, but also encompasses prayer. Here again we see the primacy of the personal in Augustine's epistemology: knowledge of God is both knowing-about and acquaintance-with. Indeed, he says, knowing-about occurs only as the result of some form of acquaintance-with.

The personal dimension of contemplation becomes yet clearer when it is identified with the purpose of the Incarnation. Augustine does not expatiate on the significance of the Word's enfleshment; nor is he concerned with the second person as the one whose role is the explication of the divine. Rather, the Word aids human knowledge of God as the object of vision: "[Christ] took a created form in which to appear to human eyes, and thereby to purify our minds for contemplating him by faith" (I.27).[24] Here he stresses the visual dimension of contemplation and portrays the act of beholding God as a preparation of the mind for faith; again, acquaintance-with and knowing-about are firmly welded together. Christ also serves, however, to point the human eye away from his incarnate form and towards the immanent Trinity: "he turns our attention to the godhead and points the minds of men upward, since to raise them up was the reason why he himself has come down" (I.27). Augustine subscribes fully to the standard patristic doctrine of deification

23. Cf. John Cavadini, "The Structure and Intention of Augustine's *De Trinitate*," *AS* 23 (1992): 109. Cavadini claims that Augustine's insistence on the infinite distance separating God and humanity, an awareness to which contemplation necessarily brings us, becomes a coincident awareness of the love of God that crossed this distance.

24. Dewey J. Hoitenga, Jr., also takes vision as Augustine's characteristic term for knowledge by acquaintance and experience, although he concurs with John Burnaby that it is inadequate ("Faith Seeks Understanding," p. 295).

and would not disagree with the notion that God became human that we might become divine. Nevertheless, Book I of the *De Trinitate* locates the purpose of the Incarnation in aiding contemplation, to the extent that this facilitation becomes the heart of Christ's mediatorial role:

> The fact is that the *man Christ Jesus, mediator of God and men* (1 Tim. 2:5) . . . is going to bring them to direct sight of God, to the *face to face* vision, as the apostle calls it (1 Cor. 13:12); that is what is meant by *When he hands the kingdom over to God and the Father,* as though to say, "When he brings believers to a direct contemplation of God and the Father." (I.16)

The Mediator, moreover, also brings knowledge of himself through contemplation: "When he brings the believers to the contemplation of God and the Father, he will assuredly bring them to contemplation of himself" (I.18). Once again, contemplation implies not only possession of theological information, but apprehension of the divine persons.

The personal element of Augustine's doctrine of contemplation also underlies his view of contemplation's end. From the passages already examined, it is clear enough that we contemplate in this life; the fullness of contemplation, however, awaits the world to come: "[in heaven] we will perceive by direct contemplation" (XV.45). Indeed, contemplation forms the very substance of paradise: "eternal life consists in that contemplation by which God is seen not to one's undoing but to everlasting joy [qua non ad poenam uidetur deus sed ad gaudium sempiternum]" (I.31); "In that contemplation, then, *God will be all in all* (1 Cor. 15:28), because nothing further will be desired of him; to be illumined and rejoiced by him will be enough" (I.20). In its perfect form, contemplation will bring communion with the divine persons, a communion that brings illumination and joy. It is because paradisal joy forms the core of contemplation that it can also transform the saints in *this* life: "it is the contemplation of [what is unchangeable and everlasting] that makes us happy or blessed" (XIII.2). It makes us happy, that is, *in via.*

Such statements will seem mere commonplaces if the reader does not bear in mind the specific content Augustine gives to contemplation, for if we associate it today chiefly with prayer, we associate it also with the vision of God in the next life. Since in theological circles paradise is an only slightly less unfashionable subject than prayer, we are not surprised to find that modern theologians have little to say of contemplation. When we recall, however, that Augustine equates contemplation with knowledge of God we realize he is not simply equating seeing God with a future consummation, but saying that happiness in *this* life consists in the knowledge of God. In Augustine's terms, therefore, to uncouple spirituality and theology implies no less than the uncoupling of this life from the next. If our perfection and consummation consist in knowledge of God, then knowledge of God, in forms including such speculative meditations as the *De Trinitate,* must form an integral part of the life of every Christian this side of heaven.[25]

Because contemplation connects the knowledge of this life and that of the next, it is centrally concerned with truth. Certainly, a perfect and immediate grasp of the truth properly characterizes the next life: "There we shall see the truth without any difficulty, and enjoy it in all its clarity and certitude. There, there will be nothing for us to seek with the reasonings of the mind, but we will perceive by direct contemplation" (XV.45). Because contemplation is a vision of the truth, enjoyed perfectly in the next life and sought in this with the "reasonings of the mind," it cannot be assimilated to the subjective and emotional varieties of spirituality that abound in our day. It is personal encounter, but not encounter with oneself, personal knowledge but not knowledge of oneself.[26] Contemplation links the search for truth with all forms of seeking God, because truth can come only from God: "the reason why it was not God the Father, not the Holy Spirit, not the trinity itself, but only the Son who is the Word of God that became flesh (although it was the trinity that accomplished this), is that we might live rightly by our word fol-

25. Thus I would reject Catherine Mowry LaCugna's claim that Augustine's contemplative approach to the Trinity led to a split between *oikonomia* and *theologia* (*God for Us: The Trinity and Christian Life* [San Francisco: Harper, 1991], pp. 7-8). It is precisely the contemplative element in his thought that permits the drawing of a close, unbreakable bond between the inner life of the Trinity and human salvation. Cf. Gilson's notion that for Augustine wisdom is always identified with happiness (*The Christian Philosophy of Saint Augustine,* p. 3) and that contemplation is the *sine qua non* of happiness (p. 8), Cooper's claim that in the final chapter of the *De Trinitate* Augustine deliberately connects his theological view of salvation with the philosophic quest for wisdom ("The Basic Philosophical and Theological Notions of Saint Augustine," p. 104), and Burnaby's idea that knowing and loving God constitute a kind of "possession" of God (*Amor Dei,* p. 252).

26. Cf. Dom Cuthbert Butler: "Truth for Augustine means not subjective or logical truth . . . but objective and ontological truth . . . [which] he ultimately identifies with Divine Being" (*Western Mysticism,* pp. 53-54). Cf. also Cavadini, who claims for Augustine that our contemplative regard is pushed outward ("The Structure and Intention of Augustine's *De Trinitate,*" p. 109), and John M. Rist: our own remembering, knowing, and loving points beyond ourselves to God (*Augustine: Ancient Thought Baptized* [Cambridge: Cambridge University Press, 1994], p. 90). *Pace* A. C. Lloyd, "On Augustine's Concept of a Person," in *Augustine: A Collection of Critical Essays,* ed. R. A. Markus (Garden City, N.Y.: Anchor, 1972 [Modern Studies in Philosophy]). Lloyd denies that Augustine says the nature of a human person is an analogy of the Trinity (p. 191) and in consequence claims: "the love, the understanding, the knowledge that chiefly interest Augustine are each man's self-love, self-understanding, and self-knowledge" (p. 204).

lowing and imitating his example; that is, by our having no falsehood either in the contemplation or in the operation of our word" (XV.20).[27] The contemplation that enables right living also enables true knowledge: the operation of the intellect is inseparable from that of the will.

Augustine acknowledges the dangers of precisely the kind of speculation he undertakes: "I am fully aware how many fancies the human heart can breed — what is my own heart, after all, but a human heart?" (IV.1). If he continues despite these dangers, it is because he trusts the One he seeks to preserve him from error:

> But what I pray for to the *God of my heart* (Psalm 73:26) is that no such fancies should spill over into these pages masquerading as solidly true, but that the only things to appear on them should be what has come to me wafted by the fresh air of his truth. . . . I breathe in his truth the more deeply, the more clearly I perceive there is nothing changeable about it . . . like the wandering fancies of our spirits, not only in time and not even in imagined space, like some of the reasonings of our minds. For God's essence, by which he is, has absolutely nothing changeable about its eternity or its truth or its will; there truth is eternal and love is eternal; there love is true and eternity true; there eternity is lovely and truth is lovely too [et cara ibi est aeternitas, cara ueritas]. (IV.1)

The reader who knows the *De Trinitate* realizes that while Augustine speaks there of the essence of God, he is also speaking of the God in three persons, for truth and love are appropriated to the Word and Spirit. The knowledge of God that he pursues in the pages of the *De Trinitate* is therefore a direct encounter with these divine persons, an encounter that not only provides knowledge, but also transforms the knower, inaugurating her everlasting joy in truth and love.[28]

Not love and knowledge distinctly and separately, but knowledge and love *in relation* binds the Trinity together in Augustine's view; in turn, knowledge and love in relation bind human persons to God through contemplation. The distinctive element of Augustine's theological epistemology, then, is

27. Timothy Maschke notes two contrasting emphases in Augustine's writings on prayer: contemplative meditation and discursive communication, implying these activities are distinct. The reading suggested here is that these two elements are united both in the contemplation that is prayer and the contemplation that is theology. Cf. "Augustine's Theology of Prayer: Gracious Conformation," p. 431, in *APFS*.

28. Cf. Donald E. Daniels, "The Argument of the *De Trinitate*," p. 53. He maintains that the argument of the *De Trinitate* moves the believer-reader's attention from topics of faith concerning the Trinity (information-about) to a place of understanding.

its proclamation of the necessary unity of knowledge and love, its refusal to *be* an epistemology in any sense recognizable to the secular mind, but rather to be an epistemology based on a personal encounter with the unity of Wisdom and Love that is the blessed Trinity.

VII. Conclusion

The *De Trinitate* has often been read as the archetypal presentation of the Western doctrine of the Trinity, less frequently, and generally less appreciatively, for its natural theology of *vestigia Trinitatis.* Its real significance, however, may lie in its conjunction of theology and anthropology, and it is at this intersection that we find the fullness of its epistemology. Augustine's treatise on the Trinity may be seen as an extended meditation on the unique nature of the knowledge of God, and it implicitly makes several claims about the distinctive character of such knowledge. First, if knowledge of the Trinity is one person's knowledge of other persons, it must differ essentially from knowledge of things or ideas. Second, if our relation to God mirrors the interrelations of the divine persons, then we are bonded to God through both knowledge and love, and these constituents of our relation to God are inseparable from one another.

The essential characteristics of personal knowledge (knowledge-about and acquaintance-with) emerge in Augustine's thought in the form of his dual emphasis on knowledge and love. Both, he insists, are essential and inseparable; the ground of their necessity and inseparability is their relation to the trinitarian persons. The weariless search for *vestigia* constitutes an attempt to find a ground for human knowledge of God by asserting that similarity which to a Neo-Platonist is the necessary condition of all knowledge. One need not accept Augustine's Neo-Platonic assumptions for the *De Trinitate's* epistemology to retain its significance and value, however. The psychological analogies function to help us *understand* the Trinity; they are the prelude to knowledge and knowledge is the precondition of any true love.

Through knowledge and love, the *De Trinitate* suggests, we are united to God as the divine persons are to one another. Augustine's treatise therefore instantiates a mystical theology, that is, one that reflects on the conditions of the possibility of humanity's union with God. Implicitly, it also states a relation between spheres of Christian life that have in our time been sundered from one another. Because personal apprehension of God must include both knowledge and love, Augustine's epistemology indicates that we cannot separate theology from spirituality, as we have done increasingly since the Enlightenment. In Augustine's terms, such a separation is not merely undesirable, it is literally impossible, because what is left after the separation is either profitless (knowledge without love) or meaningless (love without knowledge).

Augustine's treatise thus chastises both contemporary theology and contemporary spirituality. To the proponents of spirituality it says that the practice of prayer, whether individual or corporate, mental or vocal, is a sham when it is drained of the engagement of the intellect. Christian spirituality, on this reading, is not a quest for the divine within, if one takes that quest to be an exploration of one's spiritual self rather than contemplation of the transcendent and triune God revealed in Scripture. Such self-awareness is certainly not Augustine's end in seeking *vestigia;* indeed, nothing could be further from the spirit of his thought. He stresses again and again the fundamental differences between God and humanity, making clear that his reflection on the *vestigia* does not assume that one can attain knowledge of God by purely natural means. The first, and greater, part of the *De Trinitate* concerns the divine Trinity, which Augustine never suggests can be known on the analogy of the structure of human consciousness. His analogies point, not to an essential similarity between humanity and God, but to the way in which human knowledge of God is necessarily conditioned by its object.

Yet if the *De Trinitate* provides a corrective to a theologically unfounded spirituality, it reproves modern conceptions of theology just as much. It suggests that theology, even at its most technical, should be firmly grounded in an understanding of the Christian life as one of both speech and contemplation, adoration and instruction. We come to God through God, and while the divinely conditioned nature of our spiritual ascent does not preclude our using our knowledge of the created as an aid in grasping the mystery of the Uncreated, we can have no authentic knowledge of God without intimacy with the One we seek to know. Likewise, the outward functions of theology, its uses for apologetic and didactic ends, do not preclude an inward function as a contemplative act.

The implications of the treatise in this respect are many. First, it suggests that a spiritually silent Christian theology is as anomalous as a theologically vacuous Christian spirituality. Contemplation is neither the statement of a set of postulates discovered by the assiduous effort of the human mind, nor some sort of doctrinally denuded reverie. Theologians need to reflect on the significance of doctrine for spiritual life, pressing the spiritual implications of their theology. Second, if theology is a species of contemplation, it must have the character of both humility and charity. Augustine is aware that he addresses those who disagree with him about the very things he believes most important. Yet the *De Trinitate* never loses its tone of adoration. It is hard to see how a contemplative theology could be polemical, let alone sneering in tone, and modern theology would do well to retrieve the conviction that as charity and truth are one in God, so ought they to be one in Christian talk about God. Thus, while the *De Trinitate* predates the need for ecumenical dialogue, it provides a model for Christian theological discussion in an age of divisions both inter-ecclesial and intra-ecclesial.

Theology understood as contemplation would also correct the anthropocentrism of much contemporary theology. Augustine indeed considers the human soul, but does so as a means to better apprehend God. Whether he begins from God revealed in scripture, as in Books I-VIII, or from humanity, as in Books IX-XV, he arrives at the same point: adoration of the Trinity. The question he answers is not the one arising from the hoary methodological debate between top-down and bottom-up procedures, but the question of theology's end, which for Augustine is the blessed Trinity alone. Contemplation is personal in the sense that it is one person's loving intellectual regard of another, not in the sense of its being individualistic or narcissistic. The object of Christian contemplation is not the self, but an Other, a trinity of persons who together are self-communicating Truth. Contemplation fosters the apprehension of God as Other, the realization that Christian truth is to be found by engagement with the Trinity, not by looking within or even by looking to creation.

Theology understood as contemplation would therefore be neither solely systematic nor solely mystical, but both simultaneously. Contemplation unites theology and prayer, and both theology and prayer may best be understood as contemplative acts.[29] Such a view is neither original nor unique to Augustine. On the contrary, the centrality of contemplation is evident in both Eastern and Western theologians from the earliest Fathers to the Middle Ages. It is modern theology that has lost the concept of contemplation, and with it the sense that the knowledge of God differs radically from knowledge of a subject or discipline. It is this contemplative character that modern theology

29. Earl C. Muller points out that for Augustine the success of the "project" of the *De Trinitate* pivots on the ability of the Christian to mount a sort of contemplative ascent that governs the latter half of the work ("The Priesthood of Christ in Book IV of the *De Trinitate*," *APFS*, p. 135). Muller's view of the kind of unity to which the treatise points — of the individual, of marriage, and of the community — nevertheless differs considerably from the kind of unity stressed here. Cf. also J. F. Worthen, "Augustine's *De trinitate* and Anselm's *Proslogion*." Augustine and Anselm are similarly concerned to create texts that not only transfer knowledge but engage their readers in the process of coming to know, that will not only inform, but rather, reform the careful reader (p. 517).

needs to recover. As a consequence of such recovery, spirituality, currently so bereft of doctrinal content, would once again be theologically grounded and nourished; in a church now so battered by the rhetoric of anger and accusation, discourse between Christians of differing views would be tempered; and above all, theology itself would be restored to its true character as a discipline of adoration.

The contemplative character of theology points to not only a disciplinary, but an existential unity. Just as the contemplation that is theology cannot be separated from the contemplation that is prayer, so an authentically Christian existence consists in a unity, in virtue of which this life is inseparably wedded to the next. We can no more rightly separate our life now from our life in the Age to Come than we can separate our minds from our wills, and the practice of theology in this life can be true only when it partakes of the contemplation of the Age to Come. To see the inseparability of this life from the next, and the centrality of contemplation in both, implies a revision to the contemporary understanding of theology: its native habitat is not the classroom, the library, or the debating chamber, but the courts of heaven. It is the rubric of contemplation that allows us to understand that theological speech in this life is inexorably bonded to the vision of God in the next. Theology understood as contemplation is therefore the consummate discipline, the discipline shaped by paradise because it belongs most essentially to paradise.

6. Baptism

A Dramatic Journey into God's Dazzling Light: Baptismal Catechesis and the Shaping of Christian Practical Wisdom

L. GREGORY JONES

In his *Letters and Papers from Prison,* Dietrich Bonhoeffer suggested that Christian theology ought to reclaim the central insights of the early church's practices of the *disciplina arcani,* or "discipline of secrecy." He believed that this discipline provided crucial space for formation and discernment appropriate to Christian living in the world on the one hand, and for protecting the mysteries of the faith from being profaned on the other. Of course, Bonhoeffer's suggestion did not arise out of speculative reflection on the Christian past; rather, he was struggling to come to terms with a German Christian culture in which Christian language and practices had become impoverished, if not completely co-opted.

Indeed, in one of his famous (and enigmatic!) passages, Bonhoeffer makes the following observation:

> Reconciliation and redemption, regeneration and the Holy Spirit, love of our enemies, cross and resurrection, life in Christ and Christian discipleship — all these things are so difficult and so remote that we hardly venture any more to speak of them. In the traditional words and acts we suspect that there may be something quite new and revolutionary, though we cannot as yet grasp or express it. That is our own fault. Our church, which has

> been fighting in these years only for its self-preservation, as though that were an end in itself, is incapable of taking the word of reconciliation and redemption to mankind and the world. Our earlier words are therefore bound to lose their force and cease, and our being Christians today will be limited to two things: prayer and righteous action among men. . . . It is not for us to prophesy the day (though the day will come) when men will once more be called so to utter the word of God that the world will be changed and renewed by it. It will be a new language, perhaps quite non-religious, but liberating and redeeming — as was Jesus' language; it will shock people and yet overcome them by its power; it will be the language of a new righteousness and truth, proclaiming God's peace with men and the coming of his kingdom. "They shall fear and tremble because of all the good and all the prosperity I provide for it" (Jer. 33:9). Till then the Christian cause will be a silent and hidden affair, but there will be those who pray and do right and wait for God's own time.[1]

Bonhoeffer was troubled that Christians had been unable to resist the Nazis and had failed to communicate the gospel of reconciliation and redemption to the world. He therefore thought that the "silence" and "hiddenness" of the discipline of secrecy would enable Christian language and practices to be purified and renewed so as to provide a more effective witness. This would involve practices of worship as well as other practices of discipleship, including "righteous action" in response to God's action in Christ.[2]

And yet, Bonhoeffer was also acutely concerned that such a discipline not involve a withdrawal from the world or some kind of secret enclave in isolation from the world. He did not want to revert to "thinking in terms of two spheres," namely the church on the one hand and the world on the other. The Church is to stand "in the middle of the village," not on the boundaries; it is to be a Church for others.[3] Likewise, Bonhoeffer thought that disciplined engagements with God cannot involve a *deus ex machina* brought in to resolve difficult questions, much less the privatized use whereby "God" is taken to mean whatever I — in my own personal spirituality — want or need it to

1. Dietrich Bonhoeffer, *Letters and Papers from Prison,* ed. E. Bethge, trans. R. Fuller, F. Clark, et al. (New York: Macmillan, 1971), pp. 299-300. The two brief references to the "discipline of secrecy" are found on pp. 281 and 286.

2. To be sure, there are some interpretive issues in Bonhoeffer's perspective, and in the passage quoted above, which I do not adequately articulate here. For a more complete discussion, including the suggestion that Bonhoeffer's account in the *Letters and Papers* had already been anticipated in his life at Finkenwalde, see my *Embodying Forgiveness* (Grand Rapids: Eerdmans, 1995), ch. 1.

3. *Letters and Papers from Prison,* pp. 282 and 382.

mean. On the contrary, disciplined engagements require the formation of people who allow ourselves to be put into question by the God of Jesus Christ, the God who is the maker and consummator of all that is. Such a formation, Bonhoeffer seemed to suggest, needs to be reclaimed; and he noted, albeit enigmatically, that the ancient church's practices of the *disciplina arcani* offer significant resources for so doing.

More recently, Stanley Hauerwas (in some writings, with William Willimon) and Alasdair MacIntyre have also turned to examples from the early church to suggest the need for new disciplines and practices of formation. For Hauerwas, this is part of his critique of what he takes to be the Church's accommodation to the cultures around it, an accommodation not so much focused — as with Bonhoeffer — on the specificities of his own cultural time and place (although it is sometimes that), as on broader judgments about political and epistemological liberalism and, most comprehensively, the accommodations that he thinks have occurred since the Constantinian turn in the fourth century. So Hauerwas's interest in the practices of the early church are part of his project of (a) emphasizing the importance of character for philosophical and theological ethics, and (b) reclaiming the significance of Christian communities centered on the story of Jesus.[4] So, for example, Hauerwas and Willimon emphasize the importance of sponsors for catechesis, and Hauerwas structures his basic course in Christian Ethics at Duke Divinity School around the liturgy.[5]

MacIntyre's appeal to the early church is more puzzling, but no less important to his project. In a passage at the close of *After Virtue* that has been frequently cited, MacIntyre suggests that the only way to cope with the "new dark ages" that are "already upon us" is to discover another — and undoubtedly very different — Saint Benedict.[6] This proposal, which to my knowledge

4. I have suggested that these two aspects of Hauerwas's overall project have never been adequately brought together. See the Introduction to my *Transformed Judgment: Toward a Trinitarian Account of the Moral Life* (Notre Dame: University of Notre Dame Press, 1990). Since that time, Hauerwas has moved in some significant ways toward doing so; however, as I will suggest below, he still has not adequately absorbed the riches of ancient Christian practices and, more specifically, their unrelenting center on the mystery of the triune God. Were he to do so, I think he could provide a more nuanced — and, I think, engaged — analysis of Christian living in relation to specific cultural contexts than is typical in his writing.

5. See Stanley Hauerwas and William Willimon, *Resident Aliens* (Nashville: Abingdon, 1989), pp. 106ff.

6. Undoubtedly part of the reason MacIntyre wrote that it would need to be a "very different" St. Benedict is that, at the time he wrote those words, MacIntyre was not a Christian. The tenor of MacIntyre's more recent writings, after his return to the Roman Catholic Church, might suggest that he thinks the Benedictine model, supplemented and shaped by a Thomistic

MacIntyre has not taken up in later writing, is linked to his comprehensive rejection of the ethics and politics of modernity — hence his reference to the "new dark ages." Further, MacIntyre's proposal hinges in crucial ways on the formative significance of *practices* — suggesting that he would not be as interested in a new Saint Benedict as he would in the practices of new — and quite different? — Benedictine communities.[7] Yet, curiously, even as MacIntyre has turned in more recent writing to a defense of Thomistic ethics and reasoning (and perhaps a modification or rejection of his appeal to Benedict?), he has not adequately attended to the ways in which specifically Christian practices, centered upon the triune God, shape conceptions of practical wisdom.

At the same time that Hauerwas and MacIntyre have been writing, the Roman Catholic Church has been reclaiming some of the practices of the ancient church in its Rite of Christian Initiation for Adults (RCIA). This has emerged, at least to a significant extent, out of the belief that people coming into the church need more extensive catechesis than they have been receiving. This is a concern that is not peculiar either to Roman Catholicism or to adult converts; the increasingly pervasive loss of Christian identity among Christians generally is a recurring topic — among seminary professors about their students, among pastors about their parishioners, and even among cultural commentators about the churches. Yet the Roman Catholic practices of RCIA are not, at least in any obvious sense, linked to the comprehensive criticisms of modernity that are found in diverse but overlapping ways in the work of Hauerwas and MacIntyre.

How, then, should we understand the diverse yet seemingly overlapping interests in the practices of the ancient church found in Bonhoeffer, Hauerwas, MacIntyre, the RCIA — and other kindred folks? Are these interests part of a similar phenomenon, namely a disenchantment with either the theory or the results of "liberal" culture or practice? Or are they emerging as the result of a perceived "end" of Christendom, and the requirement of new (or renewed) modes of practice to deal with these changes? Are they signs of

---

ethics, is more serviceable than he suggests in *After Virtue*. See *After Virtue*, 2nd ed. (Notre Dame: University of Notre Dame Press, 1984), p. 263.

7. MacIntyre's definition of *practices* is as follows: "by a 'practice' I am going to mean any coherent and complex form of socially established cooperative human activity through which goods internal to that form of activity are realized in the course of trying to achieve those standards of excellence that are appropriate to, and partially definitive of, that form of activity, with the result that human powers to achieve excellence, and human conceptions of the ends and goods involved, are systematically extended." MacIntyre further suggests that his notion of practices must be situated within the narrative order of a single human life, and within traditions. See Alasdair MacIntyre, *After Virtue*, 2nd ed., p. 187.

either a new "sectarianism" or, in their focus on liturgy and tradition, a new "conservatism"? Or, less comprehensively, are they a return to neglected resources that can enrich our practices of Christian living? Or, perhaps, are they actually independent interests that only partially overlap with one another, suggesting that no single explanation will suffice?

At the same time, we also need to ask whether the interests are warranted. Are there significant things to be learned from the practices of the ancient church for our own time? If so, what are they? Are there dangers to be avoided? If so, what are they? Even the ways in which I have phrased these latter questions, however, already betray a methodological judgment about our relation to the past: that is, I suggest that we need to engage these practices found in the Christian tradition neither to glorify (and hence reify) the past, as if the issues dealt with then did and now do settle the issues, nor to caricature (and hence dismiss) the past, as though our forebears have nothing to teach us. Rather, we ought to engage the past in order to discern in the power of the Spirit, throughout the successes and failures of our histories, the ongoing genesis of the Church's life — and to draw appropriate analogies from that discernment for our own situations, contexts, and lives.

Of course one of the problems is that, at least in their published writings, few people concerned with Christian ethics — including Bonhoeffer, Hauerwas, and MacIntyre — have actually engaged in a sustained analysis of the practices of the early church. And most commentators on the RCIA have focused on its "liturgical" or its "educational" implications, failing to see how it might invite or even require a reshaping of key understandings within Christian theology and ethics.

I will suggest that there are remarkable implications and insights to be gained from our engagement with these texts and practices, insights for which we have been prepared by MacIntyre's emphasis on practices and traditions and Hauerwas's on the formation of character. Further, I think that the ancient practices of baptismal catechesis offer significant resources for us to rethink issues in Christian ethics where contemporary practices have become impoverished and scholarly debates have reached dead ends (or began in cul-de-sacs!). They also can help us to re-envision the shaping of Christian living in provocative and — dare I say it — exciting ways. Most comprehensively, they do so by locating Christian life in the context of the *telos* of fellowship with God. As Gregory of Nyssa put it, "To have but one purpose in life: to be called servants of God by virtue of the lives we live."[8]

8. Gregory of Nyssa, *The Life of Moses,* trans. Abraham J. Malherbe and Everett Ferguson (New York: Paulist, 1978), II.315, p. 134.

However, discovering the resources of these ancient practices of baptismal catechesis involves returning — or perhaps turning for the first time — to an examination of those texts and practices. Hence, in my first section I briefly describe the broad shape of the third- and fourth-century catechumenates. I then explore, via some programmatic suggestions, ways in which the practices of baptismal catechesis might help us reorient some of our contemporary debates within theological and philosophical ethics (as well as in other disciplines). In my conclusion, I also offer a brief assessment of why people such as Bonhoeffer, Hauerwas, and MacIntyre (and the whole program of the RCIA) have become interested in these practices — and how these practices might reshape some of our interests.

I. A Dramatic Journey: Ancient Practices of Baptismal Catechesis

The first thing that must be said is that there is no single ancient catechumenate, much less a single pattern of practices of baptismal catechesis. And, to make matters worse, we do not even have full-scale descriptions of any specific set of practices; what we have are catechumenal lectures and sermons delivered by some significant figures to congregations in their geographical areas (and the practices referred to within those lectures and sermons), along with other data gleaned from scattered sources: letters, Church-order books, hymns, and the like.[9]

Even so, there is enough extant material to be able to make some significant generalizations about these ancient practices. Though the diverse catechumenates — both diachronically over several centuries and synchronically across different geographical regions — had some different emphases, they also shared some broad commitments and practices. Further investigation and explication would be needed to sort out the important divergences

9. Thomas M. Finn has collected representative examples of these materials into two volumes, complete with introductions to each piece. See his *Early Baptism and the Catechumenate: West and East Syria,* and *Early Baptism and the Catechumenate: Italy, North Africa, and Egypt* (Collegeville, Minn.: The Liturgical Press, 1992). See also the texts from Cyril of Jerusalem, Ambrose, John Chrysostom, and Theodore of Mopsuestia that are reprinted in Edward Yarnold, S.J., *The Awe-Inspiring Rites of Initiation: The Origins of the R.C.I.A.* (Collegeville, Minn.: The Liturgical Press, 1994). For a significant "ethnographic" description of catechumenal practices in fourth-century Jerusalem, see *Egeria's Travels to the Holy Land* (Jerusalem: Ariel Publishing House, 1981).

A useful secondary analysis of many of these texts is found in Enrico Mazza, *Mystagogy,* trans. Matthew J. O'Connell (New York: Pueblo, 1989).

among the catechumenates (e.g., the extent to which initiation into the practice of baptism or Eucharist preceded explanation of the practice).

My description will focus on the catechumenate in Augustine's North Africa at the end of the fourth century and the beginning of the fifth, though many of the descriptions would apply to other catechumenates as well.[10] I focus on Augustine's engagements with the catechumenate for four reasons: first, because of his importance through the history of Christianity, particularly in the West; second, because of his pivotal influence in discussions of Christian ethics and politics, including our own contemporary situation; third, because the catechumenate I will describe takes place considerably *after* the so-called "Constantinian settlement" of the early fourth century, thus redirecting some of the discussion about practices among "early Christians"; and fourth, two helpful secondary descriptions of the North African catechumenate have appeared in recent years, providing useful summaries of often complex and disparate materials.[11]

At the heart of ancient practices of baptismal catechesis is the conviction that Christian living involves a dramatic journey of conversion, a process of turning — typically over time, and with testing — from one way of life to another. This journey typically moved through four stages, which Finn summarizes as follows: "(1) a period of preparation that emphasized instruction and testing and involved personal struggle; (2) penultimate preparations for baptism also characterized by instruction, testing, and ritual struggle; (3) baptismal immersion; and (4) post-baptismal 'homecoming' celebrations, which included the eucharist."[12]

In this context I can only offer brief descriptions of each of these stages, attempting throughout to highlight some of the salient features of these practices and texts. The first period was when those who had become seriously interested in Christianity would seek basic instruction in the Christian faith. Those whose interest increased were then entered into the catechumenate, signaled by inscription. This included formal questioning concerning the person's intention, making the sign of the cross on the forehead, exorcism, imposition of hands,

10. Indeed, Augustine's practices in North Africa were undoubtedly influenced by his own participation as a catechumen under Ambrose in Milan, Italy.

11. See Thomas M. Finn, "It Happened One Saturday Night: Ritual and Conversion in Augustine's North Africa," *Journal of the American Academy of Religion* 58, no. 4 (Winter 1990): 589-616; and William Harmless, S.J., *Augustine and the Catechumenate* (Collegeville, Minn.: The Liturgical Press, 1995). I am indebted to both for helping guide me through the thickets of Augustine's writings on these issues, and my descriptions of the North African catechumenate will closely follow Finn's compact summaries.

12. Finn, *Early Baptism and the Catechumenate*, p. 3 in both volumes.

and consumption of a tiny bit of salt. Being designated as "catechumens" meant that they could be present at worship for scriptural readings and homilies, though they would be dismissed prior to the Eucharist in order to preserve the mysteries (hence the designation of the "discipline of secrecy").

During this first period as catechumens, the focus was on instruction and a gradual inclusion into the Christian community. In fourth-century North Africa, the process typically took two years. Augustine's explanation for the lengthy time was succinct: "What is all that time for, during which they hold the name and place of catechumens, except to hear what the faith and pattern of Christian life should be?"[13] As Augustine's comment suggests, it is crucial to interpret the notion of "instruction" broadly. The "instruction" the catechumens would receive included learning Scripture through study and hearing homilies (indeed, Augustine would sometimes direct homilies specifically to catechumens and sometimes advert to the catechumens within a homily directed more broadly), *and* the shaping of their affections — "educating desire," as Robert Wilken has felicitously termed it — *and* being mentored in actual Christian living.

The homilies and other instruction in Scripture were designed to entice people into the dramatic narrative of God with God's people. Augustine recognized that people might initially show interest in Christianity for a variety of reasons, including fear or as a consequence of dreams. Whatever the reasons that brought people to interest in Christianity, Augustine sought to transform their desires through nourishment from Scripture. He used biblical characters as examples, and drew on his rhetorical training to stir genuine delight in his listeners.[14] The focus of Augustine's instructions in Scripture was not simply the mind, but the mind *and* the heart, directed toward the enjoyment of fellowship with the triune God.[15]

In addition to this "formal" instruction, catechumens were assigned sponsors whose task it was to model Christian living and to apprentice the catechumens during this period of formation. As Augustine proclaimed in

13. Augustine, *De fide et operibus,* 6.9, cited in Harmless, *Augustine and the Catechumenate,* p. 156.

14. The following passage from Origen would not have been an uncommon view among people in the early church: "Genuine transformation of life comes from reading the ancient Scriptures, learning who the just were and *imitating* them," to which he shrewdly appended the caveat, "learning who were reproved and guarding against falling under the same censure" (*Homilies on Jeremiah,* 4.5, cited in Robert L. Wilken, "Moral Formation in the Early Church," unpublished typescript, p. 10).

15. See Augustine's exposition of this theme in his *On Christian Doctrine,* trans. D. W. Robertson, Jr. (New York: Macmillan, 1958). Despite the misleading English version of the title, this is a crucial treatise for understanding Augustine's approach to the formation and education of Christians generally.

one of his sermons, "Christ is announced through Christian friends."[16] As this apprenticeship occurred, it was presumed that the catechumens' patterns of life would exhibit — albeit often slowly and painfully — transformations in their thinking, feeling, and living. Finn refers to a passage from Augustine's near-contemporary Quodvultdeus, in which Quodvultdeus chided both catechumens and Christians who wanted to keep in view both the saving scriptural "spectacles" of mystery and miracle and the withering far-from-scriptural spectacles of theater, racetrack, and the fights.[17]

Catechumens who appeared ready for baptism were encouraged to submit their names at the beginning of Lent. Those who did so began the second pivotal stage in their journey.[18] Those who became formally enrolled did so as part of a liturgy in which Psalm 42 [Septuagint Psalm 41] would be sung, including the famous words: "As a deer longs for flowing streams, / so my soul longs for you, / O God. / My soul thirsts for God, / for the living God. / When shall I come and behold / the face of God?" (Psalm 42:1-2). This liturgical practice linked the process of enrollment to the catechumens' transformation of desire — to live in communion with the triune God.

Those who enrolled were identified as "competentes." During Lent, there was a time of formal questioning about their lives; significantly, Augustine followed Hippolytus in asking the questions not directly to the catechumens, but to the sponsors. Yet Augustine used these questions not simply for testing; they also served as an occasion for Augustine to learn about the people's experiences to help him rhetorically in shaping his catechesis.[19]

The focus of this second period was on prayer, further instruction in Scripture, exorcism, and a strict observance of Lent: no wine, no meat, no baths, no public entertainment, and celibacy within marriage.[20] During this time the homilies in worship focused particularly on moral formation. As Augustine put it in a sermon to competentes, "We teach with words, you make progress with your deeds."[21] This theme, which focused on the

16. Augustine, cited in Harmless, *Augustine and the Catechumenate*, p. 152.

17. See Finn, "It Happened One Saturday Night," p. 591.

18. As the number of people affiliated with Christianity increased, a problem appeared: many catechumens would delay baptism for extensive periods. This was a status of "nominal" Christianity, neither pagan nor subject to the full expectations of being Christian; in the East, John Chrysostom and Gregory of Nazianzus used both scathing criticism and enticing rhetoric to discourage delays in baptism and to encourage becoming formally enrolled.

19. See the discussion in Harmless, *Augustine and the Catechumenate*, pp. 113-14.

20. See the discussion in Finn, "It Happened One Saturday Night," p. 591, with references.

21. Augustine, Sermon 226.1; translation mine (with thanks for assistance to Angela Russell Christman).

competentes, also had an effect on the congregations more generally. After all, baptismal catechesis served not only to initiate new persons into the dazzling light of God's reign, it also could renew the practices of the larger congregation.[22]

More generally, the Lenten period combined for the competentes an intensive period of renunciation with a continuous deepening of their formation in relation to the triune God. The renunciations entailed both an inward cleansing and an outward mission toward engaging injustice. Often this renunciation of the devil was linked to the Exodus narrative, identifying the work of the devil with Pharaoh and the people's sins with the Egyptian armies drowned in the Red Sea. In the following passage describing baptism in the context of forgiveness, Augustine wove together a complex set of biblical images about overcoming sin and evil through the Exodus and the cross:

> Your sins will be like the Egyptians following the Israelites, pursuing you only up to the Red Sea. What does up to the Red Sea mean? Up to the font, consecrated by the cross and blood of Christ. For, because that font is red, it reddens [the water]. . . . Baptism is signified by the sign of the cross, that is, by the water in which you are immersed and through which you pass, as it were, in the Red Sea. Your sins are your enemies. They follow you, but only up to the Red Sea. When you have entered, you will escape; they will be destroyed, just as the Egyptians were engulfed by the waters while the Israelites escaped on dry land.[23]

As Augustine preached this, he drew his listeners into the dramatic narrative of God's dealings with God's people. The hearers were invited to see themselves as participants in a grand "theodrama" (to deploy von Balthasar's term), and to renounce sin and evil wherever it is found.

Most dramatically for the competentes, the renunciation of sin and evil involved both exorcisms and the event known as the "scrutiny," a physical and psychological examination that culminated in the renunciation of the devil and all his works. Quodvultdeus described the rite as follows:

> From a secret place you were each presented before the entire church, and then with your head bowed, which was proudly upright before, and stand-

22. Note Augustine's description that in his sermons he presented a "cross-weave" of doctrine and of moral admonition and that "both were given to catechumens, both to the faithful"; in this way, the "catechumens were instructed," while the "faithful were roused from forgetfulness" (*De fide et operibus,* 7.11, cited in Harmless, *Augustine and the Catechumenate,* p. 156).

23. Augustine, Sermon 213.8, cited in Harmless, *Augustine and the Catechumenate,* p. 282.

> ing barefoot on goat skin, the scrutiny was performed on you, and while the humble and most noble Christ was invoked, the proud devil was rooted out of you. All of you were humble of demeanor and humbly you pleaded by praying, chanting and saying, "Probe me, Lord, and know my heart" (Psalm 139:3). Then the competens [sic] says: "I renounce the devil, his pomps, and his angels."[24]

The result of the rite of scrutiny was that, in Augustine's words, the competentes were "free from their former master *(immunis)* and healthy *(sanitas)* in body and heart."[25]

As Lent moved toward Holy Week, the competentes received instruction in both the Creed and the Lord's Prayer. In North Africa, instruction in the Creed would involve both memorization of the actual words (typically, guided by their sponsors) and instruction concerning their meaning. Part of the reason for memorization was that it helped to preserve the secrecy of the mystery; but, more deeply, Augustine thought that memorizing the Creed would help them internalize the truth of God and God's ways.[26] Referring to Jeremiah 31 and the law written on the heart, Augustine observed:

> The creed is learned by listening; it is written, not on tablets nor on any material, but on the heart. He who has called you to his Kingdom and glory will grant that, when you have been reborn by his grace and by the Holy Spirit, it will be written in your hearts, so that you may love what you believe and that, through love, faith may work in you and that you — no longer fearing punishment like slaves, but loving justice like the freeborn — may become pleasing to the Lord God, the giver of all good things.[27]

For Augustine, doctrinal clarity is crucial and must be set in the context of Christian living, learned and discerned in the context of other practices. That is, for Augustine there was a reciprocal relation between Christian living and understanding the Creed: "May this belief imbue your hearts and guide you in professing it. On hearing this, believe so that you may understand, so that by putting into practice what you believe you may be able to understand it."[28]

24. Quodvultdeus, *Sermo de symbolo* 1.1.4-7, cited in Wilken, "Moral Formation in the Early Church," typescript p. 16.

25. Augustine, cited in Finn, "It Happened One Saturday Night," p. 597.

26. See Augustine's account of his own recitation of the Creed at his baptism in Book VII of the *Confessions.*

27. Augustine, Sermon 212.2, cited in Harmless, *Augustine and the Catechumenate,* p. 276.

28. Augustine, Sermon 214.10, cited in Harmless, *Augustine and the Catechumenate,* p. 277. Augustine's formulation here has broader implications in his work concerning the im-

The competentes already had been learning to pray, but during the week preceding baptism instruction in the Lord's Prayer was a particular focus. Augustine's instructions tended to focus most on the petition concerning forgiveness. In part, this is because of its prominence in Matthew's text (Matt. 6:14-15); but in part it was because he knew that lack of forgiveness was a local vice, and so this petition seemed "especially applicable" to the people. Indeed, Augustine noted in one of his sermons that his people tended to bring their fierce resentments and their desires for revenge to prayer: "Each day, people come, bend their knees, touch the earth with their foreheads, sometimes moistening their faces with tears, and in all this great humility and distress say: 'Lord, avenge me. Kill my enemy.'" Augustine insisted that his listeners recognize that their enemies were also children of God, and told them that, when praying for those enemies, "Let your prayer be against the malice of your enemy; may his malice die, but may he live. . . . If his malice should die, then you would have lost an enemy and gained a friend."[29]

Augustine emphasized that God would forgive them only if they also forgave others. Further, Augustine stressed that the Lord's Prayer offered a "daily baptism" for forgiveness, noting that he too was a sinner who needed the cleansing of forgiveness: "You might ask, 'And you, too?' I [must] answer back: 'Yes, me too!' 'You, reverend bishop — you, a debtor?' 'Yes, I am debtor as you are.'"[30] And Augustine also linked prayer to practice, most typically by linking the importance of forgiveness to justice — specifically, loving the neighbor through sharing material resources.

On Easter morning, the third stage of the journey occurred: the baptismal immersion itself. Finn describes the drama of this event:

> 1) baptismal water was consecrated; 2) the competentes processed to the font while chanting the now familiar Psalm 41 (42); 3) they removed their garments (the course leather penitential tunic); 4) they responded to a final inquiry into their faith and firm will as they stood waist-deep in the font, and 5) they were immersed three times in the name of the Father, of the Son, and of the Holy Spirit. When they emerged the bishop imposed his hand on them, anointed their heads with chrism, and traced the sign of the cross on their foreheads, probably also with chrism. The newly bap-

---

portance of authority in relation to reason, an issue particularly pertinent to his arguments with the Manicheans. It also suggests the importance of "submitting" to participation in disciplined practices as a necessary part of learning to understand what it means to be a Christian.

29. Augustine, Sermons 56.13; 211.6; and 56.14; cited in Harmless, *Augustine and the Catechumenate,* pp. 290-91.

30. Augustine, Sermon 56.11, cited in Harmless, *Augustine and the Catechumenate,* p. 293.

> tized then dressed in white, including a linen head cover. They then received a baptismal candle and the embrace of the congregation.[31]

After the baptisms were completed, they celebrated their first Eucharist, where the newly baptized received a cup of milk and honey. After that service, the newly baptized returned later on Easter morning for a second Eucharist (and perhaps in the afternoon for a third). In Augustine's homilies for the whole congregation on Easter morning, he pointed to the newly baptized, noting that they themselves had become the first day of a new creation; they who "were once darkness" were now "light in the Lord" (Eph. 5:8).[32] And he called them to live in that light.

With the celebration of these Eucharists on Easter Sunday, the newly baptized had moved into the fourth stage of their journeys of conversion. As a part of their "homecoming," the newly baptized received a new name to signify their new life in Christ. Further, their homecoming typically included liturgies and continuing instruction over a period of eight days. For those eight days, they continued to wear white robes and came each day for a celebration of the Eucharist, including a homily. The newly baptized were given pride of place in these liturgies, as their white garments testified to the completion of their journey into the dazzling light of God's reign. They served as living icons of God's new Creation.

The primary concern of Augustine, and others in his position, at this point was whether the people would continue to walk in the ways of light after this catechetical journey into baptism had been completed.[33] As Augustine saw it, the only cloud on the horizon was the question of how to keep unstained the inner renovation symbolized by their robes, which they would wear for the last time on the octave day of their baptism: would they also put away what had been accomplished in baptism?[34] Augustine reminded the congregation that the neophytes would continue to need mentoring as they ventured forth into the world without their robes.

> You see: today, the *infantes* mix with the faithful — as if flying out of the nest. It is necessary then that we birth-laborers address them. As you know,

31. Finn, "It Happened One Saturday Night," p. 594.

32. See Augustine, Sermons 225 and 226; see also the discussion in Harmless, *Augustine and the Catechumenate,* pp. 313-14.

33. It is important to remember, however, that their journey of conversion would never be fully complete; it would continue as an ongoing process throughout Christian living, as Augustine's reference to the Lord's Prayer as a "daily baptism" signifies.

34. This is the focus of Augustine's sermons 259 and 260. I am indebted to Finn, "It Happened One Saturday Night," p. 594, for this way of phrasing Augustine's concern.

> brothers and sisters, when young swallows . . . begin to fly out of the nest, their mothers flap around them noisily and, with dutiful chirpings, testify to dangers their children face.

Further, Augustine was more worried about the influence unfaithful Christians would have on these neophytes than he was about the effects of pagan society. In the same sermon, he noted: "We know that many who are called 'faithful' live badly and that their mores do not square with the grace they have received; that they praise God with the tongue and blaspheme him with their lives."[35] Augustine also warned the neophytes about specific vices and "thorns" they needed to guard against, including business fraud and usury, drunkenness and luxurious living, lying and gossip, consulting fortune tellers and wearing amulets, fornication and adultery.

Even amidst the dangers, many of the newly baptized continued along the journey of holiness toward full communion with God. Indeed, by the time the catechumens had passed through the various stages of baptismal catechesis, they not only desired new life in Christ, they had already begun to see transformations occurring in their lives — transformations accomplished by the Holy Spirit, yet not apart from the disciplines and practices the new believers had been initiated into through their catechumenate.

Even so, Augustine did not offer the newly baptized any illusions about life on the far side of baptism; drawing on the Exodus imagery so common in baptism, he reminded them that while they had crossed the Red Sea, they were not yet in the Promised Land. Desert wanderings still lay ahead of them. Yet Augustine reminded the neophytes that they had been initiated into eschatological living; he pointed to the Octave, the eighth day, as a symbol for the new life in the Kingdom: "Today is a great sacrament, [a sign] for us of unending joy. Today itself will pass away, but the life it symbolizes will not pass away. . . . For this day, the Octave, symbolizes the new life at the world's end."[36] This eighth day, the day of Christ's resurrection, thus focused the neophytes' attention on the destiny — the *telos* — of human life: the unending

35. Augustine, Sermon 376A.2, cited in Harmless, *Augustine and the Catechumenate,* p. 332. Note also the following passage from John Chrysostom in the Christian East: "I see many after their baptism living more carelessly than the uninitiated, having nothing particular to distinguish them in their way of life. It is, you see for this cause, that neither in the market nor in the Church is it possible to know quickly who is a believer and who an unbeliever; unless one be present at the time of the mystery, and see the one sort dismissed, the others remaining within — whereas they ought to be distinguished *not by their place, but by their way of life.*" *In S. Matthaei evangelium,* 4.14, cited in Harmless, p. 74.

36. Augustine, Sermon 259.1-2, cited in Harmless, *Augustine and the Catechumenate,* p. 334.

joy of fellowship in communion with the triune God. As he called them to keep their "concentration fixed on the eighth day," so he also reminded them of the power and the importance of eschatological living — particularly on behalf of the poor.

Overall, this dramatic journey of baptismal catechesis highlighted the centrality of initiation into the spectacular drama of God's creating, redeeming, and consummating work. Thomas Finn draws on Quodvultdeus's description of the "new spectacles" of Christian life to describe the process as follows: "Here in Roman Africa at the end of the fourth century and in the early fifth the ritual drama of baptism and its Lenten preparations were the *spectacula christiana* — the new theater, the new racetrack, and the new boxing ring. It is difficult to overestimate the impact of this long-extended ritual drama on convert and community alike."[37] Through a combination of scriptural preaching and teaching, formal instruction, dramatic ritual, spiritual direction, and apprenticeship in the deeds of holy living, the practices of baptismal catechesis fostered a spectacular vision — and, more importantly, embodiment — of what it means to become part of the journey into the reign of God's dazzling light.

II. Living in God's Dazzling Light: The Shaping of Christian Practical Wisdom

The ancient practices of baptismal catechesis, exemplified in this description from late fourth- and early fifth-century North Africa, display many of the themes that have been reintroduced into contemporary philosophical and theological ethics by such scholars as MacIntyre and Hauerwas. There is an emphasis on particular practices, situated within the narrative order of a single human life (albeit one that reaches a dramatic turning point in the journey of conversion), located within a more comprehensive vision of a specific tradition's conception of the Good. Moreover, there is a clear sense that the formation of character is crucially important, and that it is formed most specifically by cultivating particular habits of thinking, feeling, and acting well. There is an emphasis on the importance of friendship and the role of exemplars in learning how to become good. And there is a clear recognition of the important theological and ethical implications of the Church's own internal life and identity.

37. Finn, "It Happened One Saturday Night," p. 595. For a firsthand description of the effect of the baptismal liturgy on a pilgrim visiting Jerusalem, see *Egeria's Travels to the Holy Land.*

In this sense, then, the description reinforces, enriches, and concretizes insights for which MacIntyre and Hauerwas have prepared their readers. As a result, perhaps we can return the ancient texts and practices of baptismal catechesis to a central place in contemporary moral inquiry and debate in ways analogous to the recovery of Aristotle and Aquinas. And, in so doing, we can find resources for further reflection on the central importance of themes such as friendships and practices, habits and character, tradition and community.

But there are also different lessons to be learned, lessons that recontextualize some of the issues raised by MacIntyre's and Hauerwas's work and that offer resources for redirecting some of the debates in contemporary theology.[38] In this context I can do little more than outline some of these constructive implications; a more complete exposition would require not only more time and space than is available for one paper, but also a more extensive discussion of issues involving interpretations of the normative positions of Augustine and Aquinas, both singly and by comparison (the latter being the preferred figure for both MacIntyre and Hauerwas).

First, these ancient practices and texts offer a *comprehensively theological focus for human life, directed toward the eschatological consummation of fellowship with the triune God.* Most obviously, this places God at the center of our practices, our thinking, and our friendships. It locates our practice, our study, and our lives in journeys of holiness marked by the ongoing transformation of our desire to know and enjoy God. Gregory of Nyssa put it nicely in *The Life of Moses:* "This truly is the vision of God: never to be satisfied in the desire to see [God]. But one must always, by looking at what he can see, rekindle his desire to see more. Thus, no limit would interrupt growth in the ascent to God, since no limit to the Good can be found nor is the increasing of desire for the Good brought to an end because it is satisfied."[39]

As such, we ought to locate Christian living within the context of what Hans Urs von Balthasar termed *theodrama.*[40] This notion is extraordinarily

38. One way in which it does so, but which I cannot describe here, is in suggesting a more complex reading of Augustine's life and thought — including his "ethical" and "political" views — than is typical in contemporary debates. In my judgment, attention to Augustine's catechumenal practices and, more specifically, to the contexts of his homilies, helps to shed light on issues in such major works as *The City of God, Confessions, On Christian Doctrine,* and *On the Trinity.* It has often been the case that interpreters of Augustine have tended to rely on one of the major works to the neglect of others; while that tendency also needs remedying, my argument emphasizes the ways in which catechetical practices of teaching and learning are integral features of the major works themselves.

39. Gregory of Nyssa, *The Life of Moses,* II.239, p. 116.

40. See Balthasar, *Theo-Drama: Theological Dramatic Theory,* trans. Graham Harrison, 5 vols. (San Francisco: Ignatius, 1988-98).

rich, and it nicely encompasses a number of crucial features. It suggests the sense of the "spectacular theater" that Augustine and Quodvultdeus thought Christianity, and specifically the practices of baptismal catechesis, exemplified. In this sense, one of the worst features of too much of Christian thinking and too many Christian communities is that they have lost any sense of being participants in an exciting drama; we have left it to Hollywood and the NBA to provide the sources of excitement.[41] Further, to become a part of the great theodrama is to recognize that we all have roles to play, and parts to learn, in the drama of which the triune God is author, director, and the lead actor. Even so, the theodrama nonetheless involves human participation, indeed the participation of the whole Creation, for its eschatological completion.

Moreover, the theodramatic character of Christian life and inquiry also breaks down the artificial disciplinary barriers that too often preclude us from seeing things more clearly in their interrelations. To see all of life in relation to the triune God who, as the Creed testifies, is both the maker of heaven and earth and the One who will bring about the life everlasting, is to recognize that our inquiries cannot be confined by disciplinary boundaries. Most directly, this suggests that — as Karl Barth insisted — Christian ethics is a task of the Doctrine of God.[42] More generally, this view requires a stereoscopic vision of theology as an activity that draws together biblical reflection, spiritual direction, liturgical clarity, doctrinal precision, aesthetic considerations, and disciplined ethical discernment and engagement.[43]

It also suggests that theology can neither be isolated from other modes of intellectual inquiry, nor allow itself to be marginalized by them. Theology needs to engage and learn from other approaches to intellectual inquiry, but it also needs to reestablish a sense of comprehensive vision in relation to God.[44] This suggests, to take one prominent example, that philosophical inquiry provides an important, even crucial, subordinate role to theological in-

41. Hauerwas's and Willimon's emphasis in *Resident Aliens* on "salvation as adventure" is an important corrective, though it needs considerably more unpacking. See especially chapter 3.

42. See Barth, *Church Dogmatics* II/2, trans. G. Bromiley et al. (Edinburgh: T. & T. Clark, 1957), esp. par. 36.

43. In this description, we might do well to take a cue from Augustine's thought, and from the centrality of aesthetic criteria in his catechetical practices, in suggesting that theology ought to be understood as a musical harmony of these diverse "instruments."

44. This is the burden of John Milbank's important book *Theology and Social Theory: Beyond Secular Reason* (Oxford: Blackwell, 1989). I think his critique is crucial, and largely persuasive; however, his constructive proposal is oversimplified and in need of a more nuanced set of descriptions of theology's relations with other modes of inquiry. I sketch some of that below.

quiry, but it ought not be treated independently (as, for example, Hauerwas tends to do) nor given priority (as, for example, MacIntyre tends to do — note his recent description of his position as "Thomistic-Aristotelianism" [which is the adjective and which the noun?], an ordering he was unwilling to change when I pressed him in conversation).[45]

Second, these ancient texts and practices offer *rich ways to deal with issues of interpreting Scripture and doctrine.* It locates the interpretation of Scripture within the context of Christian living, both individually and as communities. Indeed, the interpretation of Scripture aims at people's performance in their lives — at wise and holy living.[46] Further, the dramatic interpretation of Scripture both immerses people in the actual texts of Scripture and offers a more complex, and more imaginative, set of practices for dealing with difficult texts than we tend to deploy.[47] Augustine described Scripture — or, more accurately, the Church in which Scripture is primarily read — as a "school," and those who come to hear Scripture read as "students of divine letters."[48] Notably, Augustine did not hesitate to acknowledge that there were texts he did not understand and avoided speaking about (notably, Matt. 12:31-32 on the sin against the Holy Spirit), although he did not stop "seeking, asking, knocking" about them.[49] This offers a model of biblical interpretation which, while it can and ought to learn from academic learning, is neither fundamentalist nor bound by academic canons. Indeed, von Balthasar's work suggests the significance of a "theodramatic hermeneutics," understanding Scripture as a "word that journeys with us" in Christian living.[50]

Further, the ancient catechumenate offers resources for immersing peo-

45. I would argue that this is, indeed, Thomas's own conception of the relations between philosophy and theology. However, that would require an extended argument in a different context; more assuredly, it reflects the judgments of such patristic writers in both East and West as Gregory of Nyssa, Augustine, and Maximus the Confessor.

46. For a more detailed, constructive proposal that develops this point, see Stephen Fowl's and my *Reading in Communion* (Grand Rapids: Eerdmans, 1991).

47. On Augustine, see especially *On Christian Doctrine;* on practices of biblical interpretation in the early church more generally, see James L. Kugel and Rowan A. Greer, *Early Biblical Interpretation* (Philadelphia: Westminster, 1986). For a rich treatment of scriptural practices in early Christian monasticism, see Douglas Burton-Christie, *The Word in the Desert* (New York: Oxford, 1993).

48. See the discussion in John Cavadini, "Simplifying Augustine," unpublished typescript, p. 9.

49. Augustine, Sermon 71.7-8, cited in Cavadini, "Simplifying Augustine," typescript p. 12.

50. Hans Urs von Balthasar, *Theo-Drama,* vol. 2, trans. Graham Harrison (San Francisco: Ignatius, 1990), pp. 102ff.

ple in Scripture yet also freeing their imaginations in their engagements with it. It does so by locating the interpretation of Scripture in relation to other practices, particularly those of the liturgy and to the catechumens' apprenticeship in Christian living.[51]

In a time when biblical literacy is particularly low even among Christians, and in which Bible studies are conducted in ways that often produce little if any appreciable increase either in the participants' knowledge of its contents or in their interpretive skills, there is much to be learned from these ancient texts and practices.[52]

Similarly, they offer an understanding of doctrine that both makes significant truth-claims and is contextualized within practices. Indeed, on this understanding the teaching and learning of doctrine is itself a *practice* in MacIntyre's sense, thus taking the notion out of the often sterile contexts in which both its adherents and its opponents in modernity have placed it.[53] In the ancient catechumenate, competentes learned the Creed in preparation for baptism; they were learning the identity of the God in whose name they would be baptized and whom they were committing themselves to follow. As Rowan Williams has suggested in a different context,

> The doctrines of Christian creedal orthodoxy are not, as is regularly supposed, insuperable obstacles to dialogue; the Incarnation of the Logos is not the ultimate assertion of privilege and exclusivity, but the center of that

51. Harmless's discussion of Augustine's sermons in *Augustine and the Catechumenate* is helpful in illuminating this point. See also the important linkages to prayer in Roberta Bondi's books, *To Pray and To Love* (Minneapolis: Augsburg Fortress, 1991) and *To Love as God Loves* (Philadelphia: Fortress, 1987). For the constructive purpose of linking scriptural immersion and imagination, an important analogy for Christians is found in rabbinic practices of interpretation; this is an issue that warrants further study, exploration, and conversation.

52. The claim about the results of Bible studies is found in Robert Wuthnow's extensive study of small groups in America. He found that more than two-thirds of the small groups in America were organized around Bible study, but that they actually did not significantly help people in their knowledge either of content or of interpretation; indeed, he found that they often ended up interpreting the Bible in more rather than less wooden ways. See *Sharing the Journey* (New York: Free Press, 1994).

53. For example, within my own tradition, the United Methodist Church, people have become preoccupied with whether one is or is not "doctrinally sound" — but the issues have tended to be put in terms of a contrast between propositions (for those in favor of doctrine) and experiences (for those who are worried about the term). There are further problems, not unrelated to confusions between doctrine and theology, but discussion of them would take us too far afield here. I address some of these issues in "What Makes United Methodist Theology 'Methodist'?," a paper forthcoming in the volumes from the Duke-Lilly Project on United Methodism and American Culture.

> network of relations (implicit and explicit) in which a new humanity is to be created.[54]

Insofar as Christian living is centered on coming to know, enjoy, and love the triune God by participating in God's activity of (re)creating a new humanity, we need the sorts of doctrinal practices that can enable people more wisely to discern who this God is and how this God is related to us, our world, and our destiny. Insofar as we do so, we will begin to learn once again that doctrine and ethics are not unrelated activities.[55]

Third, these ancient texts and practices suggest that *initiation into the Christian tradition shapes a "habitus," a whole pattern of learning to think, feel, and live well as holy people.* This habitus is shaped by fundamentally theological convictions, most centrally those concerning God but also by the ways in which those convictions give shape to beliefs and practices about, for example, forgiveness.[56] The specific texts and practices of the ancient catechumenate also reflect the importance of integrating disciplined patterns of thinking, feeling, and living in an embodied way of life. In the midst of contemporary temptations to think that Christianity is primarily about "being nice," or about having a "personal spirituality," the disciplined character of thinking (and, hence, also of speaking) is particularly important.[57] At the same time, however, we have been all-too-tempted, particularly in modernity, to neglect the importance of shaping virtuous passions and desires — of learning to be properly affected. This insight goes back to Aristotle, and it has been emphasized in particularly important though diverse ways in recent feminist thought and in relation to the arts and music. The important theo-

54. Rowan Williams, "Trinity and Pluralism," in *Christian Uniqueness Reconsidered,* ed. Gavin D'Costa (Maryknoll, N.Y.: Orbis, 1990), p. 11.

55. Two recent books have begun to describe doctrines in relation to practices in some significant ways. See James Wm. McClendon, *Doctrine: Systematic Theology,* vol. 2 (Nashville: Abingdon, 1994), esp. pp. 21-62; and Christopher Morse, *Not Every Spirit? A Dogmatics of Christian Disbelief* (Philadelphia: Trinity Press International, 1994). A more technical, philosophical study that is important on these issues is William Christian, *Doctrines of Religious Communities* (New Haven: Yale University Press, 1987). See also Stanley Hauerwas's essay "On Doctrine and Ethics," in *The Cambridge Companion to Christian Doctrine,* ed. Colin Gunton (Cambridge: Cambridge University Press, 1997).

56. See my discussion of this in *Embodying Forgiveness.*

57. Note, for example, the rich complexity reflected in Augustine's comment: "the very desire with which you want to understand is itself a prayer to God" (Augustine, Sermon 152.1, cited in Cavadini, "Simplifying Augustine," typescript p. 1). Or, as one of the characters in Chaim Potok's *In the Beginning* phrases it, "A shallow mind is a sin against God." I am grateful to Mary Boys for this reference.

logical insight, one emphasized in the early church particularly by Gregory of Nyssa, Augustine, and Maximus the Confessor (among many others), is that without the ongoing transformation of our desires and the cultivation of holy affections we will not be able to cling to God in ways appropriate to holy living and saving knowledge.[58]

Further, this shaping of our thinking and of our feeling is embodied; that is, this shaping is contextualized in patterns of life and ritually signified by particular actions within the liturgical practices of the catechumenate (e.g., the kiss of peace, anointing with oil, marking the sign of the cross on the forehead, even the baptismal immersion itself). Yet no priority is necessarily given to one over the others; embodied living may give rise to new thinking or new ways of feeling, just as new patterns of thinking or feeling may stir one to new ways of living.[59]

More comprehensively, this habitus also provides a way of life that integrates rules/laws, goods, and virtues. Particularly in recent years, people have turned to themes such as character and virtue as important resources either to be set alongside an account of Kantian rules or a utilitarian understanding of goods, or to replace them. But an adequate approach to ethics needs to show how all three are interrelated; and, I think the habitus sustained by practices of baptismal catechesis does so by emphasizing the dynamic interrelations of law, virtue, and goods in lives oriented toward loving communion with the triune God.[60] This certainly ought to include an account of the "natural law" — universally applicable norms to which all people ought to assent — but such an account needs to be situated within an overarching theological

58. For some instructive commentary on these issues, see Robert L. Wilken, "Loving God with a Holy Passion," in his *Remembering the Christian Past* (Grand Rapids: Eerdmans, 1995), pp. 145-63.

59. To be sure, we may want to dissent from specific conceptions of the passions found in some of these writings, just as we may want to dissent from some practices in relation to embodiment. But at least the patterns recognized the seriousness of a whole range of issues about our identity as embodied, passionate, and thoughtful people that we are only now beginning to grapple with again.

60. Pope John Paul II's encyclical *Veritatis Splendor* is a remarkable document on moral theology, and there is much to commend it — including, most specifically, its overall *theo*logical shape. Even so, apart from disagreements I would have over its treatment of some specific issues, there are three weaknesses to its structure that are worth mentioning at this point: (1) despite its theological focus, its vision of the *telos* of the Christian life is put too much in terms of law (with the correlative claim of God as lawgiver) rather than in terms of communion with the triune God (with the correlative claim of God as love); (2) while the encyclical appropriately identifies the importance of obedience to law, it fails adequately to articulate the significance of virtues for Christian life; and (3) it does not adequately stress the eschatological character of Christian discernment.

argument; more specifically, it requires a description of how the natural law is learned and discerned in the context of our calling to communion with the triune God.[61]

Fourth, these ancient texts and practices offer *a distinctive theological conception of teaching and learning as joint inquiry.* For Augustine, this conception is grounded in the Incarnation.

> . . . Christ came mainly for this reason: that we might learn how much God loves us, and might learn this to the end that we might begin to glow with love of him by whom we were first loved, and so might love our neighbor at the bidding and after the example of him who made himself our neighbor by loving us.[62]

This provided the pedagogical structure of Augustine's teaching. As such, Augustine as the teacher and those who were his students were bound together in the joint inquiry of learning to know God and, more specifically, to know how much God loves us. This joint inquiry was directed to the end that we would actually *glow* with the love of God — and so might manifest that in love of our neighbors. This conviction shaped both Augustine's homilies and his other writings, including especially the *Confessions* and *On the Trinity.*[63]

In this light, Augustine stressed the reciprocal character of teaching and learning in the catechumenate. As he put it, "So great is the power of sympathy, that when people are affected by us as we speak and we by them as they learn, we dwell in the other and thus both they, as it were, speak in us what they hear, while we, in some way, learn in them what we teach."[64] There was thus an important dimension of embodied friendship in the relationship between teachers and learners. This was no mere transmission of information, though it certainly included that; more centrally, what was taught and learned were the inextricable interrelations between the words spoken and the lives lived.[65]

61. MacIntyre has made some important suggestions on this latter point, but unfortunately his account remains too abstracted from a theological context. See especially *Whose Justice? Which Rationality?* (Notre Dame: University of Notre Dame Press, 1988) and *Three Rival Versions of Moral Enquiry* (Notre Dame: University of Notre Dame Press, 1990).

62. Augustine, *De catechizandis rudibus,* 3.6, cited in Harmless, *Augustine and the Catechumenate,* p. 129.

63. This is one of the central reasons why Augustine's thought, even in his major works, needs to be seen in relation to his catechumenal practices and especially his homilies.

64. Augustine, *De catechizandis rudibus,* 12.17, cited in Harmless, *Augustine and the Catechumenate,* p. 266.

65. For a more extended account of one example of friendship and the practices of teaching and learning in the early church, see Robert L. Wilken, "Alexandria as a School for Training

This reciprocal dynamic of teaching and learning was contextualized as joint-inquiry because, in the most fundamental sense, both teachers and learners were in need of learning. After all, Christ is the true teacher, the one who, as Augustine put it in one of his sermons, made the cross his professorial chair.[66] Or, as he indicated in another sermon:

> Your graces know that all of us have one Teacher, and that under him we are fellow disciples, fellow pupils. And the fact that we bishops speak to you from a higher place does not make us your teachers; but it's the one who dwells in all of us that is the Teacher of us all. He was talking to all of us just now in the gospel, and saying to us what I am also saying to you; he says it, though about us, about both me and you: *If you remain in my word* — not mine, of course, not Augustine's, now speaking, but his, who was speaking just now from the gospel. . . .[67]

Augustine thus described himself as a fellow-inquirer. More broadly, Augustine suggested elsewhere that even the preacher is a "petitioner before he is a speaker"; before one begins to preach, "he should raise his thirsty soul to God, in order that he may give forth what he shall drink, or pour out what shall fill him."[68]

Further, in his questioning of the catechumens, Augustine drew on their responses to help form the rhetoric of his own sermons. In so doing, Augustine was not simply "popularizing" his theological insights that could be found elsewhere; he was recontextualizing his inquiries themselves in order to help his fellow-inquirers move along the path of inquiry into the mystery of God. His task was to teach in ways that his listeners could understand, and to address the sorts of questions with which they were concerned. This suggests that, whatever the topic, Augustine engaged in a theological approach to teaching and learning modeled most clearly on the humility and the *caritas* of Christ.

To be sure, Augustine was obviously also capable of engaging people at the highest level of intellectual inquiry and in the most technical intellectual debates. Further, in the development and exposition of his views he utilized

---

in Virtue," in *Schools of Thought in the Christian Tradition,* ed. Patrick Henry (Philadelphia: Fortress Press, 1984), pp. 15-34.

66. Augustine, Sermon 234.2, cited in Harmless, *Augustine and the Catechumenate,* p. 326.

67. Augustine, Sermon 134.1, cited in John Cavadini, "Simplifying Augustine," unpublished typescript, p. 10. I am indebted to Cavadini's analysis in this paper, and to conversation with him, for my understanding of the dynamics of Augustine's teaching.

68. Augustine, *On Christian Doctrine,* IV.15.32, p. 140.

genuine learning wherever he could find it, drawing on the classical traditions of the virtues, rhetoric, and philosophy, as well as historical investigations and political theories. It was in this that Augustine — schooled as he was in intensive Christian catechesis (both as a teacher and as a learner), contextualized in terms of Christian living understood as lifelong joint inquiry — entered into critical conversation with other modes of inquiry.[69]

Fifth, these ancient texts and practices stress *the eschatological character of discernment.* Christians claim to have discerned the Truth revealed by God in Jesus Christ; even so, though we see, it is but through a glass, darkly (1 Cor. 13:12). It is important to stress both sides of this equation; both that we see, and that there is much that cannot be seen. Put theologically, we desire to know the unknowable God. In the face of skeptics who claim that nothing can be known, we need to stress that there are sure and reliable guides for belief and conduct — most centrally, the Truth found in Jesus Christ.[70]

Yet in the face of those who think that knowledge is easily secured, or that any of us is in possession of the Truth, we need to stress that we continue to struggle to see things clearly; indeed, we must continually unlearn our own partial perspectives as we seek — as fellow-inquirers with others, both diachronically and synchronically — to see things less unfaithfully, less partially, and more in harmony with the God in whom alone the fullness of Truth is to be found. Particularly useful here is von Balthasar's position of drama between "epic" and "lyric." Drama provides a way to make a universal claim that does not presume a "God's-eye" view: everyone is on the stage of God's drama because it overarches everything. This means that there is no way off of the stage; we cannot adopt the director's or the playwright's perspective. We do have a "script," but it is only revealed to us by the "prompter" in the play, the Holy Spirit.[71]

That is, the mysteries of faith are such that no one, no matter how educated, can come to full understanding in this life. As Augustine put it, all —

69. This is, in one sense, an obvious point; yet Milbank's constructive proposal in *Theology and Social Theory* would have been better had he better integrated into his account Augustine's practice — and, in some sense, had he better integrated his own practice of learning from other modes of inquiry. Unfortunately, critics of Milbank have often given too much away in the other direction, suggesting that theology simply is one discipline among others.

70. For further exposition of the claim that for Christians truth is primarily identified with a person, see Bruce D. Marshall, "'We Shall Bear the Image of the Man of Heaven': Theology and the Concept of Truth," *Modern Theology* 11, no. 1 (1995): 93-117.

71. On von Balthasar's description of the Holy Spirit as the "prompter" in the play, see *Theo-Drama,* trans. Graham Harrison (San Francisco: Ignatius, 1992), p. 533. I am indebted to my colleague Fritz Bauerschmidt for the insights from von Balthasar in this paragraph.

preacher and hearer alike — are "little ones to be educated." Or, in reference to John 1:1-2, Augustine asked, "Who can work it out? Who can observe it, who contemplate it, who think fitting thoughts about it? Nobody."[72] We see, but through a glass darkly, as we apprentice ourselves to Christ the true teacher under the guidance of the Holy Spirit.

A close corollary to this emphasis is grounded in Augustine's conception of the self as involved in the ongoing task of unlearning sin and learning what it means to be known and loved by God. The catechumenate emphasizes the ways in which the self is put into question by God, even while being given new life as a gift from God; and Augustine's own conception of human life recognizes that our joint inquiry will involve ongoing, communal, eschatologically shaped discernment of where "I" am, where "I" have come from, and where "I" am headed. Hence our faith, and our claim to know the unknowable God, are inextricably linked to our own need for further inquiry, further unlearning and learning, deeper apprehension of the mystery of God made known in love for humanity.

The eschatological character of our discernment is directly related to the sixth and (for purposes of this paper) final set of implications from these ancient texts and practices: they offer us a clear recognition that *Christian living requires renunciations and adhesions from all of us.* One of the most starkly realistic features of the baptismal catechumenate is its confrontation with forces of evil and injustice, understood both within particular individuals and more broadly in social and cultural contexts and, indeed, the cosmos. To be sure, we may have disagreements with our forebears — and even among ourselves — about precisely *what* ought to be renounced and what ought to be affirmed. Hence the significance of our ongoing discernment, and of engaging in discussion and debate about how to understand and embody faithful living in communion with God amidst the perplexities of specific social contexts and the inextricably particular biographies of each of our lives. For Bonhoeffer, the renunciation of the Nazis was clear and obvious; yet what that renunciation meant specifically for him to do, however, was not nearly so obvious — and continues to foster debates into the present.[73] So also for the rest of us, there are some renunciations that are relatively easy — though no less important — and some adhesions that are equally clear; there are others that are more difficult to discern, much less to embody.

72. Augustine, Sermons 88.14, 225.3; both cited in Cavadini, "Simplifying Augustine," typescript p. 17.

73. For my analysis of Bonhoeffer's life on these issues, see chapter 1 of *Embodying Forgiveness.*

III. Conclusion: Christian Living in Complex Social Settings

I have suggested throughout this essay that the ancient texts and practices of baptismal catechesis offer rich resources for us to rethink issues in Christian life and thought where contemporary practices have become impoverished and scholarly debates have reached dead ends (or began in cul-de-sacs!), and to re-envision the shaping of Christian living in provocative and exciting ways. Though I have not been able to defend any of my suggestions with adequate precision or exposition, they point in fruitful directions.

In conclusion, I want to return to the questions about why there is renewed interest in these ancient texts and practices. Obviously, in one sense the RCIA has been developed out of a perceived need for richer and deeper catechesis. Its liturgical and educational possibilities seem quite significant — and, at least in broad outline, ecumenically so. Further, it seems that a recovery of the importance of catechesis is emerging precisely at this juncture because of the increasingly pervasive sense across the traditions that the nature and shape of Christian identity can no longer (if it ever could!) be assumed to be clear to most people. In part, this is because the heirs of the Enlightenment downplayed the importance of such themes as character, virtue, and formation — indeed, on some Enlightenment conceptions of the self, there is little need for reflection on the formation of particular modes of feeling, acting, or thinking. So, in response to the relative neglect of these important issues, these texts and practices can — at least in some respects — offer us resources that enable us better to deal with forming and educating Christians for faithful living in communion with God.

But a deeper concern that some people might have is that the interest in these texts and practices arises not just as a way of remedying the failures of some liberal theories, but of engaging in a more comprehensive critique of liberal societies. After all, Bonhoeffer radically rejected the Nazi society around him, and Hauerwas and MacIntyre have both offered stringent and comprehensive critiques of liberal societies. So the question needs to be asked bluntly: Are these ancient texts and practices inextricably related to a rejection of the particular cultural patterns or social settings in which the Church finds itself?

To be sure, there are patterns and practices in the ancient catechumenate that suggest a sharp discontinuity between the Church and the world. There is a dramatic discontinuity of turning from the practices and habits of the old way of life — its patterns of thinking, feeling, and living — and turning in baptism to a dramatically new way of life. This is enacted in the notion of the discipline of secrecy itself, and also in the sharp contrasts between cultural practices (e.g., the theater, the boxing ring, and other spectacles) and those appropriate to Christian living. Further, catechumens were required to renounce many features of the culture from which they were coming. As the competentes prepared for baptism, they found themselves on the threshold between the culture they were leaving and the one they were hoping to enter.[74] These discontinuities are part of what appeals to people worried about Christian accommodation to cultural norms and practices.[75]

However, there is nothing to presume that such sharp contrasts are intrinsic to either the theory or the practices of the baptismal catechumenate. Those who are baptized are sent into the world to live as Christian disciples, and there is no reason not to presume that — at least in some contexts — they could affirm many features of the societies in which they live. After all, the triune God who is our *telos* is none other than the One who created and providentially upholds all there is. To be sure, Christians would also, almost invariably, need to engage in prophetic criticism of many features of the societies in which they live; for, on this side of the fullness of God's reign, evil and sin and injustice continue to persist even in societies that are less unjust than others. So the problem ought not to be that these practices are sectarian; indeed, the very logic of the practices propels the newly baptized "back" into the world.[76] And, parenthetically, it is important to remember that Augustine was more worried about those who had been catechized and baptized being corrupted by unfaithful Christians than by pagans or particular cultural or social presumptions.

Rather, the relevant concerns ought to be focused in different directions. Those troubled by Hauerwas's emphasis on the Church, or by MacIntyre's account of the moral and intellectual virtues and the importance of practices and traditions, ought to explain how they can provide for the formation of Christian character better — or why these are not crucial themes for understanding Christian living. In my judgment, the practices of ancient baptismal catechesis go a good distance toward specifying, enriching, and concretizing Hauerwas's and MacIntyre's claims through a theological understanding of formation — albeit one which, at least in some respects, challenges aspects of their claims.

74. See the discussion in Finn, "It Happened One Saturday Night," pp. 599-601.

75. Though it should be noted that the issue is not, or at least not simply, a "Constantinian" one — the patterns of the catechumenate in North Africa described in this paper occur a century or more after the Constantinian settlement began.

76. Indeed, this is also true of Hauerwas, despite the oft-repeated charges that his position is "sectarian." Though Hauerwas sometimes describes his positions in unfortunate ways, his overall position (and his own habits of engagement) militate strongly against a charge of "sectarianism."

On the other hand, those troubled by the comprehensive claims of Hauerwas's or MacIntyre's critiques ought, rightly in my judgment, to stress the importance of making more nuanced and specific accounts than Hauerwas and MacIntyre tend to do of what ought to be renounced, what ought to be adhered to, and why. These issues encompass particular vocations that ought to be encouraged or renounced, as well as determinations about what sorts of cultural or political involvements are required, permitted, tolerated, or prohibited. These must be analyzed and adjudicated carefully; and the very practices learned in and through baptismal catechesis ought to provide all Christians with resources for making the sorts of discriminating judgments in relation to law, goods, and virtues that are the hallmark of Christian practical wisdom. Embodying such wisdom is one way in which to fulfill Bonhoeffer's wise insistence that the Church should not exist on the margins of any cultural or social context, but must be found in the middle of the "village."

Of course the deepest question is *how* Christians participate in conversations with others who do not share Christian convictions. This is not only the predicament of liberal societies; it has been part of the agenda that has faced Christians in many times and places — and is, in some sense, intrinsic to the biblical narratives themselves.[77] Here I think both the practices — including those of teaching and learning — and the theological convictions found in ancient baptismal catechesis can provide significant help. Augustine learned from other disciplines and drew on wide repertoires of cultural resources in his thinking and teaching; further, he thought there were some exceptionless norms, such as the prohibition against lying, to which all people ought to be

77. Gene Outka offers some significant reflections concerning the relevance of Augustine's thought for contemporary debates in his "Augustinianism and Common Morality," in *Prospects for a Common Morality,* ed. Gene Outka and John P. Reeder (Princeton: Princeton University Press, 1993), pp. 114-48. There is much in this essay that I think is very important and insightful. Even so, Outka's argument is weakened by three factors: (1) he fails adequately to attend to issues of learning and discernment in Christian life (and, more particularly, his account of Augustine neglects the role of the Church), which has important implications for both the description and the appropriation of the "universality" of the rules themselves; (2) despite Outka's own prioritizing of the biblical narratives in relation to more generally applicable or universal norms (see p. 140), the order of his exposition moves in the opposite direction; and (3) Outka's failure to attend to the catechetical practices of teaching and learning, and the role of the Church's liturgy, leads him to overstate the case about Augustine's so-called pessimism. Outka nicely describes both our identities as social creatures and the corruption of that sociality through sin; but he needs also to attend to the ways in which that corruption is to be unlearned through the practices of the Church. In this sense, I am insisting on a more "Catholic" reading of Augustine's thought than Outka provides.

expected to conform.[78] Further, Augustine was attentive to the needs, experiences, and perspectives of those to whom he preached and taught; in so doing, he called upon the richest rhetorical resources he could deploy. Christians today need the same kinds of rhetorical flexibility, whether those encountered are unbelievers or adherents of other religious traditions.[79]

In order to do so, however, Christians need to be immersed in the language and practices of Christian living — to unlearn the destructive patterns of speech and life that are all too often typical, and to cleanse ourselves of the trivialization of Christian speech and life so often found even in our churches and ourselves. In these ways, baptismal catechesis can silence us, and provide us ways in which to learn to engage in redemptive speech and silence in our relations with others — even when we find ourselves using rhetorical resources not explicitly Christian. Those worried about the particularity of Christian convictions or of Christian life are right, at least in one sense, that we need to be "open to the world." After all, there is truth to be learned, and beauty to be enjoyed, throughout God's good Creation. Yet we will be most genuinely open to the world, most authentically able to enjoy God's good Creation, and to enter into conversation with diverse others, when we have been nurtured in the particularities of the faith to enable us also to discern wisely that which is truly of God's Spirit from all other spirits.[80]

So, for example, Rowan Williams offers a rich meditation to Uxbridge judges and lawyers on the possibilities and limits of understanding the administration of "justice" in British society. He notes that "doing justice" begins in our effort to respond to the reality of one another, which demands that we see one another as God sees us. He goes on to observe:

> The vision of God is the cornerstone of justice: when we know ourselves to be before God, we know ourselves to be the object of a costly and careful attention, searching out the whole of our truth, accepting it and engaging with it; we experience the way that grace opens our eyes to what we'd rather not face in ourselves, gently brings us back to confront our failures

78. See the instructive comments in Outka, "Augustinianism and Common Morality," esp. pp. 119-21.

79. For an instructive Augustinian account of how to deal with religious pluralism, see Charles T. Mathewes, "Pluralism, Otherness, and the Augustinian Tradition," *Modern Theology* 14, no. 1 (January 1998): 83-112.

80. It is, I think, not insignificant that many of the people most concerned about being "open to the world" are themselves people who have received intensive formation — either as priests and religious or through disciplined communities of lay Christians — and thus may take the importance and availability of Christian formation too much for granted.

> honestly, gathers up what's fragmented and forgotten. In the light of that divine attention, we know what we must offer to each other and what we need from each other — truth sustained by grace. Augustine believed that justice in society was unthinkable without 'doing justice' to God, returning God's attentive, loving gaze in silence and in praise. A society that doesn't understand contemplation won't understand justice, because it will have forgotten how to look *selflessly* at what is other.

Understanding, then, that administering justice "is a ministry of the truth of God's life to our imaginations, whether we know it or not," Williams concludes by specifying the importance of the lawyer's vocation — and draws analogies to doctors and artists:

> All are called to attention, immersion in particulars, and to uncovering for others a truth they could not know for themselves. And the lawyers may understand, perhaps, that 'doing justice' can be a healing art, restoring becomes harder and harder, the more we cease to take it for granted that God is to be honored. Ultimately, all that can be said by the Christian about justice rests on the doctrine of God, not simply as the God whose truthful love is directed towards us, but as the God whose very life is 'justice', in the sense that Father, Son and Holy Spirit reflect back to each other perfectly and fully the reality that each one is, 'give glory' to each other. . . . So the Uxbridge Magistrates' Court and its local equivalents point us towards the contemplation of the Holy Trinity, and that contemplation, with all that it says about truth and reciprocity, grounds, for the Christian, the vision of a just society. Administering justice is a ministry of the truth of God's life to our imaginations, whether we know it or not.[81]

Williams's analysis offers our society the richly textured reflections on a common theme that is all-too-often lacking, even when Christians use biblical language such as justice or love. I suspect that Williams offers judges and lawyers more insight — or perhaps, a more specifically formulated opposition — on issues of what it means to administer "justice" precisely because he has immersed himself in the texts, practices, and language of Christian faith and life. Put in the language of this paper, those who embark on dramatic journeys into God's dazzling light are the ones most likely to offer the sort of Christian exercise of practical wisdom that our churches, our cultures, and our world desperately need.

81. Rowan Williams, *Open to Judgement* (London: Darton, Longman and Todd, 1994), pp. 245-46.

In that sense, then, perhaps Christians can be of most service to others and to our societies — and provide a richer context for Christian living — to the extent to which we genuinely center all of our formation and our living, wherever we find ourselves, in the mystery of the triune God. For as Gregory of Nyssa put it in the fourth century,

> Since the goal of the virtuous way of life was the very thing we have been seeking, and this goal has been found in what we have said, it is time for you, noble friend, to look to that example and, by transferring to your own life what is contemplated through spiritual interpretation of the things spoken literally, to be known by God and to become his friend. This is true perfection: not to avoid a wicked life because like slaves we servilely fear punishment, nor to do good because we hope for rewards, as if cashing in on the virtuous life by some business-like and contractual arrangement. On the contrary, disregarding all those things for which we hope and which have been reserved by promise, we regard falling from God's friendship as the only thing dreadful and we consider becoming God's friend the only thing worthy of honor and desire. This, as I have said, is the perfection of life.[82]

82. Gregory of Nyssa, *The Life of Moses,* II.320, p. 137.

7. Interpretation

Toward a Rehabilitation of the Vestigia Tradition

DAVID S. CUNNINGHAM

In the middle section of this book, we have been examining particular practices that contribute to our "formation in knowing the Trinity." Contemplative prayer and the baptismal catechumenate are clear examples of how this formation can take place. Both these practices require an agency that is both human and divine: we pray, but the Spirit prays through us; we baptize, but the sacrament is made efficacious by God. This twofold conception of agency will continue to play a role in the present chapter, as we inquire into whether *interpretation* might be included among those practices through which we are formed in our knowledge of the triune God.

Most of us tend to think of interpretation as formative for such knowledge primarily when its object is the Bible, the liturgy, or the history of the Church. These fundamental sources for knowing the Trinity have been explored in the first section of this book. In this chapter, we inquire into the question of whether interpretation in a broader sense — that is, our interpretation of the created order — can contribute to our "knowledge of God."

At first glance, this may seem a strange question to ask. Christian doctrine has traditionally asserted that our knowledge of God must find its ultimate source in God, not in observations about the world. This assertion would seem to be placed in jeopardy by a claim that the knowledge of God can be generated by human efforts to interpret the created order. But I want to assure any skeptical readers that I have no intention of joining ranks with those modern theologians who seem to have become disciples of Feuerbach — arguing, essentially, that our knowledge of God is a purely human construction, and that we need to start inventing some new beliefs that conform to the spirit of the present age. As Nicholas Lash dryly observes, "there are surely less cumbersome ways of being an atheist than to use the paraphernalia of Christian language and imagery simply to express the form of our alienation."[1]

On the other hand, some accounts of the knowledge of God seem to imply that it can be instilled in human beings without any action whatsoever on our parts — as though the ways that we *receive* revelation, and the categories through which we interpret God's word, have no impact whatsoever on our knowledge of God. Such claims are not limited to naïve forms of fundamentalism; they are implied by *any* suggestion that certain elements of our knowledge of God are obvious, unmediated, or unchangeable. We are cautioned against such claims by the fallible, all-too-human character of the filters and assumptions we employ as we seek to listen to the voice of the Other.

But whether the knowledge of God is described as a product of the divine will or of human speculation, an "either/or" mentality is often at work: such knowledge is presumed to come *either* from God *or* from us. Our role is characterized either as "purely active construction" or "purely passive reception." But surely such characterizations are themselves figments of our highly dichotomized imaginations. The process of revelation is essentially an act of communication; and like any communicative act, it requires more than a speaker who is properly attuned to the preconceptions of the audience. It also requires recipients who are willing actively to listen and to grasp whatever knowledge might be thereby made available to them.

My thesis is that, even though God remains the ultimate source of all our knowledge of God, *our own interpretation of the created order* can become a disciplined ecclesial practice which — like the practices of contemplative prayer and baptismal catechesis — can contribute to our formation in the knowledge of the Trinity. However, as also with prayer and baptism, such knowledge cannot be expected to result from just *any* form of the practice; interpretation must take on certain contours, and accept certain limitations, if it is to become formative in this way. This essay offers one example of such interpretation: the ancient and venerable practice of recognizing analogous structures between the created order and the triune God.[2]

1. Nicholas Lash, "Ideology, Metaphor, and Analogy," in *The Philosophical Frontiers of Christian Theology: Essays Presented to D. M. MacKinnon,* ed. Brian Hebblethwaite and Stewart R. Sutherland (Cambridge: Cambridge University Press, 1982), pp. 68-94; here, p. 87.

2. The central sections of this chapter are drawn from parts of chapters 2 and 3 of my book *These Three Are One: The Practice of Trinitarian Theology* (Oxford and Cambridge, Mass.: Blackwell, 1998). They have been significantly rewritten for this volume.

After a brief analysis of the differing means by which we come to know God, I will offer an evaluation of the long-standing theological tradition of the *vestigia trinitatis,* especially as it developed in the writings of St. Augustine. Augustine was not the first to employ the *vestigia,* but he was certainly prolific in employing them, and he also undertook a theoretical examination of their usefulness; he thus provides us with a convenient place to begin. I will then turn to the critical assessment of this tradition, especially in the early work of Karl Barth. After offering an analysis of Barth's argument, I will provide my own evaluation of the significance of this tradition for today. Throughout this discussion, we will discover that a contemporary appropriation of the *vestigia* tradition will require renewed attention to the role of the Holy Spirit in guiding the practices of the interpretive community called Church.

Levels of Revelation

I want to affirm, at the outset, that the definitive focal point for God's revelation is the person of Jesus Christ. By entering the world in human form, God provides us with the most complete and definitive knowledge of God that we can hope to have. On the other hand, however, this "complete and definitive" form of revelation comes not as a statement, nor as a set of propositions, but as a *human being.* Hence, the knowledge thereby made available to us is marked by all the ambiguities inherent in any knowledge that we gain from or through another human being. In order to "come to know" something through the life of another, we have to interpret that person's words and actions, to ask for clarification (when it is possible to do so), and to rely on the testimony of others. In Christ, God is revealed to us — but this is obviously not the end of the story. We must still *interpret* what the apostles saw with their eyes, what they looked at and touched with their hands.

Fortunately, we are not left wholly to our own devices in order to do so. A single, isolated act of communication — however definitive it may be — would not be sufficiently attentive to our limitations as "receivers" of revelation. We are free and fallible beings, and an adequate knowledge of God cannot be assured (or perhaps even expected) by one definitive act of unveiling — just as an adequate attitude of reverence toward God cannot be assured by one definitive act of superabundant donation (i.e., the creation of the world). Rather, God provides us with ongoing interpretive guidance; this is part of the mission of the Holy Spirit, who enlivens the Church to proclaim the Word and administer the sacraments. These ongoing ecclesial practices help to give shape to our encounter with Christ, such that we learn to read the biblical narratives as God would have us read them — as testifying to Christ as the definitive point of contact, the "one true light" of divine revelation. So our knowledge of God certainly *begins* with the mission of the Word; but it does not *end* there. After all, many have read the biblical narratives in wholly privatized ways, and have then barricaded themselves away in the company of their "own personal Jesus." Knowledge of God requires a communally normed reading of the biblical narratives that is made possible within the Spirit-filled Church.

But this is not quite all. The knowledge of God, given to us in the incarnation of the Word and interpreted to us through the pouring out of the Spirit, must still be rendered intelligible, concrete, and persuasive. This task requires us to draw on the widest possible range of resources and tools, to "take every thought captive to obey Christ" (2 Cor. 10:5). We believe that God's creation of the world — this act of loving, superabundant donation — is ultimately done for the sake of the incarnate Word; "all things have been created for him" (Col. 1:16). And because God is the source of all things, there is a certain sense in which the whole world expresses, and thereby resembles, God.[3] This should not be confused with "natural" theology as it is sometimes understood, i.e., knowledge that human beings can have of God without God's prior action. There can be no purely natural knowledge of God, for there is no pure nature; the world is not a "naturally occurring phenomenon." Nature is always graced, always *being* graced, by God. So any knowledge of God that we can glean from the world is also graced, and continues to be graced, by God.

The difficulty, of course, is that with each successive description of revelation that I have offered here (Christ, the Church, the world), the focus becomes less sharp. Even though we have no perfect picture of Christ (we do not have a definitive "face"), we do have enough narrative material to hypothesize about a norm — even if the specifics of this norm are constantly being contested. The work of the Church, however, is carried out by human beings; thus, even though this work is animated by the Spirit, the knowledge of God that is mediated through Word and Sacrament requires careful discernment, in order to distinguish true knowledge from the highest aspirations of particular interpreters. When we turn to the world at large, the focus becomes still less distinct. If *everything* can give us knowledge of God, then this knowledge loses its specificity and becomes banal. If God can be known through everything, then God has no specific identity.

3. Bruce D. Marshall, "'We Shall Bear the Image of the Man of Heaven': Theology and the Concept of Truth," *Modern Theology* 11, no. 1 (January 1995): 93-118; here, 112. These matters are elaborated with great clarity in Marshall's *Trinity and Truth* (Cambridge: Cambridge University Press, 2000), chapters 5 and 9. My thanks to him for access to the manuscript.

Under what conditions, then, can the created order help give shape to our knowledge of God? It can do so when it is studied by those *who have already recognized* the revelatory character of Christ, and who live within the Spirit-filled community. Affirming this claim need not compromise the centrality of the Incarnation in the formation of our knowledge of God — as long as we approach the practice of interpretation in careful and disciplined ways, such that it can become revelatory of the same Truth that we have come to know through the gospel. Indeed, all three "levels of revelation" (as they are described here) require us to practice disciplined interpretation, in different ways. The interpretation of the created order is not the same as the interpretation of Jesus Christ; but the differences between the two are not as significant as they might appear. Both activities require us to think carefully about methods and norms; and both can be productive of the knowledge of God (but only if they are understood as the work of the Spirit in the context of the Church).

An appropriate model for our interpretation of the created order has been laid out by St. Augustine. He was under no illusion that one might be able to deduce the precise nature of God from an examination of the material world. He examined that world in the light of Christ, guided by the Spirit and from within the Church; thus he interpreted the world according to certain beliefs, practices, and knowledge that had already shaped his understanding of God and of God's creation. Nevertheless, he recognized that our theological knowledge could be given new shape — that it could become more educative for the faithful, more intelligible to outsiders, and more persuasive to everyone — if we were to interpret the created order as bearing certain analogies to its Creator. He thereby helped give shape to a theological tradition that has exercised the hearts and minds of some of the most notable theologians of the Christian era — though they have not all reached the same verdict concerning its value.

Augustine's Approach[4]

In Book 13 of the *Confessions,* Augustine complains briefly about the endless debates and quarrels in which Christians seem to be engaged concerning their various speculations on the Trinity. He suggests an alternative:

4. An analysis of Augustine's approach, accompanied by a surplus of citations, appears in Étienne Gilson, *The Christian Philosophy of St. Augustine,* trans. L. E. M. Lynch (New York: Random House, 1960), pp. 210-24 and the notes at pp. 348-59 [ET of: *Introduction à l'étude de Saint Augustin,* 3. éd., Études de philosophie médiévale (Paris: Vrin, 1949), pp. 275-98].

> I wish that human disputants would reflect upon the triad within their own selves. These three aspects of the self are very different from the Trinity, but I may make the observation that on this triad they could well exercise their minds and examine the problem, thereby becoming aware how far distant they are from it.[5]

Here Augustine sounds a theme that he will take up again, in much greater detail, in *De Trinitate.* There, he draws on Romans 1:20 in particular as an invitation to offer a triadic reading of structures in the created order — but one that refers back, constantly, to the triunity of God: "As we direct our gaze at the creator by understanding the things that are made, we should recognize the Trinity, whose mark appears in creation in a way that is fitting."[6]

The word that I have here translated as *mark* is the Latin *vestigium,* from which we also derive the English word *vestige.* In English, it has two standard definitions: (1) a visible sign of something that is no longer physically present, or (2) a very slight amount of one entity that is present in another. Unfortunately, neither of these definitions is wholly satisfactory as a rendering of Augustine's concept. The first one would depict a God who creates the world and then abandons it (leaving us the task of deciphering the divine fingerprints); the second one would suggest that God places little bits of divinity into the created order, vaguely reminiscent of some of the gnostic redeemer myths. Since neither of these clusters of meaning can adequately describe Augustine's project, I will not use the English word *vestige* to describe it. In fact, the two definitions contribute to a false dichotomy — suggesting that God must either be "in" creation in some sort of quasi-pantheistic sense, or else that God must be wholly absent from creation, like a divine watchmaker who now has better things to do. Neither story is the Christian story; we believe that the God who created the world (as something radically other-than-God) is the same God who became flesh in order to redeem the world, and who is poured out on all flesh in order to sanctify the world. God's full-scale engagement and involvement (with that which is not God) cannot underwrite a sharp dichotomy of identity-or-absence. God is wholly other than the world, yet constantly involved with it.[7]

5. Augustine, *Confessions* XIII.xi; trans. Henry Chadwick (Oxford: Oxford University Press, 1992), p. 279.

6. Augustine, *De Trin.* VI.10(12): *Oportet igitur, ut creatorem per ea quae facta sunt intellectum conspicientes, trinitatem intelligamus, cuius in creatura, quomodo dignum est, apparet vestigium.* Translation (slightly altered) from *The Works of Saint Augustine: A Translation for the 21st Century,* vol. 5, *The Trinity,* ed. and trans. with an Introduction by Edmund Hill, O.P. (Brooklyn, N.Y.: New City Press, 1991), p. 213.

7. Here it may be useful to consider the traditional category of divine "missions" — the in-

In an attempt to avoid the "presence-or-absence" dichotomy posed by the typical uses of the English word *vestige,* I have instead employed the word *mark.* Even though a person who "made a mark" or "left a mark" is no longer *physically* present, the very act of deliberately "leaving one's mark" can imply both an *interest* in the other (a mark can be left *for* someone) and a degree of *personal involvement.* These latter aspects of the word's usage suggest that the *source* of the mark can continue to have an influence — perhaps even a certain "presence" — in spite of certain signs of "absence." In employing the phrase "triune marks," I may not evoke all the resonances that Augustine hoped to call to his readers' minds by means of the phrase *vestigia trinitatis;* nevertheless, this translation seems an improvement over the current alternatives.

As is well known, Augustine goes on in the later books of *De Trinitate* to offer a large number of threefold *vestigia:* the lover, the beloved, and love; the mind, its knowledge, and its love; memory, understanding, and will; man, woman, and child; and many others (twenty different ones are listed in the index to a recent translation of *De Trinitate*).[8] Some of these Augustine mentions only briefly, then quickly discards; others he develops at great length. In every case, though, he eventually observes that the particular *vestigium* fails to mirror the Trinity perfectly, and that each one has specific inadequacies in addition to the more general point that no *vestigium* can provide a complete and unmistaken account of that which produced it. "There are not a number of such trinities, experience of some of which could enable us . . . to believe that the divine Trinity is similar."[9]

Augustine picks up the same theme, in a more condensed form, in *The City of God.* Here, he suggests that the doctrine of creation itself grounds the expectation that *vestigia* will appear in creation.

> If the divine goodness is nothing other than the divine holiness, then certainly we are being reasonably diligent, and not excessively presumptuous, in inquiring whether, in the works of God, this same Trinity is not suggested to us (in an enigmatic form of speech, intended to catch our atten-

---

carnation of the Word and the sending of the Spirit. The word *mission* itself tends to evoke *engagement* in spite of *otherness;* "going on a mission" requires us to care enough about a task to leave our comfortable surroundings and venture into foreign territory.

8. Joseph Sprug, indexer, in Hill, ed., *The Trinity, s.v. trinities,* p. 469.

9. *quasi multae sint tales trinitates, quarum aliquas experti sumus, ut . . . illam quoque talem esse credamus. . . . Quod utique non ita est. De Trin.* VIII.8, trans. from *Augustine: Later Works,* ed. John Burnaby, Library of Christian Classics, vol. 8 (Philadelphia: Westminster Press, 1955), p. 46.

> tion) whenever we ask of each creature: "Who made it? And by what means? And why?"[10]

Augustine then discusses the role of the whole Trinity in creation, suggesting that the Three[11] correspond, respectively, to the three questions that he raises at the end of this passage: they are maker, means, and purpose. Consequently, says Augustine, "the whole Trinity is revealed to us in its works."[12] He notes echoes of this revelation in the created order, and especially in humankind — created in the image of God.

In encouraging us to "read the created order" with attention to its triune marks, Augustine is not suggesting that the creation will "lead us" to its Creator. Rather, he believes that, if we become *active interpreters* of the world around us, our knowledge of God will become sharper, more acute. When we inquire about the maker, the means, and the purpose of creation, the wholly other God is, in some sense, "made present" to us — albeit in veiled and cryptic ways. In the very process of our interpretive acts, God's triune character is enigmatically suggested to us. God is neither immanent in creation nor simply absent; rather, God is active in creation in ways that have certain effects, such that one might reasonably speculate on the relationship between the created effects and the One who produces them.

Augustine's description of the *vestigia* tradition can provide a model for our practices of interpreting the created order. It has three key facets. First, it requires that we have already come to know God's very specific form of revelation through Jesus Christ. Second, it assumes the ongoing guidance of the Spirit, who helps us to evaluate the analogies that we develop and refers us back to Christ as the touchstone. And finally, it is not a practice to be undertaken by isolated individuals. All of our views of the created order are limited, in various ways; we can only begin to achieve a sense of the whole if we come into conversation with other members of the believing community — persons who have experienced the acts of God in Christ and in the Spirit.

10. . . . *ut in operibus Dei secreto quodam loquendi modo, quo nostra exerceatur intentio, eadem nobis insinuata intellegatur trinitas, unamquamque creaturam quis fecerit, per quid fecerit, propter quid fecerit.* Augustine, *De civ. Dei* XI.24; my translation.

11. The use of the phrase "the Three" is my tentative solution to the vexed question of what substantive to use to describe that of which there are three in God. For a critique of the contemporary English alternatives, and a justification of this term as a substitute, see *These Three Are One*, pp. 27-29.

12. *universa nobis trinitas in suis operibus intimatur.* Augustine, *De civ. Dei* XI.24; trans., altered, from that of Marcus Dods in *The City of God* (New York: The Modern Library, 1950), p. 369.

But this is to anticipate my conclusion somewhat. At the moment, we are about to discover that our apparently pleasant path through Augustine's commendation of the *vestigia* tradition has led us into a theological minefield. For despite the good use to which Augustine and many others have employed this tradition, it has been the subject of significant critique. Indeed, it is often dismissed as a relic of the theological past; Colin Gunton, for example, speaks of the "famous and futile quest for analogies of the Trinity in the created world." Their "weakness," he claims, "is their employment as attempts to illustrate the divine Trinity: the world is used to throw light on God, rather than the other way round."[13] The familiar dichotomy once again rears its head: the assumption seems to be that theological knowledge has its origins *either* in God alone, *or* in the world alone — and that the former is legitimate while the latter is illegitimate. This further implies that the practice of *interpreting the created order* cannot actually contribute to our knowledge of God; for this would be to usurp a task that is properly God's alone. In order to explore at greater length this commonly held view, I turn to its detailed presentation in the early work of Karl Barth.[14]

Barth's Objection

Barth argues that the root of the doctrine of the Trinity is the threefold form of revelation; God is, as it were, the subject, verb, and object of a sentence centered on the word *reveal.* Barth does not seek to *deduce* the doctrine of the Trinity from this threefold form of revelation; only through the biblical witness, he argues, can we move from a recognition of the threefold nature of revelation to the doctrine of the Trinity itself.[15] Before going on to discuss that doctrine, however, Barth pauses to consider the tradition of the *vestigia trinitatis,* wondering whether we might here have a second "root" of the doc-

13. Colin Gunton, "Trinity, Ontology, and Anthropology: Towards a Renewal of the Doctrine of the *Imago Dei,*" in *Persons, Divine and Human,* ed. Christoph Schwöbel and Colin Gunton (Edinburgh: T. & T. Clark, 1991), p. 55, n. 18; see also Colin Gunton, *The One, the Three and the Many* (Cambridge: Cambridge University Press, 1993), p. 144, n. 23.

14. I focus on Barth's early work because it provides the sharpest example of a critique of the *vestigia* tradition. Barth's later work seems much more supportive of the sort of interpretive practice that I seek to develop in this chapter; see note 31 below.

15. Karl Barth, *Church Dogmatics,* 4 vols. in 14 parts (Edinburgh: T. & T. Clark, 1958-1969), volume I/1, section 8.2 ("The Root of the Doctrine of the Trinity"). Further citations abbreviated *CD;* citations of the original German text, *Die Kirchliche Dogmatik* (Zollikon-Zürich: Evangelischer Verlag, 1932-1968), are abbreviated *KD.*

trine of the Trinity that could be placed alongside that of the biblical witness, accessible to human reason without the aid of revelation.[16]

Barth worries that this may be a slippery slope: if we can find God's triunity in the created order, then our knowledge of the triune God might come not only through divine revelation, but also through *reason;* and if also through reason then perhaps through reason *primarily;* and if primarily, perhaps *only* so. Or again, revelation might be merely a confirmation of something that can be adequately known through the natural order; and if so, the resulting "knowledge" would be of human aspirations, not of the "wholly other" creator God. For Barth, the very idea of a *vestigium trinitatis* raises the specter of the reduction of theology to anthropology.

But since the *vestigia* have traditionally played so large a role in Christian theology, Barth cannot dismiss them without comment. He examines a variety of *vestigia,* grouping them into five categories: phenomena from nature, from culture, from history, from religion, and from the life of the soul. At first, Barth seems willing to allow the employment of the *vestigia* within particular constraints, that is,

> as an interesting, edifying, instructive and helpful hint toward understanding the Christian doctrine, not to be overrated, not to be used as a proof in the strict sense, because we need to know and believe the Trinity already if we are really to perceive its *vestigia* as such in the microcosm and the macrocosm, but still to be valued as supplementary and non-obligatory illustrations of the Christian Credo which are to be received with gratitude.[17]

This passage, I think, provides an excellent description of the benefits afforded by the *vestigia* tradition. Barth cites Irenaeus, Augustine, Peter Lombard, and Thomas Aquinas as all having recognized the importance, both of the construction of *vestigia,* and of keeping this caveat firmly in mind.

Overall, then, Barth's initial treatment of the *vestigia* seems to be a positive one. When theologians sought to talk about the Trinity, he says,

> they opened their eyes and ears and found they could and should venture to refer, with this end in view, to spring, stream and lake, or weight, number,

16. "The concern here was with an essential trinitarian disposition supposedly immanent in some created realities quite apart from their possible conscription by God's revelation. It was with a genuine *analogia entis,* with traces of the trinitarian Creator God in being as such, in its pure createdness" (*CD* I/1, 334 [*KD* I/1, 353-54]).

17. *CD* I/1, 338 [357-58].

> and measure, or *mens, notitia,* and *amor* — not because these things were in and of themselves suitable for the purpose, but because they were adapted to be appropriated or, as it were, commandeered [*angeeignet, sozusagen erobert zu werden*] as images of the Trinity, because those who knew God's revelation in Scripture thought they might be given the power to say what, in and of themselves, they naturally do not say and cannot say.[18]

Barth's words *appropriated* and *commandeered* provide something of the flavor of what I will eventually propose as a contemporary rehabilitation of the *vestigia* tradition. Interpreting the created order as bearing "triune marks" requires us to appropriate and commandeer certain elements and structures of creation for theological purposes. This is clearly something that *we* do — an interpretation, a construal or construction, a way of "narrating" the created order. Again, I would emphasize the *post hoc* character of this approach, as does Barth; it is properly undertaken by those who know God's revelation in Scripture, rather than by persons expecting the *vestigia* to provide some form of unmediated access to the knowledge of God. Interpreting the created order does not provide anyone with a revelational shortcut — the sort of thing expected by those "seekers" who tumble over the wall in *The Pilgrim's Progress.* On the contrary: only those who have trod the long and difficult path of the King's Highway will reach their goal; only they "know how to look" for the marks of the Maker.

And yet, in his own rhetorical context, Barth had witnessed a good many people "tumbling over the wall": using something very much like the *vestigia* tradition as a shortcut, as a second (or first, or only) root of the Christian doctrine of God. The safeguards, limits, and caveats — inserted, almost unanimously, by the theologians who had employed this approach — were being ignored, and the *vestigia* were being used to reason from the created order back to the nature of God (perhaps even to the complete exclusion of God's revelation in Israel and in the Church).[19] Too often, Barth thought, the *vestigia* have been treated as an independent proof; and what they proved, ultimately, was another god, "an epitome, a supreme principle of the world and ultimately of human beings."[20] Thus, if there is to be a *vestigium trinitatis,* according to Barth, it can only be "the form which God Himself in His revelation has assumed in our language, world, and humanity."[21] Only by focusing

18. *CD* I/1, 340, trans. slightly altered [*KD* I/1, 359-60].

19. *CD* I/1, 341-41 [360-61].

20. *CD* I/1, 342, trans. slightly altered [*KD* has "Menschen," 361].

21. *CD* I/1, 347 [367]; earlier (334 [353]), the locus of this true *vestigium* is specified as "the form that God assumes in His unveiling as the Son or Word."

on Christ as the one true *vestigium* can we be sure of moving from God's revelation to our knowledge, rather than the other way around. Thus, because of the potential dangers of the *vestigia* tradition, Barth denounces it — and, as we will see shortly, does so in extraordinarily vehement terms.

Barth's early condemnation of the *vestigia* tradition has been overwhelmingly influential. For example, Colin Gunton's quick dismissal of the tradition, noted above, is made much easier by Barth's influence. Barth's notion that there can only be one true *vestigium trinitatis* has been taken up explicitly by Eberhard Jüngel, who argues that only in this way can our discussions of trinitarian doctrine be prevented from lapsing into groundless speculation.[22] Roman Catholic theologians have been generally less willing to follow Barth here, given their differing views on analogy — as Walter Kasper observes.[23] Yet Kasper himself implicitly accepts Barth's recasting of the *vestigia* by agreeing that "the real *vestigium trinitatis* is therefore not the human being but the God-human Jesus Christ."[24]

Given Barth's own theological context, his concerns were understandable. He had witnessed, in the Nazi-sympathizing theology of the "German Christian" movement, a relatively successful effort to disconnect the doctrine of God from its grounding in the biblical narratives of salvation history, and to connect it to an Aryan mythology that would help to undergird the Third Reich. To the extent that the tradition of the *vestigia* provided any degree of aid and comfort to this murderous and idolatrous process, it certainly deserved the full force of Barth's critique.[25]

And yet, one has to wonder whether Barth — in his laudable effort to block every possible theological route traveled by the Nazification of Christianity — did not occasionally tend to eliminate the good along with the bad.

22. Eberhard Jüngel, *God as the Mystery of the World,* trans. Darrell L. Guder (Grand Rapids: Eerdmans, 1983), section 22, pp. 343-68 [ET of: *Gott als Geheimnis der Welt,* 3e. Aufl. (Tübingen: J. C. B. Mohr, Paul Siebeck, 1977), pp. 470-505].

23. Walter Kasper, *The God of Jesus Christ,* trans. Matthew J. O'Connell (London: SCM Press, 1983), p. 273 [ET of: *Der Gott Jesu Christi* (Mainz: Matthias Grünewald Verlag, 1982), p. 332].

24. Kasper, *The God of Jesus Christ,* p. 273, trans. altered [*Mensch, Gott-Mensch:* 333]. See also Hans Urs von Balthasar's surprising anxiety on this issue in *Theo-Drama: Theological Dramatic Theory* (San Francisco: Ignatius, 1990-1995), (hereafter *T-D*), III: 508 [ET of: *Theodramatik* (Einsiedeln: Johannes Verlag, 1973-1983), (hereafter *TD*), II/2: 466] — though his worries concern content (the importance of avoiding modalism and tritheism) rather than form. A more positive evaluation appears at *T-D* III: 525ff. [*TD* II/2: 480ff.] and elsewhere.

25. Looking back on this era, Barth notes his concern not only about Christianity's political corruption by the Nazis, but also its theoretical corruption by "a long period of very dubious thought and utterance in Protestantism as a whole" (*CD* IV/3/1, 86).

We can accept that, in Barth's own era, the *vestigia* tradition had been put to such evil purposes that it was perhaps best to forgo it altogether. Yet this acceptance does not entail that it must be forgone in all times and all places — nor that its careful employment necessarily leads to the kinds of consequences to which, in a badly bastardized version, it led in Nazi Germany. As the ancient Sophists knew, *any* argument can be put to evil use by a person of bad character; this does not necessarily speak against the argument itself.

Assessing Barth's Critique

Barth is certainly right to suggest that the development of "triune marks" is a risky business, in that there will always be some potential for reading them the wrong way around. But theology must always take risks; so if we are to accept Barth's condemnation of this traditional theological practice, we could reasonably expect to be shown that the risk is real and significant, and that it extends beyond the particularities of his own context. Yet Barth never really explains when or how the classical tradition "crossed the line" and sought to use the *vestigia* as an independent proof. He certainly cites a number of Christian theologians who have described various *vestigia;* but as noted above, he also admits that they seem to have gladly accepted the caveat that one must always move from God to the *vestigia,* not the reverse. None of them seem to use the idea as any kind of independent proof of the doctrine. Where shall we look in order to find such widespread abuse of the *vestigia?*

Interestingly, Barth does not cite many of the arguments of the German Christians as evidence of this move.[26] Undoubtedly, he believed that his objection would carry more weight if it were understood as a broader critique of the tradition, rather than a charge aimed specifically at his own *particular* theological enemies. But this leaves him few specific cases to cite as the downfall of the tradition, since most Christian theologians (as Barth himself notes) employed it with care. Instead, Barth makes reference to "the development of anthropological speculation by way of Descartes and Kant to Schelling and Hegel and finally and logically Feuerbach"[27] — though one would hardly expect the standard safeguards on the use of the *vestigia* to be in place for these thinkers. The only direct reference to a Christian theologian who "went too

26. Of course, we need to recall that the first volume of *KD* was published in 1932. At *CD* I/1, 337 [*KD* I/1, 356], Barth does mention (in his lengthy listing of various *vestigia trinitatis*) Moeller van der Bruck's application of the idea of a "third kingdom" to the political sphere in his book *Das dritte Reich* (2nd edition, 1926, p. 13).

27. *CD* I/1, 343 [*KD* I/1, 362].

far" is one B. Keckermann, whose 1611 systematic theology is quoted as moving from an observation about the nature of humanity to a claim about the necessity of God's triune nature.[28]

Clearly, Barth was not basing his entire case against the *vestigia* tradition on the error of one relatively obscure seventeenth-century writer; he believed that it has had much more profound and wide-reaching negative consequences. Otherwise he could not have gone on to minimize, and even to trivialize, this long-standing theological tradition — describing it as "trifling," "a game that cannot yield serious results," and speaking of "the feeling of frivolity that we can hardly avoid in its presence."[29] He believes that, even when undertaken with the best intentions, it is likely to lead us astray. At the heart of his objection is the claim that, since everything that can be known of God can be known through revelation, there is no reason to look for enigmatic hints about God in the created order. It is a case, he believes, of nothing to be gained and everything to be lost.

This objection, in my view, is flawed — not only theologically, but also in its account of the process of communication. It does not consider the degree to which, in any communication event, both the speaker and the audience must contribute (in different ways, to be sure) to the production of knowledge. Only some such admission can account for the differing ways that a single speech (or text) can be heard (or read) and interpreted by varying audiences. Moreover, from a theological perspective, Barth's account seems to describe revelation as a zero-sum game, in which it is assumed that the control of the whole process is *either* entirely in God's hands *or* entirely in our own.[30] This, I would suggest, is an inadequately *incarnational* account of the knowledge of God.[31] God's willingness to "take the world into the divine

28. Barth quotes the Latin text at 343 [362]: *quam est necessarium, hominem esse rationalem, . . . tam est necessarium in Dei essentia tres esse personas.*

29. *CD* I/1, 344 [363].

30. Whether or not this "either/or" is firmly in place for the early Barth is a matter of some dispute. Bruce McCormack, for example, finds Barth tending toward a more incarnational account as early as the *Göttingen Dogmatics.* See *Karl Barth's Critically Realistic Dialectical Theology: Its Genesis and Development 1909-1936* (Oxford: Clarendon Press, 1995), esp. pp. 327-28.

31. In *How to Read Karl Barth: The Shape of His Theology* (New York: Oxford University Press, 1991), pp. 185-224, George Hunsinger argues quite convincingly that Barth's account of double agency bears a "Chalcedonian" character. But I think this tendency develops over time in the *Dogmatics;* it does not seem to be especially evident in I/1, and especially not in Barth's treatment of the *vestigia,* to which my remarks here are directed. At the very least, I would argue that the necessarily "asymmetrical" nature of double agency is, in I/1, so heavily balanced in God's direction that human agency is eclipsed. But for the later Barth, Hunsinger is quite right. With respect to the *vestigia* in particular, see the discussion in *CD* IV/3/1 on the created order as

bosom" by becoming flesh serves as both a warrant and a hermeneutical key for offering adequate interpretations of the created order's triune marks. In what follows, I will attempt to unpack these claims a bit.

Barth admits that our understanding of revelation is an equivocal matter, and that one must use the tools available within the created order to witness to God's revelation. Yet he draws a sharp distinction between revelation itself (which is always God's alone) and the human responses to revelation, namely proclamation and dogmatics.

> Theology and the Church, and even the Bible itself, speak no other language than that of this world which is shaped in form and content by the creaturely nature of the world and also conditioned by the limitations of humanity: the language in which human beings as we are — as sinful and corrupt human beings — wrestle with the world as it encounters us and as we see and try to understand it. The Bible, the Church and theology undoubtedly speak this language on the presupposition that there might be something in it, namely, that in this language God's revelation might be referred to, witness might be given, God's Word might be proclaimed, dogma might be formulated and declared.[32]

Here, Barth certainly allows for our need to use fallen language to witness to God. What is missing, however, is any clear sense of the human role in *receiving* revelation — hearing it, understanding it, coming into conversation with it.[33] Barth's minimization of the human role in this process is clear even from the language that he sometimes uses to arrange the biblical concept of revelation — the language of "veiling, unveiling, and impartation." All three of these activities minimize the role of the audience; its members can only "stand by and watch" as the mystery of God is veiled or unveiled. Indeed, in the case of "impartation," the audience wouldn't even have to be watching.[34]

---

the *theatrum gloriae Dei,* within which "secular parables" can "speak a word of truth" and "lesser lights" can illumine the path, insofar as they conform to the one Truth, the "one true light" (pp. 86-165).

32. *CD* I/1, 339 [*KD* I/1, 358]; translation altered to first-person plural where Barth has generic third-person singulars.

33. Many commentators have criticized passive accounts of the reception of revelation, in Barth and in others; see, e.g., John Milbank, "Can a Gift Be Given? Prolegomena to a Future Trinitarian Metaphysic," *Modern Theology* 11, no. 1 (January 1995): 119-61, particularly 141-42; Kathryn Tanner, *God and Creation in Christian Theology: Tyranny or Empowerment?* (Oxford: Blackwell, 1988), pp. 90-104; Stephen H. Webb, *The Gifting God: A Trinitarian Ethics of Excess* (Oxford: Oxford University Press, 1996), pp. 98-104 and 177-80.

34. Compare the more active role assigned to the audience (in this case, the audience of a dramatic event) in Balthasar, *T-D* I: 308-13 [*T-D* I: 286-91].

Again, I do not want to deny that, in Barth's own rhetorical and theological context, he had good reason to minimize the human role in the reception of revelation. I simply want to ask whether the specificity of his context should be used to put a stop to the productive theological conversations that the *vestigia* tradition has generated across the centuries — and to its potential for helping us think seriously about the "interpretation of the created order" as a formative Christian practice. I would certainly insist, with Barth, that the source of revelation must be God, not a projected set of human aspirations. Nevertheless, I would argue that not only proclamation and dogmatics, *but also the human reception and interpretation of God's revelation,* must occur within the "creaturely nature of the world" and be "conditioned by the limitations of humanity." Revelation is not revelation unless it is revealed *to* someone; this, in turn, requires active *reception* on the part of the recipient. Revelation cannot bypass the human will, as though it were medicine injected with a syringe.

To put the matter differently: the verb *to reveal* does indeed share the threefold structure of other transitive verbs (revealer, act of revealing, and that which is revealed: subject, verb, and object) — just as Barth describes it. But unlike many such verbs, it also requires a fourth element: the one *to whom* the revealer reveals (indirect object — dative case). Thus, the grammar of "revealing" actually bears a fourfold character, for it is incomplete without the active participation of those who *receive* it. If the grammar of the word *reveal* tells us something about God's triune life, then it also tells us something about our active role as witnesses to, and potential participants in, that life.

And precisely because of our role as witnesses and participants, the Holy Spirit and the Church must come into sharper focus than Barth allows in his discussion of divine revelation.[35] If we came to know God in the wholly passive manner of a patient who is waiting to be given medication, then our ongoing relationships with God and with others would be largely irrelevant. In this "passive" mode of reception, the "medicine" (in this case, knowledge of God that is imparted — "prescribed" — directly by God) would be expected to have certain effects, and to do so wholly independently of whether we understood ourselves as members of a community or as isolated individuals. Our task would be to pick up the medicine, take it home, and measure out the stated dosage in the privacy of our rooms.

But if the reception of revelation is an *active* endeavor, requiring consid-

35. Barth's more general tendencies in this direction are nicely summarized in Robert W. Jenson, "You Wonder Where the Spirit Went," *Pro Ecclesia: A Journal of Catholic and Evangelical Theology* 2, no. 3 (Summer 1993): 296-304.

ered judgments of the heart and mind on the part of the recipient, then it cannot be a private affair. It is less analogous to taking a prescription drug, and more analogous to some forms of physical therapy: the doctors prescribe the treatment, but the patients must be willing to respond actively. They will need the faithful support of a loving community, and a good relationship with the doctors and therapists, in order to make progress. Similarly, in the theological context, a person's formation in and by the community of belief becomes an essential and critical aspect of the process of reception and interpretation. One cannot be expected to "hear" the revelatory Word rightly, nor to "read the signs of the times," unless one has already been formed by the Christian narratives and habituated into certain ecclesial practices, such as baptism, worship, and mutual care.

The whole creation speaks and testifies to the glory of God — and quite specifically, to the *triune* God. But this fact alone does not guarantee that *communication* is taking place; words can be spoken and remain unheard. Potential hearers must somehow "learn the language" through which God can be known; the school in which they do so is the Church, and their tutor in these lessons is the Holy Spirit. The Spirit teaches the Church to see and hear what others cannot.

I do not mean to suggest that this emphasis on the *active reception* of revelation is wholly absent from Barth's work. It is more salient, for example, when he speaks of this reception through the language of "hearing" (a metaphor that suggests a much more active role for the audience than does the language of "unveiling" or "imparting"). But at least in the early Barth, our "hearing" is not really integral to the revelational event; it is always something like "overhearing." While his own context may have given Barth some good reasons to think in these terms, it may have also prevented him from recognizing the real value of a careful and nuanced employment of the *vestigia* tradition as guiding our interpretation of the created order. Because of his suspicions about any theology that awarded a significant agential role to humanity, he saw interpretation as a divinely ordered event, rather than a practice in which we play an active role.

Whose Interpretation Is It, Anyway?

Just how thoroughly Barth works to remove human agency from the interpretive process can be seen in a discussion with which he ends his section on the *vestigia.* Barth sets up a distinction between the activities of *interpretation* and *illustration* — the first being a legitimate enterprise, and the second, an illegitimate one. (His use of *interpretation* here requires some explanation: he is not referring to the theological interpretation of the created order, as I am describing that enterprise in this chapter. Rather, he is referring to all attempts to interpret or illustrate God, Christ, or various theological concepts — attempts that use the language of the created order as an explanatory structure.) The distinction between interpretation and illustration, as Barth employs the terms, will turn out to be the different roles they allot to human agency.

Barth begins ever-so-mildly: the difference between them, he says, is that "Interpretation means saying *the same thing* in other words," whereas "Illustration means saying the same thing *in other words.*" He admits that "where the line is to be drawn between the two cannot be stated generally," but nevertheless insists that "there is a line."[36] But this unspecifiable line becomes urgently important as the paragraph continues and gathers steam. Eventually "illustration" is aligned with the process of "proof" — precisely what the contributors to the *vestigia* tradition emphasized they were *not* doing. (Of course, Barth wisely does not offer an outright accusation in this respect; he simply raises the possibility in the minds of his audience, mentioning "the power to illustrate revelation" and then adding a casual-sounding "and who knows but what we should say at once its power to prove it.")[37] Indeed, by the time the paragraph is over, Barth will have aligned interpretation with everything that is right and good (theology, faith, and right worship), whereas illustration will have been successfully associated with — among other things — mere anthropology, unbelief, and idolatry![38] The rhetorical brilliance of Barth's moves throughout this paragraph should not be denied; what began as a simple difference in emphasis (on "the same thing" or on "other words") has now become the difference between truth and falsehood.[39]

But the distinction does not have this absolute character.[40] As Barth's own definition indicates, it is a matter of judgment; the two sentences that he uses to describe interpretation and illustration are, of course, grammatically and syntactically identical. They differ in the location of the emphasis; and

36. *CD* I/1, 345 [*KD* I/1, 364].

37. *CD* I/1, 345 [*KD* I/1, 364].

38. *CD* I/1, 345 [*KD* I/1, 364-65].

39. Passages like this brilliantly exemplify Barth's rhetorical skill, as explored in Stephen H. Webb, *Re-Figuring Theology: The Rhetoric of Karl Barth* (Albany: State University of New York Press, 1991).

40. One could differentiate the two categories formally; interpretation appears to make a stronger claim for the adequacy of its articulation of reality. But in this case one would expect Barth to be more cautious about interpretations, since even though they are created by human beings, they claim to be the "same" as what is revealed.

emphasis (as all good rhetoricians know) is not a property of words, or meanings, or any other momentarily stable feature of language. Rather, emphasis is placed by writers and speakers, who make judgments about the persuasive power of various forms of emphasis, and implement them accordingly. Ultimately, Barth's distinction between interpretation and illustration is based on his own assessment of a theological claim's legitimacy. If Barth considers it an adequate account of revelation, it is an interpretation (and thus it is theology, leading to faith and right worship); if inadequate, it is an illustration (and thus it is anthropology, leading to unbelief and idolatry).

Clearly, Barth would *like* his audience to believe that illustration is corrupted by the intervention of human agency, whereas interpretation is not. He wants to describe interpretation as the *appropriate* human response: God is allowed to speak and human beings do not get in the way. But interpretation, too, requires human agency; otherwise one would just repeat the text or narrate the event, letting it "speak for itself" rather than offering an interpretation. This becomes obvious in Barth's various portrayals of the dangers of illustration; each of these "dangers" apply equally to interpretation.[41]

Ultimately, illustration and interpretation both require a *human* agent. This is precisely the feature of "interpretation" that Barth would like to minimize — though he does not claim explicitly that interpretation can avoid human agency. In fact, he may recognize a problem here; he admits that his own discussion of the threefold character of revelation failed to protect itself against the suspicion that it "might be using an illustration and playing a little game with a supposed *vestigium trinitatis*."[42] But Eberhard Jüngel seems much more confident that the human factor can be removed completely from the process of revelation:

> Interpretation protects the sameness of revelation in that it brings revelation (and only this) *as* revelation to speech. Illustration endangers the sameness of revelation in that it brings *with* revelation *also* language *(nomina)* as revelation to speech. But where also language *(nomina)* as revelation is brought to speech along with revelation, revelation is no longer protected as revelation *and* language no longer as language.[43]

41. Illustration is described as diminishing revelation, in that "we set a second thing alongside" it; we fail to trust "its self-evidential force"; and we assume that it "must be buttressed and strengthened and confirmed by something other than itself." But these all apply to interpretation as well as to illustration, since interpretation uses (as Barth plainly allows) "other words" (*CD* I/1, 345 [*KD* I/1, 364]).

42. *CD* I/1, 345 [365].

43. Eberhard Jüngel, *The Doctrine of the Trinity: God's Being Is in Becoming,* trans. Horton

Jüngel here attempts to use the distinction between *speech* and *language* to suggest that revelation can take place without the corrupting influence of language. But surely this is more weight than the "speech/language" distinction can bear. That the source of revelation is divine, we need not doubt; but it cannot be brought to speech without the very *human* structures of language. Interpretation is not something that revelation "does." It is, manifestly, something that human beings do — in the power of the Spirit to be sure, yet without eclipsing human agency.[44]

In a lengthy footnote, Jüngel attempts to clarify his distinction through a discussion of the way that revelation "captures" language. The goal of interpretation, it would seem, is to reiterate the process of revelation capturing language, rather than to focus exclusively on the text itself as a static residue of the event of capture. Although Jüngel does not say so explicitly, he seems to align Barth's positive evaluation of "interpretation" with the hermeneutical interest in "the *capture* of the language by revelation as it becomes perceptible in the captures (texts!). Hermeneutics attempts so to preserve revelation as revelation and language as language precisely where revelation takes place, i.e., where God comes to speech."[45]

Clearly Jüngel (like Barth) would like to get around the thorny problem of language, and to claim that revelation uses language in such a way that all human linguistic activity is excluded. If it were possible to achieve this end, it would serve the very useful function of eliminating the Feuerbachian critique of revelation as the height of human striving, since it would take the agency of revelation completely out of the hands of human beings. But I rather doubt that the "divine" and "human" ("revealing" and "receiving") elements of revelation can be so neatly sorted into discrete linguistic categories. And even if it could, this would not suffice as a Christian doctrine of revelation; for an adequately *incarnational* account of revelation must allow both the human and the divine elements to play their proper role.

In this respect, neither Barth nor Jüngel allows the Incarnation to become the operative motif. For both of them, interpretation is "fully divine," but it is not "fully human." It is something that God does for us, something over which God must exercise final control, rather than something in which both divine and human agency are present. For Barth and Jüngel, the Incar-

Harris (Edinburgh: Scottish Academic Press, Ltd., 1976), pp. 13-14 [ET of: *Gottes Sein ist im Werden*, 2e. Aufl. (Tübingen: J. C. B. Mohr, Paul Siebeck, 1966), pp. 24-25].

44. On the human activity essential to the process of interpretation, see Nicholas Lash's essays "What Might Martyrdom Mean?" and "Performing the Scriptures," both of which are reprinted in *Theology on the Way to Emmaus* (London: SCM, 1986).

45. Jüngel, *Doctrine of the Trinity*, p. 14, n. 43 [*Gottes Sein*, p. 25, n. 43].

nation is limited (in a surprisingly literalistic fashion) to the person of Jesus; he is the only real *vestigium trinitatis*. But for most of the ancient authors, the Incarnation — far from limiting the search for *vestigia* — actually *warrants* that search. Indeed, it reduces the likelihood that it will be converted into the kind of vain speculation that Barth and Jüngel fear. On the contrary: because the Incarnation teaches us something about the *character* of God, it gives us the confidence to interpret the created order — to "read the signs of the times" — in accordance with our conviction that, in Christ, "all things hold together" (Col. 1:17).

Interpreting Boldly

Interpretation of the created order can be an appropriate Christian practice, and one that helps to form us in knowing the Trinity, insofar as we allow Christ to teach us how to "read" the world's triune marks, and to effect this teaching by providing us with a keynote and example. Secure in this knowledge, we can interpret the created order boldly, drawing attention to those triune marks that seem most obvious to us. We can do this with confidence, since the nature of God's relationship with the world has already been revealed to us through Christ.

This is not to say that such a practice is without risks. Barth is right to observe that the tradition can be abused as a warrant for allowing human conceptions of God to eclipse the concrete narratives of God's ongoing involvement with the world though Israel, Christ, and the Church. Thus, the positive lesson to be learned from Barth's critique is that these concrete narratives cannot be allowed to fade into the background. They must always be the starting-point of any Christian doctrine of God.

On the other hand, there seems to be no reason to accept Barth's conclusion that there is nothing to be gained from the search for *vestigia*. By way of summary, three points can be offered here. (1) The knowledge of God is not an all-or-nothing affair. Even if we agree with Barth that the revelation of God in Christ is the ultimate source of our knowledge of God, it does not necessarily follow that this knowledge is made clear to us, nor that we understand it, nor that we are persuaded of its truth and its relevance. Even if the *vestigia* produce no wholly new knowledge, they can help to give shape and clarity to what has already been made known to us. In this sense they can be an aid to dogmatics and proclamation. (2) The reception of revelation, like the hearing of any word, requires human thought and action. Consequently, the search for *vestigia,* when done with adequate attention to the concrete narratives of the Christian faith, is not fundamentally different from (for example) reading the Bible as preparation for preaching a sermon. In each case, the theologian seeks to be attentive to the revealed word of God — but also to be attentive to the created order, and to employ human language to interpret (and/or illustrate!) divine revelation. (3) We believe in an engaged, relational God who does not abandon the world; having created us, God remains active, gracing us with the power to respond by faith to the redemptive and sustaining love that God freely gives us. This belief has implications for our understanding of revelation. Having revealed to us something of the divine life, God does not abandon us to "figure it all out for ourselves," but remains at work in the created order, providing a context within which we may hear, understand, and be persuaded by God's self-revelation.

In my view, these three points are at the heart of the *vestigia* tradition as it has been practiced by Augustine, Bonaventure, Luther, and many others throughout the history of Christianity. Augustine, for example, does not begin his *De Trinitate* with a discussion of *vestigia.* Only after seven full books — in which he begins with the biblical narratives and develops an account of the divine relations, the trinitarian missions, appropriated and proper actions, and similar elements of the doctrine of God — does he turn to the created order and construe it as marked by God. And as he does so, he constantly refers the reader back to the missions of the Word and the Spirit as touchstones of theological adequacy, so that the *vestigia* never drift off into abstract speculation. And while he admits that none of his analogies is perfect, he hopes that at least some of them will provide his readers with greater clarity and understanding about the triune God.

If we allow the *vestigia* tradition to serve as the model for our interpretation of the created order, it can become a formative element of Christian practice. "Knowing the triune God" is very different from the almost instantaneous appropriation of knowledge that is so sought-after in our culture. One does not come to know God through the acquisition of some nugget of information, any more than one comes to know other human beings by listening to their voice-mail recordings or surfing briskly over their websites. It is, rather, a lengthy process of give-and-take, one that requires us to be *in relation with* the one whom we would come to know. It requires that we listen, yes; but it also requires that we respond, that we try to express what we think we've heard, that we offer a provisional conclusion that is always open to reshaping and refining by the Other. The kind of active interpretation I have described here encourages us to call upon the power of the Spirit that has shaped us as members of the Body of Christ, allowing that formation to guide us in the long and complex process of coming to know the triune God.

I conclude this chapter with a description of three specific ways in which I believe theological reflection would prosper were it to embrace more fully the kinds of interpretive practice I have described here. First, I think that doing so would address the failure of nerve from which theology has so often suffered in assuming that other disciplines are better able to understand the created order. Marx complained that "philosophers have only interpreted the world"; but in recent decades, theologians have managed to do even less: they have blithely accepted someone else's interpretation of the world as "factual" and have largely abdicated their own interpretive power. The Christian narrative and Christian practices provide a perspective from which to view the world, a perspective that Christians hold to be *true.* Hence there need be no "bad conscience" concerning some supposed "objective reality" that lies just outside the theologian's reach. As John Milbank puts the matter, "there is no independently available 'real world' against which we must test our Christian convictions, because these convictions are the most final, and at the same time the most basic, *seeing* of what the world is."[46]

Second, a more consistent practice of interpretation would allow us to highlight the role of the Spirit and the Church as the primary agent and the primary locus of the knowledge of God. If we understand human beings as called not just passively to receive revelation but actively to interpret it, then we must acknowledge that their theological formation and the shape of their spirituality will have a considerable impact on what they "hear." The practices of the believer — and of the whole Church — then take on immense significance, in that they dispose a person in particular ways toward a "right hearing" of the Word and an adequate interpretation of the world. For example, those communities that include a catechumenate in their practice of adult baptism are helping to form Christian believers who can "interpret boldly" the world around them. And those Christians whose lives are shaped by the traditions of contemplative prayer have another reason for confidence in their interpretations. (The previous two chapters of this volume explore these practices in considerable detail.) These are but two examples of the ways in which the Church becomes a space in which the Holy Spirit can work to make us both *active* and *passionate* in our interpretation of the created order.

Finally, the kind of interpretive practice that I have outlined here has significant implications for Christian ethics. If we are called not just to "accept" the versions of the world that we are handed by "other experts," but rather to envision it anew through explicitly theological categories, then we can also re-

46. John Milbank, "The Poverty of Niebuhrianism," in *The Word Made Strange: Theology, Language, Culture* (Oxford: Blackwell, 1997), pp. 233-54; here, p. 250.

envision our interactions with the world. For example, in the West, the science of economics and the world of business have interpreted the distribution of wealth and the causes of poverty in particular ways; but this is no warrant for Christians to prostrate themselves before these interpretations. The relational life of the triune God, in which one of the Three is always "giving place" to another, would suggest a very different assessment of modern economic circumstances — and would point us toward new ethical demands.[47] Similarly, as Christians, we are called not simply to accept the world's definition of "insiders" and "outsiders," but to welcome into our midst even those who are generally regarded as "strangers." (The final three chapters in this book explore various nuances of this claim.)

To engage in the practice of interpretation is not to divorce theology from the concrete narratives that stand at the center of the Christian life. However, such interpretation can help to make those narratives clearer, more relevant, and more persuasive. What we gain, in the process, is not "new" knowledge of God, but a new perspective for Christian belief and Christian action — even while recognizing that both are ultimately motivated by "what was from the beginning, what we have heard, what we have seen with our eyes, what we have looked at and touched with our hands, concerning the word of life" (1 John 1:1).

47. An excellent beginning is that of M. Douglas Meeks, *God the Economist: The Doctrine of God and Political Economy* (Minneapolis: Fortress Press, 1989). See also D. Stephen Long, *Divine Economy: Theology and the Market* (London and New York: Routledge, 2000). For the language of "giving place" in trinitarian theology, see Rowan Williams's new book on the Trinity, forthcoming in the series Edinburgh Studies in Constructive Theology, published in the U.S. by William B. Eerdmans.

III. DISPUTED QUESTIONS ON KNOWING THE TRINITY

8. The Wounded Body

The Spirit's Ecumenical Work on Divisions among Christians

JAMES J. BUCKLEY

Whose Spirit, Which Church?

Presume that the Spirit makes God known through particular practices of the Church — especially (recalling earlier chapters) Scripture and its uses, the baptismal catechumenate and the eucharistic Supper, humble and heroic service to the world, personal gifts of the Spirit unpredictably poured forth, and other such passions and actions. Presume also that persons are formed through such practices in such a way as to be able to know God now and in eternity. Spirit, Church, and knowledge of God are, then, intimately if asymptotically related. That is, the Church exists as gift of the Spirit — and the knowledge of God is given in and with the practices of this Church.

However, here's a strong objection. What shall such persons do with the fact that their knowledge of God is shaped not only by the Spirit but also by a divided Church — a Church divided, for example, by unreflective passions and customs as well as by seemingly thoughtful heresies and schisms (e.g., 1 Cor. 11:18-19)? This, of course, is not a question about possible worlds; it is a question about Christians today and our circumstances. These divisions of the Church jeopardize my initial presumption that the Holy Spirit is at work in the Church in a way that yields knowledge of God. What then?

One possibility is that the Holy Spirit would inspire a "movement called 'ecumenical'" longing for "the one visible church of God" — a movement that "began within the churches and ecclesial communities of the Reformation" and was joined (or appropriated) by Orthodox and eventually Roman Catholic churches.[1] I take John Paul II to articulate a common Christian (and not only my own Roman Catholic) hope when he affirms an irreversible commitment to "the ecumenical venture" as embracing sundry principles as well as practices: common conversion to the triune God, continual reform of the entire Church as well as personal holiness and martyrdom, prayer together as well as theological dialogue, cooperation in our service to neighbor and other such practices local and international.[2] (I will frequently speak of "ecumenical venture" rather than "ecumenical movement" to distinguish my topic from the corruptions introduced by what I will call below "the age of ecumenicity.") By "the ecumenical venture" I will mean not primarily a movement of church officials and academics and bureaucrats but a movement of God's pilgrim people — a complex movement in which there are different charisms for different individuals and groups. In all these ways, ecumenical venture promises a way beyond a divided Church, beyond the opposition of Orthodox and Catholic and Evangelical and other churches and communions to each other.

Nonetheless, we are again faced with a strong objection. Against those tempted to substitute ecumenical movement for the Church's mission, it is crucial to remember that this movement also has its failures. It is less often a reconciliation of our unity and division (the first two paragraphs above) than its reiteration on a smaller scale — a sort of counter-sacrament. In other words, like the divided churches, "the ecumenical movement" is not simply a site of communion and consensus but also a site of conflict over its own goals and means. For example, is the ecumenical movement a paradigm of how to live with and think about others, or is it "part of an outlook which is not ready to accept difference and the Other" — a movement that privileges unity and consensus over diversity and conflict, the nature of the Church over its mission to the world, even "the Church's self-absorption" over our common conversion to the triune God? Little wonder that ecumen-

1. The first half of the sentence is from Vatican II, "Decree on Ecumenism (1964)," paragraph 1, while the second half is from John Paul II, "Ut Unum Sint (1995)," paragraph 65 (English translation slightly revised). For the former, see Norman Tanner, ed., *Decrees of the Ecumenical Councils* (London: Sheed & Ward and Washington, D.C.: Georgetown University Press, 1990), vol. 2, p. 908; for the latter see *Acta Apostolicae Sedis* 87, no. 11 (November 1995): 921-82 and the translation in *Origins* 25 (1995): 49-72.

2. "Ut Unum Sint," paragraph 3.

ical movement is periodically — including now — said to be in crisis, or eclipsed by indifference.[3]

Such objections raise a large set of issues. Responding to them would require a full-scale theology of the Spirit and the Church's mission in the world. But I think there is also a need for something more modest — a relocating of ecumenical movement in the midst of the work of the Spirit on the practices and teachings of the Church. My central claim will be that a necessary condition for holding together the asymptotic and broken relations between Spirit, Church, and knowledge of God will be to take seriously the ecumenical venture as *a movement of the Spirit* — where the genitive "of" is (first) subjective as well as (second) objective. That is, first, there is no ecumenical movement prior to *the Holy Spirit who moves it, or us* — and our participation in this movement depends crucially on how we respond to (including identify) this Spirit. Each of the three sections below relies on one traditional identification of the Spirit, asking how it might embody the Spirit's ecumenical venture — the Spirit who speaks through the prophets, who teaches all things, and so who indwells our wounded body. Second, the Spirit's ecumenical venture is a movement in and on *our wounded materiality* — our narratives, our teachings, our practices as God's sinful creatures being patiently healed. Each of the following sections will focus on one aspect of our wounded materiality, the abiding wounds of Christ's body — the way we wallow in our most painful memories and cling to our most deeply conflicting teachings and practices.

By essay's end, as we take seriously the ecumenical venture as a movement of the Spirit, we will have a theology of ecumenical venture as the Spirit prophetically preserving our painful memories in ways that heal, teaching us ecumenical "tactics" in word and deed inseparably, concealed in the Church's wounded body as a way of revealing the body of a crucified messiah, a temple being rebuilt and raised from the dead.

A. Painful Memories and the Spirit Who Speaks through the Prophets

The major irony of the modern ecumenical movement is that it arose as the traditional divisions among Christians seemed to be eclipsed by divisions be-

3. Michael Root, "Ecumenical Theology," in *The Modern Theologians: An Introduction to Christian Theology in the Twentieth Century*, 2nd edition, ed. David Ford (Oxford: Blackwell, 1997), pp. 549-50. See also the Institute for Ecumenical Research (Strasbourg), *Crisis and Challenge of the Ecumenical Movement: Integrity and Indivisibility* (Geneva: WCC Publications, 1994).

tween the Church and the world — a world that is often indifferent if not hostile to that Church. Indeed, Peter Berger once told the story of the modern age as an "age of ecumenicity" necessarily countervailed by an "age of the rediscovery of confessional heritages" — where "necessarily" is the necessity of a new market situation in which Christianity is no longer a monopoly but one product among many.[4] For this "age of ecumenicity," our past disputes can hardly be part of our present market appeal; these disputes are thought to be irrelevant to the joys and griefs of the modern world. We can "get along with" each other now, so why bother with our past divisions? Indeed, it often seems part of the logic of such an age that the Christian ecumenical movement must be appropriated as one movement among a more universal ecumenical movement that includes all religions as well as the broader philosophical and political and ecological movements of our time.[5]

The notion that we are more ecumenical than previous eras is, I think, another exercise in modern *hubris*. Long ago H. R. Niebuhr reminded us of the social sources of denominationalism — churches more visibly identifiable as modern economic classes and regions and races than by conversion to the triune God.[6] "Modernity" from this point of view looks no more like "an ecumenical age" than did "premodernity." But this "age of ecumenicity" only too often arrogantly presents itself as an Age of the Spirit that transcends the Ages of the Father and the Son, a new age filled with new content.[7]

On the other hand, "the age of confessional heritages" argues that (or acts as if) this wider ecumenical movement is in fact the demise of Christian identity, ecumenicity (catholicity) overwhelming particularity. Who (it is asked) is the "we" who shall engage in this wider movement? Do we have our own voice on the modern religious, philosophical, political stage? What we need (one confessional-denominational argument might go) is the revival of an-

4. Peter L. Berger, *The Sacred Canopy: Elements of a Sociological Theory of Religion* (Garden City, N.Y.: Doubleday, 1967), esp. pp. 141-48.

5. For the competing theologies behind ecumenical movement in the twentieth century, see the essays in Michael Kinnamon and Brian E. Cope, eds., *The Ecumenical Movement: An Anthology of Key Texts and Voices* (Geneva: WCC Publications and Grand Rapids: Eerdmans, 1997), ch. 1.

6. H. Richard Niebuhr, *The Social Sources of Denominationalism* (New York: World Publishing Company, 1929). The fact that Niebuhr's prescription is more liberal Protestant at this stage of his life than trinitarian does not undercut his diagnosis.

7. We also need to remember the truth in proposals that we live in a new age of the Spirit, namely, that "the future stands open beyond the present is a particular parable of the Holy Spirit" (Hans Urs von Balthasar, "Improvisation on Spirit and Future," in *Creator Spirit: Explorations in Theology*, vol. 3, trans. Brian McNeil, C.R.V. [San Francisco: Ignatius, 1993], pp. 135-71 [here, p. 146]). I will return to this by essay's end.

other era — biblical, patristic, medieval, and/or reformation — combined with just enough *ad hoc* cooperation among Christians to resist the corruptions of modernity. Again, an age of confessional heritage does not have to go this way. The turning of the world from the Church could be the Spirit's way of turning the Church toward the world, including toward "the disorder of secular politics and economics."[8] But there can be little doubt that only too often the confessional age moves in dialectical counterpoint to the rhythms of an ecumenical era.

No wonder, then, that ecumenical movement might be criticized as either akin to a bureaucratic corporation destined to merge the particularities of local businesses (Christianity as finally "ecumenical" over against the divisions inherited from Christendom) or a last gasp of old-fashioned Christendom (Christianity *as* "confessional heritage" over against modernity). On either view, John Paul II's irreversible commitment to the ecumenical venture would have to be viewed with deep suspicion.

Note that, in this scenario, "the ecumenical movement" and confessional-denominational counter-movements are primarily *passive* movements, less something that Church *does*, practices, or engages in than a movement *required of them* by peculiarly modern circumstances. There is more than a little truth to this story. But it also suggests that, unless the ecumenical venture has a deeper intelligibility, indifference to it will win out in the end. What is missing?

Serious divisions among Christians involve events that have happened in the past, historical memories, painful memories that require healing.[9] And ecumenical movement therefore requires knowing these events, recovering the memories of our divisions, and so remembering our wounded body. "And so"? How does knowing past events and acquiring a memory of our divisions contribute to re-membering our wounded body? Only (I propose) if "the ecumenical venture" does not embody another division among Christians — this time between an Age of Ecumenism and an Age of Confessions, liberals and conservatives, revisionists and postliberals. Ecumenical movement must be part of a narrative larger than itself if it is to be a history without the pains of division, or the pains of division with no promise of healing. Let me consider these alternatives.

8. Karl Barth, *Church Dogmatics,* ed. G. W. Bromiley and T. F. Torrance, trans. G. W. Bromiley (Edinburgh: T. & T. Clark, 1961), vol. 4, pt. 3, first half, pp. 35-38.

9. John Paul II's "Ut Unum Sint" speaks of "painful recollections" (#52) and "a healing of historical memories" (#88), "banishing from us the painful memories of our separation" (#102). Compare G. R. Evans, *Method in Ecumenical Theology: The Lessons So Far* (Cambridge: Cambridge University Press, 1996), ch. 5 (Historical Method).

"Knowing past events" surely includes knowing what modern people call "history." For example, it includes knowing those heresies and schisms that constitute the inescapable background to New Testament gospels and epistles. It includes knowing the division between Greek and Latin Christians — a schism that climaxed in mutual excommunication in 1054 and reverberated in centuries of mutual recrimination and isolation. It requires knowing the divisions between Catholic and Evangelical Christians in the sixteenth century — divisions that again climaxed in mutual condemnation but ultimately yielded increasing confessional chauvinism or indifference about such matters. And there are also other divisions — divisions among Greeks prior to the split with the Latin West; divisions within Evangelicals and Catholics after the sixteenth-century reformations, divisions by nation and race and class.

However, confronted with this history, should we not more truthfully say that the story of the Church *is* the history of its divisions, the history of its self-inflicted pain, or a battle to the death between true Church and false? Pressed to one conclusion, what moderns call "history" would then become what postmoderns call "genealogy," i.e., the recital of the Christian past as a story of our eternally recurring death, whether embraced in nihilistic sadness or joy.[10] "Genealogy" thus defined, far from being an obscurantist academic theory, is the story of our divisions told by those who despair over their healing. It is not so much a theory as a practice — the practice of habitual suspicion of reconciliation, or a deep doubt that genuine healing can occur in the world as it is and as we create it.

But, some would rightly protest at this point, it is at least as important to remember that the wounded body is not *constituted by* such wounds. There have also been reconciliations among Christians. We might think of the unity-in-diversity that *preceded* divisions between Greek and Latin, Catholic and Protestant.[11] We might also think of posthumous efforts to heal the divisions. There were efforts to heal the Greek-Latin schism throughout the Middle Ages, just as there were periodic efforts to reconcile Catholics and Protestants in the sixteenth centuries and after. Indeed, what we have called "the ecumenical movement" is such a movement of reconciliation. It may even be

10. For the contrast between Enlightenment "history" and Nietzschean "genealogy," see Alasdair MacIntyre, *Three Rival Versions of Moral Enquiry: Encyclopedia, Genealogy, and Tradition* (Notre Dame: University of Notre Dame Press, 1990). Taking genealogy seriously is taking seriously what Abraham Heschel once called "another ecumenical movement, world-wide in extent and influence: nihilism" ("No Religion Is an Island," *Union Seminary Quarterly Review* 21 [1966]: 117-33).

11. Vatican II's "Decree on Ecumenism" is a classic example of this narrative strategy; see paragraphs 14 and 19.

the most striking such movement in the history of Christianity, at least since the formation of the biblical canon. But it is not an absolute novelty.

I think that this story of communion *prior* to and even *subsequent* to division is important. However, it is at this point that our memories of reconciliations again risk forgetting the pains of division. We are tempted to forget that these past divisions are not mere facts or historical memories but *painful* memories — memories of painful slights and more serious bodily wounds. For example, Steven Ozment contends that modern historians by and large regard the Reformation "as a very modest spiritual movement . . . and, when compared with the social and political revolts of the century, a very minor event in its history."[12] However, when Ozment goes on to disagree with such modern historians and to argue that "Protestants" constituted "the birth of a revolution," he offers a narrative that cuts the Reformation from its Catholic past, even going so far as to almost glorify the Reformation's "shedding the spiritual truths of yesterday as if they were just another bad investment or failed love affair."[13] "Modern historians" thus provide grist for the mill of indifference to Catholic-Protestant divides, while Ozment's alternative account could yield despair over the contemporary ecumenical movement.

But the point applies well beyond relations among Christians. We each have memories of injustices done and suffered, betrayals of love, falsehoods committed and truths omitted. We all have such painful memories. And we also know how we only too often live through such pain: by forgetting. In short, on these terms, we have either unity of memory *without* pain of division (akin to an Age of Ecumenicity) — or preservation of the memory of division *without* healing the pain (an Age of Confessional Heritages). We seem to be back to the very divide with which we began this section.

Before proposing a way beyond this divide, I do not wish to downplay the importance of knowing when to forget.[14] We sometimes forget pain because

12. Steven Ozment, *Protestants: The Birth of a Revolution* (New York: Doubleday, 1991), p. 219.

13. See David S. Yeago, "'A Christian, Holy People': Martin Luther on Salvation and the Church," *Modern Theology* 13, no. 1 (January 1997): 102-4; see also the essays in Carl E. Braaten and Robert W. Jenson, eds., *The Catholicity of the Reformation* (Grand Rapids and Cambridge, U.K.: Eerdmans, 1996). The majority report (Reformation as Minor Event) and the minority report (Reformation as Revolution) conspire to support a tale of the Reformation as the victory of private judgment over Christendom — a pyrrhic victory that leads to modern individualism. This is not incompatible with the story of the Reformation as told by Vatican I (Norman Tanner, *Decrees of the Ecumenical Councils*, vol. 2, pp. 804-5); it is not yet integrated (we might say) with the story Vatican II begins to tell.

14. This is one of the important themes throughout Gregory Jones, *Embodying Forgive-*

it is violence done to or by us — a violence (we might think) that we must hand on in the name of truth. The danger of *remembering pain* is that our history may become the story of the violence we have done to each other. We may then tell a story in which our history not only includes such pain and violence but *is* such pain, violence, and even death. In still other words, as I suggested earlier, what moderns call "history" will turn into what postmoderns call "genealogy" — not only a history *of* division and pain and death but history *as* division and pain and death.

Particularly in the face of the despair of postmodern genealogy, I do not want to rule out some kinds of forgetfulness, as when God promises a day when our sins will be remembered no more (Jer. 31:34) and Paul says "I forget the past and I strain ahead for what is still to come . . ." (Phil. 3:12, 13).[15] Indeed, sometimes it is good (as Paul VI and Patriarch Athenagoras did in 1963) to "regret and remove from memory and from the midst of the Church the sentences of excommunication" their churches had issued against each other.[16] But this kind of forgetting is not avoidance of painful memory. Instead it is (as Paul said) inseparable from the future we strain toward, aim for, yearn for. How?

But if the story of the Church is neither history without pain nor pain without end, whence the healing of these storied pains? Everything will depend on which of these memories are broadest and deepest. And this (as the earlier references to Jeremiah and Philippians suggest) will depend on "what is still to come" — the telos or eschaton of our memories. Here, I suggest, is where Christians must remember the profession of the First Council of Con-

---

ness: A Theological Analysis (Grand Rapids: Eerdmans, 1995), and Miroslav Volf, *Exclusion and Embrace: A Theological Exploration of Identity, Otherness, and Reconciliation* (Nashville: Abingdon, 1996).

15. See Paul VI's 20 September 1963 letter to Patriarch Athenagoras in *Towards the Healing of Schism: The Sees of Rome and Constantinople,* ed. and trans. E. J. Storman, S.J. (New York and Mahwah, N.J.: Paulist Press, 1987), p. 52; and Joseph Cardinal Ratzinger, "General Orientation with Regard to the Ecumenical Dispute about the Formal Principles of Faith," in *Principles of Catholic Theology,* trans. Sister Mary Frances McCarthy, S.N.D. (San Francisco: Ignatius, 1987), pp. 205, 211.

16. *Towards the Healing of Schism,* pp. 126-29; John Paul II, "Ut Unum Sint," paragraph 52. For a different strategy with the Catholic-Protestant condemnations, reminding the churches of the condemnations and then proposing why the condemnations might *no longer* apply (without ruling out the possibility that they once did and may come to do so again), see Karl Lehman and Wolfhart Pannenberg, eds., *The Condemnations of the Reformation Era: Do They Still Divide?* trans. Margaret Kohl (Minneapolis: Fortress Press, 1990); Karl Lehman, ed., *Justification by Faith: Do the Sixteenth-Century Condemnations Still Apply?* trans. Michael Root, William G. Rusch, and J. Francis Stafford (New York: Crossroad, 1997).

stantinople: "the Holy Spirit who spoke through the prophets." That is, among Christians for whom Scripture is common source of our faith,[17] both New and Old Testament are crucial — where "testament" signals God's abiding covenant, and where "Old" does not mean "out of date" but enduring and perduring, "seasoned" (like God's testament with Israel), preserving painful memories in a way that heals.

For example, as Ephraim Radner argues, "Israel's history of treason and idolatry" — from Israel's apostasy after the Exodus through the divisions of the kingdoms and the exiles — is a "type" (1 Cor. 10:11) of a divided Church. Israel figures the demise of divided churches akin to the fallen kingdom in exile. But Israel's prophets are those who speak *against* Israel *on behalf of* Israel, bringing the narrative of God's promises to Israel to bear on faithless generations as they gather a holy remnant purging its members for the last days — a penitent community refined for the future by remembering the promise and sin of its history. Without such a reading of the life and death of Israel, Christians are left with fewer tools for "understanding of the divinely informed character of our intrinsically problematic ecclesial existence as a fractured body."[18]

On this reading, far from succumbing to the temptation to identify Israel as the bearer of God's judgment and the Church as bearer of God's mercy, Israel is also figure of God's mercy — as the Church must bear God's judgment. As George Lindbeck has put it, when the Church was a replacement rather than an expansion of Israel, the result was devastating. "The stories of unfaithfulness and the thunderings of the prophets were read as directed first against Jews, second against heretics, and third against unrighteousness in professedly Christian societies. The real church, however that was defined, could not be culpable of wickedness comparable to that of Israel before Christ, nor of Jewry *post Christum*." Thus, a "critical leverage against Christian triumphalism of every kind, but especially against anti-Judaism" was lost. The mistake, Lindbeck

17. Needless to say, the appeal to the biblical rule is not ecumenically neutral. I here presume the theology of Scripture sketched by David S. Yeago in Chapter 3 above.

18. Ephraim Radner, "The Cost of Communion: A Meditation on Israel and the Divided Church," in *Inhabiting Unity: Theological Perspectives on the Proposed Lutheran-Episcopal Concordat*, ed. Ephraim Radner and R. R. Reno (Grand Rapids: Eerdmans, 1995), pp. 134-52. I had completed this essay before the appearance of Radner's *The End of the Church: A Pneumatology of Christian Division in the West* (Grand Rapids and Cambridge, U.K.: Eerdmans, 1998). This was providential, for my effort withers before Radner's brilliant and unrelenting call to repentance of a body that cannot recognize its own wounds. I am by training, if not disposition, more inclined to what Radner calls Vincent de Paul's "mode of activism" (p. 354), but I too would hope for embrace.

notes, was Catholic as well as Protestant. Christians "either assumed with the Catholics that the church does not sin in itself but only its members or, with the Protestants, that it ceases to be the true church when it does. Both positions, it can be argued, are triumphalistic. They make impossible that combination of unbreakable communal loyalty despite unflinching recognition of unbearable communal sins characteristic of Jesus and the prophets."[19]

Much more would have to be said to support fully this contention. We would have to show how Israel's major and minor prophets spoke *against* Israel *from the midst* of her history, so that prophetic criticism of Israel's divisions served God's promise that Israel would be a blessing unto the nations. We would also need a rereading of the gospels as narratives of the Jewish Prophet who irreversibly and unsurpassably enacts Israel's return from exile and suffers the consequences on our behalf.[20] And then we would need to read the traditional disputes among Christians against the background of Israel's prophets, sifting our own true and false prophets, measured against Jesus' prophetic office. For example, we need to discover a tradition of the Church as a story that distinguishes differences from conflicts, pseudo-conflicts from genuine ones, our conflicts from those of previous generations.[21] This narrative, I should add, would have elements of both history and genealogy sketched above — a narrative that privileges the painful divides of Greeks and Latins, Catholics and Protestants, modern classes and nations against the background of their common history before their divisions and their genuine but failed efforts at reconciliation afterwards. Such (we might say) is the work of ecumenical historical (and genealogical) theologies. But it is also the task of pastors and parents and teachers who aim to learn and teach the story of the Church in charity and truth. The narrative of these divisions is not dispensable "historical background" policed by specialists — but neither is it a story without end, as if the painful memories of divisions was the final word, policed by those suspicious of any reconciliations.

19. George Lindbeck, "The Gospel's Uniqueness: Election and Untranslatability," *Modern Theology* 13, no. 4 (October 1997): 423-50 (here, pp. 436, 443). The appeal to Israel does not play a role in John Paul II's "Ut Unum Sint" (except for a brief appeal to Ezekiel 37:19, 23 in paragraph 5).

20. For a good recent treatment of Jesus as an internal critic of Israel, see N. T. Wright, *Jesus and the Victory of God: Christian Origins and the Question of God,* vol. 2 (Minneapolis: Fortress Press, 1996), e.g., p. 595.

21. As Robert Jenson puts it, the "church can and must discover and practice her temporal continuity as *dramatic* continuity, the kind of continuity that constitutes Aristotle's good stories" (*Unbaptized God: The Basic Flaw in Ecumenical Theology* [Minneapolis: Fortress Press, 1992], pp. 141, 145).

But the central point I wish to make in this section is modest: the typological pertinence of the story of divided Israel for the painful memories of the divided Church is that this is one way *the Holy Spirit speaks through these prophets* — not only by promising the Messiah but by preserving the painful memories of division as Israel does, i.e., in a way that promises their healing. The Spirit thus converts us to remember Israel, preserving our betrayals as a condition for genuine healing. Such is one way the Spirit moves ecumenically, and calls us to do the same.

B. Practices, Teachings, and the Pedagogy of the Giver of Life

Narratives that neither ignore nor perpetuate our divisions are a necessary but not sufficient condition of ecumenical movement. They are a necessary condition because, without them, we will be tempted to suppress our painful memories, or elevate them to the final word — in the one case promoting indifference over our divisions and in the other defeatism over ecumenical movement.[22] But they are not sufficient because our division, like our unity, is not of a single sort. There are, for example, opposed "practices" (e.g., personal, sacramental, political) as well as opposed "teachings" (e.g., about God, the Church, and the world). If so, the divisions we narrate and the communion we seek will have as ingredients different and opposed practices and teachings in different times and places.[23]

Note that I just said "for example." I do not mean that all divisions among Christians can be neatly lumped as divisions over teachings and practices (heresies and schisms, some might say). In fact, because our divisions embody sin, they have no fully intelligible taxonomy. This is why such divisions must ultimately be taken up one by one. Nonetheless, I take "practices and teachings" as an example because their relation has become a deep problem in our time — a problem that shapes how we engage in and think about the ecumenical venture. That is, some (often the same ones who would have us choose between "an ecumenical age" and "an age of a rediscovery of confessions") would have us choose between whether ecumenical movement is a matter of practices *or* teachings. Thus, some are tempted to think that our divisions are exclusively opposed teachings (i.e., beliefs, dogmas, truth-claims

22. For these unacceptable options, see John Paul II, "Ut Unum Sint," paragraph 79.

23. Rather than *define* what I mean by practices and teachings here, I am going to let the *examples* I give below suffice. I have tried to give more careful descriptions in *Seeking the Humanity of God: Practices, Doctrines, and Catholic Theology* (Collegeville, Minn.: The Liturgical Press, 1992), index (under "practices" and "doctrines").

about God and the world, Jesus and the Spirit, justification and sanctification, the church and its sacraments, personal and political faith and love, or so on); if so, the argument goes, no amount of common practice can overcome such opposed teachings. Or others might think that, because we share common practices (e.g., personal experiences, baptismal catechumenate, and/or communal service to the world), opposed teachings make little difference. At the extremes such people will reduce ecumenical movement to convergence on teachings (raising the question "What do these teachings have to do with our practice?") or convergence in practice (raising the question "What do these practices have to do with our opposed teachings?"). Even worse, we will divide up the ecumenical tasks, handing conflicting teachings over to theologians and conflicting practices to pastors and more ordinary folk. In all these cases, a divide opens up between "what we teach" and "what we do," between the truth-claims we make and the lives we lead, between theological dialogue and a dialogue of love, or (as I shall say) between our teachings and practices.[24]

The contention of this section is that neither option — separating teachings and practices from each other or collapsing them into each other — does justice to the pedagogy of the Spirit, i.e., the particular way that the Spirit teaches (e.g., John 14:26). Consider some results of dialogues between Catholics and Evangelicals over their sixteenth-century disputes.[25]

First, the American Lutheran–Catholic discussions presume a different "history of the question" than the modern historians and genealogists I mentioned in the previous section.[26] That is, they do not presume (or deny!) that the sixteenth century was a beginning of our more modern world — but neither do they presume that the sixteenth century is a time of irreversible death for one side or the other. Instead, they offer a narrative that centers on how sixteenth-century Christians like Luther or the Tridentine bishops viewed their dispute, in the context of the larger Christian tradition. The central dis-

24. See also Michael Root on the tension between "the practical character of ecumenical theology" and "the more general commitment of all theology to truth" in "Ecumenical Theology," pp. 544, 551; and G. R. Evans, *Method in Ecumenical Theology: The Lessons So Far*, pp. 9-16 (Theology and Practice).

25. I use "Evangelical" for what are more often still called "Protestants" (particularly Lutheran and Reformed). In what follows, I rely heavily on the succinct reading of the logic of the dialogues in Robert W. Jenson, *Unbaptized God: The Basic Flaw in Ecumenical Theology.* But I will not try to summarize or assess Jenson's book here, as I tried to do briefly in *The Thomist* 58, no. 4 (October 1994): 677-82.

26. "Justification by Faith (Common Statement)," in *Justification by Faith: Lutherans and Catholics in Dialogue*, VII, ed. H. George Anderson, T. Austin Murphy, Joseph A. Burgess (Minneapolis: Augsburg Publishing House, 1985), ch. 1.

pute, in the minds of the disputants, was over justification, e.g., the meaning and truth of Paul's teaching that "we know a person is justified not by the works of the law but through faith in Jesus Christ" (Gal. 2:16). But one twentieth-century common ground among Catholics and Evangelicals (if Robert Jenson is right) is the recognition that the sixteenth century was not asking Paul's question (about how God can establish his righteousness among us Jews and Gentiles), Greek Orthodox questions (about deification), Latin Augustinian questions (about grace and our individual salvation), modern questions about political and intellectual freedom, or postmodern questions about the intelligibility and practicality of any of these worlds.[27]

What, then, was the sixteenth-century dispute? To make a long story very short, the dispute over justification was twofold: What does it mean that *a person is justified through faith* in Jesus Christ — and how ought Christians "place" *the teaching that* persons are so justified amidst other claims or teachings?[28] The first was an argument over the comprehensive shape of the Christian life before God — e.g., practices of and teachings about penance and indulgence. The second was over the "theological-systematic weight" of the doctrine, e.g., whether the sixteenth-century doctrine was or was not essential to the gospel.[29] The first dispute led to arguments over the goodness of creation and free will, the breadth of sin, and the depth of God's grace in our lives; the second dispute led to arguments over the authority of Scripture, tradition, churchly office, and our conflicted practices and experiences of justification.

In still other words, the first was a debate over what we might call a "primary doctrine" (e.g., a belief or precept about God, the world, and human life) and the second a debate over a "governing doctrine" (i.e., a doctrine about how to identify, rank, or relate primary doctrines).[30] The confusion between the two has itself caused considerable confusion, particularly when the arguments over Scripture and tradition developed their own life independently of the arguments over justification that spawned them. But my point here is that

27. Jenson, *Unbaptized God*, pp. 22-23. Why pay attention to *their* question if it is not *Paul's* and not *ours* (or, at least, not some of ours)? Because they too are the Church, even though they are neither Paul nor us.

28. Jenson, *Unbaptized God*, p. 21.

29. Jenson's translation of *theologische Stellenwert* in "The Malta Report" (*Unbaptized God*, p. 21).

30. William A. Christian, Sr., *Doctrines of Religious Communities: A Philosophical Study* (New Haven and London: Yale University Press, 1987). "Primary doctrines" are obviously embedded in practices of teaching in diverse contexts; "governing doctrines" are embedded in the (second-level) practice of thinking about such primary teachings. My focus in this essay is on "primary doctrines" because they are, well, primary.

the separations between teaching and practice I mentioned above are obviously foreign to this way of characterizing the Reformation disputes. Clearly the Reformation disputes were arguments over a thick nexus of teachings *and* practices. What, then, are contemporary heirs of these disputes to do?

Given this narrative, a first step in untying the Gordian knot was to relate the Reformation disputes to a larger and common christological tradition. As the American Lutheran–Catholic dialogue articulates the key rule,

> our entire hope of justification and sanctification rests on Christ Jesus and on the gospel whereby the good news of God's merciful action in Christ is made known; we do not place our ultimate trust in anything other than God's promise and saving work in Christ.[31]

The location of the sixteenth-century dispute in this christological context is of a piece with its location in a narrative of the larger Christian tradition. From this point the dialogues show the way this profession has enabled Catholics and Lutherans to understand each of the other's beliefs and practices surrounding justification. But what is particularly crucial for my purposes is that this christological rule or teaching does not deny difference between Lutheran and Catholic practices and teachings. What are called "contrasting concerns and patterns of thought" exist. The contrasting *practical* concerns have to do with two different ways Christians take their engagement *by God.* Lutherans "focus on safeguarding the absolute priority of God's redeeming word in Jesus Christ" and Catholics focus on "acknowledging the efficacy of God's saving work in the renewal and sanctification of the created order." The contrasting patterns of *thought* (or teaching) have to do with different ways Christians take *their* engagement by God. Lutherans think of sinners standing *coram Deo* (before God), focusing on the discontinuous and even paradoxical ways we ought to speak before the face of God; Catholics think of creatures and sinners progressively transformed by God's infusion of saving grace. Such practical concerns and teachings "may in part be complementary and, even if at times in unavoidable tension, not necessarily divisive."[32]

But there are other kinds of differences, sometimes called "fears" each side has about the other's teaching and practice. Thus, Catholics fear that Lutherans disregard the benefits of God's love, while Lutherans fear that Catholics might

31. "Justification by Faith (Common Statement)," paragraphs 4, 157; Jenson, *Unbaptized God,* pp. 18f.; Root, "Ecumenical Theology," p. 548; cf. *Condemnations,* p. 36.

32. "Justification by Faith (Common Statement)," paragraphs 94, 95, 102, 105. On the formula "complementary rather than opposed," see Vatican II's "Decrees on Ecumenism," paragraph 17 (Tanner, *Decrees of the Ecumenical Councils,* vol. 2, p. 917).

"throw believers back on their resources."[33] The insistence that we take account of our fears and hopes is another of those points at which a dichotomy between teachings and practices (here, the *teaching* of justification and our *practical* emotions and passions) breaks down. (Why) should either side presume that their competing fears will outweigh their complementary concerns? Consider how these complementary concerns and competing fears emerge in their diverse and competing practices of, and teachings about, the Eucharist.

Much to the surprise of many in local congregations and parishes, Catholic and Evangelical theologians have found themselves able to agree on "Christ's real, living and active presence" in a Eucharistic meal that is "the sacrament of the body and blood of Christ, the sacrament of his real presence."[34] However, when pressed for the link between "the body and blood of Christ" and Christ's "real presence," Catholics insist on the persistence of this presence in the bread and wine, while Protestants worry that such a persistence will turn Christ's personal presence into a mere "thing." Yet (Jenson points out) all agree that bread and wine "remain" sacramental body and blood "for the purpose of communion," including key practices that go with it, especially communion of the sick; and all agree to "respect the practices and piety of the others" in reserving or consuming the eucharistic elements.[35] Note that this convergence, if genuine, is a convergence of *practices* (e.g., communion of the sick; reservation of the bread and wine) as well as *teachings* (e.g., confession of Christ's sacramental presence).

Can this convergence suffice? Not standing alone, for both sides have painful memories of the Catholic teaching that the Eucharist is a sacrifice, and its correlative practices. But, once again, many Christians today would be surprised to learn that Catholics and Evangelicals find themselves agreeing that the Eucharist is sacramental sacrifice. As the Groupes des Dombes put it,

> In giving himself in the Eucharist to the Church, Christ sweeps the church along in his own movement to the Father. A movement of consecration and renunciation, of life through death. So he makes the church participate in his praise of the Father and in his power of intercession for the salvation of the world. Thereby the churchly Body of Christ the High Priest, is manifested and fulfilled as a priestly people.[36]

33. "Justification by Faith (Common Statement)," paragraphs 98-101.

34. *Baptism, Eucharist and Ministry,* Faith and Order Paper No. 111 (Geneva: World Council of Churches, 1982), paragraph 13; quoted in Jenson, *Unbaptized God,* p. 26.

35. *Baptism, Eucharist and Ministry,* paragraphs 15 and 32; Jenson, *Unbaptized God,* ch. 2.

36. Groupe des Dombes, *L'acte sacerdotal du Christ dans l'activité sacerdotale de l'Église* (1962), translated in Jenson, *Unbaptized God,* p. 37.

Admittedly, when pressed for the link between Christ's sacrifice and ours, Catholics and Evangelicals often divide on the question of the extent to which the Church is not only a passive *subject* but also an active *agent* of this sacrifice. This is a very deep disagreement because it is mutual dissent over what constitutes Christian practice — our (passive) subjectivity or our (active) agency. But Jenson again suggests that this disagreement is illusory if "the great high-priestly intercession before the Father is that of the *totus Christus*, of Christ with and as his Body of the Saints . . ." (p. 43). That is, we offer Christ's body — we offer as the ones offered by the Head.

But, despite the suggestion that such concerns are complementary rather than competing, now the fear arises that the issue is more specific — not the agency of Christ and the Church but the ministry of the priest. Here we have "a displacement of the problematic" into issues not as *central* for the sixteenth-century reformers, Catholic or Protestant: *teachings* about and *practices* of churchly office — priestly, episcopal, and petrine.[37] At this point the divisions appear even more intractable, for the increasing fragmentation of Evangelical churches after the Reformation and the increasing centralization of the Catholic Church (climaxing in Vatican I) seemed to each side to prove their earlier condemnations of the other. Each side (we might say) contended that it had a "history" and the other had only a "genealogy" (i.e., a story of its death). If this is true, we can understand (without agreeing with) those who contend that traditional matters of controversy hide or disguise deeper differences that surely cannot be overcome.[38]

But even on these issues that became more controversial after the sixteenth century (frequently forgetting their original context in debates over justification in the sixteenth century), Jenson notes the remarkable convergences that have occurred in the twentieth century. For example, all agree that the context of ordained ministry is "*the ministry of the whole people of the church*, in its sending to the world."[39] Further, all agree that *ordained ministers* (pastors) "are representatives of Jesus Christ to the community," to speak *over against* the community *from within* the community.[40] And all this can be professed without denying that orders emerged contingently in the history of the Church or that their emergence is (or may be) "irreversible."

It might seem that this consensus on teachings about and practices of ordained ministry would fall apart over episcopacy and papacy. But not (Jenson

37. Jenson, *Unbaptized God*, pp. 43-44 (quoting Walter Kasper).

38. Jenson, *Unbaptized God*, p. 7.

39. *Baptism, Eucharist and Ministry*, paragraphs 1 and 5; Jenson, *Unbaptized God*, p. 47.

40. *Baptism, Eucharist and Ministry*, paragraph 11; quoted in Jenson, *Unbaptized God*, p. 51.

suggests) if an episcopal pastor of the Church as communion of saints engages in "care for diachronic and synchronic unity *in* the local flock and *between* local flocks." And not if Roman primacy or Petrine ministry is the indefectible pastorate over *the universal Church* — an office *from within* the entire Church and its ordained (episcopal) ministry that may speak *over against* us, all of us.[41]

We could go on. But let me pause. My concern here is not to argue for these convergences, although I am largely persuaded by them. My point is that it is impossible to separate the "practices" and "teachings" of such proposals. Indeed, these teachings are chiefly about *practices* — the practices ingredient in being the Church: celebration of Word and Sacrament, the ministerial ordering of the Church around its eschatological mission, our fears of and trust in each other. Shall we say then that they are convergences of sacramental and ecclesiological *practices* to which correspond (perhaps unfortunately) no *teachings?* This, too, would be odd, for it is hard to say what it means to share such practices if we do not at least share some teachings about what it means "to share a practice" — unless one could show that there is a "practice" unshaped by any beliefs, or "teachings." The fact is that the case for ecumenical "convergence" on these issues can hardly be characterized as a convergence on either practices *or* teachings. It is more accurately characterized as a movement back and forth between practices and teachings on which we disagree (and agree) to practices and teachings on which we agree (and disagree).

At this point I touch on complex issues in metaphysics and epistemology about the relationship between the lives we lead and the beliefs we hold. As Bruce Marshall suggests, our thinking about the relations between "teachings" and "practice" is interwoven in complex ways with our convictions about the triune God who creates and saves us in Word and Spirit.[42] That is, "[o]nly the Spirit whom Jesus sends from the Father can *teach us* to recognize in the narratively identified Jesus the Father's own icon, and to interpret and assess all of *our beliefs* accordingly." And the "school in which the Spirit teaches us these hard won skills" is the Church. But the schooling is not just schooling in such teachings or beliefs (e.g., from catechism classes at home and in local congregations to college, university, and seminary seminars). It is such schooling only as we also learn to engage "in a rich and distinctive array of *practices and attitudes*, including worship and prayer in the name of the triune God, and love of neighbor after the pattern of Christ."[43] The pedagogy of

41. Jenson, *Unbaptized God*, ch. 6 (the quotation from p. 68 [my emphases]).

42. Bruce D. Marshall, "What Is Truth?" *Pro Ecclesia* 4 (1995): 404-30.

43. Marshall, "What Is Truth?" p. 423. Emphases in quotations are my own.

the Spirit is a schooling in specific teachings *and* practices — personal dispositions, sacramental praying, and love's politics along with correlative teachings and beliefs. The Spirit is in ecumenical movement in both ways,[44] teaching us "all things" (John 14:26), teachings and practices inseparably — teaching us, then, to assess our beliefs according to the gospel narratives in the Church, for the world.

Consider an objection: What about the fact that most Christian communities do not know about the convergences in teachings and practices summarized above? This is sometimes called "the problem of reception" and it is tempting to describe it as "the problem of relating converging *teachings* to the *practices* of the churches." But this is a mistaken description of the problem of reception. As Michael Root has suggested, once we have proposals purporting ecumenical consensus, what is needed is more careful thought about "the criteria by which ecumenical texts and proposals are judged" *along with* "a more subtle understanding of the significance and nature of the churches as they actually exist."[45] "Criteria" for judging proposals is admittedly a more theoretical need, while understanding of "the churches as they actually exist" is a more practical need; the former can only be addressed by disciplined schooling in evangelical truth, and the latter only by equally disciplined practical involvement in the life of the Church catholic. It cannot be said that our theologians currently have too much pastoral knowledge of "the churches as they actually exist" — or that pastors who understand "the churches as they actually exist" have "criteria" for judging ecumenical proposals that are consistent locally and more universally. But it is at least clear in principle what is needed: against the background of *narratives of our divisions* aimed at healing painful memories, we will need to articulate *authentic teachings* that speak to and can be spoken by *the churches as they actually exist.*

Indeed, it is precisely at this point — at the point where assent to and dissent from practices and teaching seem equally balanced — that the ecumenical practices and teachings I mentioned in the introduction become absolutely crucial. They are (I suggest) tactics for filling this gap between (i) the practices

44. There may be an analogy between "both ways" and Jean Zizioulas's contrast between a (Latin) "pneumatology conditioned by christology" and (Greek) "christology conditioned by pneumatology," between ecclesiologies of a Church *dispersed* in history and of a Church *assembled* for eucharistic *epiklesis* in "Implications ecclésiologiques de deux types de pneumatologie," in *Communio Sanctorum: Mélanges offerts à Jean-Jacques von Allmen* by B. Bobrinskoy, C. Bridel, et al. (Genève: Labor et Fides, 1982), pp. 141-54.

45. "Ecumenical Theology," p. 552. On this score, it matters not whether the proposals are from bilateral and multilateral discussions among academic theologians and bishops — or from the most insignificant and powerless of local churches. All must be heard, and assessed.

and teachings of the churches "as they actually exist" and (ii) the practices and teachings needed for those same churches to engage in "continual reformation" of the way they "actually exist," i.e., continuous conversion to the triune God. In still other words, they are practices and teachings suitable for filling in the divided and divisive interstices between our "basic but partial unity" and "the visible unity which is required and sufficient"[46] — filling them in with continual conversion to God, continual reformation of our own churches, patient nurture of practices of prayer and martyrdom, practical cooperation in missionary activity and matters of social justice, theological dialogues, etc. Such teachings are not about dispensable practices. But neither are they autonomous practices amounting to creation of a new church or Age of the Spirit, so that an "ecumenical" church engages in these practices *rather than* heeding the Scriptures, celebrating Word and Sacrament, ordering its ministries for bold and humble service to the world. They are more like what Michel de Certeau calls "tactics" rather than what he calls "strategies"; they are less a "place" of their own than they are "spaces" within the Church's "place."[47] The "ecumenical venture" is not what we do in place of being Catholic, or Evangelical — and it does not cease when we learn, once again, that we disagree over various practices and teachings. Ecumenical venture is what ought to happen precisely when different and opposed practices undercut or threaten to undercut the unity and diversity of Christian teaching and practice.

Thus, continual conversion to God's triune *communio* is the central condition for continual reform of our own churches; continual reform of *our own* churches is a condition for heeding calls to repentance from our brother and sister churches — as this heeding is the condition for delivering calls of our own to them. We pray together because it is important in itself and because it moves us toward common baptismal and eucharistic prayer. We respond to the Spirit's personal charisms because they are important in themselves and because they move us toward being a communion of saints, equipped for holiness and martyrdom. We cooperate on matters of social justice both because such common work is important in itself and because "unity of action leads to the full unity of faith."[48] We engage in theological

46. "Ut Unum Sint," paragraph 78 ("Ab hac primaria unitate, at haud tamen integra, ad visibilem necessariam and sufficientem . . .").

47. Michel de Certeau, *The Practice of Everyday Life*, trans. Steven Rendell (Berkeley: University of California Press, 1984). I borrow this understanding of de Certeau from F. C. Bauerschmidt, "The Abrahamic Voyage: Michel de Certeau and Theology," *Modern Theology* 12, no. 1 (January, 1996): 1-26; Bauerschmidt also offers useful warnings against "reifying" the distinction between strategies and tactics.

48. "Ut Unum Sint," paragraphs 40, 43.

discussions both because they are important in themselves and because thereby we train ourselves in "confessing the one faith" together in our time, in full agreement with the Spirit (Acts 15:28).[49]

My aim in this section has not been to argue that the churches should consent to the practices and teachings sketched here (although I think they should so consent). I have also been less interested in resolving the full range of metaphysical and epistemological questions about the relationships between teachings and practices than ruling out some ways of separating them — ways that are inimical to genuine ecumenical movement. Ecumenical venture is a movement of practices and teachings under the pedagogy of a particular Spirit — the Spirit whom Jesus sends from the Father and who teaches us (inter alia) the tactics it takes to be a community that nurtures genuine knowledge of God — the communal practices that yield genuine teachings.

C. The Spirit Concealed in the Wounded Body

But the last allusion to the Acts of the Apostles raises a final problem. Suppose we agree on the importance of the narratives of Israel, Jesus, and the Church — narratives that embody our fidelities and infidelities in ways that promise healing of our painful memories, like the way the Spirit speaks through the prophets. Suppose, further, that we take up our divisions one by one, agreeing on both the practices and teachings that constitute our identity as a Spirit-formed body of Christ, the work of the Spirit being neither pure theory or pure practice. Suppose we then engage in ecumenical "tactics" aimed at filling the gap between our partial unity and our sufficient unity — tactics at once local and inter-local, undertaken by saints and pastors and theologians as well as more ordinary folk. But what is "sufficient" consensus — and how will we know when we have it? Even better, taking "the Council of Jerusalem" as exemplary, how will we know when we can say "it seems good to the Holy Spirit and to us" to lay upon each other no greater burden than "things necessary" (Acts 15:28)?

At no point does my initial presumption become more important, and more problematic. That is, I initially said that there is no ecumenical movement prior to *the Holy Spirit who moves it, or us* — and our participation in this movement depends crucially on how we respond to (including identify)

49. *Confessing the One Faith. An Ecumenical Explication of the Apostolic Faith as It Is Confessed in the Nicene-Constantinopolitan Creed (381),* Faith and Order Paper No. 153. New Revised Version (Geneva: WCC Publications, 1991).

this Spirit. On one level, this presumption arises out of a narrative in which *the disputes* in Christendom between Greek and Latin, Catholic and Evangelical, all came about against the background of *common faith* in God's Trinitarian *communio.*[50] That is, ecumenical movement is about the narratives and practices and teachings necessary and sufficient for visible unity, or reconciled diversity. But this movement depends on the triune God's movement toward us — a movement that, in turn, calls for our continual conversion to the triune God. Ecumenical movement that does not insist on the centrality of hope of communion with God's triune unity-in-diversity risks capture by "ecumenical" and "confessional" counter-movements, finding unity by forgetting painful divisions or remembering painful divisions with no hope of healing, sacrificing opposed teachings to supposedly common practices or opposed practices to teachings only "theoretically" held in common.

Yet this appeal to the Spirit is hardly immune to dissent. Indeed, as with distinctions in the previous sections, it seems to trap us. On the one side are those who might insist that past debates over the Latin creed's profession that the Spirit proceeds from the Father and the Son *(filioque)* and the eucharistic prayer for the Spirit *(epiklesis)* so crucial to Greek Orthodox are either insuperable obstacles, or are symptoms thereof. On the other side are those for whom such disputes as well as the doctrine of the Trinity itself are a problem and who recommend it be, if not eliminated, at least marginalized — those for whom even "Spirit" is too anthropomorphic to represent "the character of the Creativity we worship."[51] We seem to be, once again, back at the beginning — an Age of Confessions pitting Greek against Latin visions of the triune God; an Ecumenical Age calling for a new Age of the Spirit. But if ecumenical movement depends on the Spirit and our identification of the Spirit, these disagreements over the Spirit are sure to jeopardize any convergence on narratives, teachings, and practices. One last time we seem to have unacceptable choices forced upon us.

50. On the importance of this turn from the christocentrism of the last part of this essay to trinitarian *communio,* see (among sources already cited) Vatican II, "Decree on Ecumenism," especially paragraphs 14 and 20; "Ut Unum Sint," especially paragraphs 57 and 66; Jenson, *Unbaptized God,* pp. 66, 77, and throughout; Root, "Ecumenical Theology," pp. 545f. For two different criticisms of this turn, see Cardinal Joseph Ratzinger and Archbishop Alberto Bovone, "Some Aspects of the Church Understood as Communion," *Origins. CNS Documentary Service* 22, no. 7 (June 1992), and Nicholas M. Healy, "Communion Ecclesiology: A Cautionary Note," *Pro Ecclesia* 4, no. 4 (Fall 1995): 442-53.

51. Edward Farley, *Divine Empathy: A Theology of God* (Minneapolis: Fortress, 1996), p. 133. Farley's book is a good statement of why revisionists retrieve the Trinity in the light of a more up-to-date god than I do (especially pp. 144-50).

The most promising theologies of the Spirit (I believe) are those for whom an open future is "a particular parable of the Spirit" (see note 7 above), while also showing that this is the same future God promises to the nations in the Israelite Jesus. Thus, on the one hand, how we envision the Spirit's ecumenical venture depends in good measure on how we envision this future work. On the other hand, the risk of appropriating the future to the Spirit is that this Spirit's work will not engage past or present. It seems to me that we are far from dealing with these issues. Precisely because we are so far, I would like to address briefly the issues, not by proposing another pneumatology but by offering a parable (or "tactic") of the often surprisingly humble ways in which the Spirit is in ecumenical movement — the parable of Flannery O'Connor's "A Temple of the Holy Spirit."[52]

The story begins with two jabbering fourteen-year-old girls (Joanne and Susan) who come to stay over the weekend with their twelve-year-old second cousin (called simply "the child") and her mother. Joanne and Susan are being educated in a convent school, whose nuns teach them silly things like saying "Stop sir! I am a Temple of the Holy Ghost!" to boys who "behave in an ungentlemanly manner with them in the back of an automobile." The two girls think this is hilarious, and call each other Temple One and Temple Two. The child and her mother disagree — the young girl deriding her cousins as "stupid idiots." This is typical of the caustic judgments of the child. She "did not steal or murder but she was a born liar and slothful and she sassed her mother and was deliberately ugly to almost everybody." She knew that (or thought that) she could "never be a saint, but she thought she could be a martyr if they killed her quick."

But the real problem was finding the two visitors something to do. Wendel and Cory Wilkins, two sixteen-year-olds interested in becoming Church of God preachers, are invited to dinner and then to take the two girls to a local fair. Their visit begins with the boys and girls engaging in a friendly duel with rival hymns. The boys sing "I've found a friend in Jesus" and the

52. In Flannery O'Connor, *A Good Man Is Hard to Find and Other Stories* (San Diego: Harcourt Brace & Company, 1983 [original 1955]), pp. 85-101. O'Connor (1925-1964) was a Southern fiction-writer whose fellow Catholics sometimes confused her with being a Protestant. Early on she was perturbed and perhaps even insulted by charges that "while my convictions might be Catholic, my sensibility appeared to be Lutheran." She later handled such jousts with irony or sarcasm: "I am glad you find me a good Protestant. That is indeed a compliment. All good Catholics have the best Protestant qualities about them; and a good deal more besides; my good deal more besides I try to keep from view lest it offend your delicate sensibilities" (Flannery O'Connor, *The Habit of Being*, ed. Sally Fitzgerald [New York: Farrar, Straus and Giroux, 1979], pp. 108, 418).

girls "Tantum Ergo Sacramentum" — the girls' singing becoming sacramental only when confronted with the boys' evangelical fervor, the boys confusing the Catholic eucharistic hymn with "Jew singing."

More importantly, after dinner they go to the fair. They return to tell the child about a "freak" in the side show who "was a man and woman both. It pulled up its dress and showed us." The "freak" also warned the girls that "God made me thisaway and if you laugh He may strike you the same way. This is the way He wanted me to be and I ain't disputing His way. I'm showing you because I got to make the best of it." The child, intrigued but with preadolescent ignorance about matters of sexuality, is puzzled. What are we to make of such anomalies in the body of Christ? She later dreams of a revival in which people utter refrains of "Amen" to the hermaphrodite's pious declarations about God's will.

The next day, as "the ivory sun . . . was framed in the middle of the blue afternoon," the child and her mother take the cousins back to the convent school. A nun greets them at the door, urging them to come to the chapel for Benediction — the para-eucharistic Catholic prayer service in the presence of the consecrated Bread. The child is not a little resentful of being trapped into praying. But soon "her ugly thoughts stopped and she began to realize that she was in the presence of God." When the priest raises "the monstrance with the Host shining ivory-colored in the center of it, she was thinking of the tent at the fair that had the freak in it."

Why she thinks this thought we only learn as child and mother head home. During this journey, the child and her mother learn that the town preachers have closed down the fair (for putting such people as "the freak" on public display, one presumes). The child looks out the window, lost in thought. "The sun was a huge red ball like an elevated Host drenched in blood and when it sank out of sight, it left a line in the sky like a red clay road hanging over the trees."

And so ends the story. What does it have to do with the Spirit's ecumenical venture? The title of the story as used by the characters shows how the simplest of teachings — this one from 1 Corinthians 3:16 ("Do you not know that you are God's temple and that God's Spirit dwells in you?") — can be made the butt of jokes in ways O'Connor could appreciate. But, by story's end, the teaching is given a deeper context. The ivory-sun has become red, reflecting not only the dust of the earth but the suffering of that same earth. And this setting red sun is cosmic *vestigia* of white bread embodied by a crucified Savior. The Spirit abides in us like temples — not because "God made us thisaway" (ecumenical Stoicism, we might say) but because the Spirit abides with our suffering bodies even as the same Spirit somehow transforms them, as Paul speaks of the Spirit who raised Jesus giving life to our mortal bodies (Rom. 8:11).

Many things ecumenical, it must be admitted, are unclear in this story. For example, in some ways, the Catholic benediction clearly outdoes the Evangelical revival of which the child dreamed, much as the girls' Latin hymns seem to trump the preacher boys' evangelical jingles — as Sacrament trumps Word. By story's end, from this point of view, the hermaphrodite is embraced by God more deeply than he/she knows — neither put on display nor taken off display as a "freak" but a temple of the Holy Spirit, concealing Christ's wounded body even as she reveals it to those like the child. The "freak" is called to neither Stoic resignation nor violent resistance but to patient endurance — an active waiting for the Spirit's work that we can hardly predict.[53] Here the Catholic O'Connor tweaks her southern Evangelical culture, as the eucharistic sacrament embodies more than the mere words of the revival — or, if not "mere words" rather than sacrament, then words that recommend Stoic submission rather than hopeful endurance of one's cross.

Yet, from another point of view, the Evangelical revival meeting and Catholic benediction seem to complement each other — perhaps abbreviated or truncated versions of Word and Sacrament, of noisy Amens and silent monstration, like the hymns to Jesus and the sacrament earlier in the story. O'Connor once said that Catholics with "intensity of belief" enter the convent and "are heard from no more," whereas Protestants live it out in the world "getting into all sorts of trouble and drawing the wrath of people who don't believe anything much at all down on your head."[54] If Jesus-hymns and biblical revivals are not enough to fully embody the Church, neither are sacramental hymns and eucharistic benedictions. Catholic benediction, abstracted from cosmic and eucharistic epiphany, cannot bear on Temple One and Temple Two in other than humorous ways. Many of my Catholic brothers and sisters are more like Joanne and Susan than the child — more apt to have a Church and sacrament that are secret refuge rather than Spirit-filled context of their lives; even at their best Catholics are more like the child who finds it easier to be a martyr than a saint.

Or perhaps there is some truth to both interpretations (one privileging Catholics, the other displaying Catholic-Evangelical complementarity) in the face of the world for which O'Connor wrote — the world of nihilists, of those

53. The distinction between the hermaphrodite's Stoic endurance and Christian hope for the hermaphrodite is, for purposes of this essay, the most important distinction in the story to learn to make. See Reinhard Hütter's notion of *pathos* in Chapter 2.

54. O'Connor, *The Habit of Being,* p. 517; cf. p. 227.

who say "God is dead," of a whole world "going through a dark night of the soul."[55] In this world, we come to each other not simply to find complementary teachings and practices (as in the preceding section of this essay) but because we lack something the other has — whether our wounds are self-inflicted or inflicted by the other.

To press the story further is to press things well beyond what O'Connor could have imagined writing before the end of Vatican II. The point here is that we are (the Church is) temple of the Holy Spirit as we are the wounded body of Christ. God did not make us "thisaway," to passively endure; we must oppose those who would, out of embarrassment or indifference, put the wounded body out of sight. The Spirit is in ecumenical movement not merely in showing us how to preserve painful memories in healing ways, not merely in teaching us that communion is communion of practices and teachings, but also dwelling in us as a temple, with all our wounds.

Conclusion

In concluding with a parable of prophetic sexual anomaly I do not wish to suggest that such wounds trump the social sources of denominationalism mentioned earlier (especially the wounds of a Church divided by economic class and nationality, ethnicity and race). I have not tried to reconcile the traditional church-divisive disputes among Christians, much less the contemporary (modern and postmodern) ones. I have tried to suggest that such traditional as well as contemporary disputes must be engaged as part of a tradition of practices and teachings larger than themselves if they are to be other than a reiteration of the very wounds they aim to heal. Otherwise they will make matters worse than the divisions among Christians of which we still need to learn to repent.

The way to do this, I have proposed, is to seek the Spirit's ecumenical venture on our wounded body. In sum, *the Spirit's ecumenical venture* is the Spirit prophetically preserving our painful memories in ways that heal, teaching us ecumenical tactics in word and deed inseparably, concealed in the Church's wounded body as a way of revealing the body of a crucified Messiah, a temple being rebuilt and raised from the dead. *Our ecumenical venture,* then, must include taking our divisions seriously enough to narrate them truthfully, working at sorting out the diverse teachings and practices at stake in such divisions, learning the tactics needed to endure the reconciled diversity sufficient for sacramental witness to the nations — even when that recon-

55. O'Connor, *The Habit of Being,* pp. 90, 92, 100.

ciled diversity is less than that for which we hope. The consensus of the Spirit and the community (Acts 15) is the consensus of a wounded body, a consensus on "things necessary," not on everything.

A risk, of course, in focusing on the Spirit's work in a wounded body is that it might domesticate our hopes, making us forget that our wounds are themselves part of a larger story. We will again stoically resign ourselves to our wounds — and thus find easy warrant for inflicting further ones. The Spirit of Jesus Christ promises more than passive acceptance: the Spirit promises Christ's return and our resurrection from the dead and eternal life with God. Holding together the Spirit's "present" and "future" would require a more full-blown theology of the Trinity than I have offered here — just as holding together our present wounds with the promised bodily resurrection would require a more full-blown theology of the Church's mission than I have offered. But I began with a quite specific problem — a crisis of divisions in the very ecumenical movement committed to overcoming the divisions of the Church. And I have proposed that, unless this movement is engaged as a venture of the Spirit, our "ecumenical age" will remain a dialectical thesis to or antithesis of confessional counter-movement — whether the confessions be ancient or modern. The Spirit's ecumenical venture calls us to more: a Church embodying Scripture in its life and thought, patiently baptizing and joyfully celebrating Eucharist, reforming our deepest fears and hopes into desires attuned with God's love, shaping us sinners into servants of God's mission to draw all the world into communion with God. Faced with our betrayal of that mission as well as our indifference, we constantly need to turn to the triune God, who seeks to continually reform us into saints and martyrs daring to hope that all will be saved, while fearing that our divisions will be held against us for all eternity.

9. Israel

Do Christians Worship the God of Israel?

BRUCE D. MARSHALL

The Trinity and the God of Israel after Supersessionism

We Christians claim to worship the God of Israel. In praise and want we call upon, and seek intimacy with, the same God who elected Abraham, Isaac, Jacob and their descendants to be his people forever, who gave this people his law through Moses, and who made David king over this people, establishing the royal line from which the promised Messiah would come. Christians claim not only to worship the God who did these things, but the same God whom Abraham, Moses, and David themselves worshiped. More than that, Christians now often recognize themselves as linked in worship to their Jewish contemporaries, joined to the descendants of Abraham by their shared claim to call upon Abraham's God. Christians, that is, increasingly regard their worship as liturgical intimacy with the same God worshiped by the Jewish people today.

At the same time, the God whom Christians worship is the Trinity: the Father, the Son, and the Holy Spirit. If the Christian claim to worship the God of Israel is true, it will therefore also be true that the God who elected Abraham, gave the law to Moses, anointed David king over Israel, and raised up

I am grateful to the Pew Evangelical Scholars Program for a grant in support of the project of which this essay is a part, and to the members of the Cardin Faculty Seminar at Loyola College in Maryland for their very helpful comments on an earlier draft of this paper.

the promised Messiah, is the Trinity. It will be true, moreover, that the God whom Abraham, Moses, and David worshiped was the Trinity, and indeed that Jews today worship the Trinity.

In the Christian community's claim to worship the God of Israel looms a deep theological problem. So, at least, I will try to show. The Jewish people's own relationship to God, and the Christian community's understanding of that relationship, are implicated in this theological difficulty. The problem, briefly put, is to understand how we Christians can coherently claim that in worshiping the Trinity we worship the God of Israel, without falling into a supersessionist view of the Jewish people.

"Supersessionism" has become a term of abuse in Christian theology, often used to label any conviction assumed to be inextricable from morally intolerable attitudes toward the Jewish people. This net is sometimes cast very widely, so that, for example, believing that Jesus is God incarnate or that God is the Trinity is *eo ipso* supersessionistic — productive of the Christian community's appalling historic persecution of the Jews.

At first sight such claims apparently presume an implausibly direct relationship between particular beliefs and particular practices. People who believe that Jesus is God and who worship the Trinity have, after all, sometimes died opposing persecution of the Jews, and people who played a leading role in genocide have often rejected or known nothing of these Christian teachings. In any case our present concern is not with whether such central Christian beliefs can be extricated from morally abominable practices, but with the plausibility of the Christian claim to worship the God of Israel in the first place. Sweeping denunciations of "supersessionism" obscure this problem rather than bring it to light.

In order to see the problem more clearly, I will use the term "supersessionism" to denote the view that the Jewish people — the fleshly descendants of Abraham, Isaac, and Jacob — ceased to be God's elect people with the coming of Christ. With this view generally go two further claims. Membership in God's people after Christ no longer depends upon descent from Abraham and circumcision, but upon faith and baptism. The church, in other words, has replaced Israel as God's elect. Moreover, God no longer bestows his electing love by a criterion of carnal descent, if indeed he ever did — the latter an idea often rejected in the Christian tradition, if not always with an untroubled conscience. Instead, the basic criteria for locating the recipients of God's electing love (not, of course, for identifying its *cause*) are those that single out the members of the Christian community, namely, once again, faith and baptism.

That the historic Christian mainstream has accepted all three of these claims, and in that threefold sense been supersessionist, I will make no attempt to demonstrate here. For present purposes, I will simply assume that the first claim just identified is a bad idea. Christians, that is, have good reasons to believe that the carnal descendants of Abraham, Isaac, and Jacob are God's elect people permanently, and not just temporarily. The coming of Christ does not, therefore, bring Jewish election to an end. By itself the assumption that Jewish election is irrevocable does not, I think, determine what one should make of the relationship between Israel and the church, or how one should understand the extent of God's electing love. For present purposes we need not try to answer these important questions.[1]

The problem with which this essay is concerned will take a bit of explaining, but we may note at the outset that it should not be confused with some other matters where Jews and Christians may differ about God. The chief issue here has not to do with whether belief in the Trinity is compatible with monotheism, though this question has animated much polemic between Christians and Jews. Nor is the problem that Jews obviously do not think the God they worship is the Father, the Son, and the Holy Spirit. Nor is it even that Old Testament Israel did not exactly seem to think this either, a point the Christian theological tradition has to a certain extent conceded, though with important qualifications. The problem to which I want to attend here has rather to do with the consistency of Christian worship and belief themselves. The liturgical identification of the church's God as the Trinity strikingly calls into question the claim, which Christian liturgies also make, that the church's God is Israel's God. In order to see how this is so, we need to think briefly about what it is to identify something, and about the way Christian liturgies typically identify the church's God.

Individuation, Identity, and Christian Worship

Christian liturgies identify the God whom they enable their participants to worship. They accomplish much else besides, but they at least enable the worshiping community to determine just whom they are calling upon when they appeal to "God." We need not decide here the interesting question whether the God whom Christians worship might also be identified without reference

1. On historic Christian supersessionism and some theological arguments against it, see Bruce D. Marshall, "The Jewish People and Christian Theology," *The Cambridge Companion to Christian Doctrine,* ed. Colin Gunton (Cambridge: Cambridge University Press, 1997), pp. 81-100; for a further argument against it see Bruce D. Marshall, *Trinity and Truth* (Cambridge: Cambridge University Press, 2000), pp. 176-79.

to the actual liturgical practices of the Christian community. It might be argued, for example, that we can locate the *Deus Christianorum* just by reading the Bible comprehendingly, or perhaps by mastering the meaning of the Nicene Creed. Regardless of whether these suggestions prove out, it is surely implausible to play off worship, Scripture, and creed (or dogma) against one another as ways to the knowledge of the church's God, since each seems deeply linked to the other two. The Bible attends extensively to injunctions for and descriptions of worship in Israel and the church, and includes many liturgical and creedal elements even when these are not explicitly identified as such (for example, quotations from hymns and primitive creedal statements in both the Old and New Testaments). Conversely, and more importantly for our purposes, the church's worship in manifold ways incorporates Scripture and creed as essential elements.[2] So the assumption about the tie between worship and the knowledge of God upon which this essay depends is a relatively modest one, namely that standard Christian worship practices are *sufficient* to identify the church's God, not that they are alone sufficient for this purpose, or even that they are necessary for it.

To *identify* a person or object *x* is to succeed in distinguishing *x* from all other persons or objects. At minimum this requires that we hit on (more precisely, that we succeed in referring to) at least one feature of *x* that no other person or object has. In the case of beings that take up space and time, this can often be done simply by specifying a particular place and time in which the person or object in question is located. "Which one is Mary Jane?" my wife asks. "The one standing under the clock, even as we speak," I reply. Should my sentence be true — should Mary Jane be standing under the clock when I utter it — and should my wife and I believe it to be true, then we will have succeeded in distinguishing Mary Jane from all other persons and objects. We will have identified her.

As this example suggests, *identifying* — or, as it is sometimes put, *individuating* — a person does not require that we have any deep knowledge of her. Identifying or individuating a person does not require, in other words, knowledge of that person's *identity*. The identity of a person consists, let us say, in whatever makes her the unique individual she is. A bit more exactly, the identity of a person *x* consists in whatever makes her the same person in different circumstances, indeed the same in all circumstances in which she might be (for example, in different places or at different times); this presumably goes for the identity of objects as well. Thus, as we will use the terms,

2. Creedal elements may be found also in Christian worship that does not use the church's ancient symbols of faith.

"identity" is a feature possessed by any individual person or object, whereas "identification" or "individuation" is an activity undertaken by persons who for various purposes want to pick out or distinguish persons and objects (for example, to know more about them).

Considerable philosophical debate surrounds the issues I have just so briefly sketched. A fully generalizable theory of individuation has proven elusive. While identifying an individual surely requires reference to at least one feature not shared with any other individual, obviously not just any feature will do in every situation. While it may be true of Mary Jane that she is the only person in the Smethport High School class of 1973 to have graduated with a 4.00 average, and while I may know this to be true of her, passing this information on will not help my wife pick her out of the crowd of people milling around the baggage claim area. Controversy arises, in other words, over what sorts of features we have to refer to in order to pick out entities of different kinds (especially as to whether identifying some, or perhaps all, entities requires specifying their spatio-temporal location), and over what sorts of features suffice to do this job. For our purposes we can let these more general problems stand, and will only try to indicate in a plausible way how Christians, especially in their worship, succeed in identifying (1) the Trinity and (2) the God of Israel.

What makes for personal identity across changing circumstances, temporal or otherwise, is yet more contested. Here we can simply record two assumptions: (1) that persons — including especially the divine persons — actually do have identities to know, and (2) *identifying* persons does not necessarily require grasping their identity, or grasping it fully. This allows us to put our central concern in a more precise way. In worship Christians identify their God as the God of Israel. It is true of our God, Christians say in their praise and petition, that he is the God of Israel. It is also true of our God, Christians say, that he is the Father, the Son, and the Holy Spirit. The question is whether these identifications are compatible — whether "is the God of Israel" and "is the Father, the Son, and the Holy Spirit," can both be true of, and so enable us to pick out, the same being.

We can perhaps frame the issue in a different way by noticing that a certain asymmetry apparently obtains between the identification of the church's God as the God of Israel and as the Trinity. As we will observe, Christian worship suggests that to pick out God as the Father, the Son, and the Holy Spirit is to apprehend God's identity, in the sense suggested above: in all possible circumstances, God is the Father, the Son, and the Holy Spirit. If this is right — if identifying the persons of the Trinity is sufficient to give us God's identity — then what makes God to be one and the same being in all possible situations is, in fact, that God is the Father, the Son, and the Holy Spirit. This implies that God is the Father, the Son, and the Holy Spirit regardless of what contingent states of affairs obtain or do not obtain, such as whether there is a created world and whether God presents himself in that world.

We may be tempted to say that being the God of Israel also belongs to God's identity.[3] But this cannot be quite right. If electing Israel belongs to God's identity, if it must be true of him in order for him to be God, then God has to elect Israel; electing Israel would just go with being God. In its own way this puts an end to the election of Israel as effectively as supersessionism, since to elect is to act freely, and an event that an agent cannot keep from occurring is not his free action.[4] At the same time, Christians (at least post-supersessionist ones) want to say that the election of Israel is not simply one among the countless things God has done, but enacts God's deepest and most unalterable intentions. God's way with Israel opens up God's own heart to human beings, as the Deuteronomic depictions of Israel's election suggest, even while they assert the contingency and freedom of God's affection for this people: "Although heaven and the heaven of heavens belong to the Lord your God, the earth with all that is in it, yet the Lord set his heart in love on your ancestors alone and chose you, their descendants after them, out of all the peoples, as it is today" (Deut. 10:14 NRSV). Thus a Christian doctrine of God needs to locate God's free election of Israel closely enough to his identity that we need to know about it in order to identify God at all — "is the God of Israel" is not simply an optional means of picking out the Christian God. But it cannot allow Israel's election to become absorbed into God's identity, and so cease to be free and contingent.

To be sure, we might be able to eliminate the asymmetry. The Old Testament probably comes closest to stating the identity of Israel's God when it relates God's name: YHWH. However one interprets the enigmatic content of

3. As R. Kendall Soulen, for example, seems to suggest: "God's identity as YHWH, the God of Israel" must be "genuinely *constitutive* for understanding God's eternal identity and ultimate purposes for creation" ("YHWH the Triune God," *Modern Theology* 15, no. 1 [1999]: 25-54; here, 26-27).

Soulen's essay provides a useful counterpoint to the present paper, since he and I agree on the need for a trinitarian theology that avoids supersessionism, but consistently disagree, I think, on how this result might actually be achieved.

4. To reach the same conclusion in a different way: it is presumably a contingent state of affairs — dependent upon God's will, not his identity — whether there is a created world at all, whether this world contains Abraham and his descendants, and whether this tribe is God's elect. Should all this belong to God's identity, none of it will any longer be contingent, since God's identity is not contingent. But Israel knows God's favor and her very existence as unexpected grace and mercy, which they cannot be unless they are contingent.

the name as revealed to Moses in Exodus 3:14, it contains no reference to Israel, but is rather a play on the verb "to be." Thus the recurrent biblical phrase "YHWH, the God of Israel," is presumably not a pleonasm, but connects the one who bears this name forever to his chief deed in time, which is to join Abraham's descendants to himself as their God (cf. Exod. 3:15). The name YHWH, if we can get any fix on what it means, thus promises to bear on the identity, as distinct from the individuation, of Israel's God in a fashion similar to that in which "the Father, the Son, and the Holy Spirit" bears on the identity of the church's God. This is of limited use in an analysis of the *liturgical* identification of God, since the name YHWH does not show up in Christian worship.[5] (In Jewish prayer books it is printed, but a substitute is uttered instead.) Of course its established stand-in "the Lord" is a liturgical commonplace, applied to the persons of the Trinity taken both collectively and one at a time — especially, following the New Testament, to Jesus Christ.

If "is YHWH" gives us God's identity, at least in principle, then our problem has to do with who God is — with God's identity — as well as with the compatibility of two different ways of identifying God. In that case the question can fairly be restated like this: can YHWH — Israel's Lord — be the Trinity? Or, for that matter, can YHWH be any one of the persons of the Trinity?

Liturgical Faith: Christian Worship as Individuation of the Trinity and the God of Israel

(A) Identifying the Trinity

Here I will not try to defend the claim that Christians worship the Trinity. Elsewhere I have argued in detail that it belongs to the deep structure of Christian liturgies to identify God as the Father, the Son, and the Holy Spirit.[6] This is evident perhaps most clearly, and from an early historical point, in the eucharistic prayer. There the gathered community, obeying Jesus' own command, celebrates a common meal by offering thanks to the Father, in remembrance of Jesus' saving death and resurrection, enabled by the Holy Spirit whom the com-

5. Except through the liturgical use of some contemporary Bible translations that transliterate it, though this probably falls afoul of the ancient stricture against speaking the divine name.

6. See *Trinity and Truth*, pp. 24-44, which also includes (pp. 35-38) a preliminary discussion of the issues under consideration in this essay. Though the argument there mainly analyzes one sample liturgy (a Lutheran one), basically the same trinitarian structure can be found, I think, across the broad spectrum of historic Christian eucharistic rites, both eastern and western.

munity invokes. The trinitarian structure of the eucharistic rite allows for considerable variation in the precise content of the thanksgiving, *anamnesis,* and invocation, but eucharistic liturgies typically attribute to the Father, Son, and Spirit certain characteristic actions that enable us to identify them.[7]

Arguably chief among these is a distinctive and irreversible pattern of missions, which begin with the action of the divine person who sends, and terminate in the completed action of the person who is sent. So the community thanks the Father for sending his Son to share our mortal flesh without reserve, and gratefully remembers that the incarnate Son completed his mission by his promise in the upper room and his free acceptance of death on Golgotha. In this way, the community joyfully recalls, the Son Jesus made his body and blood available for all time to his gathered people as the food and drink of their shared meal. And the community likewise calls upon the Father to send the Holy Spirit, whose work it is to join this people to the crucified and risen Jesus, who gives his very self in the elements they eat and drink.

Since one person can send another, but not himself (sending is not a reflexive act; I do not send myself, but simply go), since the Father is never sent, but sends the Son and the Spirit, and since the eucharistic characterization of the sending of the Spirit presupposes the mission of the Son, it seems like this pattern of missions is sufficient to distinguish the persons of the Trinity from one another, and from the community that calls upon them. The missions of the three thus allow us to identify them. According to a long and broad (albeit sometimes contested) theological tradition, by way of this pattern of missions we may also grasp the identities of the divine persons. The relations to one another that their missions exhibit give us features not only unique to each, but which each has in all possible circumstances — regardless, in particular, of whether they decide to create a world and whether any of them are sent into that world.[8]

But in any case the Nicene Creed explicitly provides, for many liturgies,

7. For a concise statement of the trinitarian shape of the Eucharist that commands wide ecumenical agreement, see *Baptism, Eucharist and Ministry,* Faith and Order Paper 111 (Geneva: WCC, 1982). For theological and historical analyses of the eucharistic liturgy from different points on the denominational compass, see Louis Bouyer, *Eucharist: Theology and Spirituality of the Eucharistic Prayer,* trans. Charles Underhill Quinn (Notre Dame: University of Notre Dame Press, 1968); Peter Brunner, *Worship in the Name of Jesus,* trans. M. M. Bertram (St. Louis: Concordia, 1968), esp. pp. 157-96, 290-311; Geoffrey Wainwright, *Doxology: The Praise of God in Worship, Doctrine, and Life* (New York: Oxford University Press, 1980); Boris Bobrinskoy, *The Mystery of the Trinity,* trans. Anthony P. Gythiel (New York: SVS Press, 1999), esp. pp. 165-96.

8. For a discussion of this point, sometimes misleadingly called the relationship between the "economic" and the "immanent" Trinity, see my essay, "The Trinity," *The Blackwell Companion to Modern Theology,* ed. Gareth Jones (Oxford: Blackwell, forthcoming).

what look like identity-constituting features of the three persons, clearly distinguished from the features they freely acquire by sending and being sent. Thus according to the Creed the one Lord Jesus Christ, who was sent to become "incarnate from the Virgin Mary" in time, was already "begotten of the Father before all time" (or as the traditional English rendering has it, "before all worlds": πρὸ πάντων τῶν αἰφώνων).[9] This relationship of begetter and begotten obtains, therefore, whether or not there is a created world or any divine missions. Begetting the Son therefore belongs to the identity of the Father, and being begotten by the Father to the identity of the Son. Likewise, though rather less explicitly, the Holy Spirit "proceeds from the Father and the Son" (in western versions of the Creed), and is at the same time "the giver of life." Further theological reflection would suggest that he must be the giver of life to the world, by way of his mission in time, and not to the Father and the Son, "before all time" (otherwise they would proceed or come forth from him, and not he from them). Among the creedal marks of the Spirit, therefore, "proceeding from the Father and the Son" apparently belongs to the Spirit's identity, and not only to the temporal mission by which we identify him (though it must surely be granted that what makes for the identity of the Spirit, and the bearing of decisions about this on the identities of the Father and the Son, is far more elusive and contested than what constitutes the identities of the other two — not least, of course, because of the dispute over the *Filioque*).

(B) Identifying Israel's God

Since Christians claim that the God whom they worship and in whom they believe is none other than the God of Israel, one would expect Christian liturgies to provide clear ways of locating Israel's God. But while Christian worship is fairly saturated with trinitarian references, the liturgical means for identifying the *Deus Christianorum* as the God of Israel are less easy to locate. Strikingly, most eucharistic prayers make no explicit reference to Israel at all. There are some exceptions. "We praise you for the grace shown to Israel, your chosen, the people of your promise: the rescue from Egypt, the gift of the promised land, the memory of the fathers, the homecoming from exile, and the prophets' words that will not be in vain."[10] Here the decisive events of Is-

9. I follow here the Greek text of the Creed of 381 in Heinrich Denzinger & Adolf Schönmetzer, *Enchiridion Symbolorum,* 36th edition (Barcelona: Herder, 1976), no. 150.

10. *The Lutheran Book of Worship: Ministers Desk Edition* (Minneapolis: Augsburg, 1978), p. 221 (Eucharistic Prayer II).

rael's history are ascribed to the Father in particular, as his saving acts. This not only indicates that the God upon whom the worshiping assembly calls is supposed to be Israel's own (at least in the basic sense that he is the God who undertook the saving acts narrated in the Old Testament), but also suggests that this God is, specifically, the trinitarian Father. The Son or Word is also, it appears, sometimes eucharistically ascribed a role in Israel's history: "We give thanks to you, O God, for the goodness and love which you have made known to us in creation; in the calling of Israel to be your people; in your Word spoken through the prophets; and above all in the Word made flesh, Jesus, your Son."[11] Since this prayer is addressed to the Father, the reference to Israel implicates him as well as the Son, and so suggests that both, or perhaps all three persons of the Trinity, are the God of Israel.

The rarity and brevity of such eucharistic references to Israel suggest, however, that we look elsewhere in Christian liturgy for an unambiguous effort to identify Israel's God.

The use of the Old Testament in the service of the word is perhaps the clearest liturgical embodiment of the church's claim to worship the God of Israel. Of the four Scripture readings now normally included in the liturgy of the word, two are from the Old Testament: first a reading from the law, prophets, or writings, followed by a psalm in the singing or reading of which the congregation normally participates. By recalling God's way with his elect people Israel, the church not only locates Israel's God, but includes itself among those to whom this God's acts of mercy and judgment, his promises and commands, are directed — these things were, as Paul says, "written down to instruct us, upon whom the ends of the ages have come" (1 Cor. 10:11). Here especially the church enacts its claim that Israel's God is its God — that Israel's God is somehow the same as the Father, Son, and Spirit whose praise and glory the church sings out.

The liturgical use of the Psalter — in which the church has consistently engaged even at its most dishearteningly supersessionistic — vividly embodies the Christian claim to worship no other God than Israel's own. Singing the Psalms, the church joins Israel past and present in thanksgiving for God's acts of mercy towards his elect, in fear before his judgment, and in supplication for his present and future help. Here too the particular actions upon which the identification of Israel's God depends are ascribed, in one fashion or another, to the Trinity in whose name this assembly worships, if not by the ancient practice of concluding the recitation of the Psalm with the *Gloria Patri*,

11. *Book of Common Prayer* (According to the Use of the Episcopal Church, 1979), p. 368 (Eucharistic Prayer B).

then by the larger trinitarian context already established by the rite, and confirmed in the eucharistic prayer. These liturgical uses of the Old Testament do not by themselves make clear exactly what role the ongoing "lover's quarrel" (in Michael Wyschogrod's phrase) between YHWH and Israel plays in the church's identification of its God — of the one whom it also picks out as the Trinity. They at least suggest, however, that YHWH's engagement with Abraham's children is in some way indispensable to the church's identification of the God whom it worships. And since the origin, development, and aims of YHWH's interaction with his people become available to us only through Jewish Scripture, comprehension of Israel's Scripture seems like a necessary condition for the church's individuation of the Trinity.[12]

That the church must have recourse to Israel — or at least to the scripturally narrated portion of Israel's history — in order to identify its God seems clear not only in Christian worship, but in the New Testament, indeed on practically every page. So the evangelist Mark, to take one example, begins to tell "the good news of Jesus Christ, the Son of God," by referring his readers to Jewish Scripture, and to events between Israel and God narrated and anticipated there: "As it is written in the prophet Isaiah . . . prepare the way of the Lord, make his paths straight" (Mark 1:1-3). The God whose "Son" Mark announces that Jesus is can thus be none other than Israel's God.

This same dependence of the church upon (scriptural) Israel was also pretty clear, or became clear, in the early church, when the Christian mainstream repudiated the efforts of Marcion and the Gnostics to expel the Old Testament from the canon of Christian Scripture. Writers like Justin, Irenaeus, and Tertullian not only insisted that the Old Testament had to be there, but that it had to come first. It could not, as Schleiermacher would later suggest, be a mere historical appendix.[13] This indicates that the narrative se-

12. To be sure, the practice of reading from the Old Testament (though not that of chanting the Psalms) has a somewhat checkered history in Christian liturgy. The use of at least one Old Testament reading in the Sunday Eucharist was standard in the ancient church, but disappeared in the Middle Ages, both east and west. The west retained the practice of reading from the Old Testament on weekdays, and in modern times has generally restored the Sunday reading, though the Eastern eucharistic rite continues to have readings only from the New Testament. For a brief discussion, with references to more detailed studies, see Peter G. Cobb, "The Liturgy of the Word in the Early Church," in *The Study of Liturgy*, ed. Cheslyn Jones, Geoffrey Wainwright, Edward Yarnold, and Paul Bradshaw, 2nd edition (New York: Oxford University Press, 1992), pp. 219-29, esp. pp. 225-27. None of this negates the claim that the scriptural rendering of YHWH and Israel is indispensable for the church's identification of its God, although it obviously thins out the liturgical enactment of that claim.

13. According to much modern theology — of this Schleiermacher is only a striking and formative example — that Jesus was a Jew, and that the writers of the New Testament express

quence of the canon is indispensable to the identification of the God worshiped by Christians. Without the narratives of God's way with Israel, so the early church seems to say, we could not pick out the Christian God on the basis of the New Testament alone. The church's dependence upon Israel for the identification of its own God is, in other words, logical, and therefore permanent, and is not merely a dispensable historical accident.

Following the Old Testament reading and the Psalm, the liturgy of the word continues, of course, with readings from the New Testament: first from the epistles and then, in a culmination often marked by liturgical ceremony, from the gospels.[14] This prompts the thought that while comprehension of the Old Testament is necessary for the church's identification of the Trinity, it is not sufficient. The New Testament is also required, above all the rendering of Jesus' life, death, and resurrection in the gospels.

The liturgy thus seems to display an important assumption about identifying the Trinity. We apparently need some way of referring to Jesus, and of distinguishing him from all other persons, if we are to identify the Trinity at all — if, that is, we are to distinguish all three persons from one another and from ourselves. As Hans Urs von Balthasar puts the claim, "distinguishing a plurality in God is only possible on the basis of the action of Jesus Christ. In him alone is the Trinity opened up and accessible."[15] Modern trinitarian theology in particular has tended to insist upon this point. Traditional reflection on these issues had, to be sure, commonly held that "the Trinity is implicitly contained in Christ."[16] An adequate grasp of who Jesus is (perhaps including knowledge of his *identity,* and not simply of features that individuate him), so this sort of remark suggests, is enough to identify all the persons of the Trinity. But the characteristic modern assumption embodies a stronger claim: not only does the right sort of reference to Jesus enable us to pick out the whole Trinity, such reference is necessary for the task.[17] With this generally goes the

---

their redemptive experience of him in the tones of Jewish Scripture, are historical accidents that Christian faith now can, and indeed should, ignore. On this see Marshall, "The Jewish People and Christian Theology," pp. 86-87.

14. Note the procession with the gospel book at the Little Entrance in the Orthodox Divine Liturgy, or the common western practice of having the gospel read only by the eucharistic celebrant, often following a procession into the congregation.

15. Hans Urs von Balthasar, *Theo-Drama,* vol. 3, trans. Graham Harrison (San Francisco: Ignatius, 1992), p. 508 (translation altered).

16. Thomas Aquinas, *Super Evangelium S. Matthaei Lectura,* 5th edition, ed. Raphael Cai (Turin: Marietti, 1951), no. 2467.

17. The standard modern assumption, in other words, is genuinely biconditional: if, and *only* if, we can (adequately) identify Jesus can we identify the whole Trinity. The less demanding traditional claim might be converted into a biconditional, given some collateral assumptions. Aquinas,

further assumption that we can identify the Trinity only when Jesus actually appears on the scene, only, that is, following his temporal advent. Nowadays this may seem too obvious for comment, but it has deep and troubling implications, as we will later observe, for a post-supersessionist attempt to account for the Christian claim to worship the God of Israel.

Christian liturgy indicates, then, that the church must identify its God in two different ways: as the God of Israel and as the Trinity. The structure of the liturgy of the word suggests with particular clarity the distinction and relation between these two ways of individuating the one God. The descriptions "is the God of Israel" and "is the Trinity," with the former arrived at chiefly by way of the Old Testament, and the latter by way of the New, play irreducibly different roles in the church's liturgical identification of its God. But each is necessary for the task, and neither alone is sufficient; for this purpose the New Testament can do without the Old as little as the Old can do without the New. Yet the truth of this suggestion turns out to be less obvious than one might have thought.

Perplexities about Liturgical Faith

Some theologians writing on questions of this kind argue that once Christians recognize their commitment to worshiping the God of Israel, they will have to drop the doctrine of the Trinity. Such suggestions form a topic in their own right; for present purposes we are assuming that Christian worship is structured by a commitment to identify God as the Trinity, a commitment as basic as the church's claim to worship the God of Israel. Having granted that, it may seem odd to worry that there might still be a problem here. The church identifies its God in two different ways, but worships only one God, so it may seem obvious that the God of Israel has to be the Trinity, and conversely.[18]

---

for example, holds that "if one of the persons is taken away, the others are taken away, because they are distinguished only by relations, which have to go together *(quas oportet esse simul)*" (*Summa theologiae* III, 3, 3, c). This implies that we cannot pick out any one of the persons of the Trinity without picking out all three. Whether this requires reference specifically to *Jesus* in order to identify the Trinity (as in the modern biconditional) depends, of course, on whether it is possible to identify the "Christ" in whom the whole Trinity is "included" without reference to Jesus. We will return to this question.

18. This seems to be Soulen's view in "YHWH the Triune God." He faults trinitarian theology ancient and modern (whether rightly we need not decide) for failing to maintain that reference to Israel is necessary in order to identify God, and insists that such reference is mandatory. "The confession that YHWH is Triune," he argues, "should be understood to mean that the One God identified by the proper name YHWH and the triune history summarized in the commu-

That Christians identify God both as the Trinity and as Israel's Lord fails, in fact, to guarantee that both of these descriptions actually locate the same being. On the contrary, it leads one to wonder whether they actually do, and if so, how. This is a familiar problem. Sometimes our use of different descriptions leads us to suppose, erroneously, that we are talking about different objects. Thus the ancients apparently thought that "the evening star" and "the morning star" were two different celestial bodies, but eventually discovered that they were the same planet. Conversely, we sometimes assume that different descriptions are simply diverse ways of talking about the same object, only to discover that our descriptions fit no one individual, but instead locate different objects. Thus an important collection of christological treatises from the sixth century, each of which was written by "Leontius," were long assumed to be the work of a single person. But two of these treatises differ in substance from the rest, and further research has led to the conclusion that they are the work not of one person, but two: Leontius of Byzantium and Leontius of Jerusalem. So if Christians are to give an account of the claim that we worship only one God, we will have to show that the two different ways in which we identify the one we worship in some way succeed in locating the same God.

In order to do this, we will presumably have to solve a problem of reference. We will need to show that the terms we use when we identify God in these two different ways are co-extensive, or have the same referent. That is: if Christians succeed in worshiping one God, whom they identify both as the Trinity and as the God of Israel, then terms referring to the Father, or to the Son, or to the Holy Spirit, or to all three, ought to refer to the God of Israel (and conversely). Should they do so, then the church's God will be the same as YHWH, the God of Israel. The church's God will be "the same as" Israel's God in the relevant sense if they are numerically identical. The Christian claim, presumably, is not to worship a God who merely resembles (or is qualitatively identical with) the God of Abraham, Isaac, and Jacob, but to worship one and the same God who elected them, and whom they themselves worshiped. There would seem to be several ways in which the God whom the church identifies as the Father, the Son, and the Holy Spirit might be numerically identical with Israel's Lord. I will here look at three, each of which has considerable support in the tradition: Israel's God might be (a) the Son, (b) the Fa-

nion of Father, Son, and Holy Spirit are one such that neither supplants nor absorbs the other, and neither exists outside nor apart from the other" (p. 47). The point of this remark, I take it, is that the descriptions "is the God of Israel" and "is the Father, the Son, and the Holy Spirit" are two different ways of identifying God, that both are necessary for the task, and that neither is sufficient. So far as I can see, Soulen thinks asserting this is enough to establish that both descriptions identify the same God — that YHWH is the Trinity, and conversely.

ther, or (c) the Trinity.[19] As I will try to suggest, however, none of these alternatives seems entirely coherent.

(A) The God of Israel Is the Son

Perhaps the most widespread approach among the theologians of the early church is to say that the God of Israel is Christ — not necessarily *Jesus* Christ quite yet, but at least the Father's Son or Word, who is going to become incarnate of the Virgin Mary. It is he in particular, and not the Father or the entire Trinity, who is the subject of the Old Testament theophanies and the bearer of the divine name in Hebrew Scripture. He appears to Moses in the burning bush, leads Israel across the Red Sea, gives the prophets utterance, and so forth. Irenaeus, for example, apparently identifies Israel's God not only with the Logos, but with Jesus himself: "One and the same head of the household has produced both covenants, namely the Word of God, our Lord Jesus Christ. It was he who spoke to Abraham and Moses, and who has newly restored our liberty."[20] Later Chrysostom takes a similar view. In the wilderness "the Jews had Christ following them, but all the more does he follow us now."[21] So also, from a different exegetical tradition, does Leo the Great. By giving the beatitudes to the apostles on a mountain, "our Lord Jesus Christ . . . showed them, from the very quality of this place and of his work, that it was he himself who had once honored Moses by speaking to him on that mountain."[22]

19. Besides binary combinations, which I will not investigate here, there is the interesting possibility that Israel's God might be numerically identical with the Spirit. So far as I am aware, no one has ever made a case for this. However, Augustine, in what is surely the richest patristic exploration of these issues (*De Trinitate,* books II-IV), several times considers the possibility. See his programmatic statement of the difficulties faced by a trinitarian interpretation of the Old Testament in *De Trinitate* II, 7, 12-13. (I follow the chapter and section divisions in *Sancti Aurelii Augustini De Trinitate Libri XV,* ed. W. J. Mountain, *Corpus Christianorum series latina,* vols. 50 & 50A [Turnhout, Belgium: Brepols, 1968]. For a translation see *The Trinity,* trans. Edmund Hill, *The Works of Saint Augustine,* part I, vol. 5 [Brooklyn: New City Press, 1991]. Hill follows the section numbers in the critical edition but devises his own chapter divisions.)

20. *Adversus Haereses* IV, 9, 1. My translation from Irénée de Lyon, *Contre les hérésies, livre IV,* ed. Adelin Rousseau, *Sources Chrétiennes,* vol. 100 (Paris: Cerf, 1965). For a usable English translation of the whole, see *The Ante-Nicene Fathers,* vol. 1 (Grand Rapids: Eerdmans, 1977), pp. 315-567.

21. St. John Chrysostom, *Baptismal Instructions,* 3, 25. Trans. Paul W. Harkins, *Ancient Christian Writers,* vol. 31 (New York: Paulist Press, 1963), p. 64.

22. St. Leo the Great, *Sermons,* 95, 1. Trans. Jane Patricia Freeland and Agnes Josephine Conway, *The Fathers of the Church,* vol. 93 (Washington, D.C.: Catholic University of America Press, 1996), pp. 394-95.

This approach not only shapes the trinitarian reflection of both Greek and Latin theologians in the ancient church, but is regularly defended in the tradition through the Reformation, and indeed into modern times. Luther, for example, while clearly familiar with some of the precision introduced into trinitarian theology by the scholastics, takes a view as bold as that of Irenaeus. "The God who led the people of Israel out of Egypt and through the Red Sea, who led them through the wilderness by the pillar of cloud and the pillar of fire . . . is precisely that God, and no other, whom we Christians call our God and Lord: Jesus of Nazareth, the son of the Virgin Mary. . . . Indeed Jesus of Nazareth, who died on the cross for us, is the God who speaks in the first commandment: 'I am the LORD, your God.'"[23] Calvin is a bit more restrained; terms designating the God of Israel in the Old Testament (e.g., "the angel of the Lord" in Judges 6–7) do refer to the person of the Word, though not yet to the Word incarnate.[24] In the century just past the Russian Orthodox theologian Sergei Bulgakov pointedly supports this idea. "If the Father creates the world by his Word, he makes use of this same Word in his counsel and his revelation in the world. That is why the immediate divine subject of the Old Testament is the same as that of the New: the second hypostasis, the Logos."[25] Karl Barth hints at this as well.[26]

This view of the matter clearly has some support in the New Testament. The Israelites in the wilderness, as Paul argues, "drank from the spiritual rock that followed them, and the rock was Christ" (1 Cor. 10:4). Several Johannine texts point in the same direction. "Abraham . . . saw my day and was glad" (John 8:56); "Moses . . . wrote about me" (John 5:46); "Isaiah . . . saw [Jesus'] glory and spoke about him" (John 12:41). Throughout the tradition advocates of the idea that the God of Israel is basically the trinitarian Son or Word have not failed to pay close attention to such passages.

23. *Von den letzten Worten Davids* (1543). *D. Martin Luthers Werke, Kritische Gesamtausgabe* (Weimar, 1883ff.) (= WA), vol. 54, p. 67, 1-3, 6-7, 12-14. For a translation of the whole see *Luther's Works,* vol. 15 (St. Louis: Concordia, 1972), pp. 265-352; here, pp. 313-14.

24. "That chief angel [is] God's Word, who already at that time, as a sort of foretaste, began to fulfill the office of Mediator" (*Institutes,* I, xiii, 10). Thus in controversy with those who deny the divinity of Christ "we shall truly say: the God who of old appeared to the patriarchs was no other than Christ" (*Institutes,* I, xiii, 27). The translations are those of Ford Lewis Battles, in John T. McNeill, ed., *Calvin: Institutes of the Christian Religion* (Philadelphia: Westminster, 1960).

25. *Du Verbe Incarné: L'Agneau de Dieu,* trans. Constantin Andronikof, 2nd edition (Lausanne: Age d'Homme, 1982), p. 91.

26. "For the Yahweh who exists this second time in a very different way, the name of Yahweh, is the form in which Yahweh comes to Israel, has dealings with it, is manifest to it." *Church Dogmatics* I/1, trans. Geoffrey W. Bromiley, 2nd edition (Edinburgh: T. & T. Clark, 1975), p. 317.

This way of looking at the matter has the considerable merit of allowing for a uniform idea of the action and the self-presentation of the triune God in both the Old and New Testaments, indeed from creation to the end of time. The Father himself never appears, but always manifests himself through his Word or Wisdom, by the action of his Spirit; this self-manifestation of course undergoes a definitive increase of clarity with the incarnation of the Word. On this view all of Scripture's talk of God basically conforms to the pattern of John's prologue: no one has ever seen God, but the only Son has made him known (compare John 1:18).

Despite its manifest attraction, this way of approaching our problem has gone considerably on the wane. The chief cause of its current neglect is no doubt the rise of historical criticism. It now seems quite implausible to suppose (despite the Gospel of John) that the writers or redactors of the Old Testament books had the trinitarian Logos — to say nothing of Mary's firstborn son — in mind when they talked about "the angel of the Lord," or used other terms referring in some fashion to Israel's God. So taking Old Testament terms designating the God of Israel as referring to the second person of the Trinity, incarnate or otherwise, seems, on historical-critical grounds, ruled out from the start.

Whether we can decide on the reference of terms in scriptural sentences (or in any other inscriptions, for that matter) by appeal to what those who wrote them had in mind, we need not settle here.[27] In any case the Old Testament naturally contains numerous terms referring to the God of Israel, and the New Testament, like Christian worship, purports to do likewise (virtually all of them borrowed from the Old). At the same time the New Testament, at least, contains terms referring to the Father, the Son, and the Holy Spirit. So it is presumably in order to ask whether terms referring to the God of Israel also refer to one, all, or none of these three, and to let the actual use of the terms decide the issue. To rule out in advance the possibility that terms for the God of Israel refer to the Father, the Son, or the Spirit, or to confine this possibility to the use of these terms in the New Testament, is simply to assume that Jews and Christians worship, and the two Testaments talk about, different gods.

But granted that we cannot decide the matter *a priori,* the idea that the God of Israel is the Logos alone still runs into trouble. It seems incompatible with one of the most basic features of the New Testament's depiction of Jesus. When Jesus addresses Israel's God in the gospels, he is not talking to himself. When, for example, Jesus cries out on the cross, "My God, my God, why have

27. For some discussion of the limits of interpretive appeals to the intentions of speakers (or writers), see Marshall, *Trinity and Truth,* pp. 91-100, 194-98.

you forsaken me" (Mark 15:34 and parallels) he can only be addressing the God of Israel, the one who appeared to Moses and delivered Israel from Egypt. Just as surely, he is not talking to himself, but to someone else — to a listener numerically distinct from himself. The gospel narrative never deviates from these rudimentary but cardinal points. Jesus never invokes as God anyone but Israel's Lord, and never talks to himself. Taken together, these two elements in the narrative mean that the God of Israel cannot simply be the same as the person of the Word or Son.

This assumes, of course, the Christian trinitarian claim that Jesus is himself the Word become our flesh. However the relationship between Jesus' human agency or operation and his divine agency or operation is to be worked out, he remains a single agent, a single acting subject or person — the "theandric" doer (as Maximus the Confessor puts it) who carries out human actions in a divine way and divine actions in a human way. When Jesus speaks to another he cannot, therefore, be addressing the Logos, since his words are the human speech *of* the Logos. In order to address the divine Logos as another, Jesus would have to be a personal agent distinct from the Logos. The drawbacks to taking Jesus' words and deeds in this "Nestorian" way (as the tradition has termed it, whether or not fairly to the historical Nestorius), making of them the doings of two acting subjects rather than one, need not concern us here. We may simply note that there is no trace in the gospels (including the Gospel of John) of speech by Jesus *to* the Logos. Barring this Nestorian recourse, the idea that the God of Israel is the same as the Logos seems to generate a more or less systematic incoherence in the basic New Testament narrative. Thus terms referring to the God of Israel apparently cannot simply be co-extensive with terms referring to the Logos, whether in or out of the flesh.

(B) The God of Israel Is the Father

For this reason a lot of recent trinitarian theology tends toward the view that the God of Israel is, among the persons of the Trinity, not the Son but the Father. In the New Testament, so defenders of this approach argue, the word "God" (ὁ Θεός) almost always refers to the Father in particular. In a few clearly demarcated cases it refers to the Son, but never (or virtually never) to the entire Trinity. At the same time, when the New Testament speaks of the God who delivers the world from evil by the death and resurrection of his own Son, it does not introduce a previously unknown deity. Instead it refers to Israel's Lord, the creator of the universe and the ruler of the covenant with his elect people. Together these two considerations imply that the God of Israel is the Father.[28]

This approach tends to be strongest at just the point where the view we have just considered is weakest: it makes good sense of Jesus' words and deeds as they are depicted in the New Testament. Taking the God of Israel to be the Father honors, one could say, the narrative logic of the gospels. When Jesus cries out to God on the cross, he is clearly addressing the same God whom he had earlier singled out as "Father" when he prayed in anguish in the garden of Gethsemane (Mark 14:32-42 and parallels). He has, moreover, already invited his followers to join him in addressing their God this way (see, for example, Matt. 6:9; Luke 11:2). The God whom Jesus and his followers address can only be Israel's Lord. So the gospel story in particular seems to provide substantial warrant for saying that the God of Israel is the Father.

This way of handling the matter also has considerable patristic support. The church fathers often regard the revelation of the Trinity not simply as progressive, but sequential. It is not so much that the three persons are at first all dimly perceived, and then distinguished with gradually increasing clarity until the incarnation of the Son and the outpouring of the Spirit fully reveal the Trinity. Rather the history of Israel as recounted in the Old Testament explicitly discloses the Father, while the Son and the Spirit each wait for definitive revelation at an appropriate time. Gregory Nazianzen classically gives voice to this outlook. "The Old Testament proclaimed the Father manifestly, the Son more obscurely. The New manifested the Son and allowed a glimpse of the divinity of the Spirit. Now the Spirit lives among us and affords us a clearer manifestation of himself."[29] Should this hold up, we will have found a simple and utterly basic way of accounting for the need to have the Old Testament come first in the Christian canon (upon which the first Christian centuries, as we have observed, so vigorously insist). By locating the Father for us, the Old Testament would prove indispensable precisely in identifying the God who sends his Son and Spirit into the world for the world's salvation. With this God the New Testament presumes a familiarity that it does not itself provide, and that can only be acquired by the Old Testament's rendering of God's way with his people Israel.

28. For an extended argument that "God" in the New Testament refers specifically to the Father, see Karl Rahner, "Theos in the New Testament," *Theological Investigations,* vol. 1, trans. Cornelius Ernst (London: Darton, Longman & Todd, 1961), pp. 79-148, esp. pp. 125-48. That the Father is also the God of Israel attracts Rahner's attention, though only in passing. Cf. pp. 102, 134-35.

29. *Oratio* 31, 26. Translated from Grégoire de Nazianze, *Discours 27-31,* ed. Paul Gallay, *Sources Chrétiennes,* vol. 250 (Paris: Cerf, 1978). For the whole in English see *The Nicene and Post-Nicene Fathers,* second series, vol. 7 (Grand Rapids: Eerdmans, 1978).

Whether or not viewed in explicitly sequentialist terms, the idea that Israel's Lord is the same as the Father finds advocates across the tradition — often among theologians who, in almost the same breath, defend the claim that the God of Israel is the Son. Thus Irenaeus urges Christians to cleave to the "rule of truth," according to which "there is one omnipotent God who created all things through his Word . . . and through his Word and Spirit does all things, disposing of, governing, and giving being to all. . . . This is the God of Abraham, and the God of Isaac, and the God of Jacob, above whom there is no other God, nor beginning, nor power, nor pleroma. This is the Father of our Lord Jesus Christ."[30] Luther sometimes makes the same suggestion. "The God of Israel has spoken to me," David says (2 Sam. 23:3). Luther comments: "Which God this speaker is we Christians know from the Gospel of John. It is the Father, who said in the beginning (Gen. 1), 'Let there be light.'"[31]

Yet while this line of argument seems compelling in its own way, there seem to be equally compelling reasons not to equate the God of Israel with the trinitarian Father. First of all this view generates its own sort of narrative incoherence. Scriptural Israel, after all, enjoys a considerable if uneasy intimacy with its God, who dwells in the midst of his chosen people and is pleased to run the universe from a particular spatial location, namely the Temple on Mt. Zion. It seems a bit odd that this same God should suddenly recede into the distance, now dwelling in "inapproachable light" (1 Tim. 6:16) and dealing with human beings only through an emissary (however exalted, indeed divine, the emissary is in his own right).

The deeper problem, though, is that equating the God of Israel with the trinitarian Father apparently makes idolaters of Christians. Israel's God, after all, claims exclusive rights to human worship; in Isaiah's language, he gives not his glory to another (cf. Isa. 42:8). If this God is simply identical with the Father, then the Son and the Spirit are not the God of Israel — not the being referred to by (or whose presence is embodied in the utterance of) the Tetragrammaton. Were that the case, then in worshiping them — in giving them glory along with the Father — Christians would worship that which is not the God of Israel, and thus give their hearts to false gods.

Writing in the early seventeenth century, the Lutheran theologian Johann Gerhard puts his finger on just this problem. The Old Testament as well as the New, he argues, has to attest the Trinity. This can be inferred in several ways, not least "from the divine prohibition in Psalm 81:10 [9]: 'Have among your-

30. *Adversus Haereses* I, 22, 1 (*Sources Chrétiennes,* vol. 264); cf. III, 6, 4.

31. WA 54, p. 36, 2-4 (*Luther's Works,* vol. 15, p. 276).

selves . . . no new God, and bow down before no foreign God.'" Israel is not to worship, and so not to identify, any new God. Therefore it cannot be that the Son and the Holy Spirit are God, but are not identified and worshiped as such until the events depicted in the New Testament have come to pass. "If the mystery of the Trinity [and not just of the Father] were entirely unknown in the Old Testament, then a new God would be introduced in the New Testament by the worship of the Son and the Holy Spirit. If the Son begins to be touched by divine worship only in the New Testament, then another God has been formed besides God the Father."[32]

(C) The God of Israel Is the Trinity

If it does not seem quite right to say that the God of Israel is just the same as either the Word or the Father, then why not say that the God of Israel is the Trinity — all three persons together? This would surely seem to offer a way of avoiding the suggestion of idolatry implicit in the view that the God of Israel is numerically identical with the Father.

Gerhard, as we have just observed, apparently takes this view, but he follows in a long tradition. Augustine in particular develops this suggestion in considerable detail. Reflecting on the theophany of the burning bush in Exodus 3, he makes the following characteristic argument. "We cannot say that the God of Abraham and the God of Isaac and the God of Jacob is the Son of God and is not the Father. Or will someone dare to deny that the Holy Spirit, or the Trinity himself, whom we believe and understand to be the one God, is the God of Abraham and the God of Isaac and the God of Jacob? For whoever is not the God of those fathers is not God *(Ille enim non est illorum patrum deus qui non est deus)*."[33] This idea becomes quite common in subsequent western theology, especially as a way of interpreting the Old Testament. So, for example, Fulgentius of Ruspe, writing about a century after Augustine: "In the sacrifices of animal victims, which the holy Trinity himself, who is the one God of the New and the Old Testaments, commanded our fathers to offer to him, there was signified the most pleasing gift of all:

32. *Loci theologici, Locus* III: *De Sanctissimo Trinitatis Mysterio* (exegesin sive uberiorem explicationem), §21, ed. Johann Friedrich Cotta (Tübingen: Georg Cotta, 1762-89), vol. 3, p. 219a-b.

33. *De Trinitate* II, 13, 23. Similarly, regarding the Sinai theophany (Exod. 20) and the appearance of God to the elders of Israel (Exod. 24:10): "all these visible and sensible realities were put forth in order to signify the invisible and intelligible God, not only the Father but the Son and the Holy Spirit" (II, 15, 25).

that sacrifice by which God the Son alone was to offer himself mercifully for us according to the flesh."[34]

Much Christian theology, as we have seen, tends to oscillate unselfconsciously between the view that the God of Israel is the Son and the view that this God is the Father. It should not be surprising, therefore, that these same theologians also often say that the God of Israel is the Trinity. With this naturally goes the thought that the Jewish people before Christ (or at least some of them) knew the Trinity, just because they knew the God of Israel. Thus early on Irenaeus argues that "Christ himself, with the Father, is the God of the living, who spoke to Moses and who was manifested to the fathers."[35] One of these fathers, of course, was Abraham, "who was a prophet and saw in the Spirit the day of the Lord's advent and the economy of his passion." Therefore "the Lord was not unknown to Abraham . . . but neither was the Lord's Father, for he learned about God from the Word, and believed him."[36] Much later Luther follows a similar pattern. He asks, commenting on Isaiah 60:19-20, "Who then is it, who says such things by the tongue of Isaiah? God the Holy Spirit, no doubt, who speaks through the prophets. He introduces the person of the Father, who speaks of the eternal light, that is, of his Son Jesus of Nazareth, the Son of David and of Mary."[37]

Arguments for this sort of claim generally have recourse to the suggestion embodied, as we have observed, in the liturgy — that reference to Jesus is sufficient, but also necessary, to identify all three persons of the Trinity. So Aquinas proposes that "in the Old Testament the Trinity of persons is expressed in many ways, for example at the very beginning of Genesis" (he cites in this connection, as many had before, Gen. 1:26).[38] The Israelites' grasp of the Trinity was, more precisely, implicated in their apprehension of Christ, since in Christ the Trinity is "implicitly contained."[39] The ceremonies by which scriptural Israel worshiped its God were the very means by which it knew Christ, and so the Trinity. "In the time of the law the mind of the faithful could be joined by faith to the incarnate and suffering Christ, and so they were justified by faith in Christ. Their observance of the ceremonies [of the law] was a way of displaying this faith, insofar as these ceremonies were figures of Christ."[40] By way of

34. *De Fide ad Petrum,* 22. *Sancti Fulgentii Episcopi Ruspensis Opera,* ed. J. Fraipont, *Corpus Christianorum series latina,* vol. 91A (Turnhout, Belgium: Brepols, 1968).

35. *Adversus Haereses* IV, 5, 2.

36. *Adversus Haereses* IV, 5, 5.

37. WA 54, p. 47, 6-9 (*Luther's Works,* vol. 15, p. 290).

38. *Summa theologiae* II-II, 2, 8, sc.

39. Cf. above, note 17.

40. *Summa theologiae* I-II, 103, 2, c.

the Levitical cult at least the "elders" *(maiores)* of Israel had explicit faith in Christ to come, although for the rest (the *minores*) this prospective apprehension of Christ was only implicit and, "as it were, clouded over."[41] It seems, moreover, as though the *maiores* in Israel knew the Trinity because they knew in advance about *Jesus* in particular ("the incarnate and suffering Christ"), though Aquinas leaves room for doubt on this score. "While the mysteries of Christ were revealed to the prophets and patriarchs, they were not revealed so clearly as to the apostles. For to the prophets and patriarchs they were revealed in a certain generality, but to the apostles they were made manifest with respect to their singular and determinate circumstances."[42]

In the seventeenth century there emerges an even stronger version of the claim that the God of Israel is the Trinity, and may be known as such even before Jesus appears on the scene. Prompted by newly arisen unitarian interpretations of Christianity, theologians of all the now firmly divided confessions try to show that the Trinity is a completely biblical doctrine. Not only may traces of the Trinity be found in the Old Testament, and knowledge of the Trinity attributed to Israel "under the law," but the Old Testament by itself is sufficient to show that God is triune, and Israel apparently knew the Trinity without any reference to Jesus — without the sort of foreknowledge, however construed, that the tradition had typically attributed at least to the *maiores.* Granted, Gerhard argues, that "the clearer revelation of this mystery was reserved for the New Testament," nonetheless "the mystery of the Trinity can and should be established *(confirmari)* not only from the New Testament, but also from the Old."[43] Gerhard does not simply argue for this *a priori* (given the Trinity, and given that there can be no "new" God, the Old Testament must attest the Trinity). Rather he goes to very considerable exegetical lengths to show that "several persons, namely the Father, the Son, and the Holy Spirit, are the true God, whom the Israelites knew and worshiped."[44] Numerous Old Testament passages (especially the creation and exodus narratives) demonstrate this all by themselves, without any reference to events depicted in the New Testament.[45]

41. *Summa theologiae* II-II, 2, 8, c. On the *maiores/minores* distinction, see also 2, 6-7.

42. *In Ephesios* 3, 1 (no. 139). *S. Thomae Aquinatis Super Epistolas S. Pauli Lectura,* vol. 2, ed. Raphael Cai, 8th edition (Turin: Marietti, 1953). Cf. *Summa theologiae* II-II, 174, 6.

43. *Loci theologici, Locus* III (exegesin), §20, ed. Cotta, vol. 3, p. 218b.

44. *Loci theologici, Locus* III (exegesin), §135, ed. Cotta, vol. 3, p. 300b.

45. For Gerhard's extremely complicated anti-Socinian reading of the creation and exodus material, see *Loci theologici, Locus* III (exegesin), §§109-46, ed. Cotta, vol. 3, pp. 283-308. He argues, to be sure, that Moses and Jacob "both saw the Son of God in human form" (§143, p. 306a) but he apparently does not mean by this that they saw Jesus; rather they beheld a temporary and prefigurative theophany of the incarnation to come.

Despite all this it is not clear, at least at first glance, that equating the God of Israel with the Trinity entirely succeeds in avoiding narrative incoherence. The problem is similar to that involved, as we have already seen, in the view that the God of Israel is the Logos. Take, for example, the Lukan story of the presentation of the infant Jesus in the Temple (Luke 2:22-24). Mary and Joseph bring Jesus up to Jerusalem (2:22) "to present him to the Lord." In this sentence κύριος — "the Lord" — clearly looks like it refers to the God of Israel, regardless of whether one takes it as an explicit stand-in, via the Septuagint, for the Tetragrammaton. It is, after all, to the Temple of Israel's God that the infant Jesus is brought, in obedience to this God's commands about the presentation of the firstborn male to him (cf. Exod. 13:2, 12), and about the ritual purification of a Jewish woman after the birth of a male child (Lev. 12:8).

If the God of Israel is the Trinity, and κύριος in this sentence refers to the God of Israel, then it seems as though this expression must also refer here to the Trinity. Of the triune God, so Christian worship of this God supposes, the infant Jesus is one of the persons, incarnate. But this means that Jesus' parents brought him to the Temple to present him to himself. And that does not seem possible. If Jesus is one of the Trinity, then he cannot really be presented *to* the Trinity.[46]

Of course on this view Mary and Joseph would have presented Jesus to the Father, and in some sense to the Spirit, as well as to himself. But while it complicates matters a bit, this observation does not really seem to avoid the problem of narrative incoherence. Here too a genuine distinction between Jesus and the God to whom the narrative relates him seems basic to what is going on. It does not make much more sense to say that Jesus is presented to himself in the Temple (even if not only to himself) than it does to say that he talks to himself in the garden of Gethsemane (even if not only to himself). Luke seems aware of this difficulty, and so later has Jesus explicitly say that the Jerusalem Temple is in fact his *Father's* house (2:49). But that the God of Israel is exclusively the Father raises, as we have observed, problems of its own.

It might seem as though this problem is easy to deal with. Of course κύριος in this passage refers to the Father in particular, and not to the Son or

46. Something similar goes, e.g., for the Magnificat (Luke 1:46-55) and the Benedictus (Luke 1:68-79). Both are hymns in praise of "the Lord, the God of Israel" (1:68; 1:46, 55), but when praising the God of Israel Mary is surely not speaking about the child — precisely the "Son of God" (1:35) — just now conceived in her womb, nor Zechariah about the "mighty savior" (1:69) whom the God of Israel has now raised up. Therefore neither can be understood — barring, once again, any Nestorian recourse — as speaking of the Logos, and so not as speaking of the Trinity.

Spirit. But the Father is one person of the Trinity, and the persons of the Trinity, while distinct, are inseparable. Κύριος here, or indeed any expression that refers to the God of Israel, therefore naturally insinuates the presence of all three persons of the Trinity. This is the point of the tradition's repeated insistence (Irenaeus and Luther have been our main examples) that while the God of Israel might primarily be Christ, or at times primarily the Father, neither person is ever Israel's God alone, but only together with the other two.

The problem, alas, is more difficult than that. This rejoinder is misleadingly ambiguous. Depending on how we disambiguate it, this reply either makes an observation that is no doubt correct, but fails to bear on the problem, or makes a claim that ends up denying the assumption it aims to support.

(1) This rejoinder might be taken for the observation that because the persons of the Trinity are inseparably united (by, for example, sharing numerically the same nature, or being constituted as persons through their ordered relations to one another), we can only identify any one of them if we can also identify the other two. In Thomas's formulation (applied here to the person of the Son), "The mystery of Christ cannot be believed explicitly without faith in the Trinity."[47] While surely correct, this observation fails to address the point at issue. Suppose an expression referring to the God of Israel also refers to the Father (as in Luke 2:22). (1) requires, in effect, that in order to refer to the God of Israel we also have to be able to pick out both the Son and the Spirit. But this does not mean that the Son and the Spirit are also referred to by *this* expression, and so, like the Father, are the same as the God of Israel. On the contrary, it presumes that they are not; the Trinity is therefore not identical with the God of Israel.

(2) It is, in other words, one thing to say that we can only refer to any one person of the Trinity if we know how to refer to the other two. It is quite another to say that when we refer to any one person of the Trinity, we *thereby* refer to the other two. If we take the present rejoinder to make this latter claim, then it loses any linguistic means for identifying the triune God at all. Unless we have expressions for each of the persons of the Trinity that do *not* refer to the other two, we will have no way to distinguish the three from one another. An expression that refers to the God of Israel, and also to one of the persons of the Trinity (like κύριος in Luke 2:22), distinguishes that person from the other two. Therefore it does not refer to the other two at all. If it did, this would not secure the belief that the God of Israel is the Trinity, but would instead eliminate it. We would be left with no expressions that both refer to the

47. *Summa theologiae* II-II, 2, 8, c.

God of Israel, and enable us to distinguish the persons of the Trinity from one another.[48]

We thus seem to have arguments in support of three different possibilities: that the God of Israel is Christ, the Father, or the Trinity. But we also have good grounds for rejecting each of these possibilities. Perhaps for just this reason Christian theology has tended to oscillate between these three different views, without settling in an entirely comfortable way upon any of them. Can we find some coherence in this unsettlement?

Does the Church Worship Israel's God?

At this point we may be tempted to give up the ghost, and say that we are confronted here with one of those mysteries that we cannot hope to understand before the eschaton. More boldly, one might suppose that the God of Israel has put his own identity at hazard in the incarnation of the Son and the outpouring of the Spirit; how these events hang together with his fidelity as Israel's God will not even be knowable (perhaps not even to God) until it all gets worked out in the end. Augustine, for one, at times seems ready to make such an appeal to mystery, at least in its milder, purely epistemic form. The God of Israel must surely be the Trinity, but how the church's identification of the three divine persons actually fits together with Israel's identification of its God is a puzzle that we may not be able to solve.[49]

Recourse to mystery is no doubt occasionally appropriate, when beliefs

48. The problem can be put the other way around, so that what the rejoinder eliminates is not our capacity to distinguish the three persons, but to tell that they are identical with the God of Israel. Our paradigm sentence is not in indirect discourse, or some other oblique context that obscures reference. Christians, as we have observed, claim to worship a single God, who is at once the God of Israel and the Trinity. This should mean, given the "purely referential" context of the paradigm in its Lukan setting, that we can substitute terms referring to the God of Israel and terms referring to the Trinity for one another *salva veritate.* That we can do this is presumably how we can *tell* that the God of Israel and the Trinity are one and the same. If, as it seems, we cannot do so, this does not mean that we have an inconsequential linguistic muddle, but that so far as we can tell, the God of Israel and the Trinity are *not* one and the same — unless, of course, we can find some way of accounting for the failure of intersubstitutivity that preserves the claim that the God of Israel is the Trinity.

49. So, once again, with regard to the Sinai theophany (cf. above, note 33): "I do not see exactly how it becomes apparent from all those things which were fearfully displayed to the senses of mortals whether God the Trinity spoke, or whether it was the Father, or the Son, or the Holy Spirit in particular *(proprie)*" (*De Trinitate* II, 15, 26). In this case, he ventures to guess, the Holy Spirit is perhaps best taken to be the subject of the theophany. For similar hesitations regarding what to make of the burning bush, see II, 13, 23.

that seem equally pressing to hold also generate conflicts that steadily resist reflective resolution. Newman, for example, observes that a scientific cosmology seems incompatible with the scriptural account of Christ's ascension ("Whither did He go? beyond the sun? beyond the fixed stars? Did He traverse the immeasurable space which extends beyond them all?"). Faced with these "two apparently discordant" sets of convictions, the appropriate course for Christians, he argues, is "not an impatience to do what is beyond our powers, to weigh evidence, sum up, balance, decide, and reconcile, to arbitrate between the two voices of God, — but . . . a conviction, that what is put before us, in nature or in grace, though true in such a full sense that we dare not tamper with it, yet is but an intimation useful for particular purposes, useful for practice, useful in its department, 'until the day-break and the shadows flee away.'"[50] Better this, surely, than to reduce the cognitive strain by prematurely discarding one or the other of the apparently conflicting beliefs, or by hastily settling for a superficial and implausible solution.

In the present case, however, the cost of recourse to mystery is especially high. We Christians want to worship a God who is at once Israel's Lord and the Trinity. Apparently we cannot do this unless the descriptions "is the God of Israel" and "is the Father, the Son, and the Holy Spirit" both pick out the same being. To invoke mystery when we have failed to find any way of lining up these two descriptions would be to say that, for all we can tell, the two descriptions are incompatible. They identify not the same God, but two different gods; in the face of this conflict, which we do not know how to resolve, we believe that they are nonetheless a single God. But if we leave it at that, why Christians ever came to think that the (triune) God they worship was the same being as Israel's Lord becomes inexplicable. The situation would be akin to that of "the morning star" and "the evening star," which people believed were two separate objects and only learned after long reflection were the same. This is the opposite of the situation with Christian worship. It has long seemed *obvious* to Christians (even if they cared about it less than they ought) that they worshiped Israel's God; only on reflection does this come to seem puzzling. Surely we have missed something, for which it would be better to look than to invoke mystery too soon.

In our attempt to explicate the Christian liturgical claim to worship the God of Israel, we have run up against a troubling linguistic fact: in Christian worship, as in the New Testament, terms designating the God of Israel do not seem to have enough fixity of reference. In the Lukan infancy narrative, for

50. The cited passages are from John Henry Newman, "Mysteries in Religion," *Parochial and Plain Sermons*, vol. 2 (London: Longmans, Green, and Co., 1869), pp. 208-9.

example, the term κύριος often refers to the Father, but sometimes to the Son (e.g., Luke 2:11); elsewhere in the New Testament it perhaps refers to the Spirit (e.g., 2 Cor. 3:17), as it clearly does in the Nicene Creed. When we read the Old Testament in trinitarian terms we find, as Augustine points out, still less fixity of reference, and even in individual cases we often have no clear way to decide whether an expression refers to any one of the divine persons in particular.

Perhaps we can cope with this linguistic fact by refining the suggestion that the God of Israel is the Trinity. This lack of referential fixity, one might argue, is just what we should expect. Mary's Magnificat, Zechariah's Benedictus, the presentation of Jesus in the Temple on Mt. Zion, Jesus' prayer to Israel's God in the garden of Gethsemane: all these continue the history of Israel's God with his people and with the world, and show it to be *semper maior* than Israel — to say nothing of the world — would have otherwise thought. In this ongoing history, we might suppose, the God of Abraham, Isaac, and Jacob has made himself available to Israel and to the world in his inmost reality as the Trinity: through Jesus' acceptance of the cross in obedience to the Father, through Jesus' resurrection by the Father in the power of the Spirit, and through the outpouring of the Spirit upon all flesh by the Father and the risen Son. If Israel's God is the Trinity, and makes himself available to the world as such in the unfolding of these particular events, then we should expect the depiction of all this in the New Testament and Christian worship to use terms referring to the God of Israel in fluid ways. Sometimes they will refer to the Father, sometimes to the Son, and sometimes to the Spirit (though as Gregory Nazianzen notes, there is little of this last explicitly in the New Testament). But they will refer exclusively to none of the three.

Looked at in this way, the apparent oscillation in Christian worship and Christian Scripture between saying that Father, Logos, and (occasionally) Spirit are the God of Israel might not signal incoherence, but rather point to the logic of the matter. We get a grip on the situation — namely, that the God of Israel is the Trinity — precisely by using terms for the God of Israel to refer now to the Father, now to the Son, and now to the Spirit, depending on the context. In just this way we come to recognize that "is the God of Israel" and "is the Father, the Son, and the Holy Spirit" both identify the same being. The lack of referential fixity in Christian discourse about the God of Israel teaches us, in other words, that the Father is the God of Israel, the Son is the God of Israel, and the Holy Spirit is the God of Israel, yet they are not three gods of Israel, but one God of Israel.

This puts us in the vicinity of a more familiar trinitarian problem. The following pattern of speech, Augustine argues, apparently embodies quite basic Christian convictions about God: "Just as the Father is God, so also the Son is God and the Holy Spirit is God . . . yet we do not say that this most excellent Trinity itself is three gods, but one God." From this and cognate cases can be gathered the more general rule — subsequently much analyzed and modified — that "whatever is said of each [of the three] with respect to themselves is taken in the singular and not in the plural of all together."[51] Adding the salutary specification "of Israel" in paradigm sentences like Augustine's would not seem to alter the logical situation. Following this paradigm, it thus seems straightforward to take the one God of Israel as the Trinity, and conversely.

Just this suggestion sometimes crops up in traditional reflection on the reference of terms for the persons of the Trinity. So, quite clearly, Gerhard: "The Father is YHWH *(Jehovah),* the Son is YHWH, the Holy Spirit is YHWH, nevertheless they are not several YHWHs *(Jehovae),* but YHWH is one," and "that one true YHWH is the Father, the Son, and the Holy Spirit, and these three persons are one true God."[52] Augustine already makes a similar argument. Israel's God proclaimed his law to his elect people (and so prefigured the coming incarnation, passion, and resurrection of the Son) by angelic theophanies (compare Gal. 3:19). "In these angels," Augustine maintains, "were the Father, and the Son, and the Holy Spirit. Sometimes the Father was indicated *(figurabatur)* by them, sometimes the Son, sometimes the Holy Spirit, and sometimes God without any distinction of person."[53]

With or without reference to Israel, this pattern of speech obviously poses a large conceptual problem. It — and so the Christian conviction that Father, Son, and Spirit are one God — appears to fall afoul of some seemingly obvious truths about identity, sometimes gathered under the label "Leibniz's Law." One such feature of identity is its commutative character. If the morning star is the same as the planet Venus, and the evening star is the same as the planet Venus, then the morning star and the evening star have to be the same as each other. Applied to the Trinity, however, this produces unhappy results; we want to say that Father, Son, and Spirit are each identical with the one God but are not identical with each other. To this problem numerous solutions have been proposed.[54] Our present purpose is not to address the problem it-

51. Augustine, *De Trinitate* V, 8, 9; cf. I, 5, 8. For a subsequent analysis that considerably qualifies Augustine's rule, see Aquinas, *Summa theologiae* I, 39, 3.

52. *Loci theologici, Locus* III (exegesin), §146, ed. Cotta, vol. 3, p. 308b.

53. *De Trinitate* III, 10, 26.

54. For Aquinas's direct address to this problem, see *Summa theologiae* I, 28, 3, ad 1; his solution is tied to claims about the way the logic of identity works when applied to relations. The

self, but simply to observe that in the end the coherence of the Christian claim to worship the God of Israel seems to coincide with the coherence of the Christian claim to worship the Trinity at all. If it makes sense to say that in locating the Father, the Son, and the Holy Spirit Christians succeed in identifying the one God, presumably it makes equal sense to say that they succeed in identifying the one God of Israel.

By extending semantic paradigms traditional in trinitarian theology, we have sought to give an account of the quite basic Christian claim that in worshiping the Trinity, the church worships the God of Israel. Whether this is a claim that Jews might be able to accept (not that God is the Trinity, but that in worshiping and believing in their Trinity Christians somehow touch, as it were, Israel's God) is another, and complex, question.[55] But we need to consider whether this defense of the Christian claim to worship the God of Israel — and indeed the claim itself — can avoid relapse into supersessionism.

The problem we have attempted to solve takes its start from the requirement, apparently embodied in Christian liturgy, that two different ways of identifying the one God must both be employed if we are actually to succeed in locating this God. Granted that the descriptions "is the God of Israel" and "is the Father, the Son, and the Holy Spirit" actually succeed in identifying the same being, and granted that recourse to the first as well as the second is necessary to identify the one God, it may seem that at least on this score, supersessionism has safely been put to rest. But obviously it has not. Granting these two claims entails that Christians cannot identify the one God without recognizing that he is Israel's Lord, but it also entails that *Jews* cannot identify the one God at all.

If both of these descriptions are necessary to identify the one God, then of course neither of them is, by itself, sufficient. This means that the God of Israel cannot actually be identified without reference to the Father, the Son, and the Holy Spirit. Referring to God's ways with the descendants of Abraham, Isaac, and Jacob is not enough. By itself this is not quite supersessionism in the sense defined at the outset — the view that the carnal descendants of Abraham, Isaac, and Jacob have ceased to be God's elect with the coming of

---

problem has recently received extensive treatments that develop Peter Geach's (controversial) notion of "relative identity"; see Peter van Inwagen, "And Yet They Are Not Three Gods but One God," *God, Knowledge, and Mystery* (Ithaca, N.Y.: Cornell University Press, 1995), pp. 222-59.

55. Traditional Judaism widely, though not universally, regarded Christian worship as idolatry. Some contemporary Jewish thinkers suggest that Christians do believe in, and perhaps succeed in worshiping, the God of Israel. See Tikva Frymer-Kensky, David Novak, Peter Ochs, David Fox Sandmel, Michael A. Signer, eds., *Christianity in Jewish Terms* (Boulder: Westview Press, 2000), e.g., pp. xvii-xviii.

Christ. The God identified in this twofold way might still be supposed to have elected Abraham's descendants forever. But requiring both descriptions in order to identify God at all has implications that surely hold fast only if supersessionism is true. Given this requirement — which not only seems to be supported by the structure of Christian worship, but often by Christian theology that aims to reject supersessionism — Jews past and present cannot locate the God who elects them without reference to the Father, the Son, and the Holy Spirit. As a result they cannot reliably identify themselves as God's elect without believing in the Trinity — without, that is, becoming Christians. Few Jews have recourse to the Trinity in order to locate God, liturgically or otherwise, and so, it seems, they cannot actually identify the God of Israel at all.

This problem arises in the most debilitating way when joined to the further assumption, generally taken for granted in modern theology, that the persons of the Trinity can only be identified once Jesus appears on the scene.[56] This generates a striking incoherence in the narrative Christians claim as their own: even scriptural Israel could not locate its God and its own election, since it knew nothing of Jesus and therefore could not identify the Trinity. This is not even supersessionism, since it deprives Israel of any access to its election, and naturally leaves one wondering why God would have elected a people to whom he provided no means of learning about their special status.

Traditional trinitarian theology had a clear eye for this narrative problem, and therefore generally argued that Israel *ante Christum* in one way or another did know about Jesus, and so could identify the Trinity. Or, in the view of a theologian like Gerhard, the Israelites could identify the Trinity even without being able to spot Jesus on the horizon (though not the God of Israel without the Trinity). In either case, the two different ways of identifying God were temporally co-extensive, so no conundrum arose from saying that both were necessary; there was in effect no point in salvation history at which only one was available. This was of course a supersessionist solution. After the trinitarian identification of God became fully explicit in Christ, so traditional views in effect supposed, most Jews stopped using the trinitarian description, and so lost the ability to identify God at all. But this was a solution that co-

56. Soulen, for example, seems to suppose that insisting upon the need for both types of identifying description in no way creates, but rather avoids, supersessionist difficulties, and that linking the identifiability of the Trinity to the temporal appearance of Jesus has no supersessionist implications. "The center of God's economy," he says, "is the death and resurrection of Jesus Christ, in whom God is revealed as YHWH the Father, Son, and Holy Spirit" (p. 48).

hered both with the Christian narrative as a whole and with the assumption that we need two ways to identify the one God.

It would be possible for trinitarian theology to avoid these unwanted supersessionist outcomes by granting that both descriptions are not in fact necessary to identify God. In order to pick the one God out, it suffices to describe him as the God of Israel. For this purpose one need not, in fact, describe him as the Father, the Son, and the Holy Spirit.

This suggestion, though, has deeply troubling resonances for much Christian theology past and present. Belief in the incarnation of the Son and the outpouring of the Spirit, and with that in the triune God, seems utterly basic to Christian faith. In order to believe that the one God just is the Trinity, so modern theology especially has often tended to suppose, you have to maintain that knowing about the Trinity is required in order to locate God at all. We may conclude with some brief reflections on whether we could jettison this last claim without thereby discarding the most basic Christian convictions about the Trinity.

Surely it will not work to say that both ways of identifying God are necessary for Christians, but not, say, for Jews. If it is impossible to spot the one God at all without reference to Father, Son, and Spirit, then Jews can no more identify God without having a grip on the trinitarian distinctions than Christians can. And conversely: if Jews can spot the one God without recourse to trinitarian descriptions — as a post-supersessionist trinitarian theology seems to require — then nobody, including Christians, needs to refer to the persons of the Trinity in order to identify God. Christians need to be able to locate the Trinity in order to be *Christians,* but not in order to locate God — lest we confine the possibility of identifying God to ourselves alone.

Does this post-supersessionist suggestion dislodge the Trinity from its central place among Christian beliefs, and turn Christians into what Rahner famously calls "mere monotheists"?[57] Here our quotidian example may again be useful. In order to succeed in identifying the morning star, a person clearly need not identify (or even be able to identify) the evening star, let alone recognize that they are the same object. But a person who also knows how to identify the evening star, and has discovered that the two are in fact the same object, knows more, precisely about the morning star, than one who only knows how to spot the morning star. Similarly, Christians might be able to grant that the God of Israel can be identified by those who do not, or cannot, identify the persons of the Trinity.

57. Karl Rahner, *The Trinity,* trans. Joseph Donceel, 2nd edition (New York: Crossroad, 1997), p. 10.

This does not at all trivialize or marginalize the distinctively Christian identification of God as Father, Son, and Spirit. By identifying the Father, the Son, and the Spirit, and by recognizing that these three are the same as the one God of Israel, Christians surely know more, precisely about the God of Israel, than can be gathered without knowing how to individuate the persons of the Trinity. This increase of knowledge surely need not be regarded as a secondary and perhaps dispensable surplus, any more than the modern astronomer's grasp of the morning star should be taken as a minor addition to that of an early-rising ancient who had never seen the evening star. So it surely seems possible to say that knowledge of the Trinity, while not necessary in order to identify God, completes and perfects the identification of Israel's God.

This seems to fit, moreover, with what we have said about the liturgy. Unlike the astronomical case, the relationship between our two ways of identifying God is not reversible. One might first identify either the morning or the evening star, and go on from there. But as Christian liturgical practice and the New Testament's talk of God indicate, identifying the Trinity presupposes locating the God of Israel. The precise nature of this presupposition — of the conceptual dependence of the church's identification of God upon Israel's — we have only partly touched on here. Granted the possibility of identifying the God of Israel without reference to the distinctions among the persons of the Trinity, this presupposition need not be taken, in what appears to be the traditional fashion, simply as a logically necessary condition. It can involve temporal priority. Therefore it seems possible to take the liturgy not, after all, as specifying two mutually necessary conditions for identifying the God whom Christians worship. Christian worship can instead be regarded as building on the one necessary condition for identifying God, already given in the Old Testament, in order to reach that fuller identification which, because explicitly trinitarian, is distinctively Christian.

If our post-supersessionist suggestion fails to make believing in the Trinity adventitious for Christians, still less does it make being the Trinity adventitious for God. We have already observed that it seems possible to identify God, like anything else, without apprehending God's *identity* — without, that is, yet laying hold of whatever makes God the same being in all possible circumstances. To say that the Jewish people may identify the one true God without referring to the persons of the Trinity is not, therefore, to suggest that God might not *be* the Trinity, or that being the Trinity is somehow not as basic to God's identity as being the one God. On the contrary, by giving descriptions that enable us to distinguish and relate the Father, the Son, and the Holy Spirit, Christian liturgy and Scripture render to us God's very identity, his inmost personal reality. Themselves instruments of the eternal Spirit, they put us in touch with "the deep things of God" (1 Cor. 2:10) — which is not, of course, to say that we have begun to plumb the depths of the triune God whom liturgy and Scripture let us describe.

These suggestions may, of course, themselves pose trinitarian problems.[58] They may also create supersessionist difficulties of their own. In any case the argument by which we have reached them perhaps indicates something of the importance, and the difficulty, of a genuinely non-supersessionist trinitarian theology.

58. For some questions about the idea that reference to the Trinity allows us to identify more fully a God whom we can locate without such reference, see my essay, "The Trinity" (above, note 8).

10. The Stranger

The Stranger as Blessing

EUGENE F. ROGERS, JR.

I will bless those who bless you, and those who curse you I will curse; and by you all the families of the earth shall bless themselves.

God's call of Abraham, Genesis 12:3

In that God became human, it has also become manifest and worthy of belief that . . . God creates, sustains and rules the world as the theatre of His glory.

Karl Barth, *Dogmatics in Outline,* p. 50

Q. What is the chief end of man?
A. The chief end of man is to glorify God and enjoy Him forever.

Westminster Confession, first question

This volume considers the thesis that the knowledge of God is adequately explicated only in the practices of God's community — or, more interestingly, that the knowledge of the community is adequately explicated only in the practices of God. By "practices of God," I mean what God does in God's triune and historical life. A thesis about the knowledge of God and the community, however, raises a number of challenges. Some of them are questions about knowledge of God apparently outside the church. If the knowledge of God belongs with the practices of the community, or if the practices of God yield the community's knowledge, what does that mean about apparent knowledge of God outside the community? Does God address the community from without? Does God address the community through those who dissent from its teaching? If people claim to address the church from without or in dissent, they may support the claim with alternative interpretations of Scripture, interpretations of God's address to the community through the created world, or both. Other essays in this volume take up the problems of how to interpret Scripture and the divisions in the church. This essay takes up the question of whether God addresses the community from the created world, a question that causes difficulties not only for the thesis of this volume, but also among the divided churches. For in classical terms it is the question of the natural knowledge of God, a corollary of the question of nature and grace, a question on which Protestants and Catholics typically disagree, and the very raising of which causes Eastern Orthodox thinkers to lose patience with false Western alternatives. To put it into trendier terms, what of the knowledge of God that is other to the community? Or in more biblical fashion, what of the knowledge of God of the stranger?

The natural knowledge of God is an issue that, left unresolved, could divide Protestant from Catholic readers of this volume while frustrating the Orthodox, for it is one of the more difficult problems remaining from the Reformation. The principle of *sola scriptura* led the Reformers to develop suspicions and polemics against a natural knowledge of God, while the tendency of German idealism to contain the world within the mind led Vatican I to insist on the intelligibility of God's creation as something outside it. The two emphases came into even greater conflict in the early twentieth century, when the Swiss Calvinist Karl Barth, perhaps the most important Protestant theologian since the Reformation, notoriously castigated Catholic natural theology as "the invention of the Antichrist,"[1] because he imagined that it put the being of God and the being of the world finally into the same category. As Barth put it elsewhere, "Natural theology was able, . . . after the rediscovery of Aristotle, to get the upper hand over medieval theology, which at last and finally became apparent in the formulas of the First Vatican Council (in the canonization of Thomas Aquinas as its supreme achievement)."[2]

In earlier work I have tried to overcome this division in the community

1. Karl Barth, *Church Dogmatics,* ed. and trans. G. W. Bromiley and T. F. Torrance, 4 vols. in 13 (Edinburgh: T. & T. Clark, 1936ff.), vol. 2, part-volume 1, p. 82; hereafter like this: II/1, 82.

2. *Church Dogmatics* II/1, 127, my translation.

that claims to know God by analysis of the conceptual categories, so that, for example, "nature" rarely means the same thing to Protestants and Catholics. That approach can succeed, but it is difficult, and the problem solved in one place is apt to pop up again somewhere else. Here I want to try a different tack, turning from the intellectual practices of the community (which show division when we consider nature and grace), to the salvific practices of God (some of which foster agreement). By the salvific practices of God I mean especially the common story of God's salvific action, starting with God's intra-trinitarian good will, and proceeding through God's covenant with Israel, the death and resurrection of Jesus, and our participation in Jesus through his Supper. The trick is to narrate, rather than analyze, the action of grace upon nature. To do that I start from the assumption that nature is other than or stranger to grace (in a sense that shifts with the story), and consider how God treats others and strangers.

Under conditions of sin, otherness is a source of hostility for us. But God intended otherness, at least some otherness, for the divine glory, and for blessing. How can we tell otherness as blessing from otherness as curse? I save analytical-conceptual discussion of nature and grace for the end, attempting first to narrate their story in terms of God's particular practices in Trinity, salvation history, and the Eucharist, three topics I take to be analogous expressions of God's love of others.

From Trinity to Trinity: Creation and Consummation

The community of God tells otherness as blessing from otherness as curse as it follows God's own concrete practices of grace and gratitude. That is, otherness may become blessing according as it follows a concrete trinitarian pattern; according as, through it, human beings come to participate more fully in the specific trinitarian community of Father, Son, and Spirit that God is. We can see analogous patterns in the trinitarian relations, in God's covenant with Israel, in God's grafting the Gentiles into that covenant "contrary to nature," in God's creation of the world, and in the relations of nature and grace. Ultimately, these patterns participate in the Holy Spirit's blessing of the love between the Father and the Son.

Karl Barth describes that pattern as one of the blessings of an Other already in the intra-trinitarian relations among Father, Son, and Spirit. "In God's own being and sphere [i.e., in God's own trinitarian life] there is a counterpart: a genuine but harmonious self-encounter and self-discovery; a free co-existence and co-operation; an open confrontation and reciprocity."[3] God lives out already *in se* a pattern of grace and gratitude.[4] When Jesus gives thanks to the Father at the Last Supper, his thanksgiving is a glimpse into an inner-trinitarian event, wherein the Father lives from giving, the Son from gratitude, the Spirit from delight. The Father offers Jesus bread and wine for his life; Jesus offers in return a brukhah, a blessing of gratitude for the Father's gifts. In identifying his body and blood with the bread and wine, Jesus offers thanks to the Father also for his life, which they support. He returns not only thanks for his life; he returns also his life itself, giving it back to the Father for the testimony and celebration of the Spirit. As it happens, the giving and blessing and feasting spill over also onto us human beings as we participate at the Great Thanksgiving, the Eucharist, that Jesus started there, inviting us bodily into God's intra-trinitarian life. Yet I save the human participation in the divine thanksgiving until later. So far this is describable as an intra-trinitarian event in which human beings need not participate.

The famous sermon is wrong that begins with God saying, "I'm lonely! I'm gonna make me a world."[5] God is not lonely; God has perfect love and community already in the triune life. Although it is true that love is incomplete à deux, that on highway bridges and carved into trees even human beings feel moved to declare their love to third parties, God does not lack even for a witness to celebrate the love between the Father and the Son. It is the office of the Holy Spirit to witness, glorify, rejoice in, celebrate, and bless the love between the Father and the Son. Thus it is that Jesus says the Kingdom of Heaven is like a wedding feast.[6] The Trinity is not, like most uses of the theme of divine marriage, the fertile union of a private two; it is a public celebration of three, a dancing day, as the old carol has it. Although we human beings learn about this pattern of exchange in God's body, in Jesus and in the Eucharist, that does not displace the real origin of the pattern in God's own life. The Trinity is the paradigm or perfect case of otherness as an exchange of gift and gratitude, that from which all other cases of gift take their derivative meaning.

The primary case of otherness, in Christian thought, is the Trinity. The

3. *Church Dogmatics* III/1, 185.

4. I owe the phrase to B. A. Gerrish, *Grace and Gratitude: The Eucharistic Theology of John Calvin* (Minneapolis: Fortress Press, 1993).

5. James Weldon Johnson, "The Creation," in Johnson, *God's Trombones* (New York: Penguin, 1955), pp. 17-20; here, p. 17.

6. Matt. 22:1-14; cf. Luke 14:16-24; Matt. 8:11; Luke 13:29, 5:34; Mark 2:18-22; Isa. 62:5; Rev. 19:9. In a distinct but related metaphor, the father also bestows a ring and a feast upon the Prodigal Son.

second case we consider is otherness not within the Trinity but outside it. Again we turn first to Barth.

> Creation is the temporal analogue, taking place outside God, of that event in God Himself by which God is the Father of the Son. The world is not God's Son, is not "begotten" of God; but it is created. But what God does as the Creator can in the Christian sense only be seen and understood as a reflection, as a shadowing forth of this inner divine relationship between God the Father and the Son.[7]

Creation, Barth continues, is therefore strictly grace; a free and unmerited benefit from the One Who loves in freedom.[8]

> The mystery of creation on the Christian interpretation is not primarily — as the fools think in their heart — the problem whether there is a God as the originator of the world. . . . But the first thing, the thing we begin with, is God the Father and the Son and the Holy Spirit. And from that standpoint the great Christian problem is propounded, whether it can really be the case that God wishes to be not only for Himself, but that outside Him there is the world, that we exist alongside and outside Him? That is a riddle. If we make even a slight effort . . . to conceive [God] as He reveals Himself to us, we must be astonished at the fact that there are ourselves and the world alongside and outside Him. God has no need of us, He has no need of the world and heaven and earth at all. He is rich in Himself, He has fullness of life; all glory, all beauty, all goodness and holiness reside in Him. He is sufficient unto Himself, He is God, blessed in Himself. To what end, then, the world? Here in fact there is everything, here in the living God. How can there be something alongside God, of which He has no need? This is the riddle of creation.[9]

Thus while it is not a matter of any external necessity that God create, nor even a matter of any internal compulsion, it is deeply characteristic of God to create, to give to another — because to give to an other is God's very life in the community of the Trinity.[10] To speak in this way of God's triune character is

7. Karl Barth, "God the Creator," in his *Dogmatics in Outline,* trans. G. T. Thompson (New York: Harper & Row, 1959), p. 52.

8. *Church Dogmatics,* II/1, thesis of §28; II/2, thesis of §32.

9. *Dogmatics in Outline,* pp. 53-54.

10. Although creation is a gift of God, creation is not itself God, so that it is a self-communication of God that is not yet a self-gift in the way that the Trinity is. See Thomas Aquinas, *Summa Theologiae* I.20.

to get beyond the horns of necessity and arbitrariness. In denying necessity we deny that creation has a source anywhere other than God's good pleasure, God's loving freedom; in denying arbitrariness we deny speculation about a god who would not have created; such a god would have had a different character from the God of Israel. The creation of the world and the trinitarian life befit each other as a characteristic act of One Who blesses an Other, Who receives that blessing, and Who delights in their mutual blessing.[11]

Thus God does not begrudge the world its existence, its freeing for response to love, its ability to bless and glorify God, and thus the possibility of coming into participation in God's own inner communion. The Christian question, Barth reminds us, is not "Is there a God?" Given that there is Jesus, there is a God. And given that Jesus has a Father and a Spirit, there is the particular God who is Father, Son, and Spirit. Rather the Christian question about God the Creator is, "Given that God the Creator is already Father, Son, and Spirit, what does God need a world for?" And the answer is, since God loves an other already within, it is characteristic of God, and therefore plausible and worthy of belief, that God should love an other also without. The reality of the love of the Father for the Son is the condition, within a trinitarian account, for the possibility of creation.[12] The reality of the blessing of the Holy Spirit upon their love is the condition for the possibility of creatures' glorifying and enjoying God. Creation is grace, not as the offspring of a *hieros gamos,* but in that particular, trinitarian pattern.

Creation is the possibility of God's eternal life of grace and gratitude, of God's unconditional response to God's self-giving also in finitude — in space and time. Space grants creaturely possibility to love. Finite creatures cannot love perichoretically, as God does, as if by interpenetration. Rather, their spatial boundaries first make love possible for them. Embrace would not be pos-

11. This way of putting the matter was inspired by a similar formulation in R. Kendall Soulen, "YHWH the Triune God," *Modern Theology* 15 (1999): 25-54, thesis 5.4. See also Soulen, *The God of Israel and Christian Theology* (Minneapolis: Fortress, 1996), esp. passages indexed under "consummation."

12. I intend this claim only *posita trinitate.* That is, I do not need or mean to say anything about the stronger and logically distinct claim (made for example by Hans Urs von Balthasar at *Theologik* II, 166, and called to my attention by Bruce Marshall) that only a trinitarian view of God could account for a positively regarded world at all or accommodate real otherness, which von Balthasar also thinks must imply problems for the cogency of creation and God's love of others on a Jewish account. The questions would be, whether von Balthasar's argument really supports the "only," and whether it is really so easy to prove that another tradition or family of traditions cannot account for something. All I need here, however, is the claim that since Christians have the doctrine of the Trinity, they will find it fitting to think about creation in the way I suggest.

sible, if human beings passed ghostlike through each other. Time, too, grants creaturely possibility to love. As Barth says, creation is the temporal analogue of the relation between the Father and the Son. Human conversation cannot take place simultaneously, but only in sequence. It takes time. It follows the divine Word at a distance. So, too, does human love. The formation of Christian households and corresponding monastic vows of stability honor the ties of love to place. The bonds of marriage and corresponding monastic vows of constancy honor the ties of love to time. Creaturely love involves making space, and taking time.[13] As God loves us, God does not grudge us space and time, but grants them to us out of the divine expanse and patience. Our time participates in the triune life as we participate in a sort of availability analogous to that which the trinitarian persons enjoy for one another.[14]

The pattern so far is this. In the Trinity, otherness is a condition for the possibility of love. God can be love, because God exists in the relationships among Father, Son, and Holy Spirit, not just two others, but also a third, a second difference, that their love might not be without celebration and blessing and witness. In creation, God enables distant but appropriate correlates to the trinitarian love-in-freedom also for human love, structured by space and time. In creation the divine intimacy can become physical nearness and temporal duration. God grants the creature a body and a history. God enables lovers to make a household and a marriage. In Eden God gave Adam and Eve a place and in their life span he allotted them time.[15]

Because God is triune, God can bless us. Because God blesses the other in God, God can bless the other without. Because God reaches out to another already within, God is not contained by the Trinity's inner life, but can reach out also to us. Because God reaches into another already within, God is not trapped beyond the world, but can reach in also to us. Because God is the one who loves in freedom, God can be the one who loves in freedom also for us. God can make time and take place. God can have a history and a body. God can make a garden and walk in it. God can choose Israel and be with her like a jealous lover. God can do this to bring creatures into the trinitarian fellowship. God can elevate creatures from Eden to glory, so that creation is not static, but always already God-moved, so that creation is not all, but more is in store even for Eden. Creation might be complete by itself, but God wills to consummate

13. For more on taking time as a theological and ethical concept, see Rowan Williams, "The Body's Grace," in *Ourselves, Our Souls and Bodies: Sexuality and the Household of God*, ed. Charles Hefling (Boston: Cowley, 1996), p. 63.

14. I developed this way of putting the matter in conversation with William Young.

15. For an argument about how allotted time is a created good, rather than a defect, see Barth's long consideration of creaturely time in *Church Dogmatics*, III/2, 437-640.

it, to bring it into fulfillment by drawing it into "that unconditional response to God's giving that God's self makes in the life of the Trinity."[16]

For the consummation of creation God chooses Israel. We see this in the promise to Abraham, at Sinai, in Amos and Hosea, and in the Song of Songs. To Abraham God makes many promises, which, quasi sacramentally, do not terminate only in created goods, but work by anagogy to prefigure the goods God has in store for Israel in the heavenly Jerusalem.[17] God blesses Abraham with land and life and by making him the father of many nations. At Sinai God declares love and choice in jealousy in the third commandment: "I the Lord your God am a jealous God."[18] The warning implicit is the warning not of a judge but of a lover; sin and redemption come in the context of God's implacable desire for consummation. In the judgment of the prophets, too, redemption is for consummation. "You have ravished my heart,"[19] God declares of Israel; "I will allure her."[20] In the Song of Songs the anagogy is complete: this is the life that God has begun and will consummate with his chosen people Israel.[21] If this part of the story is heard only as prefiguring the drama of sin and redemption in Jesus, we neglect to identify God by God's final intention; we neglect to identify God by consummation where consummation is most densely plotted and most richly begun. Israel actually possesses — possesses while yearning — polity with God, community with God[22] — the very stuff of anagogy, which sees in the Bible the types (technically, anagogues) of heavenly realities, the New Jerusalem.

16. Williams, "The Body's Grace," p. 59.

17. For more on anagogy, see Rogers, "Supplementing Barth on Jews and Gender: Identifying God by Anagogy and the Spirit," *Modern Theology* 14 (January 1988), pp. 43-81.

18. Exod. 20:5. Cf. among many other passages Exod. 34:14: "you shall worship no other God, for the Lord, whose name is Jealous, is a jealous God" (NRSV). — Name christologies often take it that God's Name is Christ (as in the Lord's Prayer). Interpreted christologically, would that passage mean that the Father is jealous for (not of) the Son, since it is the Son who marries the church?

19. Song of Solomon 4:9a.

20. Hosea 2:14.

21. For more, see Denys Turner, *Eros and Allegory: Medieval Exegesis of the Song of Songs,* Cistercian Studies Series 156 (Kalamazoo, Mich.: Cistercian Publications, 1995).

22. See Soulen, *The God of Israel and Christian Theology,* on consummation; Michael Wyschogrod, "Israel, the Church, and Election," in *Brothers in Hope,* ed. John M. Oesterreicher (New York: Herder and Herder, 1970), pp. 79-87; Wyschogrod, *The Body of Faith: Judaism as Corporeal Election* (Minneapolis: Fortress, 1983); David Novak, *The Election of Israel* (Cambridge: Cambridge University Press, 1995); Eugene F. Rogers, Jr., "Selections from Thomas Aquinas's Commentary on Romans [9–11]," translation of excerpts with an introduction, in *The Theological Interpretation of Scripture: Classic and Contemporary Readings,* ed. Stephen E. Fowl (Oxford: Blackwell, 1997), pp. 320-37.

Sin and Redemption as Subplot

Under conditions of sin, the plot thickens, or more exactly a subplot opens. Space can become separation and time can lead to divorce. Can grace and gratitude survive in finitude? Here they have limits. Difference becomes distance that can strain love and end it. Duration can become a burden, and death can cut it short. "Till death do us part" (cf. Ruth 1:17): a promise becomes a threat. The Song of Songs (8:6) asserts, "Love is stronger than death." Is it? Otherness becomes the wall of hostility. Can God tear it down? God has begun to bring free creatures into the trinitarian fellowship. Will God complete what God began?

"This is my body," God says in Jesus, "broken for you." God takes a body and lets death have it, lets hostility have its way with it. In the breaking of the bread, God's body also is broken; more, the trinitarian fellowship is broken, because with the crucifixion the trinitarian fellowship is broken — threatens to break, or promises to: the Son says to the Father, "My God, my God, why have you forsaken me?" (Mark 15:34) and the Father loses the Son to death. In the breaking of bread, too, the body of God opens up — to let us in, to admit us to the Trinitarian communion at its point of greatest vulnerability, at its time of greatest risk. The Eucharist — the Great Thanksgiving — is the intra-trinitarian exchange of grace and gratitude carried out in the face of death and shared with us who are subject to it. Jesus gives thanks to the Father for his grace, and he shares the grace of the Father, and the opportunity for gratitude, also with us, in his death. Is love stronger than death? The story is not over, but God would complete what God began even on the night in which he was betrayed. On that night we come to participate in the unconditional response to God's self-giving that the Son makes to the Father even unto death. A vain attempt, perhaps; a deathbed wedding.

The Spirit is the witness of the love between the Father and the Son. At the crucifixion this love is stretched, as it were, to the breaking point. Yet like the witness at a wedding, whose office it is not only to celebrate the marriage but to safeguard and uphold it, the Spirit has still its role to play. "If the Spirit of the One Who raised Jesus from the dead dwells in you, the One Who raised Christ Jesus from the dead will give life to your mortal bodies also through the Spirit that dwells in you."[23] The Spirit is the Giver of life; the Father raises the Son, the Son arises, and the Spirit restores their bond, this time with a dif-

23. Romans 8:11. I owe my attention to this verse also to David Yeago, *The Faith of the Christian Church* (Lutheran Theological Southern Seminary, 1992), p. 119. Cf. also Robert Jenson's treatment in *The Triune Identity* (Philadelphia: Fortress, 1982), p. 44.

ference: having been admitted to the trinitarian exchange of grace and gratitude, which is the trinitarian communion and Eucharist, in the breaking open of Christ's body, we participate too in the reintegration and resurrection of that body, and as the Spirit flows between the Father and the Son it now flows — detours perhaps — also through us (us human beings? or us Gentiles?). There is now no part of the world godforsaken, because the Spirit did not forsake the Son, in whom alone the Father sees those created in his image, and in whom alone the Father sees sin. It is in the Spirit, the Giver of life, which flows through our mortal bodies also, that love is stronger than death. The love stronger than death is not an abstract power, it is a particular person, the Spirit. The Spirit that blesses the love between the Father and the Son remains a source of blessing even in the face of death. In the process the other to God within God, the Spirit, overcomes the other to God that God is not, or evil. The other that is curse is overwhelmed in the other that is blessing. The dialectical inclusion by which God determines the lost cause of the human being for God's own cause, by which God determines the sad lot of the human being for God's own lot, by which God chooses God for this way and work, changes everything for the cause and lot and way of the other. By the God of Abraham, now, all the nations — all the others — of the earth may bless themselves.

This volume concerns the practices of God in the knowledge of the Church, and here it must be said that the Eucharist is the ecclesial practice that best corresponds to the divine blessing of an other, since it corresponds to the divine giving and receiving of gift. At the Last Supper, the Father blesses the Son with the means of his bodily and spiritual sustenance, the bread and wine. The Son blesses the Father, in Jewish fashion, for these gifts. The Son blesses the Father also in the return of these gifts, in the offering up of his body again to the Father. In the Johannine discourse, the Son anticipates the sending of the Spirit. And in the Church's sacramental practice, the Spirit enables all of us there gathered to bless the marvelous exchange of blessing between the Father and the Son, which enables us to be caught up again into that exchange, in which we were created to participate. Alexander Schmemann gives an account of the Eucharist that both explicates it as blessing, and overcomes the dichotomy between nature and grace:

> [T]he unique position of man in the universe is that he alone is to bless God for the food and the life he receives from Him. He alone is to respond to God's blessing with his blessing. The significant fact about the life in the Garden is that man is to name things. . . . [I]n the Bible a name . . . reveals the very essence of a thing . . . as God's gift. . . .

> To name a thing, in other terms, is to bless God for it and in it. And in the Bible to bless God is not a "religious" or a "cultic" act, but the very way of life. God blessed the world, blessed the man, blessed the seventh day (that is, time), and this means that He filled all that exists with His love and goodness, made all this "very good." So the only natural (and not "supernatural") reaction of man, to whom God gave this blessed and sanctified world, is to bless God in return, to thank him, to see the world as God sees it — and in this act of gratitude and adoration — to know, name, and possess the world. . . . [The human being is] first of all "homo adorans." . . . He stands in the center of the world and unifies it in his act of blessing God, of both receiving the world from God and offering it to God — and by filling the world with this eucharist, he transforms his life, the one that he receives from the world, into life in God, into communion.
>
> The world was created as the "matter," the material of one all-embracing eucharist. . . .[24]

The Eucharist is the sacrament of blessing not only as the consummation of creation, but also as redemption from sin. For with sin, the freedom lost is the freedom to be blessed and to bless; the thing ruined is primarily the gift of God's body, and yet God does not give up the plan to feast us, even under conditions of sin, for God wants to complete what God began. Herbert's poem "Love (III)" has Love ask whether the companion lacks anything at the feast: "'A guest,' I answered, 'worthy to be here.' And quick-eyed Love replied, 'You shall be he.'" That makes sin a subplot, complication in the eucharistic plot — is that all?

The subplot of sin is an episode in God's story with the world that fails to make sense, a misuse of freedom that no longer counts as freedom but as absurdity and perversion. According to Anselm, freedom is the ability to pursue the good for its own sake.[25] God has this ability absolutely, since God's reason, the Logos, is infinitely able to recognize and create good, and God's will is infinitely able to pursue it. Creatures, by God's gift, participate in this ability not absolutely but dependently. In the medieval example, freedom is the cane by which we lean upon God, our ground, to stand morally and ontologically upright. In sin we "use" the cane to trip ourselves headlong: but such an abuse of freedom does not count as a proper "use," transforming the "cane" into an obstacle. Or in a modern example, it is as if a teenager, having just learned to drive, discovers only a very small box under the Christmas tree. Inside is a key,

24. Alexander Schmemann, *For the Life of the World* (New York: National Student Christian Association, 1963), pp. 4-5.

25. Anselm of Canterbury, *De libero arbitrio.*

the ability to drive, and outside sits a new car with a big red bow. Key clutched stiff between thumb and forefinger's knuckle, he races outside — and plunges the key deep into the tire. He likes it so much that he does it again and again, until the car is resting on its axles. That hardly counts as a use of the freedom to drive the car. It leaves things ruined and absurd.

God's story, the Logos, must re-absorb such stories into itself, renarrating them as ones in which freedom is restored.[26] The body becomes a place not of life but of death, and the body God offers us in Jesus we treat not with blessing but with violence. We curse him by hanging him on a tree. In the person of the Logos, the Story par excellence, God retells the story of trinitarian love by turning the curses of others back into blessing for them. The body we crucify in the great Un-Eucharist becomes, at the Last Supper, a gift for us once again and in advance. God tells the story so that we recover the freedom we lost, the freedom for gift and gratitude, the freedom to bless God for God's blessings.

The eucharistic reversal is perhaps too familiar to shock. Phyllis Trible has recovered its risk and terror. In Judges 19 we read, "So the man seized his concubine, and put her out to them; and they knew her, and abused her all night until the morning." Having found her lying on the doorstep, dead or alive it does not say, "he took a knife, and laying hold of his concubine he divided her, limb by limb, into twelve pieces, and sent her throughout all the territory of Israel" (19:25b, 29). Although Trible's explicit thesis is that the passage calls us to repentance, her implicit thesis is christological. In a few scattered phrases she subtly retells the story, the more powerfully because she calls no attention to the procedure. "Truly, the hour is at hand, and the woman is betrayed into the hands of sinners," she comments, citing Mark 14:41. "At the end of the section," she continues, "safety within the house has lost to danger without. Yet only the concubine suffers the loss. No one within comes to her aid. They have all fallen away in the darkness of night (cf. Mark 14:26-42)."[27] Several pages later, these lines appear: "Her body has been broken and given to many. Lesser power has no woman than this, that her life is laid down by a man."[28] It is stories as terrible as these of which the Eucharist practices God's retelling.

In using Trible that way, I have picked out and raised to prominence suggestions that she makes fleetingly and sometimes with irony. She means to

26. I owe my attention to renarration to David Hart.

27. Phyllis Trible, "An Unnamed Woman: The Extravagance of Violence," in her *Texts of Terror* (Philadelphia: Fortress, 1984), pp. 65-91; here, p. 76.

28. Trible, p. 81.

suggest, and not to emphasize. She hopes to gain more by a rhetoric of understatement against a theology of the cross that, by an irony of its own, takes the place of moral seriousness and repentance. Facile references to the cross and the Eucharist can domesticate and prettify violence, too easily dispensing sublimation and forgiveness, overlooking the necessity of judgment and change of life. Yet if the cross and Eucharist do not turn judgment into blessing, then the story is not retold. The only solution, if the cross brings forgiveness, is that the resurrection brings judgment.

In the Jewish tradition of atonement, practiced person to person in the ten days between Rosh Hashanah, the New Year, and Yom Kippur, the Day of Atonement, when the gates of atonement are closed, God forgives the sins committed against God — but not the sins that one human being commits against another: for those one must ask forgiveness of the one wronged. A crime such as the one depicted in Judges seems to trap both the victim and the criminals in their fates. She cannot return to life, and they cannot repent before her. Rowan Williams suggests that the resurrection of Jesus has part of its meaning within such a system.

> [T]he primary stage in preaching the resurrection [is] to recognize one's victim as one's hope. . . . The Jesus who is [in Acts 4:12] preached as the sole source of salvation is the particular victim of that court. If any insight may be generalized out of this saying, it is that salvation does not bypass the history and memory of guilt, but rather builds upon and from it. . . . I am not saved by forgetting or cancelling my memory of concrete guilt. . . . And so I must look to my partner: to the victim who alone can be the source of renewal and transformation.[29]

So the Eucharist is not the domestication of violence and easy forgiveness. Under the sign of the resurrection, it enables Jesus to meet his victimizers face to face. The one they had betrayed, denied, abandoned, condemned, and crucified, is back again, walking the streets, before their faces. The victim will not stay dead. The story of the victim's terror becomes the story of the victimizers' terror. The unnamed woman, the holocaust victim, meets and judges the executioners. Jesus meets and judges them with — forgiveness. They must live differently — and they may, because the resurrection restores their victim as the one in whom alone there is judgment, and therefore hope. This confrontation might also become part of eucharistic practice, if we took seriously Jesus' suggestion that we go and be reconciled with our brother be-

29. Rowan Williams, "The Judgement of Judgement: Easter in Jerusalem," in his *Resurrection: Interpreting the Easter Gospel* (London: Darton, Longman and Todd, 1982), pp. 11-12.

fore we place a gift upon the altar. Why? Because bringing gifts to the altar participates in the eschatological movement toward the feast where we shall meet our victims face to face.

We are now in a position to begin re-asking the initial questions of this essay. What does the story practiced in the Eucharist mean for those the Church has encountered as other than itself, as strange to itself: Gentiles, Jews, philosophers, nature itself — those whom human beings now name, not in order to bless, but in order to curse?

1. It is crucially necessary for the Church to acknowledge its overwhelmingly Gentile nature, in order for it to appreciate appropriately the grace of God. We Gentiles, as Kendall Soulen puts it, have no God of our own. We worship an other God, a God strange to us, the God of Israel,[30] and we are strangers within their gate. We are not God's first love, not those of whom God is jealous, not those to whom God is betrothed, with whom God has made and renewed a covenant. We Gentiles are so foreign to the God of Israel that Paul can say that God acts "contrary to nature," *para phusin,* in grafting us in.[31] A phrase more liable to provoke, the same one Paul uses earlier in the letter only to describe homosexual activity, is difficult to imagine. Does Paul mean to compare God's activity to homosexual activity? Or does he at least mean to let the phrase stand, echoing, setting up unsavory comparisons in the reader's mental ear? Both the first and the second *para phusin* have to do specifically with Gentiles. The first use, like the second, distinguishes not a modern class of people, homosexuals, but a biblical class of people, Gentiles, and distinguishes them not from heterosexuals, but from Jews. In Romans 1 Paul lets his readers regard homosexuality as a characteristic Gentile sin of excess, one that they could temporarily pride themselves on avoiding, until chapter 2 comes in with what Richard Hays has called Paul's "rhetorical sting operation,"[32] according to which Jews turn out also to be without excuse. The rhetorical sting operation has a further whip of its tail in store. By Romans 11, the God of Israel has shown solidarity with these Gentiles. God associates with them, eats and drinks with them; in the modern idiom we would even say that God is sleeping with the enemy — the phrase is not too strong, for God seeks to make the Jews "jealous." In both cases *para phusin* more strictly means "in excess of nature";[33] Paul sees the activity that characterizes God,

30. Soulen, "YHWH the Triune God," p. 45.

31. Romans 11:24. I owe my attention to this passage to Richard Hays.

32. Richard Hays, "Relations Natural and Unnatural: A Response to John Boswell's Exegesis of Romans 1," *Journal of Religious Ethics* 14 (1986): 184-215.

33. Dale B. Martin, "Heterosexism and the Interpretation of Romans 1:18-32," *Biblical Interpretation* 3 (1995): 332-55.

like the activity that characterizes the Gentiles, as excessive, profligate, prodigal. The sting is this: in saving the Gentiles, God shows solidarity with something of their nature, the very feature that had led the Jewish Paul earlier depicted to distinguish himself from them: their excessive sexuality. Although the metaphor of ingrafting is agricultural, it is also one about households. What is "natural" is that God should love God's natural children, that is, the children of God's covenant with Israel. What is natural is that the domestic olive — the olive of the household and economy of God — should bear domestic fruit. And yet God loves also the Gentiles — wild olives, adopted children. Strange children: idol-worshipers whom God had given up to desires in excess of nature, *para phusin.* According to Paul, divine and Gentile profligacy are both *para phusin.* God saves the Gentiles — most Christians, who are not Jews — by adopting to God's purposes a Gentile characteristic. Just as God saved flesh by taking it on and defeated death by dying, here God saves those who act in excess of nature by an act in excess of nature. We Gentiles owe our very salvation to God's unnatural act. That is how much grace it is.

2. Another import of the passage is that Paul defines "nature" in terms of covenant. Although Barth does not talk about the passage as I do, it could serve as a prooftext for his axiom that creation is the external ground, the theater, of the covenant, and the covenant is the internal ground, the plot, of creation. Nature and grace are no sheer opposites. Nature is for something, is oriented toward something, is dynamic, not static. This is not because an independent nature anticipates grace, the creature reaching up Babel-like to God. It is because nature and grace, creation and covenant, are two moments of one grace. Their separation is relative, not absolute.[34] Otto Pesch has observed: "it is easy to overlook: the justification of the sinner is no 'new' dispensation of God's, but the carrying out of God's creatorly will over against the rebellious

34. This relativism goes in spades for the relative distinction that Paul seems to make between the natural and the unnatural, the Jew and the Gentile in Romans 11. In particular, it denies a supersessionist reading of that dialectic. Paul is not being particularly innovative when he portrays God in this way, because by a familiar dialectic he is being particularly rabbinic. Jews, too, know God's "unnatural" choices — of barren women and second sons. The rabbis qualify the rhetoric of natural children of Abraham — which I owe to Michael Wyschogrod — with a story according to which Abraham succeeded in killing Isaac, so that children of Isaac are precisely unnatural, children of a resurrection (see Jon D. Levenson, *The Death and Resurrection of the Beloved Son: The Transformation of Child Sacrifice in Judaism and Christianity* [New Haven: Yale University Press, 1993]). For both Christians and Jews, grace is unnatural, but also naturalizing. God's grace both acts upon us, as if from without, and most intimately involves us, as if from within. God's gracious engagement of us in our own salvation, rather than leaving us out of it, takes hold of even (or precisely) our most "natural" impulses — such as eating bread. (I owe this qualification to Peter Ochs.)

human creature. The dimensions of nature that remain *un*disturbed are therefore to be conceived of as the effectiveness already in advance of the grace that saves."[35] It is one gift divided for purposes of human analysis into two parts, one plot sectioned for purposes of temporal drama into two acts. Nature might have stood alone; God might have set it loose to run by itself; God might not have intended any more for nature than that it should play itself out in Eden. Were nature static in that way, it would not be at risk, at least, not in a way that involved God's self-commitment to it. But that was not God's plan. Nature was to be dynamic, open to change, to elevation, to friendship with God, and also to risk. Nature as God in fact bestowed it is not free-standing, stable, upright by itself. By nature creation leans upon grace. Of this leaning of nature upon grace, of this lack of natural uprightness, we may say, if not of sin itself, "O happy fault, that merited such and so great a Redeemer."

Nor are nature and grace, after all, biblical categories. If we cast about for a biblical dichotomy of similar range, one that divides all divine and human relations into two parts, we discover that we have seen it already: it is the categorization of Jews and Gentiles. Jews and Gentiles are already in relation. From the promise to Abraham God's blessing already embraces both. And yet creation itself is tied to God's history with the Jews, the stage for that drama. For the whole history of Israel is measured by generations; names of fathers and sons mark out its chronology, and the begats of the King James Version (the plan of *toledoth*) sum up the passage of time. From Abraham to Moses and Moses to David we have not numbers of years primarily, but generations. From David to Christ forward again we have generations as the principle of connection and continuity. The generations of God's people measure God's history too. And back from Abraham we also have generations. Before Abraham was, God was at work. Before the covenant, God was preparing it, all the way back to Adam and Eve, so that Adam and Eve, as Genesis tells it, become not so much the progenitors of the human race, as the prehistory of Israel. And it does not stop with the first parents. The Priestly writer of Genesis has a vision bold enough to include the creation of the world within the compass of God's history with Israel, as he says: "These are the generations of the heavens and the earth" (Gen. 2:4). The chronological device of the generations assimilates all created things, from the very beginning, into the history of Israel.[36] The history of grace embraces nature; nature does not embrace grace.

35. Otto Hermann Pesch, *Die Theologie der Rechtfertigung bei Martin Luther und Thomas von Aquin: Versuch eines systematisch-theologischen Dialogs* (Mainz: Matthias-Grünewald, 1967), p. 526.

36. Gerhard von Rad, *Old Testament Theology*, trans. D. M. G. Stalker, 2 vols. (New York: Harper & Row, 1962), vol. 1, pp. 138-39.

The embrace of nature, and even un-nature, by grace, if properly narrated (the embrace of Esau by Jacob, the virgin by the Spirit, the Gentiles by the olive-grafter) can overcome certain technical problems of what the German theologians call *Kontroverstheologie,* the theology of controversy. At the beginning of this essay I posed the problem between nature and grace as one between Protestants and Catholics, in which Protestants exercise suspicion about arguments from nature, Catholics insist on them, and the Orthodox throw up their hands in frustration. So far I have attempted to recast that problem narratively, by retelling the Christian story of God's triune life and love of the world with the nature-grace problem in nearer or more distant view, instead of trying to solve it analytically. The retelling of the narrative, however, allows us to return to the analytical categories from a fresh point of view.

Thomas Aquinas, the theologian whom Barth identifies as starting the development of natural theology crowned by Vatican I, turns out, properly understood, to be just as open as Barth to a reading in which God's revelation is first of all of God's own self, as Barth and Vatican II agree.[37] Thomas is not as explicit, to be sure, but he did not share Barth's polemical climate. Thomas, too, makes God's revelation primarily of God's own self, just when he defines theology as an Aristotelian science. For Aristotelian science looks quite different when Thomas finishes with it. The true knowledge or *scientia* of God belongs properly to God only, which God shares with the blessed in heaven, and on earth with Christ alone. Christ's teaching is, like all teaching, the "activity of making known." This activity of making known is, in God's case, the incarnation, the taking on of flesh as a remedy for sin.[38] In this activity of making known, the activity of God's own humanity, the making known accomplished by an Aristotelian demonstration, of syllogisms, is a real but pale participation.[39] Because Christ humanly possesses the *scientia Dei,* he can be for us "the demonstration of the Father," and, in his flesh (historical and eucharistic) our *via,* or way, into God.[40] The famous so-called "proofs for the existence of God," called by Thomas the "five ways,"[41] are *viae* of this sort again

37. Dogmatic Constitution on Divine Revelation, "Dei Verbum," I.2. See Barth's commentary in his book *Ad limina apostolorum: An Appraisal of Vatican II,* trans. Keith R. Crim (Richmond, Va.: John Knox Press, 1968).

38. Cf. Victor Preller, *Divine Science and the Science of God* (Princeton: Princeton University Press, 1967), p. 253.

39. Eugene F. Rogers, Jr., *Thomas Aquinas and Karl Barth: Sacred Doctrine and the Natural Knowledge of God* (Notre Dame: University of Notre Dame Press, 1995), pp. 58-70, 162.

40. *Summa Theologiae* III.9.2, I.42.6 ad 2, I.2 proemium.

41. *Summa Theologiae* I.2.3.

by participation, distant and remote, having such efficacy as they may or may not possess because they are derivative and distant Christology.[42] At the beginning of the *Summa* Thomas defines sacred doctrine as a science, in that it "proceeds from first principles."[43] First principles, as Thomas interprets Aristotle, are not just propositions about, say, how birds fly, but also the facts about the world described in those propositions, the principles by which birds fly.[44] The first principles of sacred doctrine come from Scripture in their propositional form;[45] but their shape in the world, by which human beings come to that beatitude, or salvation, which is the knowledge of God enjoyed by the blessed in heaven, is the sacred humanity of Christ.[46] Yet this procedure does not make sacred doctrine an exceptional science, one that manages only sneakily to claim to proceed from first principles, even if divine revelation is not what Aristotle had in mind by a first principle. On the contrary a first principle is a small-*r* revelation, something that Aristotle imagined as at once enlightening the mind and animating the world. If Thomas knows the very source of all light and animation, then that is no exception to Aristotle's teaching about first principles, but its unrecognized foundation. Sacred doctrine is not the less Aristotelian science for proceeding from revelation; all sciences proceed from a revelation. Rather, by proceeding from revelation sacred doctrine is science par excellence; other Aristotelian sciences become merely pale reflections of it.[47]

This pattern is an old and familiar one in Christian thinking. It is the pattern by which God is not opposed to things human, but first puts them back together by assuming flesh. Barth too prefers this pattern, according to which the human nature in Christ is not free-standing, not a person in its own right, but borne by the person of the Logos "enhypostatically," for re-integration and repair.[48] Theology can assume philosophy into itself because God can assume

42. Rogers, *Thomas and Barth,* p. 162.

43. *Summa Theologiae* I.1.2.

44. Terence Irwin, *Aristotle's First Principles* (New York: Oxford, 1988), p. 7. See also Alasdair MacIntyre, *First Principles, Final Ends, and Contemporary Philosophical Issues* (Milwaukee: Marquette University Press, 1990), p. 4.

45. *Summa Theologiae* I.1.3, I.1.8, II-II.1.2.

46. *Summa Theologiae* III.9.2. "The human being is a rational creature capable of that beatific cognition, insofar as the human being is [ordered] to the image of God. But human beings are led to that end by the humanity of Christ." For commentary see Preller, p. 253, and Rogers, *Thomas and Barth,* p. 68.

47. Rogers, *Thomas and Barth,* p. 27. See also Michel Corbin, *Le chemin de la théologie chez Thomas d'Aquin* (Paris: Beauchesne, 1972), pp. 717-18.

48. For argument see Bruce McCormack, *Karl Barth's Critically Realistic Dialectical Theology: Its Genesis and Deveopment, 1909-1936* (Oxford: Clarendon, 1995), pp. 327-74.

flesh. Only because God takes on flesh can it be again truly human. Only because logic wittingly or unwittingly participates in the Logos is it truth-bearing. Only because demonstrations participate, wittingly or unwittingly, in the demonstration of the Father by the Son can they be valid. Only when the five ways participate wittingly or unwittingly in the Way can they lead to God. Only when the Aristotelian sciences participate wittingly or unwittingly in the science of God do they proceed from real first principles. Sacred doctrine can use philosophy as the Israelites can despoil the Egyptians, and as God can assume flesh. In Thomas's hands, secular reason can become a eucharistic practice, that is, one that receives all human knowledge as blessing and returns it as blessing to God. For in the bread and wine of the Eucharist it encounters God's divine humanity become against all odds a source of blessing. This is true even, or especially, of human knowledge that theology has historically mistaken as other than blessing — the astronomy of Galileo, the biology of Darwin, the philosophy of Feuerbach, the political theory of Marx, the psychology of Freud, the sociology of Durkheim. Like the metaphysics of Aristotle, they are good insofar as they are true; they are true by participation in the Truth; and they participate in the truth because the Truth took on flesh and dwelt among us — circling this sun, descended from those apes, having that religious hunger, under those economic conditions, possessed of such an id and superego, experiencing God in his society. For Durkheim was precisely right, Christian theologians ought to say, just on account of the incarnation: God is in society. God is among Jews and Gentiles, because God was in Jesus reconciling the world. The practice of God's presence in society (as on the earth, in the body, and related to all subjects of study) is again the Eucharist, by which God opens up the triune life to all flesh. The adoring, wondering work of the human thinker in whatever discipline is a participation, however distant and remote, in this grace and gratitude.

When human beings bless God in all their activities, mental and physical, they participate in Christ's work of making God known and the Holy Spirit's work of blessing the life of gift and gratitude that the Son shares with the Father.[49]

49. A longer version of much of this essay appears to a different purpose in Eugene F. Rogers, Jr., *Sexuality and the Christian Body: Their Way into the Triune God* (Oxford: Blackwell, 1999), pp. 195-219 and 249-68.